THE WORLD ALMANAC

ROAD TRIPPERS' GUIDE TO

NATIONAL PARKS

5,001 THINGS TO DO, LEARN, AND SEE FOR YOURSELF

WORLD ALMANAC BOOKS

World Almanac books may be purchased in bulk at special discounts for sales promotion, corporate gifts, fund-raising, or educational purposes. Special editions can also be created to specifications. For details, contact the Special Sales Department, 307 West 36th Street, 11th Floor, New York, NY 10018 or info@skyhorsepublishing.com.

Published by World Almanac, an imprint of Skyhorse Publishing, Inc., 307 West 36th Street, 11th Floor, New York, NY 10018.

The World Almanac™ is a trademark of Skyhorse Publishing, Inc. All rights reserved.

www.skyhorsepublishing.com

10 9 8 7 6 5 4 3 2 1

Text by John Rosenthal
Interior design by Chris Schultz
Cover by David Ter-Avanesyan
Cover photographs by Shutterstock

Library of Congress Cataloging-in-Publication Data is available on file.

Print ISBN: 978-1-5107-6846-8
Ebook ISBN: 978-1-5107-6847-5

Printed in China

Contents

AN INTRODUCTION TO NATIONAL PARK SYSTEM DESIGNATIONS V

CALIFORNIA 1
Yosemite National Park.. 2
Golden Gate National Recreation Area 6
Joshua Tree National Park 9
Point Reyes National Seashore 13
More to See in California 16

THE PACIFIC NORTHWEST 27
Olympic National Park 28
Mount Rainier National Park.. 34
Crater Lake National Park.. 39
Denali National Park and Preserve 44
More to See in the Pacific Northwest 49

THE SOUTHWEST 65
Grand Canyon National Park 66
Zion National Park 71
Bryce Canyon National Park... 76
Glen Canyon National Recreation Area 80
More to See in the Southwest 84

THE ROCKY MOUNTAINS 109
Yellowstone National Park 110
Grand Teton National Park 116
Rocky Mountain National Park 120
Glacier National Park.. 125
More to See in the Rocky Mountains.. 129

THE MIDWEST 137
Indiana Dunes National Park 138
Gateway Arch National Park... 142
Cuyahoga Valley National Park.. 146
Mount Rushmore National Memorial... 150
More to See in the Midwest 153

THE SOUTH 175
Great Smoky Mountains National Park 176
Hot Springs National Park.. 181
Gulf Islands National Seashore... 185
Chattahoochee River National Recreation Area....................................... 189
Natchez Trace Parkway.. 192
More to See in the South... 196

THE NORTHEAST 219
Acadia National Park 220
Boston National Historical Park..224
Cape Cod National Seashore..230
Parks of New York Harbor 234
Gettysburg National Military Park 238
More to See in the Northeast 242

THE CAPITAL REGION 263
The National Mall and Memorial Parks..264
Assateague Island National Seashore..269
Blue Ridge Parkway 273
Colonial National Historic Park..278
More to See in the Capital Region 281

U.S. ISLANDS 305
Hawai'i Volcanoes National Park...306
Haleakala National Park...311
Pearl Harbor National Memorial 315
Virgin Islands National Park 318
More to See in U.S. Islands..322

CANADA..329
Banff National Park 330
Jasper National Park...335
Pacific Rim National Park Reserve 340
Fundy National Park..344
Prince Edward Island National Park..347
Saguenay-St. Lawrence Marine Park..350
Yoho National Park..353
More to See in Canada...358

INDEX 375

An Introduction to National Park System Designations

The United States National Park System encompasses 423 different sites covering more than 85 million acres (34 million hectares). Each site has been designated by Congress as being of such national significance as to justify special recognition and protection. Within the Park System are 19 different types of sites, ranging from Pennsylvania's Benjamin Franklin National Memorial (a 20-foot statue of the founding father) to Alaska's 8,323,146-acre (3,368,258-hectare) Wrangell-St. Elias National Park. Here is a brief description of each type of site overseen by the National Park Service.

AREAS OF NATURAL VALUE

National Parks are the large natural wonderlands that most people imagine when they think about the National Parks. National Parks usually provide a wealth of opportunities for outdoor recreation. They contain a large variety of resources and encompass large land or water areas to help provide adequate protection of those resources. As of April 2021, there were 63 National Parks, including Yosemite and Grand Canyon.

National Monuments (84) are intended to preserve at least one nationally significant resource.

They are usually smaller than and lack the diversity of attractions of National Parks.

National Parkways (4) preserve roadways in scenic areas from commercial development. They are not designed for high-speed travel, but rather as routes for leisurely driving. Some national parkways travel through other units of the National Park System.

National Preserves (19) are established primarily for the protection of certain resources. Activities like hunting and fishing or the extraction of minerals and fuels may be permitted if they do not jeopardize the natural values.

National Reserves (2) are similar to National Preserves. Management may be transferred to local or state authorities.

National Rivers (4) and **Wild and Scenic Riverways** (10) preserve free-flowing streams and their immediate environment with at least one remarkable natural, cultural, or recreational value. They must flow naturally without major alteration of the waterway by dams, diversion, or other alteration. Besides protecting and enhancing rivers, these areas provide opportunities for outdoor activities.

National Seashores (10) and **National Lakeshores** (3) preserve the natural beauty of shoreline areas and islands, while providing

water-oriented recreation. Although national lakeshores can be established on any natural freshwater lake, the existing three are all located on the Great Lakes.

National Scenic Trails (3) are generally long-distance footpaths winding through areas of natural beauty.

AREAS OF HISTORIC IMPORTANCE

National Historic Sites (74) preserve places of historic importance. They are usually smaller than **National Historic Parks** (61), which have greater physical extent and complexity. The lone **International Historic Site** (Saint Croix Island, ME) is important to both U.S. and Canadian history.

National Battlefields (11), **National Battlefield Parks** (4), **National Battlefield Sites** (1) and **National Military Parks** (9) curate areas associated with American military history.

National Memorials (31) are sites or structures that are primarily commemorative.

National Recreation Areas (18) were originally areas surrounding reservoirs impounded by dams built by other federal agencies. In recent years, they have come to include other lands and waters set aside by Congress for recreational use, many of them in urban centers.

CALIFORNIA

Yosemite National Park

It's hard to believe that pictures don't do justice to a place that has been photographed as extensively as Yosemite. But your first glimpse of **Yosemite Valley** proves that no Ansel Adams calendar can fully convey the majesty, the grandeur, the spectacle that is Yosemite.

There's something about seeing Yosemite in person that causes even seasoned world travelers to come to a screeching halt. In fact, so many people were doing exactly that on the **Wawona Road** leading into the Valley that the Park Service had to add a **Tunnel View** parking lot and pedestrian promenade to accommodate all the visitors taking selfies of the view Adams made famous. **El Capitan, Cathedral Rocks,**

Tenaya Canyon, and **Bridalveil Falls**—names you've heard for years—start to fill the horizon. Then your eyes settle on **Half Dome**, that bisected ice-cream scoop of granite that is the definitive feature of Yosemite. It's no wonder that 90 percent of Yosemite visitors spend all their time in this tiny but riveting sliver of the park.

Many, especially those with strollers, make a beeline for **Lower Yosemite Falls**. A wheelchair-accessible path meanders through a grove of cedars and ponderosa pines before depositing visitors at a spacious viewing area where they can feel the spray from **North America's tallest waterfall**. Spring is the best time to enjoy this view; by mid-summer, this

Fast Facts

Established: 1890
Acreage: 761,748 (308,268 hectares)
Visitors (2019): 4,422,861
Visitor Centers): Big Oak Flat Information Station, Mono Basin Scenic Area, Tuolomne Meadows, Wawona (summer only), Yosemite Valley
Nearest Major Airport: Fresno Yosemite Intl. (FAT)
Nearest Major Highways: CA-41, CA-120, CA-140
Fees: $35/vehicle.
Accessibility: Download the park's comprehensive accessibility guide from nps.gov/yose for information about access to attractions and facilities for people with a variety of disabilities. Yosemite also has a Deaf Services Program and a visitor's guide for people with aphasia.
Contact Information: 209-372-0200 www.nps.gov/yose

Yosemite Valley, as seen from Tunnel View

gushing cascade slows to a trickle before drying up completely each fall.

The ambitious might pursue the six-hour trek to **Upper Yosemite Falls**, or spend all day scaling **Half Dome** (permits, available only through a lottery, are required, so plan far in advance). Mere mortals, on the other hand, can take the gentle four-mile trail around **Mirror Lake,** with its stunning views of Half Dome. The **Mist Trail** and the **John Muir Trail** are two of the Park's most popular hikes. Both trails take visitors 2.4 miles (3.9 km) and 1,000 vertical feet (305 m) to **Vernal Fall** and continue another 3 miles (4.8 km) and 1,000 more vertical feet to the top of **Nevada Fall**.

Like all things of beauty, the Valley is exceedingly popular. Particularly on weekends, everything fills up quickly: the campgrounds, parking lots, even the shuttle buses that are

The best views of iconic Half Dome are from Glacier Point.

meant to reduce traffic in the Valley. Weekends are a good time to get out of the Valley and explore the rest of park, which encompasses over 1,100 square miles (184,031 sq km).

Crowds disappear amid the towering sequoias at the **Mariposa Grove of Giant Trees** at the southern end of the park. An easy three-mile trail meanders through the trees (literally *through*

Yosemite Falls is at its most active in the spring.

3

Giant trees at Mariposa Grove are big enough to walk, or even drive, through.

The Ahwahnee Hotel seems almost carved out of the surrounding rock.

the trees, as several redwoods have hollowed-out bases wide enough to walk through).

Glacier Point Road, which traces the south rim of the valley, is typically buried under snow from October to May, accessible only for **cross-country skiing**. In summer, though, it's a leisurely hour-long drive to **Glacier Point**, which offers glorious vistas of the entire Valley below. (Late afternoon is the perfect time for photos with Half Dome in the background.) Similarly grand views can be had by hiking the mostly uncrowded trails that branch off from Glacier Point Road. The trailhead at **McGurk Meadow** is the jumping off point for the four-mile round-trip walk to **Bridalveil Creek** and the more strenuous 8.2-mile (13.2-km) round-trip hike to **Dewey Point.**

You'll have even more pristine wilderness practically to yourself if you visit during the short window between the opening of the **Tioga Road** (late May or early June, depending on snowfall) and the summer onslaught. A spectacular driving tour in and of itself, the 47-mile (75-km) road cuts through the north edge of the Valley and brings you to lightly visited areas of the park like **Siesta Lake**, **White Wolf Campground**, **Tenaya Lake**, and **Tuolumne Meadows**. The view of the back side of Half Dome from **Olmsted Point** is like nothing you've ever seen on a calendar.

No visit to Yosemite is complete without a stop at the **Ahwahnee Hotel**, perhaps the most famous of all National Park lodges. Built in 1927 as a way to lure the rich and famous to Yosemite and persuade them to support the National Park System (it worked!), it occupies the premier perch in the Park, with drop-dead gorgeous views of the surrounding Valley. The interior sights aren't too shabby, either: walk-in fireplaces made from the same granite as the impressive façade, ceilings built from logs twice the size of telephone poles, and fine Native American artwork throughout. Room rates are as steep as the trek up El Capitan ($600 a night in high season), but there's no charge for being a looky-loo and non-guests can still enjoy lunch or dinner in the **Ahwahnee Dining Room.**

Don't Miss This . . . Suggested Yosemite Itineraries

Day One: Start your day at **Lower Yosemite Falls**, North America's tallest waterfall. Then rent bikes at Yosemite Valley Lodge and see the Valley on two wheels. Stop for lunch at **The Ahwahnee Hotel**. Spend the afternoon climbing the **Mist Trail to Vernal Fall**, or even keep going all the way to **Nevada Fall**. Get back in your car and make the hour-long drive up **Glacier Point Road** in time to take photos of **Half Dome** at sunset.

Day Two: Pack a lunch and drive south to the **Wawona** section of the park. Walk the easy 2-mile (3-km) **Grizzly Giant Loop**, which passes by Yosemite's oldest living tree, and *through* the **California Tunnel Tree**. For a longer hike, follow the 6.2-miles (10-km) **Mariposa Grove Loop** past the **Telescope Tree**, to the top of **Wawona Point**, and back. In the afternoon, head to **Wawona Stables** for a two-hour horseback ride along a pioneer wagon road, or a five-hour ride to **Chilnualna Falls**.

Day Three: Spend the morning walking the **Valley Loop Trail**, for knockout views of **El Capitan** and **Bridal Veil Falls**. The full loop is 6.6 miles (11 km) but you don't have to go all the way around if you'd prefer a shorter outing. In the afternoon, take the shuttle bus to **Curry Village** and rent a raft for a 3-mile (5-km) float down the **Merced River**.

Day Four: Get out of the Valley and explore the quiet northwest corner of the park near **Hetch Hetchy Reservoir**. The 4.6-mile (7.4-km) **Wapama Falls Trail** traces the reservoir's shoreline to (where else?) **Wapama Falls**, which flows almost year-round (unlike many of the cascades in the Valley, which dry up by summer). Or drive the entire 60-mile (100-km) length of **Tioga Road** (summer only), stopping along the way for unexpected perspectives of sights you've only seen from the **Valley Floor**, and for uncrowded walks around lakes and through wildflower-filled meadows. The **Tenaya Lake Trail** is an easy 3.4-mile (5-km) flat walk around the south shore of **Tenaya Lake**.

Horsetail Fall usually flows only during winter.

Golden Gate National Recreation Area

If you've spent any time in San Francisco, chances are you've been counted among the tens of millions of people who visit the Golden Gate National Recreation Area every year. This massive urban park encompasses 37 different sites on both sides of the **Golden Gate Bridge.** Among its jewels are several other sites within the National Park System, such as **Muir Woods National Monument**, **Fort Point National Historic Site**, and **The Presidio of San Francisco**. It also includes **Alcatraz Island**, a.k.a. "The Rock," where notorious prisoners like Al Capone and George "Machine Gun" Kelly Barnes served time. Ferries to the island prison leave hourly from Pier 33. The excellent self-guided **audio tour** (available in 11 languages) lends an eerie soundtrack to the former jailhouse.

The GGNRA is home to 19 different ecosystems and more than 2,000 plant and animal species. And it supports more activities than a Disney cruise. Hike 1,901 feet (579 meters) from sea level to the top of **Montara Mountain** at **Rancho Corral de Tierra**. Bike along

Golden Gate Bridge at sunset

Alcatraz Island

Windsurfers and kiteboarders share the water below the Golden Gate Bridge.

the **Bolinas Ridge Trail**, a 10.5-mile (16-km) loop that starts in **Samuel Taylor Park**. View seals, whales, and porpoises as you ascend the short trail to the **Point Bonita Lighthouse**. Cast for salmon and lingcod on **Baker Beach**. Spot spotted owls and other wildlife at **Muir Woods National Monument**.

Tour the Cold War–era **Nike Missile Site** in the **Marin Headlands**. Catch sunset (and maybe a glimpse of migratory raptors in fall) from Hawk Hill. Ride a horse to the ocean on the **Tennessee Valley Trail**. Scramble down the bluffs to the windy beach at **Fort Funston**. Tour the ruins of the **Sutro Baths**, an erstwhile indoor

Cliff House

The Marin Headlands are a mostly undeveloped stretch just north of the Golden Gate Bridge.

aquatic playground that once attracted tens of thousands of visitors every year. Step into the **Camera Obscura** in front of the **Cliff House**, a century-old (but now vacant) restaurant site on a dramatic perch at **Lands End**, the northwestern-most point of San Francisco. Marvel at the daredevil **windsurfers and kiteboarders** (you can join them if your skills are up to the challenge) who catch air underneath the Golden Gate Bridge. Or pack a picnic and spend the entire day at **Stinson Beach**.

The opportunities for outdoor recreation don't end at dusk. **Beach bonfires** are permitted (in fire rings) at **Muir Beach** from 9 a.m. to one hour after sunset, and at **Ocean Beach** from 6 a.m–9:30 p.m. between March 1 and October 31. Four different campgrounds in the Marin Headlands welcome overnight guests. With its secluded wooded setting and spectacular views of the bridge, **Kirby Cove Campground** fills up the fastest.

The most accessible campground, **Bicentennial**, is just a short stroll from the Battery Wallace parking lot. The other two campgrounds require visitors to hike in. **Haypress Campground** is just ¾ miles (1.2 km) from the Tennessee Valley Trail Parking Lot; a stay at remote **Hawk Campground** involves a 2.5-mile (4-km) uphill hike. All four campgrounds are small, so reservations are a must.

GGNRA is perhaps the most dog-friendly unit in the National Park System, with dozens of trails and beaches that welcome canine friends, and a handful of locations where four-legged visitors can run free. The most popular of these is **Crissy Field**, a former military airfield that has been transformed into a greenbelt with walking paths, a tidal marsh, and a dog beach.

Crissy Field

Joshua Tree National Park

Joshua Tree's proximity to Los Angeles—the park is only about 150 miles (240 km) from America's second-largest city—plays a large part in its popularity among visitors. But its unique rock formations and curious flora make it worth a trip from anywhere.

Start with the park's namesake, *Yucca brevifolia* as it's known in Latin. The local indigenous Cahuilla people called it *humwichawa*, the Southern Paiutes referred to it as *sovarampi*, and the Serranos deemed it *choormartsh*. All three groups prized the plant's roots and leaves for making baskets and sandals; they also made food from the buds, flowers, and seeds.

The name Joshua Tree came from Mormons from Utah in the mid-19th century, who saw a likeness to the Old Testament figure with arms outstretched in supplication, leading acolytes to a new promised land. Twenty-first

A lone Joshua tree in Joshua Tree National Park

Rock climbing is one of Joshua Tree's most popular activities.

century visitors might observe a resemblance to truffula trees, the flora Dr. Seuss created for *The Lorax*.

Joshua trees can be found throughout the American southwest, but rarely in such high concentrations as within this park. One could easily spend a day just wandering the park by foot, car, or bicycle, from one copse to another, in search of the tree with the most bizarre arrangement of branches.

Joshua Tree's moon-like rock formations make it one of the premier climbing destinations in the country. **Trashcan Rock** (so named because the multiple cracks around the cylindrical perimeter evoke a grooved metal trashcan) is one of the most accessible spots, both for

its abundance of beginner-level climbs and its proximity to **Park Boulevard**, Joshua Tree's main drag. **The White Cliffs of Dover** require a little more walking to get to the base, but the reward is a wonderland of routes, with fanciful names like **Ace of Spades**, **Popular Mechanics**, and **Search for Chinese Morsels**.

There are also hundreds of other locations throughout the park where no climbing experience or gear is necessary to scramble from one pile of smooth granite to another in search of the finest perch. Short trails lead to landmark formations like **Skull Rock** (which truly lives up to its name), **Split Rock**, **Cap Rock**, **Arch Rock**, and **Jumbo Rocks**. Even driving through the park

A short hike to Skull Rock is a great introduction to the park.

Cholla cacti in the Colorado desert section of Joshua Tree.

offers an exceptional viewing experience of this transfixing desert landscape.

What makes Joshua Tree unique is its location in the midst of three distinctly different ecosystems. The southern and eastern section of the park is **Colorado Desert,** an extension of Arizona's Sonoran Desert. Cacti and other succulents thrive in its low elevation and hot, dry climate. The northern half of the park is **Mojave Desert,** high desert, subject to more frequent rainfall, and the habitat of the namesake Joshua trees. The third ecosystem, the **Little San Bernardino Mountains,** runs along the southwestern edge of the park. It is home to peaks topping 4,000 feet (1,200 m)

Arch Rock

Joshua Tree allows views of the entire Milky Way.

in elevation and evergreens like pinyon pine and California juniper. It's possible to drive through all three ecosystems in a single day, or even to hike through one in the morning and one in the afternoon.

The **Bajada Nature Trail** (0.25 miles/0.4 km) and the **Cholla Cactus Garden** (0.25 miles/0.4 km) both offer easy introductions to the variety of plants that thrive in the Colorado Desert's forbidding environment. Wear closed-toe shoes—prickly chollas have sharp spikes! The short hike up **Mastodon Peak** (3 miles/4.8 km) loops around an old gold mine. To make a day out of it, tack on the **Lost Palms Oasis Trail** (7.5 miles/12 km total), which starts out easy, then descends into a canyon of California fan palms. The climb out of the canyon can be strenuous on hot days.

In the Mojave, warm up with a 30-minute stroll around **Cap Rock**, one of the best places to see Joshua trees. The **Black Rock** area at the northwestern corner of the park is home to several longer options, including the short but occasionally steep **Hi-View trail** (1.3 miles/2 km), the slightly more challenging **West Side Loop** (4.7 miles/ 7.6 km), or the 1,100-foot (335-m) climb to the panoramic views at **Warren Peak** (6.3 miles/10.1 km).

The best immersion into the Little San Bernardino Mountains range is on the 5.5-mile (8.9-km) drive from **Hidden Valley** up to **Keys View**. The amazing panoramic views take in more than 50 miles (80 km) of the San Andreas Fault, from Mount San Gorgonio to the Salton Sea.

Many of Joshua Tree's most popular attractions are concentrated in the Hidden Valley area in the middle the park. **The Barker Dam Nature Trail**, an easy 1.1-mile (1.6- km) loop, passes one of the few areas where water collects after a winter rain. The seasonal moisture supports a variety of lush flora that in turn attracts wildlife like birds, reptiles, and the occasional bighorn sheep.

The hike to the summit of **Ryan Mountain** is just 3 miles (4.8 km) round trip, but gains 1,069 feet (326 m) in elevation. It's a great place to take in the desert sunset, which is apt, since it's often too hot to hike this trail in the middle of the day.

After the sun goes down, it's time for stargazing. With minimal light pollution, the night skies around Joshua Tree enable visitors to witness the entire **Milky Way**. **Orion** is visible in winter, along with **Gemini** and **Taurus**. August consistently brings the **Perseid Meteor Shower.**

Point Reyes National Seashore

Point Reyes has been attracting visitors for nearly half a millennium, since Sir Francis Drake became the first European explorer to set foot on the peninsula. He encountered a land the Coast Miwok people had treasured for thousands of years for its plentiful food and fresh water. The Park Service has re-created a traditional **Miwok village** at **Kule Loklo** (Bear Valley), a short walk from the **Bear Valley Visitor Center**.

After Drake claimed the land for England, more explorers and traders followed, often with disastrous results. The treacherous waters and the thick fog claimed dozens of ships, starting with the Spanish galleon **San Agustin**, which wrecked on

Fast Facts

Established: 1972
Acreage: 71,055 (28,755 hectares)
Visitors (2019): 2,265,301
Visitor Centers: Bear Valley, Kenneth C. Patrick, Point Reyes Lighthouse
Nearest Major Airport: San Francisco Intl. (SFO)
Nearest Major Highways: US-101, CA-1
Fees: $0
Accessibility: Download the 24-page accessibility guide at www.nps.gov/pore/planyourvisit/upload/guide_accessibility_2017.pdf
Contact Information: 415-464-5100 www.nps.gov/pore

Point Reyes is famed for miles of wild, undeveloped shoreline.

A steep staircase to Point Reyes Lighthouse

the beach across **Drakes Bay** in 1595 on its way back from the Philippines.

This tragedy-filled history was the impetus for one of the Seashore's most enduring attractions: the **Point Reyes Lighthouse**, built by the U.S. Lighthouse Service in 1870. For 105 years, it helped mariners navigate the rocky shores, but it did not stop every ship from crashing into shore. The **Point Reyes Lifeboat Station**, built in 1889, housed the first responders of their era: men who went out in small boats to rescue wreck survivors.

Both the lighthouse and lifesaving station have been decommissioned and replaced by more modern technology. But they still serve as museums of Point Reyes's history. They're both at the far western end of the peninsula, a long pastoral drive from the main entrance. Visitors traveling between the two sites can descend a steep 54-step staircase to **Sea Lion Overlook**, where gray whales and nesting Brandt's cormorants may also share the stage with a large population of California sea lions. **Elephant Seal Overlook**, located on Drakes Bay closer to **Chimney Rock**, is where females of the species come ashore each January to birth their pups and males throw their weight around to establish dominance.

Tomales Point, at the far northern reaches of the Seashore, is home to a different kind of wildlife: tule elk, a subspecies of elk native to California. Hunting and cattle ranching nearly drove the tule elk to extinction during the 1800s, but thanks to the preservation efforts of a single farmer, the statewide population has been restored to nearly 6,000. Since the Park Service reintroduced the elk to the Tomales Point reserve in 1978, the population has expanded to more than 600 animals, enough to populate hundred-strong sub-herds further south on Drakes Beach and **Limantour Beach.**

The best elk viewing is during the fall rut, or mating season (August–October), when males bugle, strut, and occasionally lock horns in pursuit of the most desirable females. It's often possible to witness tule elk without even leaving the parking lot at **Historic Pierce Point Ranch**, a holdover from Point Reyes's years of dairy cattle ranching. The elk are also attracted to the spring at **White Gulch**, reachable on foot via a relatively flat, 2-mile (3.2-km) hike on the **Tomales Point Trail** to **Windy Gap**. From there, it's another 3 miles (4.8 km) to the 270-degree ocean views at **Tomales Bluff**. Wind, fog, steep ascents and descents, and a narrow trail that can be overgrown and hard to follow

Elephant seals return each year to Drakes Beach.

Sculpture Rock Beach is prime tidepooling territory at low tide.

make this section for seasoned hikers only.

Birders flock to the 2-mile (3.2-km) round-trip hike through **Abbotts Lagoon**, where ducks, raptors, and black-shouldered kites are plentiful in fall and winter. Threatened western snowy plovers make their nests here. Spring brings wildflowers like California poppies and Tidy Tip asters to the open grasslands.

The **Laguna** and **Coast Trails** take different routes from the **Point Reyes Hostel** on Limantour Road to Santa Maria Beach, making it possible to link them together for a 5-mile (8-km) loop. The **Coast campground** at the south end of the beach has 12 sites that can accommodate up to six people each, and 2 larger campsites. All campgrounds in Point Reyes are backcountry sites accessible only by foot or boat; vault toilets, a water faucet, picnic tables, and charcoal grills are the only facilities.

Mt. Wittenberg, the highest point in the park at 1,407 feet (429 m) is accessible by several trails. The easiest way up is by taking the **Sky Trail** to the **Horse Trail** to the **Z Ranch Trail**, a 4.3-mile (6-km) round-trip with just 740 feet (226 m) of elevation gain. The ascent via the **Bear Valley Trail** is only a little bit longer in distance, but has twice the elevation gain (1,300 feet/396 m).

The Bear Valley trail is one of the most popular in the Seashore, in part because it begins at the **Visitor Center** at the main park entrance, in part because it's the most direct route to the ocean, and in part because the first 3 miles (5 km) are open to bicycles. It's about 5 miles (8 km) each way through Douglas fir forest and meadows to reach **Kelham Beach** and the **Coast Trail** that parallels the water.

Point Reyes boasts 80 miles (129 km) of magnificent beaches, but they're mostly for admiring from shore. The rough waters that have claimed so many ships over the years also make swimming a risky proposition. The frigid temperatures (usually around 50°F/10°C) can cause hypothermia; sneaker waves can be strong enough to drag an adult out to sea; and rip currents can make it hard to get back to the beach. Falling rocks and landslides from the unstable bluffs above many of the beaches are a hazard of walking too close to the edge or the base of a cliff.

A visitor center, bathrooms, bookstore, and parking lot make **Drakes Beach** one of the Seashore's most popular strands. An annual Sand Sculpture Contest takes place around Labor Day weekend. Intricate rock formations are the namesake sculptures at **Sculptured Beach** at low tide, making this area prime **tidepooling** terrain. Heavy surf pounds the broad sands all along **Point Reyes Beach**, also known as the Great Beach or Ten-Mile Beach, (even though it's actually 11 miles/18 km long). Leashed dogs are permitted in multiple stretches, and people are welcome to stroll the entire length of this breathtakingly undeveloped shoreline. A short (0.6 mile/1 km) stroll along a marsh ends at the giant sand dunes at **Kehoe Beach**, at the northern end of Point Reyes Beach. The cliffs north of Kehoe Beach feature a dramatic transition from smooth Laird sandstone to rougher granite.

Tule elk abound on Tomales Point.

15

MORE TO SEE IN CALIFORNIA

Cabrillo National Monument

Fast Facts

Established: 1913
Acreage: 159 (64 hectares)
Visitors (2019): 761,485
Nearest Major Airport: San Diego Intl. (SAN)
Nearest Major Highways: I-5, I-8
Fees: $20/vehicle; $10/pedestrian or cyclist
Accessibility: www.nps.gov/cabr/planyourvisit/
accessibility.htm has extensive information for
visitors with physical disabilities, hearing loss,
impaired vision, cognitive issues, and service animals.
Contact Information:
619-557-5450
www.nps.gov/cabr

The intertidal habitats here are among the most
sensitive in the world. The monument is named
for Juan Rodriguez Cabrillo, the Iberian explorer
who claimed this coast for Spain in 1542. Old
Point Loma Lighthouse is restored to its most
active period—the 1880s. Remnants of World War
II coastal defense batteries dot the landscape. In
winter, the monument's high perch makes it ideal
for spotting migrating gray whales.

Cabrillo Point overlooks San Diego.

César E. Chávez National Monument

Fast Facts

Established: 2012
Acreage: 117 (47 hectares)
Visitors (2019): 16,490
Nearest Major Airport: Los Angeles Intl. (LAX)
Nearest Major Highways: CA-58, CA-223, I-5
Fees: $0
Accessibility: Most facilities are wheelchair
accessible, except the replica of a migrant worker's
camp home.
Contact Information:
661-823-6134
www.nps.gov/cech

Widely recognized as one of the most important
Latino and labor leaders in the United States during
the 20th century, César E. Chávez led farm workers
and supporters in the establishment of the century's
first permanent agricultural union. His leadership
brought sustained international attention to the
plight of the U.S. farm workers and secured higher
wages and safer working conditions.

Channel Islands National Park

Fast Facts

Established: 1938/1980
Acreage: 249,561 (100,994 hectares)
Visitors (2019): 409,630
Visitor Centers: The main visitor center is on the
mainland, in Ventura; visitor contact stations are
located on Anacapa Island, Santa Barbara Island,
and Santa Cruz Island.
Nearest Major Airport: Los Angeles Intl. (LAX)
Nearest Major Highways: CA-1, US-101
Fees: $0.
Accessibility: The remote and rugged character
of the Channel Islands make them largely
inaccessible to people with most physical
disabilities. To protect indigenous wildlife,
service animals must be screened before coming
ashore on Santa Cruz, Santa Rosa, or San Miguel
Islands. Some park brochures and publications
are accessible to people with hearing loss or
impaired vision.

Channel Islands National Park

Contact Information:
805-658-5700
www.nps.gov/chis

The park consists of five islands off southern California: San Miguel, Santa Rosa, Santa Cruz, Anacapa, and Santa Barbara, including the surrounding marine waters. Access to all of the islands is via Island Packers ferry (www.islandpackers.com) from Ventura or Oxnard Harbors or a Channel Islands Aviation flight (www.flycia.com) from Camarillo Airport. There are no services or lodging on any of the islands. Visitors must bring their own camping gear, food, and water. Nesting sea birds, sea lion rookeries, and unique plants inhabit the area. Archaeological evidence of substantial populations of Native Americans can be found throughout the islands.

Death Valley National Park
Fast Facts
Established: 1933/1994
Acreage: 3,373,063 (1,365,030 hectares)
Visitors (2019): 1,740,945
Visitor Center: Furnace Creek
Nearest Major Airport: Harry Reid Intl. (LAS), Las Vegas, NV
Nearest Major Highways: CA-190, US-395, US-95 (Nevada side)
Fees: $30/vehicle; $15/pedestrian or cyclist. Entry valid for seven days.
Accessibility: Many facilities and attractions were built before current accessibility standards, so while they may be negotiable, they may not fully meet federal standards. Visit www.nps.gov/deva/planyourvisit/accessibility.htm for more information.
Contact Information:
760-786-3200
www.nps.gov/deva

The largest national park in the lower 48 states, this desert park contains mountain ranges, sand dunes, dry lake playas, and many desert springs. It includes the lowest elevation point in North America and holds the record for the hottest temperature ever recorded (130°F/54°C, in August 2020). The area includes the grandiose Scotty's Castle, a Spanish Mediterranean mansion named for a famous local prospector and rogue of the 1930s. The Nevada section is home to the protected Devils Hole pupfish, a tiny desert fish endemic to this underground habitat.

Moon over Death Valley

Basalt formations at Devils Postpile National Monument

Devils Postpile National Monument

Fast Facts

Established: 1911

Acreage: 800 (324 hectares)

Visitors (2019): 147,864

Visitor Center: Ranger station only

Nearest Major Airport: Reno-Tahoe Intl. (RNO), Reno, NV

Nearest Major Highways: US-395.

Fees: $8/adult, $4/children aged 3-15; (free for kids aged 2 and under) to ride the shuttle bus from Mammoth Lakes Village or Mammoth Mountain Adventure Center. $10/vehicle when shuttle is not running.

Accessibility: One campground and two bathrooms are ADA-compliant. Most trails are not wheelchair accessible.

Contact Information:

760-934-2289

www.nps.gov/depo

Preserves and protects the glacially exposed columns of the Devils Postpile, the scenic Rainbow Falls, and the wilderness landscape of the upper Middle Fork San Joaquin River in the Sierra Nevada for scientific value, public interest, and inspiration. Hot lava cooled and cracked some 100,000 years ago to form basalt columns 40 to 60 feet (12 to 18 m) high resembling a giant pipe organ. The John Muir Trail and Pacific Crest National Scenic Trail traverse the monument.

Eugene O'Neill National Historic Site

Fast Facts

Established: 1976

Acreage: 13 (5 hectares)

Visitors (2019): 2,944

Visitor Center: Accessible only as part of a reservations-only tour.

Nearest Major Airport: Reno-Tahoe Intl. (RNO), Reno, NV

Nearest Major Highway: I-680

Fees: $0. All visitors must be picked up by a National Park Service shuttle from the town of Danville (reservations required).

Accessibility: All shuttle buses are equipped with wheelchair lifts. A video of the upstairs is available to visitors who cannot climb stairs. Visit www.nps.gov/euon/planyourvisit/accessibility.htm for more information.

Contact Information:

925-838-0249

www.nps.gov/depo

The playwright Eugene O'Neill and his wife Carlotta were living in a San Francisco hotel when they had this house built for them on a 158-acre (64-hectare) ranch. O'Neill lived here from 1937 to 1944, during which he wrote two of his most enduring plays: *The Iceman Cometh* and *Long Day's Journey Into Night*.

Fort Point National Historic Site
Fast Facts
Established: 1970
Acreage: 29 (8 hectares)
Visitors (2019): 1,421,349
Nearest Major Airport: San Francisco Intl. (SFO)
Nearest Major Highway: US-101
Fees: $0
Contact Information:
 415-556-1693
 www.nps.gov/fopo

This classic brick and granite mid-1800s coastal fort is the only one of its style on the west coast of the United States.

John Muir National Historic Site
Fast Facts
Established: 1964
Acreage: 344
Visitors (2019): 40,725
Nearest Major Airport: San Francisco Intl. (SFO)
Nearest Major Highways: I-80, I-680, CA-4
Fees: $0
Contact Information:
 925-228-8860
 www.nps.gov/jomu

The site preserves and protects the home and portions of the Alhambra Valley agricultural estate where John Muir lived, worked, and was buried. It aims to memorialize and connect people with Muir's global legacy as an influential naturalist, writer, and champion for protecting national parks and wild lands.

Kings Canyon National Park
Fast Facts
Established: 1890/1940
Acreage: 461,901 (186,925 hectares)
Visitors (2019): 632,110
Visitor Centers: Cedar Grove, Grant Grove

Zumwalt Meadows in Kings Canyon National Park

Nearest Major Airport: Fresno Yosemite Intl. (FAT)
Nearest Major Highways: CA-180, CA-198, CA-245
Fees: $35/vehicle; $20/individual. Fee includes access to adjacent Sequoia National Park (see below).
Accessibility: Visit www.nps.gov/seki/planyourvisit/upload/SEKI-Accessibility-Guide_03-2020-508.pdf for extensive information about accessible areas within the park.
Contact Information:
 559-565-3341
 www.nps.gov/seki

Administered jointly with the adjacent Sequoia National Park, Kings Canyon preserves an area of wilderness that includes two enormous canyons of the Kings River and multiple peaks of the High Sierra Nevada topping 10,000 feet (3,048 m). The wide range of elevations within the park supports a diversity of wildlife: birds, black bears, snakes, lizards, and mountain lions, but also bats, mule deer, and pikas: small, round relatives of rabbits.

Lassen Volcanic National Park
Fast Facts
Established: 1907/1916
Acreage: 106,589 (43,135 hectares)
Visitors (2019): 517,039
Visitor Center(s): Kohm Yah-mah-nee, Loomis Museum (summer only).
Nearest Major Airport: Sacramento Intl. (SMF)
Nearest Major Highways: CA-36, CA-44, CA-89
Fees: $30/vehicle in summer; $10/vehicle in winter; $15/pedestrian or cyclist year-round

Snow on Mount Lassen

Accessibility: Download the Lassen Accessibility Guide at www.nps.gov/lavo/planyourvisit/upload/Accessibility-site-bulletin-web.pdf
Contact Information:
530-595-4444
www.nps.gov/lavo

Lassen is home to all four types of volcanoes found in the world: shield, composite, cinder cone, and plug dome. The last cinder cone eruption was more than 350 years ago, but Lassen Peak's plug dome erupted intermittently from 1914 to 1917. Steaming fumaroles, mudpots, sulfurous vents, and boiling springs attest to the smoldering volcanic activity that continues just below the surface.

Lava Beds National Monument
Fast Facts
Established: 1925
Acreage: 46,692 (18,896 hectares)
Visitors (2019): 109,630
Nearest Major Airport: Rogue Valley Intl. (MFR), Medford, OR
Nearest Major Highways: CA-139; US-97
Fees: $25/vehicle; $15 individual
Accessibility: The caves and most of the trails have uneven surfaces and are not accessible to visitors in wheelchairs.

Contact Information:
530-667-2282
www.nps.gov/labe

Over the last half-million years, the Medicine Lake shield volcano has spewed forth molten rock and lava here, creating an incredibly rugged landscape with diverse volcanic features. Spelunkers can explore the caves left behind by the flowing lava. During the Modoc War, 1872–73, a small band of Native Americans used the area as a natural fortress.

Manzanar National Historic Site
Fast Facts
Established: 1992
Acreage: 814 (329 hectares)
Visitors (2019): 97,380
Nearest Major Airport: Fresno Yosemite Intl. (FAT)
Nearest Major Highways: US-395
Fees: $0
Contact Information:
760-878-2194
www.nps.gov/manz

Known as Manzanar War Relocation Center during World War II, this site in California's Owens Valley was one of 10 camps where more than 110,000

Twilight at Pinnacles National Park

Japanese Americans were relocated and interned. The replica buildings and exhibits of Block 14 recreate daily life of the interned population.

Mojave National Preserve
Fast Facts
Established: 1994
Acreage: 1,542,741 (624,325 hectares)
Visitors (2019): 841,516
Visitor Center(s): Barstow Headquarters, Hole-in-the-Wall Information Center, Kelso Depot
Nearest Major Airport: Harry Reid Intl. (LAS), Las Vegas, NV
Nearest Major Highways: I-5, I-40
Fees: $0
Contact Information:
   760-252-6100
   www.nps.gov/moja

This massive, minimally developed site protects the fragile habitat of the desert tortoise and other wildlife, vast open spaces little changed by humans, and historic mining, ranching, and railroad scenes such as the Kelso railroad depot. Other jewels of the desert include sand dunes, cinder cone volcanoes, a large Joshua tree forest, and carpets of spring wildflowers.

Muir Woods National Monument
Fast Facts
Established: 1908
Acreage: 554 (224 hectares)
Visitors (2019): 812,073
Nearest Major Airport: San Francisco Intl. (SFO)
Nearest Major Highways: CA-1, US-101
Fees: $15/person plus $8.50 to park or take the shuttle into the park from Sausalito, Marin City, and the Pohono Park & Ride Lot. Reservations are required.
Contact Information:
   415-388-2596
   www.nps.gov/muwo

This virgin stand of old growth coastal redwoods was named for John Muir, writer and conservationist. Part of the Golden Gate National Recreation Area, its trails are popular day hikes for San Francisco residents and tourists or can be combined with trails in adjacent Mt. Tampalpais State Park to make a longer trek.

Pinnacles National Park
Fast Facts
Established: 1908/2013
Acreage: 26,686 (10,799 hectares)
Visitors (2019): 177,224

Nearest Major Airport: Norman Y. Mineta San Jose Intl. (SJC)

Nearest Major Highways: CA-146, CA-25, US-101. There is no route between the east and west entrances.

Fees: $30/vehicle; $15/individual

Accessibility: Visitor centers and restrooms are ADA accessible, but most of the trails are steep and rocky. An exception is the Prewett Point Trail, near the western entrance.

Contact Information:
831-389-4485
www.nps.gov/pinn

Volcanic eruptions 23 million years ago left behind spire-like rock formations 500 to 1,200 feet (152 to 366 m) high, as well as two talus caves and a landscape that serves as refuge for a wide variety of species. The unique rock formations attract climbers of all ability levels throughout the year. From March to May, the park is awash in wildflowers in a riot of colors.

Port Chicago Naval Magazine National Memorial

Fast Facts

Established: 2009

Acreage: 5 (2 hectares)

Visitors (2019): 830

Nearest Major Airport: San Francisco Intl. (SFO)

Nearest Major Highways: I-680, CA-242

Fees: $0. All visitors must take the shuttle from the John Muir National Historic site. Reservations are required.

Contact Information:
925-228-8860
www.nps.gov/poch

This memorial preserves the site of the deadliest home front disaster of World War II, honoring 320 Americans killed by a munitions explosion on July 17, 1944. Most of the dead were Black service members in the racially segregated Navy. The largest naval mutiny in U.S. history ensued, and the subsequent trial catalyzed desegregation of the U.S. armed forces.

Giant redwoods at Redwood National Park

Redwood National and State Parks

Fast Facts

Established: 1968
Acreage: 138,999 (56,250 hectares)
Visitors (2019): 504,722
Visitor Centers: Crescent City, Hiouchi, Thomas H. Kuchel, Prairie Creek, Jedediah Smith
Nearest Major Airport: Rogue Valley Intl. (MFR), Medford, OR
Nearest Major Highway: US-101
Fees: $0
Accessibility: More than a dozen trails, campgrounds, or picnic areas are ADA accessible, but not all. A limited supply of beach wheelchairs with balloon-like wheels are available on a first-come, first-served basis.
Contact Information:
  707-464-6101
  www.nps.gov/redw

Coastal redwood forests with virgin groves of ancient trees, including the world's tallest, thrive in the foggy and temperate climate. The park includes 40 miles (72 km) of scenic Pacific coastline, as well as vast prairies, oak woodlands, and wild rivers. Its vast size makes it a good park for exploring by car, bicycle, or electric bike, with scenic drives through a variety of ecosystems.

Rosie the Riveter/World War II Home Front National Historical Park

Fast Facts

Established: 2000
Acreage: 145 (59 hectares)
Visitors (2019): 50,404
Nearest Major Airport: San Francisco Intl. (SFO)
Nearest Major Highway: I-580
Fees: $0
Contact Information:
  510-232-5050
  www.nps.gov/rori

This site commemorates the contributions of the civilians, especially women and minorities, who supported World War II on the home front. Sites open to the public include the Rosie the Riveter Memorial, a shipyard, a Ford jeep and tank assembly plant, war worker housing, and the SS *Red Oak Victory*, the last surviving ship built in the Kaiser Shipyards.

Rosie the Riveter Museum

San Francisco Maritime National Historical Park

Fast Facts

Established: 1988
Acreage: 50 (20 hectares)
Visitors (2019): 4,016,598
Nearest Major Airport: San Francisco Intl. (SFO)
Nearest Major Highways: I-80, US-101
Fees: $15 per person to board the historic vessels.
Contact Information:
  415-561-7000
  www.nps.gov/safr

A fleet of historic vessels at Hyde Street Pier in the Fisherman's Wharf neighborhood commemorates the achievements of seafaring Americans. Other attractions include a small craft collection, a maritime museum and research center, and the WPA-era Aquatic Park historic district.

Santa Monica Mountains National Recreation Area

Fast Facts

Established: 1978
Acreage: 156,670 (63,402 hectares)
Visitors (2019): 707,566
Nearest Major Airport: Los Angeles Intl. (LAX)
Nearest Major Highways: CA-1, US-101
Fees: $0
Accessibility: Mostly inaccessible to wheelchairs.
Contact Information:
  805-370-2301
  www.nps.gov/samo

This recreation area in Los Angeles's backyard offers rugged mountains, a coastline with sandy

The General Sherman Tree at Sequoia National Park is the largest in the world.

Nearest Major Airport: Fresno Yosemite Intl. (FAT)
Nearest Major Highways: CA-190. CA-198, US-395
Fees: $35/vehicle; $20/individual. Includes entry to adjacent Kings Canyon National Park.
Accessibility: Visit www.nps.gov/seki/planyourvisit/ upload/SEKI-Accessibility-Guide_03-2020-508. pdf for extensive information about accessible areas within he park.
Contact Information:
559-565-3341
www.nps.gov/seki

Administered jointly with Kings Canyon National Park, Sequoia is home to great groves of giant sequoias, including the General Sherman tree, the world's largest. Mount Whitney, the highest mountain in the continental U.S. and the most-climbed peak in the Sierra Nevada range, lies on Sequoia's eastern edge (special permits required).

Whiskeytown National Recreation Area
Fast Facts

Established: 1972
Acreage: 42,503 (17,200 hectares)
Visitors (2019): 687,159
Nearest Major Airport: Sacramento Intl. (SMF)
Nearest Major Highways: I-5, CA-299
Fees: $25/vehicle; $15/individual.
Accessibility: The visitor center, park headquarters, restrooms, and two fishing piers are accessible to wheelchairs.
Contact Information:
530-242-3400
www.nps.gov/whis

The crystal clear waters of Whiskeytown Lake give the area its name and a multitude of outdoor recreation opportunities. Whiskeytown also preserves historic sites that highlight the dramatic effects of the Gold Rush on this rugged, mountainous landscape.

beaches and rocky shores, chaparral-blanketed canyons with abundant wildlife, and the 67-mile (108-km) Backbone Trail. The area preserves L.A.'s rare Mediterranean-like ecosystem while also protecting historical sites like Paramount Ranch and the Satwiwa Native American Indian Culture Center.

Sequoia National Park
Fast Facts

Established: 1890
Acreage: 404,063 (163,518 hectares)
Visitors (2019): 1,246,053
Visitor Centers: Foothills, Giant Forest, Lodgepole, Mineral King Ranger Station

THE PACIFIC NORTHWEST

Olympic National Park

Fast Facts

Established: 1909/1938
Acreage: 922,650 (373,384 hectares)
Visitors (2019): 3,245,806
Visitor Centers: Olympic, Hurricane Ridge, Hoh Rain Forest, Kalaloch Ranger Station, Quinault Rain Forest Ranger Station, Staircase Ranger Station, Storm King Ranger Station
Nearest Major Airport: Seattle-Tacoma Intl. (SEA), Seattle, WA
Nearest Major Highways: US-101 forms a ring around the park.
Fees: $30/vehicle; $25/motorcycle; $15 cyclist/individual. All passes are valid for 7 days. Campsites $20/night.
Accessibility: Visit www.nps.gov/olym/planyourvisit/accessibility.htm for an extremely detailed accounting of the accessibility of buildings, campsites, and trails.
Contact Information: 360-565-3130 www.nps.gov/olym

Tucked into the Northwest, separated from the rest of the contiguous 48 states—and even the rest of Washington state—by a maze of bays, inlets, straits, and canals, Olympic National Park is a world unto itself. The park occupies the majority of the Olympic peninsula and includes a thin corridor along the Pacific Coast apart from the rest of its protected lands.

It's often said that Olympic is three parks in one, but that's understating the case by at least half. A towering 7,980-foot (2,432-m) snow-capped mountain peak at the center of the park, thousands of acres of temperate rain forest, and 65 miles (105 km) of wild Pacific coastline do indeed form three discrete environments. But in and around them are cozy pockets, coves, lakes, and passes, largely unconnected to one another except by the two-lane road (US-101) that rings the park. As you drive this loop, you'll encounter half a dozen or more signature brown highway signs alerting you to yet another finger of the park for exploring. Almost anywhere you go in the park, keep an eye out for massive Roosevelt elk, which can grow to more than 1,100 pounds (500 kg).

Start your visit at the park's main visitor center, just south of the quirky gateway town of **Port Angeles**, reached via a three-hour drive from Seattle and Tacoma, or by 45-minute ferry ride from Victoria, BC, Canada, across the Strait of Juan de Fuca. Ask a ranger about visibility at **Hurricane Ridge**, a 45-minute drive up a narrow winding (but paved) mountain road. On a clear day, you'll get magnificent views of the mountaintops to the south and west and the Canadian islands across the Strait to the north. But on a rainy or foggy day, don't bother. All you'll see is mist. You can check conditions on the park service webcam before setting out; just do a browser search for Hurricane Ridge Webcam.

A handful of hiking trails leave from the **Hurricane Ridge Visitor Center**, some going up to nearby peaks, others descending into subalpine lakes and valleys. In spring, wildflowers sprout up in the subalpine meadows, often attracting blacktail deer. The **Heart O' the Hills Campground**, 12 miles (19 km) back on the main road, is the nearest place to pitch a tent; Port Angeles also has numerous lodging options.

In spring and summer, wildflowers frame the view from Hurricane Ridge.

Low nitrogen levels make the waters of Lake Crescent nearly transparent.

Twenty miles (32 km) west of Port Angeles sits the glacier-carved **Lake Crescent**, whose nearly transparent blue-green waters result from extremely low levels of nitrogen, limiting the growth of algae and other plants. You can see straight to the bottom, even at depths of 60 feet (18 m). Crescenti and Beardslee rainbow trout, two species found nowhere else in the world, are among the prized hauls for fly-fishers (catch and release only). The outstanding **Certified Green Restaurant** at **Lake Crescent Lodge** is an idyllic place for locally sourced breakfast, lunch, dinner, or any excuse to sit and enjoy the lake view. For a closer look, you can rent **boats**, **canoes**, or **paddleboards** at the front desk and travel the lake for several miles in either direction.

Two short but worthwhile walks leave from the lodge: the 0.6-mile (1 km) **Moments in Time** self-guided nature trail, and the 1.8-mile (2.9-km) round-trip through old growth forest to **Marymere Falls** (90 feet/27 m). Longer options include a steep (3.4 miles/5.5 km each way) climb to **Aurora Ridge**, and the paved, pancake flat **Spruce Railroad** trail on the opposite side of the lake. The railroad trail is open to **bicycles** and leashed dogs, so you'll likely have company. Spruce Railroad is part of the **Olympic Discovery Trail**, a 70-mile/113-km (and growing every year) route between Port Angeles and the Pacific Coast, so you can travel as far as you like before doubling back. Most folks do that right around **Devil's Punchbowl**, a favorite swimming hole about 1 mile (1.6 km) from the restrooms at the trailhead.

The Lake Crescent area is also a good base for exploring the **Sol Duc River Valley** just west of the lake. Turn off US-101 at Sol Duc-Hot Springs Road and head south for 8 miles (13 km) until you see signs for **Salmon Cascades**. In late summer, you might see chinook and coho salmon leaping up the Sol Duc River to spawn; cutthroat trout and steelhead swim upstream in winter and spawn in spring. Four miles (6 km) beyond this pullout is **Sol Duc Hot Springs and Resort**, a hotel and adjacent campground (open from March to October) with a full-service restaurant and a spa where you can get a massage, take a dip in the freshwater swimming pool, or soak in one of three large outdoor mineral pools fed by nearby hot springs. Admission to the pools is complementary for hotel guests; day trippers can pay for a 90-minute session.

A short trail leads to Sol Duc Falls.

The resort and campground sit amidst the **Seven Lakes Basin**, an area of old growth rain forest rich with lakes and waterfalls. The most popular trail starts at the end of the paved road and meanders 0.8 miles (1.3 km) to **Sol Duc Falls**, one of the most iconic cataracts on the peninsula. For a longer hike, you can take the **Lover's Lane Trail** from the resort to the falls. Both of these walks have minimal elevation gain. For an uphill hike, climb 2.6 miles (4.2 km) to **Mink Lake** or 3.8 miles (6.1 km) to **Deer Lake**.

Thru-hikers with backcountry permits can trek overland 23 miles (37 km) from Sol Duc Valley to the **Hoh Rain Forest Visitor Center**, cresting **Bogachiel Peak** along the way. But most visitors will need to drive back down to US-101, stray into the Olympic National Forest, then re-enter the park at Upper Hoh Road. The 72-mile (116-km) trip takes about two hours without traffic. Break up the drive with a stop in Forks, WA, the only town of any size on this side of the park, where you'll find a full-service grocery store and a handful of lodgings and restaurants.

Heavily laden trees in the Hall of Mosses

In September, if you're lucky, you might hear male elks bugling in search of a mate.

Unless you arrive early in the day, you'll probably be surrounded by other visitors as you walk the 1-mile (1.6-km) **Hall of Mosses** loop. It's popular for a reason; it has one of the densest concentrations of old growth forest. Several kinds of mosses blanket the hemlocks, spruce, red cedars, and the occasional Douglas fir, while multiple species of ferns carpet the forest floor. Many of the trees in the Hall of Mosses are so jacketed they look like the haunted forest from *The Wizard of Oz*. The mossiest trees are usually maples, which are able to share more nutrients with the mosses than the evergreens. Sometimes maple branches will break from the weight of so much

moss. In September, the rain forest is a propitious place to hear male elk bugling during their mating season.

The nearby **Spruce Nature Trail** makes a nice complement to the Hall of Mosses, traversing an amazing variety of terrain over its short 1.2 miles (1.9 km). It's replete with nurse logs: fallen timbers out of which new trees have taken root. In some cases, the original log has rotted away, and tall offspring stand in a straight line called a colonnade. The **Hoh River**, which runs parallel to the Spruce Trail, and is cloudy with glacial snowmelt. It stands in stark contrast with crystal clear **Taft Creek**, which streams through the Nature Trail and the Hall of Mosses, its waters

having been filtered of detritus by the rain forest soil, sand, and gravel.

To experience the mystical **beaches** at the far western edge of the park, you'll want to keep an eye on the tides. The beaches are best viewed at low tide, when there's little chance of getting trapped by incoming waves. The parking lots at most beaches list the tide schedule, but there's little point in driving all the way out to the edge of the country if there's no beach to walk on. **Rialto Beach**, 14 miles (23 km) west of Forks, is the quintessential Olympic beach, with sea stacks rising up from the ocean and shores littered with giant drift logs that flowed down river only to be returned to the beach by

Rialto Beach is the quintessential Olympic beach.

the ocean's pounding waves. Enterprising visitors have built rudimentary forts and miniature cabins out of fallen logs. From Rialto, you can walk 1.5 miles (2.4 km) north past **Split Rock** to the sea-carved arch of **Hole-in-the-Wall**.

Ruby Beach, 27 miles (43 km) southwest of Forks, is another iconic beach, and a terrific place to spot bald eagles. The prosaically named **Beach 4**, another 4 miles (6.4 km) south, is prime tidepooling territory. Sea stars, anemones, and other marine wildlife get trapped in the rocks until the next high tide can wash them back out to sea. Wear sturdy shoes.

The **Lake Quinault** region, in the southwest corner of the park, is popular throughout winter for its world-class trout and salmon fishing, but in other seasons, it's a little less frenetic than other parts of the park. It has something for

everyone: fishing and boating in the lake, which is warm enough for swimming in summer; nature trails through the rain forest; waterfalls that wouldn't

look out of place in Hawaii; the world's tallest Sitka spruce tree (perhaps not as impressive as it sounds); hiking and backcountry camping in the delightfully

Building a driftwood fort is a cherished pastime on many of Olympic's beaches.

Olympic beaches are stellar spots for spotting marine life at low tide.

named Colonel Bob Wilderness; and the 1926 **Lake Quinault Lodge**. Franklin Roosevelt's 1937 stay at the Lodge is often cited as the impetus for Olympic's designation as a National Park a year later; the lodge's dining room is named in his honor. Some of the terrain in the Quinault region is technically Olympic National Forest, rather than the national park, and the lake itself is administered by the Quinault Indian Reservation.

The gauge outside Lake Quinault Lodge measures rain in feet, not inches.

Mount Rainier National Park

America's fifth National Park often feels like a massive game of Chutes and Ladders. The ladders are the dozens of hiking trails that ascend the 14,410-foot (4,392-m) mountain from all sides. The chutes, meanwhile, are the countless waterfalls that carry snowmelt from the summit down to pristine streams, rushing rivers, and glassy lakes. In spring and late summer, wildflowers turn the meadows a different brilliant color each month.

Tying them all together is the **Wonderland Trail**, a 93-mile (150-km) route that encircles the mountain, climbing and falling through the various regions of the park as it makes its circuit. Much of the Wonderland Trail traverses terrain far from the nearest roads, but it darts in and out of some of the park's more accessible areas, enticing visitors to sample its numerous charms. Even if you're only up for a mile-long hike, you're likely to overlap some portion of the Wonderland Trail.

Most visitors arrive from Seattle, Tacoma, and other points west, entering the park at the **Nisqually Gate**; they're rewarded with a knockout view of the majestic mountain just 6 miles (10 km) later, usually from the front porch of the **National Park Inn**, the only lodging in the park that's open year-round. The adjacent **Longmire Museum** is named for the man who developed his mining claim here in the 19th century and saw its potential as a vacation destination. The 0.7-mile (1-km) **Trail of the Shadows** loop is a sort of outdoor museum, meandering past the springs that first attracted visitors and the

Fast Facts

Established: 1899
Acreage: 236,381 (95,660 hectares)
Visitors (2019): 1,501,621
Visitor Centers: Henry M. Jackson (Paradise), Longmire Museum, Sunrise, Ohanapecosh, Carbon River Ranger Station
Nearest Major Airport: Seattle-Tacoma Intl. (SEA), Seattle, WA
Nearest Major Highways: I-5, US-12 (south side), WA-123 (east side), WA-165 (northwest side), WA-706 (main entrance)
Fees: $30/vehicle; $25/motorcycle; $15 cyclist and individual. All passes are valid for 7 days. Campsites $20/night.
Accessibility: Buildings are generally accessible but even paved trails are usually too steep for visitors to negotiate in wheelchairs.
Contact Information: 360-569-2211 www.nps.gov/mora

cabins and other structures they left behind.

Christine Falls is easily visible from the main park road, tempting many drivers to stop and gawk. Don't be one of them. There's a parking area just beyond the falls, where you can stroll to a viewpoint that's better (and safer) than on the narrow bridge. Eight miles (13 km) beyond Christine Falls is **Narada Falls**, popular enough to have its own full-sized parking lot. One of the nicest aspects of Mt. Rainier is how many of its trails connect points of interest to one another. Case in point: the 1.6-mile (2.6-km) segment of the Wonderland Trail that connects Narada Falls to **Reflection Lakes**. Take this

Visit Reflection Lakes early on a sunny morning to see the mountain reflected in the lake's surface.

Christine Falls

hike early in the morning for two views of the mountain: one above the waterline and another upside down on its glassy surface.

From Narada Falls, it's a winding 3-mile (5-km) drive up the serpentine road to the Paradise area, the unofficial center of the park, and home to the main **Henry M. Jackson Visitor Center**. The ever-popular **Skyline Trail** leaves from the visitor center; the 1-mile (1.6-km) round-trip walk to **Myrtle Falls** is paved but too steep for wheelchairs to negotiate without assistance. More adventurous hikers can climb the steep (1,700 feet/ 518 m of elevation gain over just 1.5 miles/2.4 km) trail past a vista of the **Nisqually Glacier** to **Panorama Point**, with its 360-degree views of the

The popular Skyline Trail ends at Panorama Point and its 360-degree views of the Tattoosh Range.

Some trees in the Grove of the Patriarchs are more than 1,000 years old.

Tattoosh Range. On a clear day, the snow-capped peaks of **Mt. Adams**, **Mt. St. Helens**, and Oregon's **Mt. Hood** are visible in the distance. A variety of other trails intersect the Skyline Loop, allowing hikes of 6 miles (10 km) or more. A less crowded option is the 5-mile (8-km) **Lakes Trail Loop**, which links Paradise with Reflection Lakes and **Lake Louise** but lacks the mountain view.

Two well-traveled attractions welcome visitors who enter the park via the **Stevens Canyon Entrance** in the park's southeast corner: the **Grove of the Patriarchs** (1.3 miles/2 km round-trip) and the **Silver Falls Trail** (1-mile/1.6 km round-trip). Parking in this area is tight, so be prepared for a hike from your car even before you hit the

trailhead. The shady Grove of the Patriarchs trail through old growth forest is a perfect escape on a hot day. The oldest (1,000 years) and tallest (300 feet/91 m)

trees, at the far end of the trail, are reached via an idyllic but rickety, **one-person-at-a-time suspension bridge** over the crystal clear waters of the

A pedestrian suspension bridge leads to the Grove of the Patriarchs.

The Tipsoo Lake area is popular for hiking and picnicking.

Ohanapecosh River. On a busy day, the wait to cross can add a half hour to your itinerary.

The Silver Falls Trail starts on the other side of the park road, descending 300 feet (91 m) through evergreens of the same sort as in the Grove of the Patriarchs, but only half as old and not nearly as tall. The designated viewpoint is impressive, but an even better view awaits 600 feet (183 m) farther down the trail. Visitors staying at the Ohanapecosh Campground can also hike the other way up the trail, 1.1 miles (1.7 km) to the falls.

The west-facing views of the mountain from the **Tipsoo Lake** area are simply breathtaking. The trail around the lake is about a mile (1.6 km), but the 3-mile (4.8 km) loop around **Naches Peak** is well worth the extra effort. The path doesn't actually go over the peak, but you won't mind.

The **White River Entrance** on the east side of the park is the gateway to the **Sunrise** area, which opened to tourism 25 years later than the rest of the park and is open only from July to late September. The views of Mount Rainier practically slap you in the face as you round the **hairpin turn at Sunrise Point**. There's usually more snow visible on Rainier's peak from this angle, which is slightly removed from the mountaintop. In their rush to get to the **Sunrise Visitor Center**, most people jump back

into their cars as soon as they get the perfect selfie from the Sunrise Point parking lot. In doing so, they miss out on the lovely **Palisades Lake Trail**. This trail is more of a chute than a ladder, descending 500 feet (152 m) into a thickly wooded dell dotted with alpine meadows. It's 1.5 miles (2.4 km) each way to **Clover Lake**, or 3 miles (5 km) each way to **Hidden Lake**. Look for wildflowers here (and practically everywhere nearby) in the spring and early summer.

Almost everyone who continues to the Sunrise Visitor Center at the end of the road walks the 1.5-mile (2.4-km) round-trip **Sunrise Nature Trail**, which boasts knockout views of the summit. The nature trail

Sunrise Point has one of the best views of Mount Rainier.

connects to longer trails along **Sourdough Ridge**: 1.5 miles (2.4 km) each way to **Frozen Lake**, 2.4 miles (3.9 km) to **1st Burroughs Mountain**, and 3.0 miles (4.8 km) to **2nd Burroughs Mountain**. To make a loop out of any of these walks, return to the visitor center via a different section of the Wonderland Trail past **Shadow Lake**. The 2-mile (3.2-km) **Silver Forest Trail** heads east, away from the mountain, so you get the views on the way back. Stop at the **Emmons Vista Overlooks** (0.6 miles/1 km from the trailhead) to see the White River dropping out of the **Emmons Glacier**.

Rainier is first and foremost a hiker's park. But the well-maintained roads are a pleasure to drive, because they were intricately planned to enhance the natural setting rather than pave over it. The roads are open to **bicycles**, but they're too narrow for most cyclists to relax while riding alongside heavy summer traffic. Bikes are prohibited on all trails except the **Westside Road to Klapatche Ridge**. But there are no places to rent bikes anywhere in the park. Fishing and boating are permitted in the park's various lakes, but you'll need to bring your own boat.

There are also precious few places to get food in the park. The national park lodges at **Longmire**, **Paradise**, and **Sunrise** have sit-down dining rooms as well as cafes selling prepackaged sandwiches and other snacks. Other than that, the only options are a few restaurants in Ashford, outside the Nisqually Entrance, or in Packwood, 12 miles (19 km) south of the Stevens Canyon Entrance. If you're planning to camp at the park, stock up before you arrive.

Nearly two-thirds of Mount Rainier's visitors arrive in the short summer season between Memorial Day and Labor Day. Many of the trails are frozen until late May, but there's a spectacular, less-crowded window in September before the snow returns. The park remains open in winter for cross-country skiing and snowshoeing, but not much else.

Crater Lake National Park

The eruption and subsequent collapse of **Mount Mazama** some 7,700 years ago created the deepest lake in the United States (1,943 ft/592 m) and a spectacle that can take your breath away. Crater Lake is fed by rain and snowmelt, but no rivers or streams carry sediment into the caldera, making it the cleanest large body of water in the world.

As gorgeous as the lake may be (and it is indeed awe-inspiring), it's a bit like the hole in the middle of a donut. There's only one way to get down to water's edge, and it requires hiking down a steep, 1.1-mile (1.7-km) trail to the shore. For that reason, most visitors prefer to admire its beauty from afar.

The best way to do that is by circumnavigating the historic **Rim Drive**. The full 33-mile (53-km) loop is usually open from July through October, but snow (an average of 43 feet/13 m every year) can make portions of the drive impassable almost any time of year. Only the 7 miles (11 km) between the two visitor centers remains open year-round, and sometimes plows have trouble keeping even that much clear. The rim drive is narrow, winding, often slowed by congestion . . . and marvelous. A total of 30 overlooks are designed

Fast Facts

Established: 1902
Acreage: 183,224 (74,148 hectares)
Visitors (2019): 704,512
Visitor Centers: Rim (summer only), Steel (closed until 2023)
Nearest Major Airport: Rogue Valley Intl.-Medford (MFR), Medford, OR
Nearest Major Highways: US-97, OR-62
Fees: $30/vehicle; $25/motorcycle; $15 cyclist and individual. Vehicle and motorcycle fees are reduced by $10 from Nov. 1 to May 21. All passes are valid for 7 days.
Accessibility: All commercial facilities, most restrooms, and some picnic areas are accessible, but most of the park is in the backcountry and inaccessible to visitors with impaired mobility.
Contact Information: 541-594-3000
www.nps.gov/crla

Discovery Point

Pumice Castle Overlook shows off a different side of the caldera.

to highlight specific views of the lake. Most of the pullouts are unnamed and therefore attract fewer visitors than the more popular named stops.

Start your circuit at **Crater Lake Lodge**, a historic 1915 hotel with 71 rooms perched on the edge of the crater. The views from the lodge's dining room are so exceptional that you might decide not to get back in your car at all. Assuming you do, though, head clockwise from there to **Discovery Point**, where gold prospector John Hillman became the first European American to set eyes on what he dubbed "Deep Blue Lake" in 1853. **Watchman Overlook** is another highlight, delivering the best views of **Wizard Island**. The island is a cinder cone within the lake that erupted some 400 years

after the initial explosion, and which itself has a crater in its middle.

Pumice Castle Overlook shows off a different side of the caldera: some visitors see the shape of a medieval castle in the eroded coral-colored pumice. The turnoff for this overlook is unmarked; look for it 1.1 miles

Phantom Ship Island is the smaller of the two islands within Crater Lake.

Pinnacles Overlook is worth a detour off the rim drive.

(1.8 km) west of **Cloudcap Overlook** or 2.4 miles (3.9 km) east of **Phantom Ship Overlook**, which is the best place to catch a glimpse of the lake's other, much smaller island. **Pinnacles Overlook** requires a 6-mile (10-km) detour from Rim Drive, but its views of colorful 100-foot (30-m) spires are worth it. The turnout for **Vidae Falls** leads not only to a 100-foot (30-m) waterfall over a glacier-carved cliff, but also to **Grayback Drive**, a gravel road popular with bikers because it is closed to motor vehicles. Bikes are also allowed on Rim Drive, but this is no leisurely ride; there are a lot of hills (3,800 ft/1,158 m of elevation change) and no shoulders.

If you don't want to do the driving yourself, hop aboard the ADA-compliant **Crater Lake Trolley** (www.craterlaketrolley. net; $29/adult aged 14 and older; $26/senior; $18/child aged 6-13). The two-hour tour hits all the highlights, with narration that helps visitors understand the geologic history of the park. Reservations are recommended.

Cleetwood Cove is almost directly opposite the Rim Visitor Center and is the only (legal) way to access the lake. The 1.1-mile (1.7-km) **Cleetwood Cove Trail** descends 700 feet (213 m), which wouldn't be so bad if you didn't have to hike

Hike 700 feet (213 m) down to the water's edge to take a boat tour of the lake.

Stop at Watchman Overlook for the best views of Wizard Island.

back up it at the end of the day. Unfortunately, there's no mule ride to carry weary walkers, but there are benches along the route. **Swimming** is permitted within 100 yards (91 m) of the rough and rocky shore, but there's no beach, and the water rarely gets above 60 °F (16 °C). To keep non-native organisms out of the pristine lake, bringing anything beyond a swimsuit—snorkels, goggles, wetsuits, canoes, kayaks, paddleboards, and the like—is forbidden.

Fishing, on the other hand is not only permitted, it's encouraged, as a way to remove **rainbow trout** and **kokanee salmon** that were introduced in the first half of the 20th century. No fish are native to the lake. No fishing license is required, and there's no limit to your catch,

but no live bait of any kind is allowed.

The main reason people go down to the lake is to see it by boat. A standard 2-hour **lake cruise** takes in Wizard Island, Phantom Ship, and other natural wonders. Or you can take the **shuttle** straight to Wizard Island and spend the day hiking, swimming, or just enjoying the view from the bottom instead of the top. Keep your eyes open for **bald eagles**, which visit frequently in the summer. Visit www.travelcraterlake.com for schedules and prices.

The old-growth forest that surrounds Crater Lake is chockablock with trails to suit hikers of all abilities. From late June through early July, the **Castle Crest Trail** (0.5 miles/ 0.8 km loop) erupts with

wildflowers fed by springs on the surrounding hillside. The trailhead is a short walk or an even shorter drive from park headquarters. Near **Mazama Village**, the 1.1-mile (1.8 km) **Godfrey Glen** loop through the forest welcomes dogs on leash and mobility-impaired visitors on all-terrain wheelchairs. The flat trail to **Plaikni Falls** (2.0 miles/ 3.2 km round-trip) starts from Pinnacles Road and ends at a lush cascade fed by snowmelt.

The moderate 2.0-mile (3.2-km) **Discovery Point Trail** traces the edge of the crater— sometimes frighteningly so— linking **Rim Village** with Discovery Point. It's one of the easier segments of the **Rim Trail**, which continues another 8 miles (13 km) north beyond Discovery Point, where it joins the Pacific

Snow can fall at Crater Lake any time of the year.

Crest Trail. The **Watchman Peak** trail gains 420 feet (128 m) in elevation over 0.8 miles (1.3 km) on its way to the historic fire tower, built in 1932 and still in use today. The **Annie Creek Trail**, a 1.7-mile (2.7-km) loop, has it all: a canyon, a creek running through it, wildflowers in summer, and occasional wildlife sightings. Big mammals are rarely seen in the park, but you might spot foxes, porcupines, coyotes, or owls.

Mount Scott is the highest point in the park (8,929 feet/2,721 m), accessible via a strenuous 4.4-mile (7.1-km) round-trip climb from East Rim Drive. The best lake views from the peak are in the morning.

Garfield Peak isn't quite as high, but the 3.6-mile (5.8-km) round-trip ascent and descent has great views along the way. Both of these trails are closed seasonally—sometimes as late in the year as July—by snow.

The **Pacific Crest Trail** crosses through the park a few miles west of the lake over its 2,650-mile (4,265-km) route from Mexico to Canada. Through-hikers who want to see the lake usually detour east at the north entrance road (for southbound hikers) or Castle Creek (for those headed north) and follow the **Rim Trail** before rejoining the PCT 18 miles (30 km) later. Park visitors who want a taste of the PCT can drive 1 mile (1.6 km)

west on OR-62 from the **Annie Spring Entrance Station** to a spot where they can join the trail.

In addition to the Lodge, **Crater Lake Hospitality** operates two **campgrounds** in the park, both open only in summer. **Mazama**, the larger of the two, is near the Annie Springs entrance, and features 214 campsites (75 for RVs), 18 electric hookups, showers, laundry, and a camp store. **Lost Creek Campground**, on Pinnacles Road, has just 16 tent-only sites, and makes up in solitude what it lacks in availability. Cold-water faucets, toilets, and food storage lockers are the only facilities here.

Denali National Park and Preserve

Denali is not like other national parks.

For one thing, it's humongous. Yellowstone, Yosemite, Olympic, Great Smoky Mountains, and Grand Canyon National Parks could all fit comfortably within its confines at the same time, and there would still be room for all of New York City's five boroughs. For another, it's intentionally undeveloped, designed by Congress to remain a primitive wilderness. That means there are no hotels within the park, and only one road, most of which is off-limits to private vehicles.

There are only a handful of marked trails, primarily around the visitor centers, and most of them less than 2.7 miles (4.3 km). But unlike in other parks, visitors to Denali are encouraged to tramp around the pristine wilderness, whack through brush, and bounce on spongy tundra mounds. There are no bridges or wooden boardwalks across streams and creeks; you're going to get your feet wet. This untrammeled wilderness makes for exceptional wildlife viewing, especially as you delve deeper into the park

Denali is open year-round, but the vast majority of visitors arrive in the short (but almost never dark) **summer season** from mid-May through early September. Private cars can travel the first 15 miles (24 km) of the park road to **Savage River**, but beyond that point, visitors must ride the park buses. Over the next 77 miles (124 km), the road climbs through low elevation taiga forest to high alpine tundra and snow-capped mountains. Hovering above it all is the eponymous 20,310-foot (6,190-m) Mt. Denali (formerly Mt. McKinley), North America's highest peak,

Denali National Park is immense, with just one through-road.

guarded by more than a dozen glaciers on all sides. On a clear day, you can see "the mountain" as early as mile marker 9.

The simplest way into the backcountry is on a **transit bus** (prices start at $38/adults aged 16 and older). These Kelly-green school buses depart from the **Denali Bus Depot** and travel to one of four destinations. The shortest excursion is the 6.5-hour round-trip to **Toklat River** (mile 53). Longer journeys make a rest stop at Toklat River and

Most of Denali is roadless, trail-less wilderness.

Buses in Denali make unscheduled stops when wildlife comes into view.

then continue to **Eielson Visitor Center** (mile 66; eight hours round-trip), **Wonder Lake** (mile 85; 11 hours round-trip) and **Kantishna** (mile 92; 12 hours round-trip). All transit buses make 15-minute rest stops every 90 minutes, and unscheduled stops when wildlife comes into view.

Specially outfitted **camper buses** have extra space to accommodate backpacks and bicycles, and are available only for visitors with campground reservations or backcountry permits. All other transit buses are hop-on hop-off, so you can flag one down anywhere along the park road as long as there is space available. Campers and hikers should carry bear spray at all times; mosquito repellent is also a good idea most of the year.

Visitors should carry bear spray at all times.

For a more guided experience, consider a **narrated bus tour**. Driven by a trained naturalist, narrated tours are designed for people who want to learn a little more about the surroundings. Narrated buses also make frequent stops for restroom breaks and wildlife viewing, but you can't hop off one bus and onto another. Painted a tan color, narrated buses are also converted school buses, so they're not as comfortable as a Greyhound, but there are plenty of opportunities to get off and stretch your legs.

The **Denali Natural History** tour is the shortest bus ride (4–5 hours), and also the least expensive ($102/adult aged 16 and older; $43/child 15 and younger). It travels 27 miles (43 km) into the park to **Teklanika River**. Wildlife viewing opportunities on this trip are not as plentiful as on longer trips, but the driver's narration and a cultural presentation by Alaska Native experts immerse visitors into the landscape, geology, and history of Denali.

The **Tundra Wilderness Tour** is a better choice if you want to see big mammals like moose and bears. It turns around at Stony Overlook, 62 miles (100 km) into the backcountry, and lasts 7–8 hours. (The bus goes only as far as Toklat River May 20–31.) The drivers do an admirable job of scouting for wildlife while keeping their eyes on the road and narrating the experience. The cost is $163/adult aged 16 and older; $74/child aged 15 and younger. To participate in ranger-led programs, you can add an excursion to the **Eielson Visitor Center**, which showcases works by the artists in residence.

For the full Denali experience, consider the 12-hour **Kantishna Experience Tour**, which travels the entire 92-mile (148-km) length of the park road to the old gold mining town of **Kantishna**. Like the Tundra Wilderness Tour, it's an excellent way to see wildlife, and it is the only tour narrated by a National Park Service ranger. The price ($240/adult aged 16 and older; $113/child aged 15 and

The northern lights are often visible from the park.

younger) includes lunch, a snack, and drinks.

All tour prices include the $15 park entry fee. There are usually morning and afternoon departure times for both the Natural History and Wilderness tours; the Kantishna tour leaves once a day in the morning. Parents should bring car seats for children under 7 years old. For more information on how to choose a tour, visit www.nps.gov/dena/planyourvisit/bus-tours.htm.

Wildlife sightings are never guaranteed, of course, but the high seats on the buses give you one of the best perches for spotting animals. There will also be dozens of other eyes on the bus scanning for bear, moose, caribou, and other species in every direction. In general, look for grizzly bears and caribou anywhere near a river, Dall sheep high on mountains, and moose in the hills north of Wonder Lake at the end of the road. You may also

Caribou are plentiful in Denali.

encounter moose in the dense forest between the park entrance and the Denali Visitor Center.

Equally elusive is the mountain itself, which sometimes hides in the clouds or behind an overcast scrim of fog. You may need to spend three or four days in

Denali before getting one with clear skies.

While you wait, you can visit the **Sled Dog Kennels**, where from June 1 to September 1, park rangers demonstrate this traditional Alaskan mode of transportation at 10 a.m., 2 p.m.,

This view is reward for climbing 1,700 feet (518 m) to the top of Mount Healy.

and 4 p.m. There's no parking at the kennels, but buses leave from the Denali Visitor Center approximately 40 minutes before each demonstration. There are no programs in winter, but if you visit between September and May, you might catch sight of a team packing up for a trip or returning from a multi-night sojourn.

Trail hiking in Denali is kind of like ordering the cheeseburger at a seafood restaurant. But for those who don't want to go off into the wild, there are a number of marked routes in the park, mostly near the Denali Visitor Center. The **Horseshoe Lake Trail** (3 miles/5 km round-trip from the visitor center) makes a loop around the lake of the same name. On clear days, you might get a glimpse of "the mountain" from the steep (1,700 feet/518 m of elevation gain over 2.7 miles/ 4.3 km each way) **Mt. Healy Overlook Trail**.

Another set of trails are clustered near Savage River, the last part of the park accessible by private car. The easy **Savage River Loop Trail** (1.7 miles/ 2.7 km round-trip) parallels the canyon carved by the river from Mount Margaret to Healy Ridge and is one of the better places to spot wildlife without boarding a bus. The **Savage Alpine Trail** leaves from the **Mountain Vista** parking area and climbs 1,400 feet (427 m) over 2.4 miles (3.9 km) before depositing you at the Savage River parking lot for a total distance of 4 miles (6.4 km) one way. Watch for Dall sheep along this trail. To save retracing your steps, take the free shuttle bus back to your car.

Denali has six campgrounds, three of which can accommodate RVs up to 40 feet (12 m), although there are no electrical or water hookups. All campgrounds have some kind of toilet facilities, and most have potable water. **Riley Creek Campground** (142 sites) is the closest one to the park entrance and is the only one open year-round. **Savage River Campground** (32 sites) is also reachable by private car at mile 13 on the Denali Park Road. Visitors who stay three or more nights at **Teklanika River Campground** (53 sites) receive special permission to drive beyond Savage River to mile 29, as long as they leave their vehicles at the campground. **Sanctuary River** (7 sites), **Igloo Creek** (7 sites), and **Wonder Lake** (28 sites) campgrounds are all tents only.

Wonder Lake truly lives up to its name.

MORE TO SEE IN THE PACIFIC NORTHWEST

ALASKA
Alagnak Wild River
Fast Facts

Established: 1980
Length: 67 miles
Visitors (2019): NA
Visitor Center: King Salmon
Nearest Major Airport: Ted Stevens Anchorage Intl. (ANC), Anchorage, AK
Nearest Major Highways: None. The park cannot be reached by road. Air taxi flights can be chartered from Anchorage and King Salmon (AKN) airports. Visit the park website for a list of licensed transportation and guide services.
Fees: $0
Accessibility: Not accessible.
Contact Information:
907-246-3305
www.nps.gov/alag

Preserves 67 miles (108 km) of the Alagnak River between Katmai Lodge and Kukaklek Lake (located within Katmai National Park and Preserve). The river is renowned for its outstanding whitewater floating, abundant wildlife, natural scenery, and sport fishing for five species of salmon.

Aleutian Islands World War II National Historic Area
Fast Facts

Established: 1976
Acreage: NA
Visitors (2019): NA
Nearest Major Airport: Ted Stevens Anchorage Intl. (ANC), Anchorage, AK
Nearest Major Highways: None. The best way to reach the islands is on the Alaska Marine Ferry service from Homer or Kodiak Island. Some charter flights are available from Anchorage.
Fees: The World War II Visitor Center charges $5 per person, $2 for those aged 55 and older, and is free to veterans. There is a $6/person ($10/family) fee to visit the National Historic Area on Mount Ballyhoo, which is privately owned by the Ounalashka Corporation.
Accessibility: Largely inaccessible. The park website has detailed information for travelers with a range of disabilities.
Contact Information:
907-644-3472
www.nps.gov/aleu

During World War II, the remote Aleutian Islands, home to the *Unangax̂* (Aleut) people for over 8,000 years, became a fiercely contested battleground in the Pacific. This 1,000-mile (1,609-km) archipelago saw invasion by Japanese forces, the occupation of two islands, a mass relocation of civilians, a 15-month air war, and one of the deadliest battles in the Pacific Theater.

Aniakchak National Monument and Preserve
Fast Facts

Established: 1978/1980
Acreage: National Monument: 137,176 (55,513 hectares); National Preserve: 464,118 (187,822 hectares)
Visitors (2019): 100
Visitor Center: King Salmon
Nearest Major Airport: Ted Stevens Anchorage Intl. (ANC), Anchorage, AK
Nearest Major Highways: None. The park cannot be reached by road. Air taxi flights can be chartered from Anchorage and King Salmon (AKN). Visit the park website for a list of licensed transportation and guide services. The preserve can also be accessed by motorboat along the Pacific Ocean coastline.
Fees: $0
Accessibility: Not accessible. No federal facilities.
Contact Information:
907-246-3305
www.nps.gov/ania

Preserves the Aniakchak Caldera, one of the great dry calderas in the world. At 30 square miles (78 square km), it's 50 percent bigger than Crater Lake. Located in the volcanically active Aleutian Mountains, the Aniakchak last erupted in 1931. The crater includes lava flows, cinder cones, and explosion pits, as well as Surprise Lake, source of the Aniakchak River, which cascades through a 1,500-foot (457-m) gash in the crater wall. There are no federal facilities at the monument or the preserve.

Bering Land Bridge National Preserve
Fast Facts
Established: 1978
Acreage: 2,697,391 (1,091,596 hectares)
Visitors (2019): 2,642
Visitor Center: The visitor center is in Nome, AK, 100 miles (160 km) away.
Nearest Airport: Nome Airport (OME), Nome, AK. Fairbanks Intl. (FAI), Fairbanks, AK, is the closest major airport, more than 260 miles (418 km) away.
Nearest Major Highways: None. The park cannot be reached by road. Most visitors arrive by private plane, air taxi, or snowmobile.
Fees: $0
Accessibility: None. Limited federal facilities.
Contact Information:
907-443-2522
www.nps.gov/bela

Preserves a remnant of the land bridge on the Seward Peninsula that once connected Asia and North America more than 13,000 years ago. Paleontological and archeological resources abound; large populations of migratory birds nest here. Ash explosion craters and lava flows, rare in the Arctic, are also present. Visitor facilities are limited.

Cape Krusenstern National Monument
Fast Facts
Established: 1978
Acreage: 649,096 (262,680 hectares)
Visitors (2019): 16,226
Nearest Major Airport: Fairbanks Intl. (FAI), Fairbanks, AK; Ted Stevens Anchorage Intl. (ANC), Anchorage, AK
Nearest Major Highways: None. Most visitors arrive by private plane, air taxi, or boat.

Fees: $0
Accessibility: None. Limited federal facilities
Contact Information:
907-442-3890
www.nps.gov/cakr

Preserves archeological sites along 70 miles (113 km) of shoreline on the Chukchi Sea, north of the Arctic Circle. More than 114 beach ridges illustrate Inupiat communities of every known cultural period in arctic Alaska, dating back some 5,000 years. The Inupiat continue to use the area today. Nearly pristine barrier islands, lagoons, and beaches provide habitat for fish, marine mammals, and migratory birds. Visitor facilities are limited.

Gates of the Arctic National Park and Preserve
Fast Facts
Established: 1978/1980
Acreage: National Park: 7,523,897 (3,044,816 hectares); National Preserve 948,608 (383,888 hectares)
Visitors (2019): 10,518
Visitor Centers: Bettles, Arctic Interagency (Coldfoot, AK), Anaktuvuk Ranger Station
Nearest Major Airport: Fairbanks Intl. (FAI), Fairbanks, AK
Nearest Major Highways: None. Most visitors arrive by air taxi or hike in from the Dalton Highway, an unpaved two-lane road with no services between Fairbanks and the park.
Fees: $0
Accessibility: The visitor centers are the only areas of the park accessible to people with impaired mobility.
Contact Information:
907-459-3730
www.nps.gov/gaar

The second-largest national park in the U.S. lies north of the Arctic Circle, protecting a large swath of the Central Brooks Range, the northernmost extension of the Rocky Mountains. The park and preserve are contiguous with Kobuk Valley National Park and Noatak National Preserve, forming one of the largest stretches of wilderness anywhere in the world and featuring jagged peaks, gentle arctic valleys, wild rivers, and many lakes.

Glacier Bay National Park and Preserve
Fast Facts

Established: 1925/1980

Acreage: National park: 3,223,38 (1,320 hectares); National Preserve: 58,406 (23,636 hectares)

Visitors (2019): 672,087

Visitor Centers: The Visitor Center and a separate Visitor Information Station are both located in Bartlett Cove, 10 miles (16 km) from the local airport in Gustavus.

Nearest Major Airport: Juneau Intl. (JNU), Juneau, AK

Nearest Major Highways: None. The park is accessible only by plane or boat. Most visitors arrive on cruise ships.

Fees: $0

Accessibility: Glacier Bay Lodge and Visitor Center are accessible, but not all trails are.

Contact Information:
907-697-2230
www.nps.gov/glba

Preserves a land of rugged mountains, calving glaciers, temperate rain forests, wild coastlines, and deep sheltered fjords in Alaska's Inside Passage. It is a spiritual homeland for the Huna Tlingit, a sanctuary for marine and terrestrial animals, a natural scientific laboratory, a premier destination for boating and outdoor recreation, and a favored stop on most cruises of the Inside Passage.

Katmai National Park and Preserve
Fast Facts

Established: 1918/1980

Acreage: National Park: 3,674,368; (1,486,964 hectares); National Preserve: 418,699 (169,442 hectares)

Visitors (2019): 84,167

Visitor Centers: King Salmon, Brooks Camp, Robert F. Griggs

Nearest Major Airport: Ted Stevens Anchorage Intl. (ANC), Anchorage, AK

Nearest Major Highways: None. The park is accessible only by boat or air taxi flights from Anchorage, Dillingham, Homer, King Salmon, or Kodiak.

Fees: $0

Accessibility: Largely inaccessible except for public buildings (including restrooms) at Brooks Camp.

Contact Information:
907-246-3305
www.nps.gov/katm

Variety marks this vast landscape of forests, lakes, mountains, and marshlands abounding with wildlife.

With unimpeded views of calving glaciers, Glacier Bay is a favored stop on many cruises of Alaska's Inside Passage.

Alaska brown bears thrive on the red salmon of Katmai National Park's lakes and streams.

The Alaska brown bear thrives here, feeding on red salmon that spawn in the lakes and streams. Wild rivers and renowned sport fishing add to the attractions of this subarctic environment where 9,000 years of human history are preserved. Here, in 1912, Novarupta Volcano erupted violently, forming the ash-filled "Valley of 10,000 Smokes," so named for the steam rising from countless fumaroles.

Kenai Fjords National Park
Fast Facts

Established: 1978/1980
Acreage: 670 (271 hectares)
Visitors (2019): 356,601
Visitor Center: The visitor center is located outside the park in the town of Seward, and is open only during summer.
Nearest Major Airport: Ted Stevens Anchorage Intl. (ANC), Anchorage, AK
Nearest Major Highways: AK-9
Fees: $0
Accessibility: The visitor center, Exit Glacier Nature Center, public-use cabins, and Exit

Fjords, glaciers, and whales are the primary attractions of Kenai Fjords National Park.

Glacier campground are all accessible. A trail to a panoramic view of Exit Glacier is also accessible.

Contact Information:
907-422-0500
www.nps.gov/kefj

Preserves coastal fjords and nearly 40 glaciers within the 800-square-mile (2,072-sq-km) Harding Icefield, the largest icefield entirely in the U.S. The park's rich, varied rain forest is home to tens of thousands of breeding seabirds; its adjoining marine waters support a multitude of sea lions, sea otters, and seals. Today, the shrinking glaciers bear witness to the effects of climate change.

Klondike Gold Rush National Historical Park

Fast Facts

Established: 1976
Acreage: 12,996 (5,259 hectares)
Visitors (2019): 1,116,161
Visitor Centers: Klondike Gold Rush, Chilkoot Trail Center (summer only). A separate unit is headquartered in the Cadillac Hotel in Seattle, WA.
Nearest Major Airport: Juneau Intl. (JNU), Juneau, AK
Nearest Major Highways: The Klondike Highway connects Skagway, AK, to Whitehorse, Canada, but not directly to the lower 48 states. Bring your passport if you're driving through Canada.
Fees: $0
Accessibility: Varies. Visit www.nps.gov/ klgo/planyourvisit/accessibility.htm for a comprehensive list of facilities that are accessible to visitors with a variety of disabilities.

Contact Information:
907-983-2921
www.nps.gov/klgo
(Also in Washington)

Commemorates the 1897–98 Klondike gold rush with historic buildings and exhibits in Skagway, the Chilkoot Trail, and portions of the White Pass Trail. The National Park Service has restored more than 20 gold-rush-era buildings in downtown Skagway that are now home to the park visitor center, a Junior Ranger activity center, several museums, and an international trail center (operated in conjunction with Parks Canada). Because so

many fortune-seekers set out from Seattle, a separate urban unit of the park is located in the historic Cadillac Hotel, within the downtown Pioneer Square Preservation District.

Kobuk Valley National Park

Fast Facts

Established: 1978/1980
Acreage: 1,750,716 (708,490 hectares)
Visitors (2019): 15,766
Visitor Center: The Northwest Arctic Heritage Center is located in nearby Kotzebue.
Nearest Major Airport: Fairbanks Intl. (FAI), Fairbanks, AK
Nearest Major Highways: None. Most visitors arrive via air taxi from the towns of Kotzebue or Bettles.
Fees: $0
Accessibility: Largely inaccessible, other than the Northwest Arctic Heritage Center, in Kotzebue, which is accessible. Visitors requiring an American Sign Language interpreter should reserve at least 10 days in advance.

Contact Information:
907-442-3890
www.nps.gov/kova

This remote park embraces the central Kobuk River valley, north of the Arctic Circle. At the northernmost extent of the boreal forest, the park protects several rivers, designated wilderness, and the Great Kobuk Sand Dunes. At a wide bend in the Kobuk River called Onion Portage, researchers have unearthed evidence of humans following a great migration of caribou for more than 9,000 years. Today, local Inupiaq Eskimos continue to harvest caribou, grizzlies, wolves, and waterfowl in the region.

Lake Clark National Park and Preserve

Fast Facts

Established: 1978/1980
Acreage: National Park: 2,619,836 (1,060,211 hectares); National Preserve: 1,410,294 (570,726 hectares)
Visitors (2019): 17,157
Nearest Major Airport: Ted Stevens Anchorage Intl. (ANC), Anchorage, AK
Nearest Major Highways: None. Most visitors arrive by air taxi, float plane, or planes on skis.

Most visitors to remote Lake Clark National Park arrive by air taxi, float plane, or planes on skis.

Visit www.nps.gov/lacl/planyourvisit/directions.htm for a comprehensive list of companies that offer air transport from Anchorage, Homer, and several smaller Alaskan cities.

Fees: $0

Accessibility: Largely inaccessible, except for the Port Alsworth Visitor Center, which has a ramp and an all-terrain wheelchair available for loan.

Contact Information:
907-644-3626
www.nps.gov/lacl

Protects the ancestral homelands of the Dena'ina people, an intact ecosystem at the headwaters of the world's largest sockeye salmon fishery, and a rich cultural wilderness. Located in the heart of the Chigmit mountains, the park and preserve contain great geologic diversity, including jagged peaks, granite spires, glacially carved lakes, and two symmetrical active volcanoes.

Noatak National Preserve
Fast Facts

Established: 1978/1980
Acreage: 6,587,071 (2,665,695 hectares)
Visitors (2019): 17,216

Visitor Center: None. The closest facility is the Northwest Arctic Heritage Center in Kotzebue.

Nearest Major Airport: Fairbanks Intl. (FAI), Fairbanks, AK

Nearest Major Highways: None. Most visitors arrive via air taxi from the towns of Kotzebue or Bettles. Visit www.nps.gov/locations/alaska/services-noatak.htm for a list of authorized guides and transportation services companies.

Fees: $0

Accessibility: Largely inaccessible, other than the Northwest Arctic Heritage Center, in Kotzebue, which is accessible. Visitors requiring an American Sign Language interpreter should reserve at least 10 days in advance.

Contact Information:
907-442-3890
www.nps.gov/noat

The Noatak River basin is the largest untrammeled mountain-ringed river basin in the nation. The preserve is a transition zone and migration route for plants and animals between subarctic and arctic environments. It is specially designated as a place for scientific study of the archeological, plant, and wildlife resources that it protects. The preserve has limited federal facilities.

Sitka National Historical Park
Fast Facts
Established: 1910/1972
Acreage: 116 (47 hectares)
Visitors (2019): 232,876
Nearest Major Airport: Juneau Intl. (JNU), Juneau, AK
Nearest Major Highways: None. The best way to reach Sitka is via the Alaska Marine Ferry service

Totem poles from Tlingit and Haida areas line the coastal trail at Sitka National Historic Park.

from Juneau. Some charter flights are available from Anchorage. Many cruise ships of Alaska's Inside Passage stop in Sitka.
Fees: $0
Accessibility: Largely accessible. The first floor of the Russian Bishop's House is accessible; tablets with a virtual tour of the second floor are available at the front desk. The walking trail through the park is wide, relatively flat, and paved with crushed gravel.
Contact Information:
907-747-0110
www.nps.gov/sitk

Preserves the fort at the site of an 1804 battle between invading Russian traders and indigenous Kiks.ádi Tlingit. Totem poles from Tlingit and Haida areas line the park's scenic coastal trail through towering spruce and hemlock trees. The restored Russian Bishop's House, originally built in 1842, is the oldest intact piece of Russian-American architecture in the U.S., and reminder of Russia's colonial legacy in Alaska. The house is located at the cruise ship tender dock in Crescent Harbor, about a 10-minute walk from the rest of the park.

Wrangell-St. Elias National Park and Preserve
Fast Facts
Established: 1978/1980
Acreage: National Park: 8,323,146 (3,368,261 hectares); National Preserve: 4,852,645 (1,963,797 hectares)
Visitors (2019): 74,518
Visitor Centers: Wrangell-St. Elias Headquarters (Copper Center), Kennecott (summer only), Chitina Ranger Station (summer only), Slana Ranger Station (summer only)
Nearest Major Airport: Ted Stevens Anchorage Intl. (ANC), Anchorage, AK; Fairbanks Intl. (FAI), Fairbanks, AK
Nearest Major Highways: AK-1, AK-4 (Richardson Highway). The only roads that enter the park are the Nabesna Road and the McCarthy Road, both of which are gravel. Note that many rental car companies forbid driving their vehicles on unpaved roads.
Fees: $0
Accessibility: The visitor center, exhibit building, theater, and restrooms are all accessible. A paved

Wrangell-St. Elias National Park

section of the boreal forest nature trail enables visitors with impaired mobility to take in grand views of the Wrangell Mountains and Copper River.

Contact Information:
907-822-5234
www.nps.gov/wrst

The biggest national park in the U.S. includes the continent's largest assemblage of glaciers and the greatest collection of peaks above 16,000 feet (4,877 m). Four major mountain ranges—the Chugach, Wrangell, St. Elias, and Alaska—converge here in what is sometimes referred to as the "mountain kingdom of North America." Mt. St. Elias, at 18,008 ft (5,489 m), is the second-tallest peak in the U.S.

Yukon-Charley Rivers National Preserve

Fast Facts

Established: 1978/1980
Acreage: 2,256,512 (913,179 hectares)
Visitors (2019): 1,114
Visitor Centers: Eagle, Alaska Public Lands Information Center (Fairbanks, AK)
Nearest Major Airport: Fairbanks Intl. (FAI), Fairbanks, AK
Nearest Major Highways: AK-5 (Taylor Highway). The border crossing into Canada's Yukon Territory along the Top of the World Highway is open in summer from 8 am to 8 pm (Alaska time) only.

Fees: $0
Accessibility: Inaccessible. The preserve was designated by Congress to remain a primitive area.
Contact Information:
907-457-3730
www.nps.gov/yuch

Located along the Canadian border in central Alaska, the preserve protects 128 miles (206 km) of the 1,900-mile (3,057-km) Yukon River and the entire Charley River basin. Old cabins and relics are reminders of the importance of the Yukon River during the 1898 gold rush. Many consider the Charley, an 88-mile (142-km) tributary of the Yukon, the most spectacular river in Alaska. The preserve has almost no federal facilities.

IDAHO
City of Rocks National Reserve

Fast Facts

Established: 1988
Acreage: 14,407 (5,830 hectares)
Visitors (2019): 99,311
Nearest Major Airport: Salt Lake City Intl. (SLC), Salt Lake City, UT; Boise (BOI), Boise, ID
Nearest Major Highways: I-84, ID-77
Fees: $0
Accessibility: The visitor center is accessible, but most campsites and trails are not. Smoky Mountain Campground, in adjacent Castle Rocks State Park, has two fully accessible campsites.

Sunset over City of Rocks National Reserve

Contact Information:
208-824-5901
www.nps.gov/ciro

Preserves a landscape of scenic granite spires and sculptured rock formations, described by early settlers as "a city of tall spires" or "the silent city." Remnants of the California Trail are still visible in the area. Recreational opportunities include rock climbing, hiking, and camping. The reserve is administered cooperatively with the Idaho Department of Parks and Recreation and has limited federal facilities.

Craters of the Moon National Monument and Preserve
Established: 1924/2002
Acreage: 464,304 (187,897 hectares)
Visitors (2019): 272,224
Nearest Major Airport: Salt Lake City Intl. (SLC), Salt Lake City, UT; Boise (BOI), Boise, ID
Nearest Major Highways: I-15, I-84, US-20/26/93

Fees: $20/vehicle; $15/motorcycle; $10 cyclist and individual. All passes are valid for 7 days.
Accessibility: The visitor center, museum, bookstore, and restrooms are fully accessible. Several sites (and the restrooms) at the Lava Flow Campground are also accessible, as are the Devil's Orchard Trail and the Snow Cone portion of the Spatter Cones Trail.
Contact Information:
208-527-1300
www.nps.gov/crmo

Lava flows from more than 2,000 years ago produced a "weird and scenic" landscape of steep cinder cones, unforgiving rocks, and lava tube caves. The monument and preserve are administered in cooperation with the Bureau of Land Management.

Hagerman Fossil Beds National Monument
Fast Facts
Established: 1988

Acreage: 4,351 (1,761 hectares)
Visitors (2019): 23,768
Nearest Major Airport: Boise (BOI), Boise, ID
Nearest Major Highways: I-84, US-30
Fees: $0
Accessibility: A paved, accessible walkway connects the visitor center with reserved parking spaces for people with impaired mobility. The restrooms are also accessible.
Contact Information:
208-993-4105
www.nps.gov/hafo

Preserves extraordinary fossils from the Pliocene Epoch, 3.5 million years ago, including the Hagerman horse, the first-ever true one-toed horse. Saber-tooth cats, mastodons, bears, camels, and ground sloths are among the more than 200 fossilized plant and animal species that have been unearthed from sediment in the Snake River Plain. The monument has limited federal facilities.

Minidoka National Historic Site
Fast Facts
Established: 2001/2008
Acreage: 396 (160 hectares)
Visitors (2019): 13,647
Nearest Major Airport: Salt Lake City Intl. (SLC), Salt Lake City, UT; Boise (BOI), Boise, ID
Nearest Major Highways: I-84, ID-25
Fees: $0
Accessibility: The visitor center is fully accessible. The trail that loops the site is not.
Contact Information:
208-825-4169
www.nps.gov/miin
(Also in Washington)

Interprets the history and cultural resources associated with the forced relocation and internment of Japanese Americans during World War II. The site includes Bainbridge Island Japanese American Exclusion Memorial in Bainbridge, WA.

Nez Perce National Historical Park
Fast Facts
Established: 1965
Acreage: 4,565 (1,847 hectares)
Visitors (2019): 216,068

Nearest Major Airport: Missoula Montana (MSO), Missoula, MT; Spokane Intl. (GEG), Spokane, WA
Nearest Major Highways: I-84, I-90, US-12, US-93, US-95
Fees: $0
Accessibility: The visitor centers at Spalding and Big Hole Battlefield have accessible restrooms and exhibits.
Contact Information:
208-843-7001
www.nps.gov/nepe
(Also in Montana, Oregon, and Washington)

A total of 38 different sites across the Northwest commemorate the Nez Perce people, whose traditional homeland once spanned the region. The National Park Service administers nine of these sites, including Spalding, Canoe Camp, Buffalo Eddy, East Kamiah, White Bird Battlefield, and Big Hole National Battlefield. The main visitor center is in Spalding, ID.

OREGON
John Day Fossil Beds National Monument
Fast Facts
Established: 1974
Acreage: 14,062 (5,691 hectares)
Visitors (2019): 197,091
Nearest Major Airport: Portland Intl. (PDX), Portland, OR
Nearest Major Highways: I-84, US-26, OR-19
Fees: $0
Accessibility: Buildings, restrooms, and picnic areas are accessible, but trails are not.
Contact Information:
541-987-2333
www.nps.gov/joda

Colorful rock formations here preserve a world-class record of plant and animal evolution, changing climate, and past ecosystems spanning more than 40 million years. The monument consists of three separate units: Clarno, Painted Hills, and Sheep Rock. Exhibits and a working lab at the Thomas Condon Paleontology and Visitor Center as well as scenic drives and hikes at all three units allow visitors to explore the prehistoric past of Oregon.

It's easy to see how the Painted Hills unit got its name at John Day Fossil Beds National Monument.

Lewis and Clark National Historic Park

Fast Facts

Established: 1958/2004
Acreage: 3,410 (1,380 hectares)
Visitors (2019): 270,993
Nearest Major Airport: Portland Intl. (PDX), Portland, OR
Nearest Major Highways: US-26, US-101
Fees: $10/adult aged 16 and older; free for children 15 and younger.
Accessibility: Varies by location. None of the trails are accessible, though some may be navigated with sport wheelchairs or motor scooters. Visit www.nps.gov/lewi/planyourvisit/accessibility.htm for a detailed accounting of accessible facilities at each of the various sites within the park.
Contact Information:
503-861-2471
www.nps.gov/lewi
(Also in Washington)

Preserves, restores, and interprets key historic, cultural, scenic, and natural resources throughout the lower Columbia River area associated with the Lewis and Clark Expedition's arrival at and exploration of the Pacific coast. Commemorates the 1805–1806 winter encampment at Fort Clatsop.

A statue of the Lemhi Shoshone guide Sacajawea stands at Lewis and Clark National Historic Park.

Oregon Caves National Monument and Preserve

Fast Facts

Established: 1909
Acreage: 4,554 (1,843 hectares)
Visitors (2019): 65,006
Nearest Major Airport: Rogue Valley Intl.-Medford (MFR), Medford, OR
Nearest Major Highways: I-5, US-199, OR-46
Fees: $0. Ranger-led tours cost $10/adults aged 16 and older; $7/children aged 15 and younger; $5/ seniors aged 62 and older. Most tours last 60 or 90 minutes and are moderately strenuous. The three-hour Off-Trail Caving Tour ($45/person aged 15 or older) is rated as strenuous.
Accessibility: Mostly inaccessible, except for Watson's Grotto, the first room of the cave, which is accessible. Walking sticks are not permitted in the caves, with the exception of visitors who have a medical requirement to use one.
Contact Information:
541-592-2100
www.nps.gov/orca

Violent geologic events spanning millions of years and the dissolving action of acidic water created "The Marble Halls of Oregon," a marble cave nestled within an unusually diverse array of rock types. The area above ground preserves a remnant of old-growth Douglas fir forest and many glacial features.

Oregon National Historic Trail

Established: 1978
Length: 2,000 miles (3,218 km)
Visitors (2019): NA
Nearest Major Airport: Western end: Portland Intl. (PDX), Portland, OR; Eastern end: Kansas City Intl. (MCI), Kansas City, MO
Nearest Major Highways: NA
Fees: $0. Some sites along the trail may charge separate admission fees.
Accessibility: Varies. Check with individual sites.
Contact Information:
541-592-2100 & 505-988-6098
www.nps.gov/oreg
(Also in Idaho, Kansas, Missouri, Nebraska, Washington, and Wyoming)

This historic trail links hundreds of sites along the route taken by pioneers migrating west in the 19th century. More than 2,000 miles (3,218 km) of trail ruts and other traces can still be seen along the trail over its six states.

WASHINGTON
Ebey's Landing National Historical Reserve

Fast Facts

Established: 1978
Acreage: 19,333 (7,824 hectares)
Visitors (2019): NA
Visitor Centers: None. The Coupeville Chamber of Commerce serves as the main visitor center. Information is also available at the Island County Historical Museum and at Fort Casey State Park.
Nearest Major Airport: Seattle-Tacoma Intl. (SEA), Seattle, WA
Nearest Major Highways: I-5, WA-20
Fees: $0. A Washington State Park Discover Pass ($1/day or $30/annually) grants visitors admission to Fort Ebey State Park, Fort Casey State Park, and Ebey's Landing State Park).
Accessibility: Largely accessible. Visitors with impaired mobility can join the gravel trail that begins at the Prairie Overlook midway through Ebey's Prairie.
Contact Information:
360-678-6084
www.nps.gov/ebla

This rural historic district preserves and protects an unbroken historical record of Puget Sound exploration and settlement from the 19th century to the present. Historic farms, still under cultivation on the prairies of Whidbey Island, reveal land-use patterns unchanged since the first European Americans arrived in the 1850s. The Victorian seaport community of Coupeville is also in the Reserve. The reserve is managed in cooperation with a trust board representing the Town of Coupeville, Island County, and Washington State Parks. Federal facilities are limited.

Fort Vancouver National Historic Site
Fast Facts
Established: 1948/1961

Aviation history is on display at the Pearson Air Museum, a unit of the Fort Vancouver National Historic Site.

Acreage: 207 (84 hectares)
Visitors (2019): 1,018,214
Nearest Major Airport: Portland Intl. (PDX), Portland, OR
Nearest Major Highways: I-5, WA-14
Fees: Entry to the site is free for all. There is a fee of $10/adult aged 16 or older (free for children 15 and younger) to enter the reconstructed fort.
Accessibility: Most buildings are accessible, except the restroom at the McLoughlin House in Oregon City, OR.
Contact Information:
  360-816-6230
  www.nps.gov/fova
(Also in Oregon)

Established on the north bank of the Columbia River in 1825, Fort Vancouver served as headquarters for the Hudson's Bay Company's vast fur trading empire in the Pacific Northwest. The site also preserves and interprets a rich legacy of American history, including emigration along the Oregon Trail, military history at Vancouver

Barracks, and aviation history at Pearson Air Museum. The McLoughlin House in Oregon City, OR, is also part of this vibrant and diverse park.

Ice Age Floods National Geologic Trail
Fast Facts
Established: 2009
Acreage: 10,240,000 (4,143,981 hectares)
Visitors (2019): 1,018,214
Nearest Major Airport: Seattle-Tacoma Intl. (SEA), Seattle, WA; Portland Intl. (PDX), Portland, OR
Nearest Major Highways: I-84, I-90
Fees: $0. Individual sites and state parks along the route may charge separate admission fees.
Accessibility: Varies. Check with individual sites.
Contact Information:
  509-237-9722
  www.nps.gov/iafl
(Also in Idaho, Montana, and Oregon)

At the end of the last Ice Age, 18,000 to 15,000 years ago, an ice dam in northern Idaho created Glacial Lake Missoula, which stretched 3,000 square miles (7,770 sq km) into Montana. When the dam burst, it released an amount of water equivalent to Lake Ontario and Lake Erie combined in just two days, flooding parts of Montana, Idaho, Oregon, and Washington. Over thousands of years, this scenario repeated itself hundreds of times. Dozens of sites along the trail preserve reminders of the floods: gigantic basalt coulees, enormous dry waterfalls, and massive boulders that were carried hundreds of miles by walls of water.

Lake Roosevelt National Recreation Area

Fast Facts

Established: 1946/1990
Acreage: 100,390 (40,626 hectares)
Visitors (2019): 1,358,818
Visitor Center: Fort Spokane
Nearest Major Airport: Spokane Intl. (GEG), Spokane, WA
Nearest Major Highways: I-90, US-2, WA-25
Fees: $0. Boat launch fees are $8/week or $45/year and can be purchased online. Camping fees are $11.50, Oct.1–Apr. 30, $23, May 1–Sept. 30.
Accessibility: Varies. The exhibits and lobby at the visitor center are accessible, but the restrooms are not. Some campgrounds have a limited number of accessible sites.
Contact Information:
509-754-7800
www.nps.gov/laro

Massive ice age floods carved the landscape surrounding this 150-mile (241-km)-long lake. The lake was formed by the construction of Grand Coulee Dam as part of the Columbia River Basin project. Today, it's a destination for swimming, boating, hiking, camping, and fishing.

Manhattan Project National Historical Park

Fast Facts

Established: 2015
Acreage: Boundaries not yet established
Visitors (2019): 27,957
Nearest Major Airport: Spokane Intl. (GEG), Spokane, WA

Nearest Major Highways: I-82, WA-24
Visitor Center: The Hanford unit visitor center is in the neighboring city of Richland, WA.
Fees: $0. Some tours or experiences may charge a separate admission fee.
Accessibility: Largely accessible. Visitors on the B Reactor and Pre-War Historic Sites tours must be able to walk short distances on uneven surfaces.
Contact Information:
509-376-1647
www.nps.gov/mapr
(Also in New Mexico and Tennessee)

The Hanford unit of this tripartite park celebrates the contributions of the Hanford Engineer Works, which produced the plutonium used in the first atomic test and in the nuclear bomb that the U.S. dropped on Nagasaki on August 9, 1945. This park was created to improve the understanding of the Manhattan Project and its legacy; it is jointly operated with the U.S. Department of Energy.

North Cascades National Park

Fast Facts

Established: 1968
Acreage: 504,781 (804,277 hectares)
Visitors (2019): 38,208
Visitor Centers: North Cascades, Golden West, Park & Forest Information Center, Wilderness Information Center, Glacier Public Service Center, Skagit Information Center
Nearest Major Airport: Seattle-Tacoma Intl. (SEA), Seattle, WA
Nearest Major Highways: I-5, WA-20
Fees: $0
Accessibility: Most visitor centers are accessible, and all have accessible restrooms, as do most campgrounds. Several boardwalk trails can be navigated by visitors in wheelchairs, including the Sterling Munro Trail and the Happy Creek Forest Walk.
Contact Information:
360-854-7200
www.nps.gov/noca

Protects an alpine wilderness of high jagged peaks crowned by more than 300 glaciers. Waterfalls cascade through forested valleys, while rivers and lakes sustain a great diversity of plants and animals. The park consists of two discrete sections, sandwiched around the **Ross Lake National Recreation Area**, which abounds in outdoor activities along the upper Skagit River, Diablo Lake, and Ross Lake. The southern half of North Cascades is contiguous with the adjacent **Lake Chelan National Recreation Area**, where the fjord-like Lake Chelan bisects the untrammeled, roadless Stehekin Valley. Two ferry companies provide passenger service to Stehekin from the town of Chelan at the south end of the lake: Lake Chelan Boat Company (www.ladyofthelake.com) and Stehekin Ferry (www.stehekinferry.com).

Diablo Lake at Ross Lake National Recreation Area

San Juan Island National Historical Park
Fast Facts
Established: 1966
Acreage: 2,146 (868 hectares)
Visitors (2019): 292,507
Visitor Center: American Camp
Nearest Major Airport: Seattle-Tacoma Intl. (SEA), Seattle, WA
Nearest Major Highways: None. Visitors must arrive by ferry from Anacortes, WA. Visit Washington State Ferries (https://wsdot.wa.gov/ferries) for schedule and fare information.
Fees: $0
Accessibility: The American Camp visitor center is fully accessible, as are some trails in that section of the park. None of the trails at English Camp are accessible. A golf cart is required to shuttle visitors with impaired mobility to and from the parade grounds.
Contact Information:
360-378-2240
www.nps.gov/sajh

With over 6 miles (10 km) of shoreline, trails, prairies, and military camps, this park commemorates the peaceful settlement of the San Juan Boundary Dispute between Great Britain and the United States from 1853 to 1872. The contretemps came to a head when an American settler shot a British-owned pig, and it escalated into a five-month-long standoff before cooler heads prevailed. The pig was the only casualty.

Whitman Mission National Historic Site
Fast Facts
Established: 1936/1963
Acreage: 139 (56 hectares)
Visitors (2019): 48,481
Nearest Major Airport: Spokane Intl. (GEG), Spokane, WA
Nearest Major Highways: I-82, US-12
Fees: $0
Accessibility: Largely accessible.
Contact Information:
509-522-6360
www.nps.gov/whmi

Preserves, analyzes, and interprets the site where Marcus and Narcissa Whitman established a Methodist mission in 1836 and attempted to convert the neighboring Cayuse people to Christianity. By 1847, the mission had become a popular stop for Oregon Trail travelers, arousing fear among the Cayuse that the new arrivals would steal their land and spread diseases to which they had no immunity. When an 1847 measles epidemic did exactly that, a group of Cayuse attacked the mission, killing both Whitmans and 12 others, and capturing more than 50 hostages. The incident sparked the Cayuse War of 1848–50 and was a major factor in the U.S. government's movement to push Native Americans onto reservations. The National Park Service has partnered with the Confederated Tribes of the Umatilla Indian Reservation to present the full, continuing story of the Cayuse Nation.

THE SOUTHWEST

Grand Canyon National Park

Fast Facts

Established: 1908/1919
Acreage: 1,201,647 (486,289 hectares)
Visitors (2019): 5,974,411
Visitor Centers: South Rim, North Rim
Nearest Major Airport: South Rim: Phoenix Sky Harbor Intl. (PHX), Phoenix, AZ. North Rim: Harry Reid Intl. (LAS), Las Vegas, NV.
Nearest Major Highways: South Rim: I-40, US-180, AZ-64. North Rim: I-15, AZ-67.
Fees: $35/vehicle, $30/motorcycle, $20/cyclist or pedestrian. All entrance fees are valid for 7 days.
Accessibility: Varies. Shuttle buses are wheelchair accessible. A comprehensive Accessibility Guide can be downloaded at www.nps.gov/grca/planyourvisit/upload/GRCA-Accessibility-Guide-2018.pdf
Contact Information: 928-638-7888 www.nps.gov/grca

Staring into the abyss known as Grand Canyon, one can't help but marvel at the power of nature. Over the course of nearly six million years, the mighty Colorado River slowly carved this massive hole in the ground, a mile (1.6 km) deep and up to 18 miles (29 km) across. Until you've seen it in person, you cannot fathom how grand Grand Canyon truly is. The island of Manhattan could fit comfortably in the canyon—crosswise! So could Washington, D.C., or the entire state of Rhode Island. It's simply impossible not to stare slack-jawed at the countless layers of colorful rocks left behind by the river's downward journey.

If you do nothing more than drive up to the South Rim and gaze into the canyon—as millions of people do each year—you will be forever humbled and enriched by the experience. One reason Grand Canyon is so crowded is that people can't tear their eyes away. No wonder it's been named one of the **seven natural wonders of the world** (an unofficial list that includes the Aurora Borealis, the Great Barrier Reef, and Mount Everest).

Grand Canyon's popularity means a trip here requires more planning than other parks, especially if you hope to stay overnight. There are only two campgrounds near the heart of the South Rim in Grand Canyon Village: the 327-site **Mather Campground** and the 123-space **Trailer Village RV Park**. The 50-site **Desert View Campground** is 26 miles (41 km) away, near the park's east entrance.

Grand Canyon Village is also home to a half-dozen hotels, including the historic 1905 **El Tovar**, and the **Thunderbird Lodge**, which boasts canyon views from many rooms. These

Until you've seen it in person, you cannot fathom how grand Grand Canyon is.

The Kiva Room at Desert View Watchtower

lodgings sell out months in advance, particularly during the busy summer months. Even more in demand are beds at **Phantom Ranch**, the only accommodations on the canyon floor. To snag a **cold-water cabin** (sleeps 2–10 people) or a space in the **hiker's dormitories**, you'll almost certainly need to enter a lottery more than a year in advance.

Additional South Rim lodgings are available in the towns of **Tusayan** (21 miles/34 km south), **Grand Canyon Junction** (29 miles/47 km south), and **Williams** (59 miles/95 km south). These too fill up quickly, so in July and August, you may have to go all the way to **Flagstaff** (80 miles/129 km south) to find a place to stay overnight.

Aside from the main park road, the busiest thoroughfare just might be the **Canyon Rim Trail**. It follows the contour of the canyon for 13 miles (22 km) from the South Kaibab Trailhead to **Hermits Rest**, where there's a small gift shop and snack bar. The route is paved all the way, and is almost entirely wheelchair accessible. A shuttle bus stops at more than a dozen landmarks

along the way, so you can catch a ride any time you tire of walking.

For a South Rim experience with smaller crowds, head east to the **Desert View** section of the park. Many visitors arriving at the south entrance blow right past the turnoff for Desert View in their rush to get to the village. This means that the sights, overlooks, vista points, and trails there have only a fraction of the people. The Desert View

Overlook is one of the few places on the South Rim where you can see the river.

The 23-mile (37-km) **Desert View Drive** is an attraction in its own right. All of the viewpoints are on the north side of the road, so to avoid making a lot of left turns, drive straight to the **Tusayan Museum and Ruin** before continuing on to the 1932 Puebloan-style stone **Watchtower**. (On your return

South Kaibab Trail is the shortest (and steepest) route between the South Rim and the Colorado River.

trip, pull over for parking lot views at **Lipan Point**, **Moran Point**, and **Grandview Point**. Or linger a while and hike the easy 2-mile (3.2-km) round-trip trail from **Shoshone Point** through ponderosa forest to a (somewhat) secret view of the canyon.

Two popular hiking trails connect the South Rim to the **Colorado River**: the 7.8-mile (12.6-km) **Bright Angel Trail** and the shorter, steeper (6.3-mile/10.1-km) **South Kaibab Trail**. Only the most experienced hikers should attempt to descend all the way to the canyon floor and back in the same day; those that do are advised to go down South Kabab and up Bright Angel. (If there's snow on the ground, the morning sun will melt it faster on South Kaibab than on Bright Angel, which can be icy.)

But there's no need to go all the way to the bottom to get a feel for the world below the canyon rim. It's less than a mile (1.6 km) each way on the South Kaibab Trail to the spectacular views at the aptly named **Ooh Aah Point**, and just 1.5 miles (2.4 km) to **Cedar Ridge**, where there's a pit toilet. The first view of the Colorado River comes at **Skeleton Point**, 3 miles (5 km) down (and the same distance back up), with 2,000 feet (610 m) of elevation loss. Rangers discourage day hikers from going any farther than this, and suggest turning around at Cedar Ridge on a warm day. The deeper you go into the canyon, the hotter it gets; a good rule of thumb is 5.5°F (3.1°C) change in temperature for every 1,000 ft of elevation change.

Because it leaves from Grand Canyon Village, the Bright Angel Trail is more popular, and isn't too steep for the first ¾ mile (1.2 km) to the **second tunnel**; another ¾ miles down is the **1.5 Mile Resthouse**, where water is available seasonally. Casual hikers should head back up from here before the steepest part of the trail begins; hardier hikers might turn around at **Indian Garden** (4.5 miles/7.2 km each way).

On both the Bright Angel and South Kaibab trails, watch out for mule droppings. (If you encounter a mule or mules while hiking, stand still, follow the wrangler's instructions, and wait until the last mule is 50 feet (15 m) past you.) The extremely popular **mule ride to Phantom Ranch** goes down the Bright Angel trail and up South Kaibab the next day. Even with a price tag of up to $700 per rider (rates vary by the number of people in your group), this mule ride is one of the most sought-after tickets in town, so book far in advance

The aptly named Ooh Aah Point, on the South Kaibab Trail

Sure-footed mules carry visitors down to the canyon floor and back.

and make sure the riders in your group meet all of the height and size requirements. The shorter, three-hour **Canyon Vista mule ride** (two hours in the saddle) takes riders along the canyon rim, and leaves twice daily from March through October, once a day November through February.

Parking spaces throughout the South Rim are almost as scarce as hotel rooms, so if you find one, you might be tempted to ditch your car and ride the **free shuttle bus**. The purple line goes all the way to a park and ride station in Tusayan, so if you're not staying in the park, you don't have to bring your car at all. And if you're staying in Williams, consider arriving at the park by train. The **Grand Canyon Railway** (www.thetrain.com) departs Williams every day at 9:30 and returns at 3:30. Rates range from $67 for a regular seat to $226 for a spot in a glass-domed car.

Another good way to get around the park is by **bicycle**. A 13-mile (22-km) **Greenway** links many of the South Rim's most popular destinations. Bikes can be loaded onto shuttle buses, so it's possible to ride the shuttle one way (say, uphill from Tusayan) and pedal back downhill. Rent bikes or electronic bikes from **Bright Angel Bicycles** (www.bikecrandcanyon), adjacent to the Grand Canyon Visitor Center. You can also rent e-bikes at **Grand Canyon Bikes** (www.bikegrandcanyon.com) near Tusayan. The ride into the park is slower on an e-bike, but when you get to the park entrance, you'll breeze right in instead of waiting in a long line of cars. And you just might spot elk along the way.

Grand Canyon's **North Rim** is less than 20 miles (32 km) away as the crow flies, but 220 miles (354 km) by car, and a world away in terms of crowds and climate. The North Rim is about 1,000 feet (305 m) higher in elevation, so it's cooler in summer (and usually inaccessible in winter). It also gets about a tenth as many visitors, so everything from parking lots to hiking trails to eateries features more elbow room.

Lodgings, on the other hand, tend to fill up far in advance because there are so few of them on the North Rim. The only indoor accommodations are the motel rooms and cabins at the historic **Grand Canyon Lodge**. Many rooms share the same stunning view enjoyed by the lodge's back patio overlooking the canyon. The **North Rim Campground** has 87 sites, none with electric hookups or showers. **Jacob Lake**, 45 miles (75 km) north of the park, also has campgrounds.

One of the easiest hikes on the North Rim is the ½-mile

Rafting down the Colorado River is a spectacular way to see the canyon.

More than a dozen authorized concessioners offer **rafting or boating trips** through the Canyon down the Colorado River. They range from 3 to 18 days, so there's a trip for every adventure and commitment level, including some that allow you to hike up to the South Rim from Phantom Ranch. Visit www.nps.gov/grca/planyourvisit/whitewater-rafting.htm for information on outfitters and on how to travel the river on your own if you dare.

Skywalk, an attraction built by the local Hualapai Tribe, is the only place where you can walk out over the canyon and look down 4,000 feet (1,219 m) through a glass-bottomed horseshoe-shaped bridge, sturdy enough to support 70 packed 747s. Skywalk is located 250 miles (402 km) west of the South Rim, in an area known as **Grand Canyon West**. While you're there, you can also take a **helicopter ride** over the canyon, go **ziplining** above a smaller canyon, or travel the Colorado River by **raft** or **pontoon boat**.

(0.8-km) round-trip **Bright Angel Point Trail**, which leaves from Grand Canyon Lodge. The trail is paved, but stairs and steep sections make it inaccessible to wheelchairs. The **North Kaibab Trail** is the only one that goes to the canyon floor. It's twice as long (14 miles/23 km) as either of the rim-to-river trails on the south side, so hikers are even more strongly discouraged from going down and back on the same day. For a shorter option, turn around at **Coconino Overlook** (1.5 miles/2.4 km round-trip, or at **Supai Tunnel** (4 miles / 6.5 km round-trip). The 3-mile (5-km) **Transept Trail** connects the Campground and the Grand Canyon Lodge without the mule poop that can sometimes plague the North Kaibab Trail. The views aren't as grand as on some other trails, but there's lots of shade and little elevation change.

The winding **North Rim Scenic Drive** takes you to views of the canyon you probably haven't seen before. It's 22 miles (35 km) to **Cape Royal**, whose panoramic views include vistas of the Colorado River's sweeping turn at **Unkar Delta**, the high ridge known as **Wotan's Throne**, and the Desert View Watchtower on the South Rim. Sunrise and sunset are popular times. On the way (or the way back), detour 6 miles (10 km) to **Point Imperial**, the highest point in the park, which overlooks both the canyon and the **Painted Desert**.

At Skywalk, 250 miles (402 km) west of the National Park, you can look down into the canyon from a cantilevered glass-bottomed bridge.

Zion National Park

Zion, a Hebrew word meaning "quiet sanctuary," tends to draw comparisons with Yosemite. Both parks feature serene natural settings with a river running through striking rock formations, almost identical visitation statistics, and more activities than a cruise ship. The one major difference between the two is the color palette. Where Yosemite is granite and gray (even in person, not just in all the black-and-white Ansel Adams photos), Zion is aflame in peaches, crimsons, and every shade of sandstone in between.

Zion is also a lot more compact than Yosemite. Almost all of its activities take place within **Zion Canyon**, the central north-south corridor carved by the Virgin River. The canyon is lined on either side by one massive rust-colored sandstone monolith after another, with glorious names like The **Court of the Patriarchs** (three peaks individually dubbed Abraham, Isaac, and Jacob) and the **Great White Throne** (6,744 ft/ 2,056 m). To ensure visitors experience nature, rather than traffic, cars are prohibited in the canyon from March through November. A free shuttle bus stops at the park's most popular attractions.

A list of hikes tops the NPS's Zion homepage, which is a pretty good indicator of what people like to do at Utah's first National Park. That applies to visitors with mobility impairments as well, who can take advantage of two paved trails of significant length. The **Pa'rus Trail** parallels the Virgin River for 1.75 miles (2.8 km) each way between the visitor center and Canyon Junction. Delicate hanging gardens flourish on the rocky cliff faces on **Riverside Walk,** which traces the Virgin River at the opposite end of the park. It's paved for just over a mile (1.6 km) north of **The Temple of Sinawava**, though some sections may be too steep for wheelchairs. For a full listing of all hikes in the park, ranked by length and difficulty, visit the website or NPS app.

If the lines for the shuttle bus into the canyon are too daunting in the morning, start your day at the **Watchman Trail** (3.5 miles/

Zion National Park

The three peaks of the Court of the Patriarchs are informally named Abraham, Isaac, and Jacob.

location opposite **Zion National Park Lodge** probably has something to do with it as well. It's 1.2 miles (1.9 km) round-trip to **Lower Emerald Pool**, 2 miles (3.6 km) round-trip if you add on the **Middle Pool**, and 2.5 miles (4 km) to visit all three. Because it leaves from The **Grotto**, rather than Zion Lodge, the 2.4-mile (3.9-km) **Kayenta Trail** is a road less traveled to the same destination. Those who hate going back the same way they came can turn any of these hikes into a 3-mile (4.8-km) loop by taking the **Grotto Trail** between the lodge and the Kayenta Trailhead.

The 5.4-mile (8.7-km) round-trip hike to **Angels Landing** isn't particularly long, and its 1,488 feet (453 m) of elevation gain isn't especially challenging, but it's not for the faint of heart. If you're afraid of heights, you won't want to brave the steep

5.6 km round-trip). It leaves from the Visitor Center and climbs 368 feet (112 m) into the surrounding foothills. Every foot you ascend, you'll see a different persimmon color of stratified rock, the result of centuries of erosion. The loop at the top brings you to **Watchman Point**,

which boasts spectacular views of **Bridge Mountain**, **Towers of the Virgin**, and the town of Springdale.

Swimming is prohibited in all of Zion's three legendary **Emerald Pools**, but that doesn't dent the popularity of two trails that lead to them. The trailhead's

The paved Pa'Rus Trail is a terrific way to enjoy the park by bicycle or from a wheelchair.

The short trail to Zion's three Emerald Pools crosses the Virgin River.

drop-offs, narrow ridges, and sections where you need to hold onto a chain handrail. If those hurdles don't deter you, however, the summit view overlooking the **Big Bend of Zion Canyon** is unrivaled. Avoid this popular trail in the height of summer, when 100°F-degree (38°C) heat and crowds make it even more nerve-wracking.

Biking is permitted on the Pa'rus Trail and all park roadways, including the 6 miles (10 km) between Canyon Junction and the Temple of Sinowava, where, from March through November, the only motorized traffic cyclists have to compete with is the shuttle bus. Do not pass a stopped shuttle bus, and pull over completely to the side of the road any time a bus approaches. Each shuttle has racks that can carry three bikes, so it's possible to take the bus uphill to the Temple of Sinawava and coast all the way back down. Rent

bikes at **Zion National Park Lodge** (www.zionlodge.com) or in the town of Springdale, just outside the main entrance, where multiple outfitters rent traditional and pedal-assist electric bikes.

Opposite the Park Lodge is the saddle-up spot for **horseback rides**. From March to October, **Canyon Trail Rides** (www. canyonrides.com) offers one-hour rides along the Virgin River ($50) four times a day or twice-daily three-hour rides that climb 500 feet (152 m) up into the west side of the canyon ($100). There's a 220-lb (100-kg) weight limit for all riders.

Where the Riverside Walk pavement ends, an only-in-Zion attraction begins: **The Narrows.** For 16 miles (22 km), the Virgin River courses through a slot canyon flanked by impossibly high walls on both sides. The only way up or down is by walking *through* the river. If you'd like to get your feet wet (literally) in the

Walter's Wiggles is a series of 20 tight switchbacks on the trail to Angels Landing.

73

Cairns placed by hikers frame the outstanding views of Angels Landing.

free unexpectedly. Numerous routes may also be closed to climbing to protect nesting peregrine falcons. Visit the Zion website or NPS app for specific regulations and to obtain permits to bivouac overnight.

Because Zion has so many different habitats, it is home to an amazing variety of **birds**. Look for **California condors** in summer and fall in evergreen and riparian woodland areas, **Cooper's hawks** in pinyon-juniper woodlands throughout the year, **bald eagles** anywhere there's water, and **kestrels** and **red-tailed hawks** just about anywhere at any time of year. Lucky birders might spot **Mexican spotted owls** before the birds spot them. **Black-chinned hummingbirds, hairy woodpeckers**, and **mountain chickadees** live and breed in the park year-round.

In addition to all the spectacles fashioned by nature, Zion is also

sport of **canyoneering**, you can splash, wade, or swim north from the Temple of Sinawava for up to 5 miles (8 km) to **Big Spring.**

To traverse the entire length of the Narrows from the top down, however, you'll need a permit as well as your own transportation to **Chamberlain's Ranch.** Permits are limited and are hard to get, so plan far in advance and reserve yours online at zionpermits.nps.gov. It is possible to walk the Narrows in about 12 hours, making a day trip feasible, if strenuous. There are also 12 **campsites** along the route, for those who are willing to risk getting their camping gear wet in the rushing river.

The river is cold everywhere, more than 6 feet (1.8 m) deep in parts, slippery on the bottom, and dangerously fast-moving at times, especially after a rainfall. Flash floods can be deadly, so check weather forecasts before venturing out. The Park Service closes access to The Narrows when the river is running dangerously high. Rental of the necessary gear for a Narrows trip—canyoneering boots, waterproof backpacks,

wooden hiking sticks, neoprene socks, and more, depending on the season—is a cottage industry in nearby Springdale.

Zion Canyon's high walls are also a hit with **rock climbers**, though most of its faces are for experts only. Desert sandstone is notoriously weak when wet, causing holds and bolts to break

Hiking the Narrows trail requires walking through the river.

home to one man-made marvel: the **Zion–Mt. Carmel Tunnel**. Completed in 1930, the tunnel required blasting through a solid mile of mountain. East of the tunnel, the russet-colored sandstone that so dominates Zion Canyon gives way to white and gray slickrock. In the area known as **Checkerboard Mesa**, giant boulders of the stuff, shaped almost like nuclear reactors, crop up along the highway like leviathan mushrooms from a Tim Burton movie.

The east end's distance from Zion Canyon makes it one of the best spots for views *of* the canyon. The **Zion Canyon Overlook Trail** starts opposite the very small parking lot just east of the tunnel. It's a mile (1.6 km) round-trip, and mostly flat, but is rated as moderate because of a series of steep switchbacks. The vistas are marvelous throughout the hike, none more so than the overlook at the end, which captures the entirety of Zion Canyon.

Don't Miss This . . . Suggested Utah Itineraries

Day One: Arrive at Zion National Park. Hike the Emerald Pools/Kayenta/Grotto Trail loop. Take the shuttle bus all the way to the Temple of Sinawava and stroll along Riverside Walk to its end at The Narrows. If it's a warm day and you don't mind getting your feet wet, walk upstream through the river as far as you dare (but not beyond Big Spring). If the water's too cold, make a note to rent waterproof gear in town and come back tomorrow.

Day Two: Hike the easy, paved Pa'rus Trail, the steep and narrow Angel's Landing Trail, or the moderate Watchman Trail. Rent bikes in town or at Zion National Park Lodge and cycle the car-free main park road. Or put your bike on the shuttle bus and let it carry you up the hill so you only have to ride down.

Day Three: Cross the Zion-Mt. Carmel tunnel into the east end of the park on your way to Bryce Canyon National Park. It's only a two-hour drive, so there's plenty of time for a stop in Red Canyon, just before you get to Bryce. It truly is redder than all the other canyons. Check out the views from Bryce Point and Inspiration Point, then check in to your lodgings in the park or in Bryce Canyon City. If there's an evening astronomy program offered, don't miss it.

Day Four: Take one more look at Bryce Canyon and try not to be transfixed by it for too long; you've got a big day ahead. Head east along Scenic Byway 12 toward Cannonville. Enjoy views of the Colorado Plateau all the way to the North Rim of Grand Canyon. Stop at Kodachrome State Park, Calf Creek Recreation Area, or any of the dozens of scenic turnouts along the route. Have lunch in Boulder at Burr Trail Grill, before continuing on to Capitol Reef National Park, which has a 72-site developed campground (reservations required).

Day Five: Explore Capitol Reef National Park. Hike or bike the numerous trails, or pick your own fruit from the apple, apricot, cherry, peach, pear, or plum orchards in the Fruita Historic District of the park.

Checkerboard Mesa

Bryce Canyon National Park

In a state replete with gorgeous southwestern landscapes, Bryce Canyon National Park arguably shines as the most stunning sight of all. Rising from the canyon floor like the bristles of a giant hairbrush are thousands of hoodoos: skinny ginger-colored limestone spires left behind by eons of erosion to once-solid rock.

A single road meanders through most of the park, linking **12 canyon viewpoints** like charms on a bracelet. Hopscotching from one to the next is on just about every visitor's itinerary, so the park has a **free shuttle bus** that runs every 15 minutes from 8 a.m. to 6 p.m. (and until 8 p.m. from late May through September). It stops at the eight most visited points of interest within the park and five locations in the gateway town just outside the park. There's even a website (www.brycecanyonshuttle.com/routes) with real-time updates of when the next bus will arrive.

All of the viewpoints of the canyon are on the left side of the road, so if you do decide to take your own car, you can avoid making a lot of left turns by driving all the way to **Yovimpa Point**, at the southern end of the park. From there, you can stop at as many overlooks as you like on the 16-mile (26-km) drive back to the visitor center.

Fast Facts

Established: 1923/1924
Acreage: 35,835 (14,502 hectares)
Visitors (2019): 2,594,904
Visitor Center: Bryce Canyon
Nearest Major Airport: Salt Lake City Intl. (SLC), Salt Lake City, UT
Nearest Major Highways: I-15, US-89, UT-63
Fees: $35/vehicle, $30/motorcycle, $20/cyclist or pedestrian aged 16 years or older. All entrance fees are valid for 7 days. An annual pass is $40. Camping fees range from $5 for the backcountry to $30 for an RV at one of the two campgrounds.
Accessibility: Buildings and viewpoints are generally accessible, but trails are not. Visit www.nps.gov/brca/planyourvisit/accessibility.htm for a full accounting of what is and isn't accessible.
Contact Information: 435-834-5322
www.nps.gov/brca

The views from Bryce Point capture the full amphitheater of Bryce Canyon . . .

. . . while the vista from Inspiration Point includes the densest concentration of hoodoos.

Bryce Point is the one in all the money shots of the park because it captures the full amphitheater of hoodoos. It's especially glorious at dawn, when the sun's rays illuminate the tops of the hoodoos before spreading an orange glow deeper into the canyon. From **Inspiration Point**, you can see three distinct strata of hoodoos, giving the impression that these rock formations might continue as corkscrews down into the center of the Earth.

Sunset Point is the best place to view the tightly packed formation known as **Silent City**, as well as **Thor's Hammer**, a top-heavy hoodoo that stands all alone just below the point. For **birdwatchers,** Cliff Swallows and White-throated Swifts like to linger here, as do hawks and ravens; Clark's nutcrackers and Steller's Jays prowl the pinecones for nuts.

Sunrise Point is the jumping off point for two moderate hikes: Queen's Garden and Tower Bridge. **Queen's Garden** is a

Thor's Hammer stands just below Sunset Point.

From the right angle, this hoodoo looks like Queen Victoria standing on a pedestal.

1.8-mile (2.9-km) round-trip out and back to the **Queen Victoria** formation. Those looking for a longer hike (and more elevation change) can combine this hike with the Navajo Loop, which takes in Thor's Hammer, **Two Bridges**, and **Wall Street**, a section at the bottom of the canyon where the spires seem as tall as skyscrapers. It's the most popular hike in the park. **Tower Bridge** is the first landmark on the strenuous **Fairyland Loop**, an 8-mile (13-km) trail with 1,716 feet (523 m) of elevation change. Turn around at the bridge for a 3-mile (5-km) round-trip with half the climbing.

The **Rim Trail** which hugs the canyon's edge between **Fairyland Point** and Bryce Point, seems like it would be the easiest walk in the park, but 1,754 feet (535 m) of elevation change makes it quite a challenge. You don't have to walk the entire 5.5 miles (9.2 km) however. The half-mile (0.8-km) section between Sunrise and Sunset Point is paved, wheelchair accessible, and open to leashed pets. The park shuttle also makes it feasible to walk one way (downhill from Bryce Point, for example), and take the bus back (uphill) the other way.

You can do the same thing if you don't like **biking** uphill. The paved **Shared Use Path** starts in Bryce Canyon City and extends for 18 miles (29 km), crossing into the park and ending at Inspiration Point. Park shuttle

The Wall of Windows

buses can accommodate two bikes at a time. As its name suggests, the shared use path is open not just to cyclists, but to skaters, skateboarders, scooter riders (non-motorized only), wheelchairs, and cross-country skiers in winter.

If you'd rather let a **horse** do the walking, book a two-hour ride with **Canyon Trail Rides** (www.canyonrides.com) down to the floor of the canyon or a three-hour ride that also visits spectacles like **The Wall of Windows, The Chessmen**, and **The Bristle Cone Pine Trees**. Riders must be at least 7 years old for the two-hour trip and 10 years old for the three-hour tour. Morning and afternoon departures are available; all horseback rides leave from the horse corral near **The Lodge at Bryce Canyon**.

The canyon goes dark at night, but that's when the sky

Scenic Byway 12, between Bryce Canyon and Capitol Reef, is an unforgettable drive.

Park rangers lead Full Moon Hikes into Bryce Canyon or along the rim.

is just starting to light up. The lack of light pollution makes Bryce one of the few places where you can see the entire Milky Way galaxy. Check the program schedule at the visitor center for nighttime programs led by Astronomy Rangers. The annual Astronomy Festival, usually held in June, consists of four days and nights of constellation tours, informative talks by experts, and a slate of family-friendly activities during the daytime.

The red rock country surrounding Bryce Canyon may lack the concentration of hoodoos, but it is no less beautiful. And a single road connects more than a dozen opportunities to soak it all in. **Utah's Scenic Byway 12** has been designated an All-American Road, which means it's one of the finest drives in the world. The road starts west of Bryce Canyon City and ends 123 miles (198 km) later in the town of

Torrey, just north of **Capitol Reef National Park**.

Roadside signs heralding a "Scenic Turnout" pop up along the road like gophers. **Kodachrome Basin State Park** got its name from *National Geographic* photographers in 1949 as they put their color film to the test against the persimmon-colored chimneys and crisp blue sky. **Calf Creek Recreation Area** features jagged cliffs, views of the **Grand Staircase Escalante National Monument**, and a 3-mile (5-km) hike to a waterfall with a pool at its base placid enough for swimming. Between Escalante and Boulder, the road sits atop a narrow ridge that falls off steeply on both sides. This 31-mile (50-km) stretch is known as the **Million Dollar Road** for the amount it cost the Civilian Conservation Corps to build it in 1935. Allow 2.5 hours of driving each way, and much more than that for sightseeing and activities along the way.

Glen Canyon National Recreation Area

Originally built as a way to store drinking water for seven southwestern states, Glen Canyon Dam had the additional benefit of creating a massive outdoor playground in the middle of a desert. At its center lies **Lake Powell,** named for John Wesley Powell, who led the first U.S. government-sponsored expedition through Grand Canyon, in 1869. The largest human-made lake in North America meanders for 186 miles (299 km), and its 1,960 miles (3,154 km) of shoreline in both Arizona and Utah offer countless opportunities for water-based recreation. Leashed pets are permitted in most parts of the park.

Lake Powell's deep turquoise waters are a major destination for **boating**. Four marinas on the lake serve boaters: **Antelope Point** and **Wahweap**, on the Arizona side, close to the dam; and **Bullfrog** and **Halls Crossing**, both in the northeast section on the Utah side. When water levels permit, the Utah Department of Transportation runs a **ferry** every two hours between Bullfrog and Halls Crossing ($25/vehicle, $15/motorcycles, $10/cyclist or pedestrian aged 6 or older).

There are also public launch ramps at each of the marinas, and two public ramps in the far northeastern corner of the park that can accommodate small vessels only. If you didn't bring your own boat, the four marinas rent anything from a kayak to a

Glen Canyon Dam created a massive water wonderland in the middle of a desert.

personal watercraft to a 12-person pontoon boat to a speedboat tricked out with everything you need for a day of **waterskiing**. And if you don't want to captain your own ship, you can sit back and relax on a **boat tour** of the lake.

Top kayaking spots include **Antelope Canyon, Labyrinth Canyon,** and **Lost Eden**, all of which are no-wake zones. The primitive camping areas at **Lone Rock Beach** and **Stanton Creek** welcome overnight kayak

Lake Powell is one of the world's premier boating destinations.

and canoe trips. **Swimming** is permitted just about anywhere except at marinas and boat launch areas. However, there are no lifeguards anywhere in the park, not even at designated swim beaches. Most swimming takes place off the back of a boat, but there are a few sandy beaches where you can walk to water's edge. Lone Rock Beach sits just across the road from a parking lot, and has toilets and outdoor showers. **Bullfrog Bay** is home to numerous strands, including **Stanton Beach** and **Hobie Cat Beach,** both of which are close to the Bullfrog marina.

Renting a **houseboat** is another Lake Powell tradition, and no special license is required. The simplest rentals start around $1,500 for a four-day trip on a 46-foot (14-m) boat with two bedrooms and one bathroom. Prices go up from there, to as much as $13,000 for a week aboard a 75-foot (23-m) luxury yacht with 5 wheelchair-accessible staterooms, 2 baths, flat screen TVs throughout, and a water slide. Visit www. antelopepointlakepowell.com for boat rentals of all kinds at Antelope Point Marina, or www. lakepowell.com for rentals at the other three marinas.

Fishing is another favored activity, both in the lake and on the river. A valid Utah, Arizona, or combination fishing license is required. Introduced species such as bass crappie, walleye, and bluegill are abundant; native fish like Bonytails, Humpback

No special license is needed to rent a houseboat on Lake Powell.

Horseshoe Bend is perhaps the most-photographed landscape in Glen Canyon National Recreation Area.

chubs, and Razorback suckers must be immediately released. In 2020, the National Park Service offered anglers a financial incentive for helping to remove invasive fish species from the waters below the dam. The park service pays at least $25 for every brown trout over 6 inches (15 cm) caught and removed from the river between Glen Canyon Dam and the mouth of the Paria River.

Wilderness River Adventures (www.riveradventures.com) operates several **rafting trips** on the Colorado River, ranging from a half-day float past Horseshoe Bend to multi-day excursions through Canyonlands and/or Grand Canyon National Parks. Horseshoe Bend trips start just below the dam at 7 a.m. and 10:30 a.m. daily and visit **Petroglyph**

Beach, **Horseshoe Bend**, **Lee's Ferry**, and **Vermilion Cliffs**.

Horseshoe Bend is the single-most photographed location in the park. A minor drawback of

rafting through this 270-degree turn is that you don't get to see the iconic wide-angle view of the entire bend. On the other hand, you don't have to compete

Lake Powell has miles of sandy beaches, many reachable only by boat.

Reflection Canyon

with the multitudes crowding the overlook for the best selfies. A 0.7-mile (1.1-km) walk each way on a paved, accessible trail takes you from the parking lot to a viewpoint 1,000 feet (305 m) above the river. The overlook is located outside the park in the city of Page, AZ, which charges a parking fee of $10/car or RV ($5/motorcycle). On the busiest holiday weekends, the parking lot fills up quickly, and visitors may have to wait for somebody to leave before they can enter.

While the lake and the river get all the headlines, the canyons surrounding them are laced with myriad trails welcoming hikers of all abilities. The Park Service does not maintain any trails in the recreation area, and scorching temperatures in summertime dissuade all but the most dedicated trekkers. But spring and fall are lovely times to stretch your legs. Dogs are permitted on most trails.

Near the Carl Hayden Visitor Center, **Hanging Gardens** (1.5 miles/2.4 km round-trip) is an easy walk with a short climb at the far end to a secret desert oasis. The 3-mile (4.8-km) **Cathedral Wash Trail** from Lees Ferry Road down to the river and back is rated as moderate-to-difficult, but only because there are a few sections where you have to scramble over rocks. Otherwise, it's a relatively flat walk through a slot canyon. Do not hike this trail

when there is a potential for flash flooding.

The only thing that makes the **Page Rimview Loop** challenging is its length. But if you're up for a 10-mile (16-km) stroll around the town of Page, AZ, you'll be blessed with tremendous views of the lake, canyon, and dam. The impossibly green fairways of the **Lake Powell National Golf Course** strike a brilliant contrast with the surrounding red rock.

Rainbow Bridge National Monument is contained within Glen Canyon National Recreation Area, accessible only by boat from Lake Powell or a 14-mile/23-km hike through Navajo land (permit required). It's just one of a half dozen federally protected lands in the immediate surrounding area. Together, they make a greenbelt stretching from eastern Utah to the southern tip of Nevada.

A number of other federally protected lands surround Glen Canyon. If you follow the Colorado River below the dam to the southwest, you'll make your way to **Grand Canyon**. The 66-mile (106 km) **Burr Trail**

Road climbs northwest through **Grand Staircase Escalante National Monument** all the way to **Capitol Reef National Park**. Once described by pioneer Josephine Catherine Chatterley Wood as "the most God-forsaken and wild looking country that was ever traveled," the Burr Trail is now almost entirely paved, and accessible to passenger cars except in the wettest conditions.

Paddle upstream on the Colorado to the northeast and you'll reach the vast expanse of **Canyonlands National Park**. The skinny key-shaped eastern section of the recreation area traces the San Juan River through **Natural Bridges National Monument** and **Bears Ears National Monument**, whimsically named for two mesas in the shape of ursine ears that peek over the horizon. A half-hour drive south of the town of Mexican Hat brings you to **Monument Valley**—not on federal land, but immediately recognizable as the filming site of countless Hollywood westerns. Together, they make for a roadtrip that has it all.

Rainbow Bridge National Monument

ARIZONA
Canyon de Chelly National Monument
Fast Facts
Established: 1931
Acreage: 83,840 (33,929 hectares)
Visitors (2019): 460,757
Nearest Major Airport: Albuquerque Intl. Sunport
  (ABQ), Albuquerque, NM
Nearest Major Highways: I-40, US-191
Fees: $0
Accessibility: Mostly accessible except the
  backcountry trails.
Contact Information:
  928-674-5500
  www.nps.gov/cach

Located on Navajo trust land that contains a
residential community, Canyon de Chelly is unique
among national park units. The National Park
Service, Navajo Nation, and canyon community
work in conjunction to manage park resources and
commingle traditional and contemporary life. The
monument preserves one of the longest continually
inhabited locations by Native American communities
in the U.S., spanning at least 5,000 years.

*The Spider Rock spire is the centerpiece of
Canyon de Chelly National Monument.*

Casa Grande Ruins National Monument
Fast Facts
Established: 1892/1918
Acreage: 473 (191 hectares)
Visitors (2019): 68,379
Nearest Major Airport: Phoenix Sky Harbor Intl.
  (PHX), Phoenix, AZ
Nearest Major Highways: I-10, AZ-287
Fees: $0
Accessibility: Mostly accessible.
Contact Information:
  520-723-3172
  www.nps.gov/cagr

Preserves a multi-story, earthen-walled structure
surrounded by the remains of smaller buildings and
a compound wall constructed by the Hohokam,
who farmed the Gila Valley in the early 1200s.

Chiricahua National Monument
Fast Facts
Established: 1924
Acreage: 12,025 (4,866 hectares)
Visitors (2019): 60,655
Nearest Major Airport: Tucson Intl. (TUS),
  Tucson, AZ
Nearest Major Highways: I-10, AZ-186
Fees: $0
Contact Information:
  520-824-3560
  www.nps.gov/chir

Stonehenge meets Easter Island at Chiricahua National Monument.

This "Wonderland of Rocks" was created millions of years ago by volcanic activity, resulting in a landscape of rare beauty. The monument includes Faraway Ranch, a restored home Swedish immigrants Emma and Neil Erickson built and improved from the late 1880s to the 1920s.

Coronado National Memorial

Fast Facts

Established: 1952
Acreage: 4,830 (1,955 hectares)
Visitors (2019): 130,328
Nearest Major Airport: Tucson Intl. (TUS), Tucson, AZ
Nearest Major Highways: I-10, AZ-92
Fees: $0
Contact Information:
520-366-5515
www.nps.gov/coro

In a natural setting on the Mexican border, the memorial commemorates the first organized European expedition into the Southwest, led by Francisco Vásquez de Coronado in 1540, and affirms ties that bind the United States to Mexico and Spain.

Fort Bowie National Historic Site

Fast Facts

Established: 1972
Acreage: 999 (404 hectares)
Visitors (2019): 7,577
Nearest Major Airport: Phoenix Sky Harbor Intl. (PHX), Phoenix, AZ
Nearest Major Highways: I-10, AZ-186
Fees: $0
Accessibility: Visitors with impaired mobility may take an alternate route to the visitor center if the 1.5-mile (2.4-km) trail from Apache Pass Road proves too difficult to navigate.
Contact Information:
520-847-2500
www.nps.gov/fobo

Preserves and interprets the focal point of the U.S. Army's military operations against the Chiricahua Apache. The site also preserves part of the Butterfield Overland Mail Route.

Grand Canyon-Parashant National Monument

Fast Facts

Established: 2000

Acreage: 1,048,321 (424,240 hectares)
Visitors (2019): NA
Nearest Major Airport: Harry Reid Intl. (LAS), Las Vegas, NV
Nearest Major Highways: I-15
Fees: $0
Accessibility: Largely inaccessible.
Contact Information:
435-688-3200
www.nps.gov/para

This rugged, remote wilderness is a three-hour drive west from the North Rim of Grand Canyon National Park, and even farther from the South Rim. But geologically, this volcanically active land deep canyons and solitary buttes is just a stone's throw away. Prehistoric trails, villages, and rock art images provide a perspective on the ancient people who once inhabited the area. There are no paved roads, so a four-wheel-drive vehicle, all-terrain tires, and at least one spare tire are a must. There is no water or cellphone service.

Hohokam Pima National Monument
Fast Facts
Established: 1972
Acreage: 1,690 (684 hectares)
Visitors (2019): 0
Nearest Major Airport: Phoenix Sky Harbor Intl. (PHX), Phoenix, AZ
Nearest Major Highways: I-10
Fees: $0
Contact Information:
520-723-3172
www.nps.gov/pima

Located on the Gila River Indian Reservation, the monument preserves the archeological remains of the Hohokam culture. Hohokam is a Pima Indian word meaning "those who have gone." There is no public access to the site.

Hubbell Trading Post National Historic Site
Fast Facts
Established: 1965
Acreage: 160 (65 hectares)
Visitors (2019): 50,285

Navajo artisans work onsite at Hubbell Trading Post National Historic Site.

Nearest Major Airport: Albuquerque Intl. Sunport (ABQ), Albuquerque, NM
Nearest Major Highways: I-40, US-191
Fees: $0
Accessibility: Mostly accessible. A ramp to the Hubbell home can be arranged in advance.
Contact Information:
928-755-3475
www.nps.gov/hutr

The oldest operating trading post on the Navajo Nation, Hubbell's is both a historic site and an active trading post, famed for its selection of authentic Navajo rugs. The Western National Parks Association, a nonprofit partner of the National Park Service, operates the trading post.

Lake Mead National Recreation Area
Fast Facts
Established: 1964
Acreage: 1,495,806 (605,331 hectares)
Visitors (2019): 7,499,049
Nearest Major Airport: Harry Reid Intl. (LAS), Las Vegas, NV
Nearest Major Highways: I-15, US-93
Fees: $25/vehicle, $20/motorcycle, $15/cyclist or pedestrian, $16/boat ($8 for seniors). All entrance fees are valid for 7 days.
Accessibility: Many accommodations have been made for visitors with disabilities. Visit www.nps.gov/lake/planyourvisit/accessibility.htm for a detailed accounting.
Contact Information:
  702-293-8990
  www.nps.gov/lake
(Also in Nevada)

Formed by Hoover Dam, Lake Mead is America's first and largest national recreation area. The lake offers opportunities to boat, fish, swim, waterski, and sail. But the lake itself represents only about 13 percent of the park. The rest is on the surrounding land, which is rich with natural and cultural resources, including nine wilderness areas, the convergence of three of America's deserts, and 1,347 recorded archaeological sites. The park includes adjacent Lake Mohave, formed by Davis Dam downstream.

Montezuma Castle National Monument
Fast Facts
Established: 1906
Acreage: 1,016 (411 hectares)
Visitors (2019): 376,254
Nearest Major Airport: Phoenix Sky Harbor Intl. (PHX), Phoenix, AZ
Nearest Major Highways: I-17
Fees: $10/ adults aged 16 and older.
Accessibility: The trail at Montezuma Well and a portion of the Castle Trail are too steep for wheelchairs. The picnic area at the castle is also inaccessible.

A bighorn sheep enjoys the views of Lake Mead.

Contact Information:
928-567-5276
www.nps.gov/moca

Built in the 1100s and 1200s, this five-story, 20-room cliff dwelling is one of the best preserved in the United States. Included is Montezuma Well, a collapsed limestone sinkhole whose high levels of arsenic and carbon dioxide prevent fish from living in its waters. But the conditions are just right for five species of invertebrates found nowhere else in the world, including the tiny amphipod, a shrimp-shaped crustacean the size of a fingernail.

Navajo National Monument
Fast Facts
Established: 1909
Acreage: 360 (146 hectares)
Visitors (2019): 49,983
Nearest Major Airport: Albuquerque Intl. Sunport (ABQ), Albuquerque, NM
Nearest Major Highways: I-40, US-160, AZ-564

Fees: $0. Free permits are required to hike to Keet Seel. Guided tours are also free.
Accessibility: Buildings are accessible, but trails are too steep for wheelchairs.
Contact Information:
928-672-2700
www.nps.gov/nava

Preserves the remains of three cliff dwellings dating back to the 12th century: Betatakin, Keet Seel, and Inscription House (closed to the public due to its fragility). Archaeological evidence unearthed in these multi-hued canyons documents human use of this region over the past several thousand years.

Old Spanish National Historic Trail
Fast Facts
Established: 2002
Length: 2,680 miles (4,312 km)
Visitors (2019): NA
Nearest Major Airport: Eastern end: Albuquerque Intl. Sunport (ABQ), Albuquerque, NM.

Montezuma Castle, a five-story cliff dwelling, has survived for more than 800 years.

Western end: Los Angeles Intl. (LAX), Los Angeles, CA.
Nearest Major Highways: I-70
Fees: $0
Contact Information:
505-988-6098
www.nps.gov/olsp
(Also in California, Colorado, Nevada, New Mexico, and Utah)

Traces the former routes of mule pack trains between Santa Fe, NM, and Los Angeles, CA. New Mexican traders moved locally produced merchandise across what are now six states to exchange for mules and horses. The trail is managed in partnership with the Bureau of Land Management.

Organ Pipe Cactus National Monument
Fast Facts
Established: 1937
Acreage: 330,689 (133,825 hectares)
Visitors (2019): 263,186

Nearest Major Airport: Phoenix Sky Harbor Intl. (PHX), Phoenix, AZ
Nearest Major Highways: I-8, AZ-85
Fees: $25/vehicle, $20/motorcycle, $15/cyclist or pedestrian. All entrance fees are valid for 7 days.
Accessibility: Mostly accessible.
Contact Information:
520-387-6849
www.nps.gov/orpi

Protects a community of Sonoran Desert plants and animals found nowhere else in the U.S. Human stories echo throughout the preserve, chronicling thousands of years of desert living. UNESCO declared the monument an International Biosphere in 1976.

Petrified Forest National Park
Fast Facts
Established: 1906/1962
Acreage: 221,416 (89,604 hectares)
Visitors (2019): 643,588

Organ Pipe Cactus National Monument

Visitor Centers: Painted Desert, Rainbow Forest Museum
Nearest Major Airport: Albuquerque Intl. Sunport (ABQ), Albuquerque, NM
Nearest Major Highways: I-40
Fees: $25/vehicle, $20/motorcycle, $15/cyclist or pedestrian. All entrance fees are valid for 7 days.
Accessibility: Mostly accessible. Some trails are too steep for wheelchairs.
Contact Information:
928-524-6228
www.nps.gov/pefo

Preserves petrified logs composed of multicolored quartz; shortgrass prairie; part of the Painted Desert; and archeological, paleontological, historic, and cultural resources documenting more than 13,000 years of human history.

Pipe Spring National Monument
Fast Facts
Established: 1923
Acreage: 40 (16 hectares)
Visitors (2019): 27,482
Nearest Major Airport: Harry Reid Intl. (LAS), Las Vegas, NV
Nearest Major Highways: I-15, AZ-389
Fees: $10/adults aged 16 and older.
Accessibility: Interiors of the historic structures are not wheelchair accessible. The fort at Winsor Castle contains four sets of stairs.
Contact Information:
928-643-7105
www.nps.gov/pisp

These springs have sustained human occupation for hundreds of years, beginning with ancestral Puebloan and Southern Paiute cultures, and later Mormon ranchers, who drastically altered the landscape and set the stage for conflict on the western frontier. The monument preserves historic structures associated with the Mormon outpost and ranching operations.

Saguaro National Park
Fast Facts
Established: 1933/1994
Acreage: 91,442 (37,005 hectares)
Visitors (2019): 1,020,226

Visitor Centers: Rincon Mountain (East district), Red Hills (West district, a.k.a. Tucson Mountain district)
Nearest Major Airport: Tucson Intl. (TUS), Tucson, AZ
Nearest Major Highways: I-10, AZ-86
Fees: $25/vehicle, $20/motorcycle, $15/cyclist or pedestrian. All entrance fees are valid for 7 days.
Accessibility: All buildings, many trails, and most picnic areas are accessible.
Contact Information:
520-733-5153
www.nps.gov/sagu

A large wilderness park with two districts that bracket the city of Tucson and its one million residents provides a unique opportunity to engage urban dwellers. Giant saguaro cacti, unique to the Sonoran Desert, cover the valley floor and rise into the neighboring mountains. Five biotic life zones are represented, from desert to ponderosa pine forest.

Sunset Crater Volcano National Monument
Fast Facts
Established: 1930
Acreage: 3,040 (1,230 hectares)
Visitors (2019): 108,379
Nearest Major Airport: Phoenix Sky Harbor Intl. (PHX), Phoenix, AZ
Nearest Major Highways: I-40, US-89
Fees: $25/vehicle, $20/motorcycle, $15/cyclist or pedestrian. All entrance fees are valid for 7 days

Sunset at Saguaro National Park

at both Sunset Crater and Wupatki National Monuments.
Accessibility: Largely accessible.
Contact Information:
928-526-0502
www.nps.gov/sucr

Preserves a cinder cone volcano with summit crater that last erupted around 1085. Its upper part is colored as if by a sunset.

Tonto National Monument
Fast Facts
Established: 1907
Acreage: 1,120 (453 hectares)
Visitors (2019): 28,853
Nearest Major Airport: Phoenix Sky Harbor Intl. (PHX), Phoenix, AZ
Nearest Major Highways: I-10, AZ-88, AZ-188
Fees: $0
Accessibility: The visitor center, museum, park store, and picnic area are all accessible, but the trails are too steep for wheelchairs.
Contact Information:
928-467-2241
www.nps.gov/tont

More than 700 years ago, the Salado Phenomena blended ideas of neighboring Native American cultures to produce a unique and vibrant society. The monument showcases two Salado-style cliff dwellings. Colorful pottery, woven cotton cloth, and other artifacts tell a story of people living and using resources from the northern Sonoran Desert from 1250 to 1450.

Tumacacori National Historical Park
Fast Facts
Established: 1908/1990
Acreage: 360 (146 hectares)
Visitors (2019): 39,704
Nearest Major Airport: Tucson Intl. (TUS), Tucson, AZ
Nearest Major Highways: I-19
Fees: $10/adults aged 16 and older.
Accessibility: The visitor center, museum, restrooms, and mission grounds are fully accessible. A wheelchair is also available for loan to any visitor.

Contact Information:
520-377-5060
www.nps.gov/tuma

Protects the ruins of three Spanish missions: San José de Tumacácori, San Cayetano de Calabazas, and Los Santos Ángeles de Guevavi. These missions serve as a doorway into the rich and complex blending of cultures within the Santa Cruz River Valley from the 17th century to today.

Tuzigoot National Monument
Fast Facts
Established: 1939
Acreage: 812 (329 hectares)
Visitors (2019): 98,538
Nearest Major Airport: Phoenix Sky Harbor Intl. (PHX), Phoenix, AZ
Nearest Major Highways: I-17, AZ-89A
Fees: $10/adults aged 16 and older.
Accessibility: The Tuzigoot Pueblo trail and the top room of the Tuzigoot Pueblo Tower are inaccessible to visitors in wheelchairs.
Contact Information:
928-634-5664
www.nps.gov/tuzi

Preserves the ruins of a large Indian pueblo that flourished in the Verde Valley between 1100 and 1450.

Walnut Canyon National Monument
Fast Facts
Established: 1915
Acreage: 3,529 (1,428 hectares)
Visitors (2019): 152,333
Nearest Major Airport: Phoenix Sky Harbor Intl. (PHX), Phoenix, AZ
Nearest Major Highways: I-40
Fees: $28/vehicle, $15/cyclist or pedestrian aged 16 years or older. Individual entrance fees are valid for 7 days; vehicle entrance fees are only valid for 1 day.
Accessibility: All buildings are accessible but the two trails are not.
Contact Information:
928-526-3367
www.nps.gov/waca

Cliff dwellings at Walnut Canyon National Memorial

Preserves dozens of cliff dwellings that were built in shallow caves under ledges of limestone by the Northern Sinagua people about 800 years ago.

Wupatki National Monument

Fast Facts

Established: 1924
Acreage: 35,422 (14,335 hectares)
Visitors (2019): 187,059
Nearest Major Airport: Phoenix Sky Harbor Intl. (PHX), Phoenix, AZ
Nearest Major Highways: I-40, US-89
Fees: $25/vehicle, $20/motorcycle, $15/cyclist or pedestrian. All entrance fees are valid for 7 days at both Wupatki and Sunset Crater National Monuments.
Accessibility: Most buildings and some trails are accessible, but not all.
Contact Information:
928-679-2365
www.nps.gov/wupa

Preserves red sandstone pueblos built by Ancestral Puebloan people from 1120 to 1250. They raised families, farmed, traded, and thrived on land seemingly inhospitable to human habitation between the Painted Desert and Arizona's northern highlands.

NEVADA
Great Basin National Park

Fast Facts

Established: 1922/1986
Acreage: 77,180 (31,234 hectares)
Visitors (2019): 131,802
Visitor Centers: Great Basin, Lehman Caves
Nearest Major Airport: Salt Lake City Intl. (SLC), Salt Lake City, UT
Nearest Major Highways: I-15, US-50, US-93
Fees: $0
Accessibility: Both visitor centers are fully accessible. The stairs and narrow passageways of Lehman Cave are challenging for visitors in

wheelchairs. The steepness of the Island Forest Trail makes it a challenge as well.

Contact Information:
775-234-7331
www.nps.gov/grba

Preserves an outstanding segment of the Great Basin, including 5,000-year-old bristlecone pines, 13,063-foot (3,982-m) Wheeler Peak, remnant rock glaciers, Lexington Arch, the darkest of night skies, and the decorated galleries of Lehman Caves.

Tule Springs Fossil Beds National Monument

Fast Facts

Established: 2014
Acreage: 22,650 (9,166 hectares)
Visitors (2019): NA
Nearest Major Airport: Harry Reid Intl. (LAS), Las Vegas, NV
Nearest Major Highways: I-15, US-95
Fees: $0
Accessibility: No federal facilities.
Contact Information:
702-293-8853
www.nps.gov/tusk

Columbian Mammoths, sloths, American lions, and camels once roamed along wetlands just north of what is now known as Las Vegas. Tule Springs Fossil Beds National Monument preserves the history of the Pleistocene Epoch and may hold clues about climate change over the past 200,000 years. It was listed on the National Register of Historic Places in 1979 for its importance in understanding paleoenvironments and for its association with important advances in archeological methods and analysis, including radiocarbon dating.

NEW MEXICO
Aztec Ruins National Monument

Fast Facts

Established: 1923
Acreage: 318 (129 hectares)
Visitors (2019): 63,777
Nearest Major Airport: Albuquerque Intl. Sunport (ABQ), Albuquerque, NM
Nearest Major Highways: US-550
Fees: $0

Aztec Ruins National Monument

Accessibility: The visitor center, restrooms, and picnic tables are accessible, but steps, narrow doorways, and steep slopes make the Aztec Ruins Trail inaccessible to wheelchairs.
Contact Information:
505-334-6174
www.nps.gov/azru

Preserves and stabilizes the remains of this large Pueblo Indian community from the 1100s, including a Great House of more than 400 masonry rooms.

Bandelier National Monument

Fast Facts

Established: 1916
Acreage: 33,677 (13,629 hectares)
Visitors (2019): 200,741
Nearest Major Airport: Albuquerque Intl. Sunport (ABQ), Albuquerque, NM
Nearest Major Highways: I-25, NM-4
Fees: $25/vehicle, $20/motorcycle, $15/cyclist or pedestrian aged 16 years or older. All entrance fees are valid for 7 days.
Accessibility: The visitor center, museum, bookshop and theater are all accessible, but the trails are not.
Contact Information:
505-672-3861
www.nps.gov/band

On the mesa tops and canyon walls of the Pajarito Plateau are the remains of Pueblo Indians' cliff houses and villages dating from the 1200s.

Capulin Volcano National Monument

Fast Facts

Established: 1916
Acreage: 793 (321 hectares)
Visitors (2019): 81,617
Nearest Major Airport: Albuquerque Intl. Sunport (ABQ), Albuquerque, NM
Nearest Major Highways: I-25, US-87
Fees: $20/vehicle, $15/motorcycle, $10/cyclist or pedestrian. All entrance fees are valid for 7 days.
Accessibility: The visitor center, nature trail, Crater Rim Overlook, and picnic area are all wheelchair accessible. All other trails are inaccessible, as is the Outdoor Classroom.
Contact Information:
505-278-2201
www.nps.gov/cavo

This symmetrical cinder cone volcano showcases the geology of northeastern New Mexico. From the rim, one can see spectacular vistas of four different states during the day. At night, one of the darkest night skies in the country creates ideal stargazing conditions.

Carlsbad Caverns National Park

Fast Facts

Established: 1923/1930
Acreage: 46,766 (18,926 hectares)
Visitors (2019): 440,691
Nearest Major Airport: Albuquerque Intl. Sunport (ABQ), Albuquerque, NM
Nearest Major Highways: I-10, I-25, US-62
Fees: $15/adults aged 16 and older. Children aged 15 and younger are free. Entrance fees are valid for 3 days. Ranger-guided tours are an additional $15 for adults (free for children aged 15 and younger).
Accessibility: The Big Room Trail is the only wheelchair accessible route into the cavern.
Contact Information:
505-785-2232
www.nps.gov/cave

Countless formations decorate huge chambers, including the easily accessible Big Room, covering 8 acres (3 ha) with a 250-ft (76-m) ceiling. The park contains at least 120 separate caves, including the nation's deepest limestone cave.

The entrance to Carlsbad Caverns National Park

Chaco Culture National Historical Park

Fast Facts

Established: 1907/1980
Acreage: 33,960 (13,743 hectares)
Visitors (2019): 47,342
Nearest Major Airport: Albuquerque Intl. Sunport
(ABQ), Albuquerque, NM
Nearest Major Highways: I-40, NM-371, NM-57
Fees: $25/vehicle, $20/motorcycle, $15/cyclist or
pedestrian. All entrance fees are valid for 7 days.
Camping costs $20/night. Reserve campsites at
least 3 days in advance.
Accessibility: Buildings are accessible, but trails are
not.
Contact Information:
505-786-7014
www.nps.gov/chcu

The massive structures built by the Ancestral
Puebloan people testify to organizational and
engineering abilities not seen anywhere else in
the American Southwest. This canyon preserves
13 major sites built between 850 and 1250 AD and
hundreds of smaller ones.

El Camino Real de Tierra Adentro National Historic Trail

Fast Facts

Established: 2000
Length: 404 miles (650 km)
Visitors (2019): NA
Nearest Major Airport: North end: Albuquerque
Intl. Sunport (ABQ), Albuquerque, NM. South
end: El Paso Intl. (ELP), El Paso, TX.
Nearest Major Highways: I-40, US-54, US-285
Fees: $0. Some sites along the route may charge an
admission fee.
Accessibility: Most sites along the trail meet
accessibility standards.
Contact Information:
505-988-6098
www.nps.gov/elca
(Also in Texas)

This 300-year-old route between El Paso, TX, and
Santa Fe, NM, commemorates the multicultural
connections, exchanges, and interactions among
residents and explorers from Native American,
Mexican, Black, and European backgrounds.

Trade and travel on the trail shaped individual lives
and communities, as well as the settlement and
development of the American Southwest. The trail
passes by 44 different historic sites.

El Malpais National Monument

Fast Facts

Established: 1987
Acreage: 114,314 (5,793 hectares)
Visitors (2019): 158,924
Nearest Major Airport: Albuquerque Intl. Sunport
(ABQ), Albuquerque, NM
Nearest Major Highways: I-40, NM 53, NM-117
Fees: $0
Accessibility: Caves and other natural features are
inaccessible to visitors in wheelchairs.
Contact Information:
505-876-2783
www.nps.gov/elma

This spectacular volcanic area features cinder cones, a
17-mile- (27-km-) long lava tube system, and ice caves.
The area is rich in ancient Pueblo and Navajo history.

El Morro National Monument

Fast Facts

Established: 1906
Acreage: 1,279 (518 hectares)
Visitors (2019): 68,867
Nearest Major Airport: Albuquerque Intl. Sunport
(ABQ), Albuquerque, NM
Nearest Major Highways: I-40, NM 53,
Fees: $0
Accessibility: The visitor center, picnic area, and
campground are all accessible. The Inscription
Trail is only accessible to visitors who use
wheelchairs with some assistance. The Headland
Trail is not at all accessible.
Contact Information:
505-783-4226
www.nps.gov/elmo

Preserves the remains of Pueblo Indian dwellings
and pre-Columbian petroglyphs. A highlight is
Inscription Rock, a 200-foot (61-m) sandstone
monolith on which are carved thousands of
messages from early travelers.

Fort Union National Monument

Fast Facts

Established: 1954
Acreage: 721 (292 hectares)
Visitors (2019): 11,063
Nearest Major Airport: Albuquerque Intl. Sunport (ABQ), Albuquerque, NM
Nearest Major Highways: I-25, NM-161
Fees: $0
Accessibility: Fully accessible.
Contact Information:
  505-425-8025
  www.nps.gov/foun

Preserves remnants of the Southwest's largest frontier fort, which played a key role in the Indian Wars and in the Confederate defeat at Glorieta Pass. A large network of Santa Fe Trail ruts is still visible on the prairie.

Gila Cliff Dwellings National Monument

Fast Facts

Established: 1907
Acreage: 533 (216 hectares)
Visitors (2019): 66,614
Nearest Major Airport: Albuquerque Intl. Sunport (ABQ), Albuquerque, NM
Nearest Major Highways: US-180, NM-15
Fees: $0
Accessibility: Buildings are fully accessible, but the trail to the dwellings is unpaved, steeply graded, and includes many steps, stairs, and ladders.
Contact Information:
  575-536-9461
  www.nps.gov/gicl

For thousands of years, groups of nomadic people used these caves on the Gila River as temporary shelter. In the late 1200s, people of the Mogollon Culture decided it would be a good place to call home. They built rooms, crafted pottery, and raised children in the cliff dwellings for about 20 years before moving on.

Manhattan Project National Historical Park

Fast Facts
Established: 2015

Acreage: Not yet established
Visitors (2019): 21,790
Visitor Centers: Los Alamos (20th Street, between Trinity Drive and Central Avenue)
Nearest Major Airport: Albuquerque Intl. Sunport (ABQ), Albuquerque, NM
Nearest Major Highways: I-25, NM-502
Fees: $0
Accessibility: The visitor center is accessible, and the park film includes captions and audio descriptions. The guided tour includes stairs and uneven terrain.
Contact Information:
  505-661-6277
  www.nps.gov/mapr
(Also in Tennessee and Washington)

The Los Alamos unit of this tripartite park preserves the laboratory where Robert Oppenheimer, Richard Feynman, and other scientists developed the theoretical and experimental tests that created the first atomic weapons. The 4.3-mile (6.9-km) Kwage Mesa Trail Loop gives visitors insight into why this remote location was chosen for the top-secret lab.

Pecos National Historical Park

Fast Facts

Established: 1965/1990
Acreage: 6,694 (2,709 hectares)
Visitors (2019): 43,834
Nearest Major Airport: Albuquerque Intl. Sunport (ABQ), Albuquerque, NM
Nearest Major Highways: I-25, NM-63
Fees: $0
Accessibility: Buildings are accessible. Trails are not completely accessible.
Contact Information:
  505-757-7241
  www.nps.gov/peco

Preserves 12,000 years of human history, including the remains of the Pecos Pueblo and many other American Indian structures, Spanish colonial missions, homesteads of the Mexican era, a section of the Santa Fe Trail, sites related to the Civil War Battle of Glorieta Pass, and a 1900s ranch.

Petroglyph National Monument features more than 25,000 designs and symbols carved by Native Americans and Spanish settlers.

Petroglyph National Monument

Fast Facts

Established: 1990
Acreage: 7,209 (2,917 hectares)
Visitors (2019): 293,957
Nearest Major Airport: Albuquerque Intl. Sunport (ABQ), Albuquerque, NM
Nearest Major Highways: I-40, NM-45
Fees: $0. Parking at Boca Negra is $1 on weekdays, $2 on weekends.
Accessibility: Buildings are accessible, but trails are not, except for the Volcanoes trail, which is partially accessible.
Contact Information:
 505-899-0205
 www.nps.gov/petr

Protects one of the largest petroglyph sites in North America, featuring more than 25,000 designs and symbols carved by Native Americans and Spanish settlers 400 to 700 years ago. The petroglyphs continue for 17 miles (27 km) along Albuquerque's West Mesa escarpment. The monument is owned and managed in partnership with the City of Albuquerque and the State of New Mexico.

Salinas Pueblo Missions National Monument

Fast Facts

Established: 1909/1980
Acreage: 1,071 (433 hectares)
Visitors (2019): 31,672
Visitor Centers: Salinas, Abó, Qarai, Gran Quivira
Nearest Major Airport: Albuquerque Intl. Sunport (ABQ), Albuquerque, NM
Nearest Major Highways: I-25, US-60
Fees: $0
Accessibility: All sites are at least partially accessible.
Contact Information:
 505-847-2585
 www.nps.gov/sapu

Preserves and interprets some of the best examples of Spanish Franciscan mission churches and convents of the 1600s still extant in the U.S., as well as three large Pueblo Indian villages.

Valles Caldera National Preserve

Fast Facts

Established: 2000
Acreage: 89,000 (36,017 hectares)
Visitors (2019): NA
Visitor Centers: Valle Grande, Valles Caldera
Nearest Major Airport: Albuquerque Intl. Sunport (ABQ), Albuquerque, NM
Nearest Major Highways: I-25, NM-4
Fees: $25 per vehicle of any kind. $15/adult aged 16 and older for those arriving by bicycle or horse.
Accessibility: Buildings are accessible, but trails are not.
Contact Information:
575-829-4100
www.nps.gov/vall

About 1.25 million years ago, a spectacular volcanic eruption created the 13-mile (21-km) crater-shaped landscape now known as Valles Caldera in the Jemez Mountains of north-central New Mexico. One of only three super-volcanoes in the U.S., the preserve is known for its huge mountain meadows, abundant wildlife, meandering streams, and extensive history of indigenous and Hispanic land use.

White Sands National Park

Fast Facts

Established: 1933
Acreage: 143,733 (58,167 hectares)
Visitors (2019): 608,785
Nearest Major Airport: Albuquerque Intl. Sunport (ABQ), Albuquerque, NM
Nearest Major Highways: I-10, I-25, US-54, US-70
Fees: $25/vehicle, $20/motorcycle, $15/cyclist or pedestrian. All entrance fees are valid for 7 days.
Accessibility: Buildings are accessible. The 0.4-mile (650-m) Interdune Boardwalk to the top of a dune is also wheelchair-accessible.
Contact Information:
505-679-2599
www.nps.gov/whsa

Gypsum gives the dunes their snowy color at White Sands National Park.

More than 275 square miles (712 sq km) of glistening white dunes rise 60 feet (18 m) into the air , creating the world's largest gypsum dunefield. Small animals and plants have adapted to this harsh environment. The park occasionally closes for missile testing at the adjacent White Sands Missile Range. Visit the website or NPS app for scheduled park closures.

TEXAS
Alibates Flint Quarries National Monument
Fast Facts
Established: 1965
Acreage: 1,371 (555 hectares)
Visitors (2019): 8,847
Nearest Major Airport: Dallas/Fort Worth Intl. (DFW), TX
Nearest Major Highways: I-40, TX-126
Fees: $0
Accessibility: The visitor center and native plants garden are both accessible.
Contact Information:
806-857-6680
www.nps.gov/alfl

Mammoth hunters visited the red bluffs above the Canadian River some 13,000 years ago to dig for colorful agatized dolomite, which they used as flint for tools. Centuries passed but the brightly hued flint never lost its value and usefulness. The quarries were dug by hand approximately 500–800 years ago, possibly with the use of bone tools.

Amistad National Recreation Area
Fast Facts
Established: 1990
Acreage: 58,500 (23,674 hectares)
Visitors (2019): 1,267,900
Nearest Major Airport: San Antonio Intl. (SAT), San Antonio, TX
Nearest Major Highways: I-10, US-90, US-377
Fees: $0. There is a $4 daily lake use pass to bring a boat onto the lake.
Contact Information:
830-775-7491
www.nps.gov/amis

Boating, watersports, camping, and fishing are the primary activities at the U.S. portion of the International Amistad Reservoir on the Rio Grande. The U.S. and Mexico jointly manage the reservoir; Americans and Mexicans in the border cities of Del Rio, TX, and Ciudad Acuña, Mexico, celebrate their shared history and culture every October during the Fiesta de Amistad (Friendship Festival).

Big Bend National Park
Fast Facts
Established: 1944
Acreage: 801,163 (324,219 hectares)
Visitors (2019): 463,832
Visitor Centers: Panther Junction, Chisos Basin, Castolon, Persimmon Gap, Rio Grande
Nearest Major Airport: El Paso Intl. (ELP), El Paso, TX
Nearest Major Highways: I-10, TX-118
Fees: $30/vehicle, $25/motorcycle, $12/cyclist or pedestrian. All entrance fees are valid for 7 days.
Accessibility: Visit www.nps.gov/bibe/planyourvisit/accessibility.htm for a full accounting of what is and isn't accessible.
Contact Information:
432-477-2251
www.nps.gov/bibe

Mountains contrast with desert at the big bend of the Rio Grande in far West Texas. The river waters rush through deep-cut canyons and the open desert, creating habitat for hundreds of bird species.

Mountains rise out of the desert at Big Bend National Park.

Big Thicket National Preserve

Fast Facts

Established: 1974
Acreage: 109,092 (44,148 hectares)
Visitors (2019): 255,926
Nearest Major Airport: George Bush Intercontinental (IAH), Houston, TX
Nearest Major Highways: I-10, US-287
Fees: $0
Accessibility: The visitor center is accessible, as are the Sundew Trail and a short portion of the Pitcher Plant Trail.
Contact Information:
409-951-6700
www.nps.gov/bith

An incredible diversity of plant and animal species coexist in this biological crossroads in southeast Texas. Hiking trails and waterways meander through nine different ecosystems, from longleaf pine forests to cypress-lined bayous.

Chamizal National Memorial

Fast Facts

Established: 1974
Acreage: 55 (22 hectares)
Visitors (2019): 38,228
Nearest Major Airport: El Paso Intl. (ELP), El Paso, TX
Nearest Major Highways: I-10, US-54
Fees: $0
Accessibility: Largely accessible, except for the outdoor stage, which lacks curb cuts and paved walkways.

Murals at Chamizal National Memorial

Contact Information:
915-532-7273
www.nps.gov/cham

Commemorates the peaceful settlement of a century-old boundary dispute between the U.S. and Mexico. A 500-seat theater, outdoor stage, and three art galleries interpret and enhance multicultural understanding.

El Camino Real de los Tejas National Historic Trail

Fast Facts

Established: 2004
Length: 2,580 miles (4,151 km)
Visitors (2019): NA
Nearest Major Airport: West end: Austin-Bergstrom Intl. (AUS), Austin, TX, or San Antonio Intl. (SAT), San Antonio, TX. East end: Alexandria Intl. (AEX), Alexandria, LA
Nearest Major Highways: I-35, US 182, US-290
Fees: $0. Some locally owned historic sites along the trail may charge admission fees.
Accessibility: Most sites are accessible, but some of the more rural stations may not be.
Contact Information:
505-988-6098
www.nps.gov/elte
(Also in Louisiana)

El Camino Real de los Tejas served as a political, economic, and cultural link between Mexico City and Los Adaes (now part of Natchitoches Parish in Louisiana). Spanish, Mexican, French, American, Black, and American Indian travelers along the trail created a mix of traditions, laws, and cultures that is reflected in the people, landscapes, place names, languages, music, and arts of Texas and Louisiana today.

Fort Davis National Historic Site

Fast Facts

Established: 1963
Acreage: 523 (212 hectares)
Visitors (2019): 51,995
Nearest Major Airport: El Paso Intl. (ELP), El Paso, TX
Nearest Major Highways: I-10, US-90, TX-17

Fees: $20/vehicle, $15/motorcycle, $10/cyclist or pedestrian aged 16 or older. All entrance fees are valid for 7 days.

Accessibility: Largely accessible.

Contact Information:
432-426-3224
www.nps.gov/foda

One of the best surviving examples of a 19th-century frontier military post, Fort Davis served travelers seeking to settle in West Texas or passing through along the Trans-Pecos section of the San Antonio-El Paso Road and on the Chihuahua Trail from 1854–91.

Guadalupe Mountains National Park

Fast Facts

Established: 1972
Acreage: 86,367 (34,951 hectares)
Visitors (2019): 188,833
Visitor Centers: Pine Springs, Dog Canyon, McKittrick Canyon, Dell City
Contact Station
Nearest Major Airport: El Paso Intl. (ELP), El Paso, TX
Nearest Major Highways: I-10, US-62, US-90
Fees: $10/person aged 16 years or older.
Accessibility: Visitor Centers are all accessible, as are the paved Pinery Trail and Manzanita Spring Trail.

Contact Information:
915-828-3251
www.nps.gov/gumo

Multiple peaks tower above the Texas and New Mexico landscapes, including Guadalupe Peak, the highest point in Texas at 8,751 feet (2,667 m). The park protects the world's most extensive Permian period fossil reef. Canyons, sand dunes, and wilderness include Chihuahuan Desert, Rocky Mountain, and Great Plains plants and animals.

Lake Meredith National Recreation Area

Fast Facts

Established: 1965/1990
Acreage: 44,978 (18,202 hectares)
Visitors (2019): 1,328,340
Nearest Major Airport: Dallas/Fort Worth Intl. (DFW), TX
Nearest Major Highways: I-40, TX-136
Fees: $0
Contact Information:
806-857-3151
www.nps.gov/lamr

Lake Meredith, created by Sanford Dam on the Canadian River in the Texas panhandle, is the setting for boating, fishing, and watersports. The area's canyons, foothills, and meadows provide opportunities for hiking and other activities. The

Capitan Peak in Guadalupe Mountains National Park

The Lockheed Jetstar on display at the LBJ Ranch is sometimes jokingly called Air Force ½.

U.S. Bureau of Reclamation cooperates in the park's administration.

Lyndon B. Johnson National Historical Park

Fast Facts

Established: 1969/1980
Acreage: 1,570 (635 hectares)
Visitors (2019): 111,972
Visitor Centers: Park Headquarters (Johnson City), Airplane Hangar (LBJ Ranch District), LBJ State Park and Historic Site (across from LBJ Ranch)
Nearest Major Airport: San Antonio Intl. (SAT), San Antonio, TX
Nearest Major Highways: I-10, US-290
Fees: $0
Accessibility: Fully accessible except for the Lockheed Jetstar, which requires climbing stairs to visit the interior.
Contact Information:
830-868-7128
www.nps.gov/lyjo

Two separate locations 14 miles (23 km) apart conserve historic properties related to the 36th president from his birth to death. Together, they provide one of most complete pictures of an American president. The Texas White House on the LBJ Ranch is the primary resource. Burial sites of the president and first lady are located on the ranch.

Padre Island National Seashore

Fast Facts

Established: 1968

Acreage: 130,434 (52,785 hectares)
Visitors (2019): 576,299
Visitor Center: Malaquite
Nearest Major Airport: George Bush Intercontinental (IAH), Houston, TX; San Antonio Intl. (SAT), San Antonio, TX
Nearest Major Highways: I-37, TX-358
Fees: $10/vehicle per day, $7/motorcycle per day, $5/cyclist or pedestrian per day. Seven-day passes are $35/vehicle, $29/motorcycle, $15 cyclist or pedestrian. An additional $5/vehicle fee is charged for use of the Bird Island Basin.
Accessibility: Beach wheelchairs that can navigate the seashore's soft sand are available for free at the visitor center.
Contact Information:
361-949-8173
www.nps.gov/pais

Protects 70 miles (113 km) of coastline separating the Gulf of Mexico from the Laguna Madre, one of a handful of hypersaline lagoons in the world. The seashore is noted for its wide sand beaches, excellent fishing, and abundant bird and marine life.

Palo Alto Battlefield National Historical Park

Fast Facts

Established: 1978/2009
Acreage: 3,442 (1,393 hectares)
Visitors (2019): 1,393
Nearest Major Airport: San Antonio Intl. (SAT), San Antonio, TX
Nearest Major Highways: I-168, TX-550
Fees: $0
Accessibility: The distance between the visitor center and the battlefield can be a challenge for visitors with limited mobility.
Contact Information:
956-541-2785
www.nps.gov/paal

Preserves and interprets the sites of the first two battles of the U.S.-Mexican War (1846–48).

Rio Grande Wild and Scenic River

Fast Facts

Established: 1978
Acreage: 9,600 (3,885 hectares)

Visitors (2019): 324
Visitor Centers: Panther Junction, Chisos Basin, Castolon, Persimmon Gap, Rio Grande (all in Big Bend National Park)
Nearest Major Airport: San Antonio Intl. (SAT), San Antonio, TX
Nearest Major Highways: I-10, US-385, TX-118
Fees: $0. Backcountry use permits required for all river use. Day use permits are free; overnight permits are $10/day. If you float the portions inside Big Bend National Park, you must pay that park's entrance fee: $30/vehicle, $25/motorcycle, $12/cyclist or pedestrian. All entrance fees are valid for 7 days.
Accessibility: Most visitor centers and some trails along the river are wheelchair-accessible.
Contact Information:
432-477-2251
www.nps.gov/rigr

Protects a 196-mile (315-km) strip on the American shore of the Rio Grande in the Chihuahuan Desert. The protected portion of the river begins in Big Bend National Park and continues downstream to the border between Terrell and Val Verde counties. The river was designated for outstanding scenic, geologic, recreational, and cultural values.

San Antonio Missions National Historical Park
Fast Facts
Established: 1983
Acreage: 948 (384 hectares)
Visitors (2019): 1,281,121
Nearest Major Airport: San Antonio Intl. (SAT), San Antonio, TX
Nearest Major Highways: I-10, I-35, I-37, I-410, TX-536
Fees: $0
Accessibility: Each of the major sites in the park is partially accessible, but there may be rough terrain, steep grades, or stairs.
Contact Information:
210-534-8833
www.nps.gov/saan

Preserves four Spanish frontier missions, part of a colonization system that stretched across the Spanish Southwest from the 1600s to the 1800s.

Concepcion is one of four missions at San Antonio Missions National Historical Park.

The park is the only UNESCO World Heritage Site in Texas.

Waco Mammoth National Monument
Fast Facts
Established: 2015
Acreage: 107 (43 hectares)
Visitors (2019): 111,331
Nearest Major Airport: San Antonio Intl. (SAT), San Antonio, TX
Nearest Major Highways: I-35, US-84
Fees: $0. Access to the Dig Shelter is $5/adult; $4/seniors, military, teachers, and students; $3/child in pre-kindergarten through 6th grade.
Accessibility: Fully accessible. Special materials available for visitors with hearing and visual impairments.
Contact Information:
254-750-7946
www.nps.gov/waco

This paleontological site is home to the U.S.'s only known nursery herd of ice age Columbian mammoths. Discoveries here include 23 mammoths, a camel, a dwarf antelope, an American alligator, a giant tortoise, and the tooth of a saber-toothed cat.

UTAH
Arches National Park
Fast Facts
Established: 1929/1971

Turret Arch, as seen through the North Window at Arches National Park.

Acreage: 76,679 (31,031 hectares)
Visitors (2019): 1,659,702
Nearest Major Airport: Salt Lake City Intl. (SLC), Salt Lake City, UT
Nearest Major Highways: I-70, US-191
Fees: $30/vehicle, $25/motorcycle, $15/cyclist or pedestrian. All entrance fees are valid for 7 days.
Accessibility: Varies. Visit www.nps.gov/arch/planyourvisit/accessibility.htm for a comprehensive list of trails and facilities that are accessible to visitors with impaired vision, hearing, and mobility.
Contact Information:
435-719-2299
www.nps.gov/arch

This red rock wonderland is chockablock with extraordinary products of natural erosion of sandstone. The stunning formations include windows, pinnacles, pedestals, giant boulders, and more than 2,000 of the eponymous natural stone arches.

Canyonlands National Park
Fast Facts
Established: 1964
Acreage: 337,598 (136,621 hectares)
Visitors (2019): 733,996
Visitor Centers: Island in the Sky, The Needles, Hans Flat Ranger Station (in the Maze region)
Nearest Major Airport: Salt Lake City Intl. (SLC), Salt Lake City, UT
Nearest Major Highways: I-70, US-191
Fees: $30/vehicle, $25/motorcycle, $15/cyclist or pedestrian. All entrance fees are valid for 7 days.
Accessibility: The visitor centers are largely accessible, but most trails are not.
Contact Information:
435-719-2313
www.nps.gov/cany

Rocks, spires, and mesas dominate the heart of the Colorado Plateau, cut by canyons of the Green and Colorado rivers. The rivers divide the park into several discrete sections, with no roads connecting them and few places to cross the rivers. Island in the

The Needles District of Canyonlands National Park may require hiking or four-wheel drive to reach.

Sky is the most accessible district; the Needles and the Maze offer more of a backcountry experience and often require hiking or four-wheel drive to reach. Prehistoric American Indian rock art and structures dot the red rock landscape. Canyonlands was designated an International Dark Sky Park in 2015.

Capitol Reef National Park
Fast Facts
Established: 1937/1971
Acreage: 241,904 (97,895 hectares)
Visitors (2019): 1,226,519
Nearest Major Airport: Salt Lake City Intl. (SLC), Salt Lake City, UT
Nearest Major Highways: I-70, UT-12
Fees: $20/vehicle, $15/motorcycle, $10/cyclist or pedestrian. All entrance fees are valid for 7 days.
Accessibility: The Visitor Center is fully accessible, but most trails are not.
Contact Information:
435-425-3791
www.nps.gov/care

Preserves more than 70 miles (113 km) of the Waterpocket Fold, a geologic uplift or wrinkle, featuring colorful sedimentary layers formed by erosion into a labyrinth of cliffs and canyons.

Towering domes of white sandstone account for the name. Archaeological evidence of prehistoric cultures and a historic Mormon pioneer settlement are also preserved. Capitol Reef was designated an International Dark Sky Park 2015.

Cedar Breaks National Monument
Fast Facts
Established: 1933
Acreage: 6,155 (2,491 hectares)
Visitors (2019): 579,861
Nearest Major Airport: Salt Lake City Intl. (SLC), Salt Lake City, UT
Nearest Major Highways: I-15, UT-143
Fees: $10/person aged 16 or older. Valid for 7 days.
Accessibility: All overlooks and the Sunset Trail are fully accessible.
Contact Information:
435-986-7120
www.nps.gov/cebr

Multicolored rock formations fill a vast geologic amphitheater, creating a spectacular landscape. Situated at over 10,000 feet (3,048 m) in elevation, Cedar Breaks offers a variety of recreational opportunities year-round. The high elevation makes the park monument a cool escape in summer, with a yearly show of colorful wildflowers. Family-friendly

The aspen forests at Cedar Breaks National Monument turn brilliant gold in autumn.

hikes trace the rim of the amphitheater, and backcountry trails navigate red rock slot canyons and waterfalls. Fall foliage paints the landscape with brilliant yellows, oranges, and reds. Winter activities include snowshoeing, cross-country skiing, and snowmobiling. The park hosts popular night sky "star parties" in summer and winter.

Golden Spike National Historical Park
Fast Facts

Established: 1957/1965
Acreage: 2,735 (1,107 hectares)
Visitors (2019): 108,154
Nearest Major Airport: Salt Lake City Intl. (SLC), Salt Lake City, UT
Nearest Major Highways: I-15, I-84, UT-83
Fees: $20/vehicle, $15/motorcycle, $10/cyclist or pedestrian aged 16 or older. Those aged 15 and under are admitted for free.

Accessibility: The visitor center and last spike site are fully wheelchair-accessible, but the Big Fill hiking trail has stairs.
Contact Information:
435-471-2209
www.nps.gov/gosp

Commemorates the completion of the first transcontinental railroad in the U.S. here on May 10, 1869, linking the Central Pacific and Union Pacific railroads at Promontory Summit, UT.

Natural Bridges National Monument
Fast Facts

Established: 1908
Acreage: 7,636 (3,090 hectares)
Visitors (2019): 88,090
Nearest Major Airport: Salt Lake City Intl. (SLC), Salt Lake City, UT

Nearest Major Highways: I-70, US-191, UT-95

Fees: $20/vehicle, $15/motorcycle, $10/cyclist or pedestrian aged 16 or older. Those under age 15 are admitted for free.

Accessibility: The visitor center and the trails to Sipapu Bridge Overlook and Owachomo Bridge Overlook are accessible. The trail to Kachina Bridge Overlook and most campgrounds are barrier-free but may contain minor obstacles or steep grades.

Contact Information:
435-692-1234
www.nps.gov/nabr

Protects and interprets three of the world's largest natural bridges, all carved out of sandstone. They are named Kachina, Owachomo, and Sipapu in honor of the Ancestral Puebloans who once called this place home. Horse Collar ruin preserves two largely intact Puebloan structures from the 14th century. Natural Bridges was designated an International Dark Sky Park in 2007.

Rainbow Bridge National Monument
Fast Facts
Established: 1910
Acreage: 160 (65 hectares)
Visitors (2019): 115,108
Nearest Major Airport: Salt Lake City Intl. (SLC), Salt Lake City, UT
Nearest Major Highways: I-70, UT-95, UT-275
Fees: Visitors to Rainbow Bridge must pay the fees for entering Glen Canyon National Recreation Area ($30/vehicle, $25/motorcycle, $15/cyclist or pedestrian aged 16 or older). There are no additional fees to visit Rainbow Bridge, but the boat tour from Wahweap Marina costs $126/adult, $80/children 3–12 years old.
Accessibility: Inaccessible

Contact Information:
928-608-6200
www.nps.gov/rabr

Contained within Glen Canyon National Recreation Area and accessible only by boat on Lake Powell (or a 14-mile/23-km hiking trail from the Navajo Nation), Rainbow Bridge protects an extraordinary natural bridge rising 290 feet (88 m) above the floor of Bridge Canyon. It is a premier example of eccentric stream erosion in a remote area of the Colorado Plateau. For many indigenous peoples in the Four Corners region, Rainbow Bridge is a spiritually occupied landscape that is inseparable from their cultural identities and traditional beliefs.

Timpanogos Cave National Monument
Fast Facts
Established: 1922/2002
Acreage: 250 (101 hectares)
Visitors (2019): 103,512
Nearest Major Airport: Salt Lake City Intl. (SLC), Salt Lake City, UT
Nearest Major Highways: I-15, UT-92
Fees: $0
Accessibility: The Visitor Center and Swinging Bridge Picnic Area are accessible. The strenuous trail to the caves is paved but likely too steep for wheelchairs.
Contact Information:
801-756-5239
www.nps.gov/tica

Three limestone caves are notable for their diverse and colorful formations, and abundant helictites—water-created formations that grow in all directions and shapes, regardless of gravity.

THE ROCKY MOUNTAINS

Yellowstone National Park

Yellowstone was the first National Park in the U.S. (and the world), but that's only the beginning of the superlatives needed to describe it. Despite being located more than 300 miles from a major city, it's consistently one of the 10 most-visited parks in the country. It's home to the largest concentration of mammal varieties in the lower 48 states (67 species) and more than 285 species of birds. More than half the world's **active geysers** (500 and counting) are within the park's boundaries, as are 1,800-plus archeological sites.

It's also ginormous. Only Death Valley and six Alaska parks have more acreage. The 44-mile (71-km) drive from **Yellowstone Falls** to Old Faithful takes close to an hour and a half, and that's not even taking into account the possibility that traffic comes to a complete stop because a herd of bison has taken over the road. A complete circuit of **Grand Loop Road**, which has many of the park's main attractions along its figure-8 shape, is a 140-mile (230-km) **driving tour** that can take more than seven hours (without stops).

Not that you'd do it without stopping, of course. Each of the park's eight developed areas is worthy of at least a few hours' visit. Do yourself a favor and plan to experience no more than one or two each day so you're not spending all of your time in the car.

Of all the national parks in the U.S., Yellowstone is the one with the greatest number of things to do. Active visitors can choose from 900 miles

Fast Facts

Established: 1872
Acreage: 2,219,791 (898,317 hectares)
Visitors (2019): 4,020,288
Visitor Centers: Albright, Canyon, Fishing Bridge, Grant, Madison Information Station and Trailside Museum, Museum of the National Park Ranger, Norris Geyser Basin Museum and Information Station, Old Faithful, West Thumb, West Yellowstone.
Nearest Major Airport: Bozeman Yellowstone Intl. (BZN), Belgrade, MT
Nearest Major Highways: I-15, I-90, US-14/16, US-20, US-89, US-191, US-212
Fees: $35/vehicle, $30/motorcycle, $20/pedestrian or cyclist. All entry fees are valid for seven days.
Accessibility: Varies extensively by location. Visit www.nps.gov/yell/planyourvisit/accessibility.htm for information about a range of accommodations in specific areas of the park.
Contact Information: 307-344-7381 www.nps.gov/yell (Mostly in Wyoming; also in Montana and Idaho)

(1,448 km) of **hiking trails** and 10 established **bike trails**. Dozens of lakes are open to **canoeing, kayaking,** and **fishing.** In winter, when snow completely blankets much of the park, opportunities arise for **cross-country skiing, snowshoeing,** and **snowmobiling.**

Then there is the thermal activity. The Yellowstone caldera is a technically a **supervolcano,** meaning it has had an eruption of magnitude 8 (the highest level) on the Volcanic Explosivity Index. (By comparison, Hawaii's

Bison and geysers are abundant throughout Yellowstone.

The Lower Falls pour through the Grand Canyon of the Yellowstone.

Kilauea is a 0 on that index; Mt. St. Helens is a 5.) More than two million years ago, the Huckleberry Ridge eruption at Yellowstone spewed 2,450 cubic km of volcanic matter into the air (enough to fill **Crater Lake** 130 times over). Scientists don't know when (or if) that kind of explosion will happen again, but they do know where visitors can reliably witness **geysers**, **mudpots**, **hot springs**, and **fumaroles**.

Old Faithful is the one everyone wants to see, a stop on 90% of all Yellowstone itineraries. Who doesn't like an eruption you can practically set your watch by? Thar she blows every 74 minutes on average. To escape the crowds (which peak at 800,000 people a month visit Yellowstone in July and August),

Old Faithful is as reliable as advertised, erupting every 74 minutes on average.

Grand Prismatic Spring may be Yellowstone's most-photographed feature.

wait for Old Faithful early or late in the day. Better yet, hike the half-mile (1 km) to **Observation Point**, where you'll share the stellar bird's-eye view of the pyrotechnics with just a handful of people.

Grand Prismatic Spring, in the **Midway Geyser Basin**, is the **largest hot spring** in the U.S., and probably the most photographed thermal feature of the park for its immense size (bigger than a football field) and the rainbow of colors that emanate out from its center. All four types of thermal fun are on display in the **Fountain Paint Pot** area north of Old Faithful. **Mudpots** don't erupt so much as simmer and bubble. The boardwalks let you walk over them without boiling your shoes. **Great Fountain Geyser**, on

Firehole Lake Drive, is the only geyser other than Old Faithful to merit eruption forecast times. **Fumaroles** are vents where the smoldering volcano below lets off steam. **Norris Geyser Basin** is the spot for a free, if pungent, facial. At **Mammoth Hot Springs**, near the park's north entrance, a vast array of fractures and fissures in the limestone allow hot water to surface, carrying dissolved carbon dioxide. When the water reaches air, calcium carbonate is deposited in the form of travertine terraces.

The Mammoth Hot Springs area is also a spectacular place to see **wildlife**, as is the Tower-Roosevelt area, which is 18 miles (29 km) east and provides a home to some of the largest herds of **bison and elk** in North America. On any given day in the **Lamar**

Valley, southeast of Tower-Roosevelt, you might see bison, **black bears, grizzlies, bighorn sheep**, elk, **mule deer**, and **pronghorns**. Their presence in turn attracts **coyotes, wolves**, and occasionally **bobcats** or **cougars**. **Moose**, on the other hand, are often spotted around the south entrance to the park and at **West Thumb**, the part of **Yellowstone Lake** closest to **Grant Village**.

Drive slowly through these and other areas where wildlife flourishes. A traffic jam on one of the park roads is usually a sign that an animal is within camera range. Park rangers will often visit the scene if a bear (or a giant herd of bison) get too close to the road. Visitors are reminded to stay 100 yards (91 m, or the length of a football field) away from bears and wolves, and

Elk love to visit Mammoth Hot Springs almost as much as people do.

coniferous forest, Yellowstone is practically an aviary. **Four owl species** have been sighted in the park. They are among the **19 breeding raptor species** found here, a list that includes **bald eagles, golden eagles, ospreys, and peregrine falcons. American kestrels** and **Swainson's hawks**, two other birds of concern to conservationists, are also found in Yellowstone. **Canada Geese** and **trumpeter swans** live here year-round.

 Hayden Valley between **Fishing Bridge** and **Canyon Village**, is one of the best places to spot water birds and raptors. Bald eagles and osprey hunt for fish along the Yellowstone River; northern harriers search the grass

25 yards (23 m) from all other wildlife.

 It's hard to find a part of Yellowstone that isn't frequented by birds. The majority of birds in the park are songbirds and woodpeckers, but with landscapes ranging from wetlands to

Wolves were re-introduced to the Yellowstone ecosystem in 1995.

for rodents. **Blacktail Ponds**, near the Montana border, and **Madison River**, near the west entrance, are also good birding spots. So too are the scores of hiking trails throughout the park. To download the Park Service's list of 20 favorite day hikes, visit the park website's "Plan Your Visit" page. **Trout Lake Trail,** in the northeast corner of the park, is an easy introduction to the park with multiple rewards. It's just 0.6 miles (1 km) each way through a Douglas fir forest to a lake jumping with trout, and there's a good chance of

spotting otters or osprey along the way. Orange paintbrush and purple larkspur dot the meadows along the **Cascade Lake Trail** (2.5 miles/4 km each way).

A typical hike to a mountain peak is an all-day affair, but not the trail to **Mt. Washburn**. The **Chittenden Road** trailhead is less than 3 miles (5 km) from the summit, with just 1,482 feet (452 meters) of elevation gain through whitebark pine forest into alpine tundra with stunted trees and blue lupines. A different route to the top from Dunraven Pass is 6.8 miles

(11 km) round-trip, passing through yellow glacier lilies in June and shocking pink Lewis's monkeyflowers in August.

Avalanche Peak isn't a very long trail, but it's one of the steeper hikes in the park, gaining 2,100 feet (640 meters) in just 2.1 miles (3.3 km). The summit presents views of the tallest and most remote peaks Yellowstone has to offer. **Seven-Mile Hole Trail** is actually closer to 10 miles (16 km) round-trip, but it's an upside-down hike, with almost all of its 2,043 feet (623 meters) of elevation gain on the way back.

Yellowstone cutthroat trout are a prized catch.

Don't Miss This . . .
Suggested Yellowstone Itineraries

Day One: Get a jump on the crowds at **Old Faithful** by visiting early in the morning. If you have time, take the short hike to **Observation Point** to see the water show among a smaller crowd. Spend the rest of the day driving up the west side of the park, stopping along the way to marvel at all the other types of thermal activity on display: **Fountain Paint Pots, Great Fountain Geyser, Firehole Lake Drive,** and **Norris Geyser Basin.** Have lunch in the **Mammoth Hot Springs** area, then wander around the intricate limestone formations or bike the mostly flat **Abandoned Railroad Bed Trail** (8 miles/13 km) or the more challenging **Bunsen Peak Loop Trail** (9 miles/14 km; 1,120 feet/335 m elevation loss and gain)

Day Two: Explore the **Tower-Roosevelt** section of the park, home to some of the largest herds of **bison and elk** in North America. Take a short hike on the **Trout Lake Trail** (1.2 miles/2 km round-trip) or a longer one on the **Garnet Hill Trail** (8 mile/12-km loop). Have lunch in the **Roosevelt Lodge Dining Room,** a rustic log cabin. In the afternoon, **ride on horseback** through the sagebrush flats of **Pleasant Valley,** into **Lost Canyon** and on to **Lost Lake.** Late afternoon rides can be combined with the **Old West Cookout,** a dinner cowboy-style, over an open campfire (there's even a covered wagon available for transportation for those who don't want to ride their own horse).

Day Three: Spend the entire day in the **Canyon Village** section of the park, home to the **Grand Canyon of the Yellowstone** and **Upper and Lower Yellowstone Falls.** Hike three miles (5 km) up to the top of **Mt. Washburn,** or all the way down to the bottom of the canyon along the challenging **Seven-Mile Hole** trail. **Canyon Village** has some of the most varied dining options in the park, including **Canyon Lodge Eatery, M66 Bar & Grill** (breakfast and dinner only), and **The Ice Creamery.**

Day Four: **Drop a line** in the **Yellowstone River, Yellowstone Lake,** or any of the dozens of other rivers, ponds, creeks, and streams in the **Fishing Bridge/Lake Village** section of the park. If you don't have your own gear, book a fishing expedition at **Bridge Bay Marina.** Boat trips range from two hours to all day, and typically include both guide and gear. If you catch any lake trout, many dining rooms in the park will cook it up for you. Landlubbers can take the scenic drive to **Lake Butte Overlook,** or travel US-20 all the way over the **Absaroka range** to the park's east entrance.

Fishing season in Yellowstone begins the Saturday of Memorial Day weekend and ends on the first Sunday in November. All anglers age 16 and over must purchase a park fishing permit ($40 for 3 days, $55 for a week, $75 for the season) from www.recreation.gov or numerous locations within the park. Regulations that support fish conservation goals vary in different areas of the park, so check the park's website or app before you drop a line in any of the park's rivers, streams, or lakes. **Yellowstone cutthroat trout** are the most commonly found native fish; nonnative species like brook, brown, lake, and rainbow trout compete with the cutthroats for food and habitat, and usually must be killed when caught.

If you didn't bring your own **boat,** you can rent everything from **canoes and kayaks** to 18-foot (5-m), 40-horsepower **motorboats** to cruise around Yellowstone Lake. **Swimming** isn't recommended, since most of Yellowstone's waters are either scalding hot springs or hypothermia-inducing mountain lakes and rivers.

The white backdrop of snow makes wildlife viewing easier in winter.

Grand Teton National Park

Grand Teton National Park is the counterpoint to Yellowstone, Donkey to Yellowstone's Shrek, Key to its Peele. And that contrast is, in many ways, key to its appeal. It's one-seventh the size of Yellowstone, as compact as Yellowstone is colossal and spread out. While Yellowstone is remote, Grand Teton is practically urban, with a commercial airport within its borders—a feature no other National Park has—and the cowboy/skiing/resort town of Jackson Hole on its doorstep.

None of this is to say that Grand Teton is any less spectacular than Yellowstone. In fact, it might be even more enchanting. The stunning craggy peaks of the Tetons have few foothills, so they rise steeply from the valley floor (or from the ultramarine Jackson Lake), surrounding visitors with one giant summit after another. And except for the lack of geysers and other thermal activity, the myriad of things to do in Grand Teton is just as endless.

Give Grand Teton a once-over by driving (or **cycling**, if you're up for it; biking is permitted on all paved roads in the park) the 42-mile (68-km) **Scenic Loop Drive**. Most people start at the Park Headquarters in Moose Junction, at the south end of the loop, and make a quick detour

Moulton Barn, in historic Mormon Row, may be the most-photographed barn in America.

The reflected view of the Tetons makes Oxbow Bend a popular stop for photography.

to the **Mormon Row Historic District**, which preserves the late-19th-century barns and homesteads of Mormon families who headed north from Salt Lake City and settled here. These days, especially at sunrise or sunset, you're likely to spot antelope in these meadows.

After returning to the loop road, you'll pass several turnouts, and unless you're in a hurry, there's no reason not to stop at each one. **Snake River Overlook**, positioned at about 4 o'clock on the circle, provides a vista made famous in 1942 by Ansel Adams. But the far better

backdrop for photography is at the Snake River's **Oxbow Bend** (at the top of the loop, just east of Jackson Lake). Photos taken here capture not only the Tetons piercing the mountain sky, but also their mirror image reflected in the water in the foreground.

Jackson Lake is a spectacular place to get out on the water in a canoe, kayak, boat, or paddleboard.

The Jenny Lake area has just about anything you could want in a national park.

At **Jackson Lake Dam,** the loop road circles back south, tracing the lakeshore for 6 glorious miles (10 km). Halfway through this segment, look for the turnoff to Signal Mountain Road, which brings you (where else?) to the top of **Signal Mountain** for an aerial view of the entire park. At around 10 o'clock on the loop, be sure to take another detour around the eastern shore of **Jenny Lake,** itself a 3-mile (5-km) scenic drive.

From the end of the one-way Jenny Lake loop, it's 8 miles (13 km) back to beginning of the Loop Drive, not counting a short detour to the **Menors Ferry Historic District,** where Bill Menor's late-19th-century **cabin and country store** still stand, along with a replica of the boat he used to ferry hunters, foragers, and lumberjacks to the wilderness across the Snake River. The delightful, dedicated **Multi-Use**

Pathway (open to **biking, skating, and walking**) parallels this section of the road all the way back to Moose Junction. And about halfway between Jenny Lake and Moose, the easy 3-mile (5-km) round-trip **Taggart Lake Trail** is a mostly flat walk to a small lake with some of the best views of the Tetons. Extend this hike to 4 miles (7 km) by adding a detour to **Beaver Creek,** or make it 5 miles (8 km) by tacking on the adjacent **Bradley Lake** before turning back.

But nobody would blame you if you cut short the drive and spent the rest of the day (or even several days) at Jenny Lake. Here is all of the Tetons in a nutshell, a jumping off point for nearly every activity you can pursue in a national park, including the possibility of seeing **moose, deer,** and **black and grizzly bears.** Accommodations options range from 51 no-frills campsites at **Jenny Lake Campground** ($36/

night; no electricity, no RVs) to the obscenely expensive **Jenny Lake Lodge and Cabins,** home to an equally pricy full-service restaurant.

Some of the park's most popular hiking trails leave from the Jenny Lake Visitor Center. The shortest is the paved, wheelchair-accessible, ⅓-mile (½-km) **Discovery Trail;** the longest, **Hurricane Pass,** is a 26-mile (42-km) round-trip trek with 4,000 feet (1,219 m) of elevation gain, and views of **Schoolroom Glacier** and **Grand, Middle, and South Teton.** Somewhere in between are the popular 5-mile (8-km) round-trip walk to **Hidden Falls,** or the slightly longer (6 miles/10 km) trip to **Inspiration Point,** for standout views of **Cascade Canyon, Teewinot,** and **Grand Teton.** Either of these hikes can be shortened by taking the **shuttle boat** back across the lake to the visitor center. The adventurous can complete the loop around Jenny Lake for a 7.6-mile (12-km) outing.

Rent **canoes or kayaks** between June and September from **Jenny Lake Boating,** the same company that operates the shuttle service as well as hour-long scenic cruises of the lake with a naturalist guide on board. To paddle the much larger **Jackson Lake,** rent boards or boats at **Colter Bay Village** or **Signal Mountain Lodge.** Several local outfitters arrange **rafting trips** or **guided fishing expeditions** down the **Snake River.** Visit the park website or app for a list of authorized concessionaires.

Wildlife being wild, opportunities to see animals can pop up almost anywhere in the park. Maximize your chances

The town of Moose is just one of many places to see moose in the Tetons.

at **Oxbow Bend (river otters, beavers, moose, bald eagles, and great blue herons)**; **Timbered Island**, southeast of Jenny Lake **(pronghorn antelope and elk)**; and **Mormon Row (bison, pronghorn, and coyotes)**. Another safe bet is just about anywhere along the **Snake River**, whose meadows are a dining room for **elk and bison**, whose

trout stocks are a feast for **bald eagles and ospreys**, and whose willows attract **beavers and moose**. The unpaved **Moose-Wilson road** is another good place to **spot moose**, and a pleasant scenic route back to the town of Jackson at day's end. Go slow to avoid the many potholes.

In addition to pikas, yellow-bellied marmots, and mule deer,

Cascade Canyon is home to multiple species of migratory songbirds, including **western tanagers, ruby-crowned kinglets**, and **yellow-rumped warblers**. A hike from **Christian Pond** to **Grand View Point** (6 miles/10 km round-trip, with 956 feet/291 meters of elevation gain) not only delivers spectacular views of both mountains and lakes; it carries the possibility of seeing and/or hearing **red-naped sapsuckers, red-breasted nuthatches**, and **dark-eyed juncos** in the old-growth Douglas fir forest, and waterfowl like **ruddy and ring-necked ducks** and **American coots** in the lakes and ponds. After nearly becoming extinct in the early 1900s, the **Trumpeter swan**, North America's largest waterfowl species, is making a comeback. Look for them in ponds and rivers throughout the park. **Great Gray Owls,** the tallest owls in North America, hunt during the daytime in lodgepole forests.

Great Gray Owls are one of the few species that hunt during the day.

Rocky Mountain National Park

If you were asked to design the quintessential Rocky Mountain landscape, you'd have a hard time crafting anything better than Rocky Mountain National Park. Home to 77 mountain peaks at 12,000 feet (3,658 meters) or higher, the park straddles both sides of the **Continental Divide**, with a breathtaking road over the top linking the two sections. The Colorado River starts here, providing fresh water to 40 million people in seven states along its 1,450-mile (2,333-km) journey to the Gulf of California.

Snow caps the park's summits year-round, and as the temperature rises, it trickles down the slopes to feed countless rivers, lakes, and streams. Coniferous forests give way to mountain meadows; deciduous trees support biologically diverse habitats. More than **28 species of birds** make their homes here, as do **141 species of butterflies**, and **60 different types of mammals**, not including humans, more than four million of whom visit annually.

Trail Ridge Road delivers an excellent overview of the park, with an emphasis on "over." It connects the two sides of the park, cresting at 12,183 feet (3,713 meters) in the middle, and crossing the Continental Divide on its way back down. The Dept. of Transportation has designated it an **All-American Road** in 1996, meaning it is in the pantheon of the nation's most scenic drives.

Over its 48 miles (77 km), Trail Ridge Road travels through three completely different ecosystems. From the gateway town of Estes Park, the road ascends quickly through

Fast Facts

Established: 1915
Acreage: 265,795 (107,563 hectares)
Visitors (2019): 4,670,053
Visitor Centers: Alpine, Beaver Meadows, Fall River, Kawuneeche, Moraine Park Discovery Center (summer and fall only), Sheep Lakes Information Station
Nearest Major Airport: Denver Intl. (DEN), Denver, CO
Nearest Major Highways: I-25, US-34, US-36
Fees: $25/vehicle or motorcycle, $15/cyclist or pedestrian. Advance timed reservations are required to enter the park from Memorial Day weekend through mid-October. Visit www.nps.gov/romo/planyourvisit/timed-entry-permit-system.htm for details on how and where to request a permit.
Accessibility: Varies by location. Visit www.nps.gov/romo/planyourvisit/upload/Access-Rocky-2014.pdf to download Access Rocky, a comprehensive 12-page guide to all of the accessible areas of the park.
Contact Information: 970-586-1206 www.nps.gov/romo

Western Tiger Swallowtails are one of 141 species of butterflies in the park.

montane forests of aspen and ponderosa pine into **subalpine forests** of fir and spruce, before climbing above treeline. For the next 11 miles (17 km), the road traverses **alpine tundra**, with sweeping vistas, a short but brilliant season for wildflowers, and a surprising amount of fauna. **Pikas**, **marmots**, **ptarmigans**, and **bighorn sheep** are common trail companions; **elk** can show up at any time. The road through the tundra is

Elk are show-stoppers everywhere in Rocky Mountain National Park.

open only from Memorial Day to mid-October.

Just north of Trail Ridge Road is **Old Fall River Road**, which opened in 1920 as the first automobile route to cross through the park's high country. Everything about this drive is a bit more extreme: the road is narrower and mostly gravel, the grade is steeper, the switchbacks are tighter, and there are no guardrails anywhere. It's open even fewer days of the year (July 4 until September), and it's one-way (east-to-west) only. Old Fall River Road ends at **Alpine Visitor Center**, the highest visitor center in the National Park System. From there, you can double back on Trail Ridge Road, or continue across the Continental Divide into the less-visited western end of the park.

Marmot fight!

The Bear Lake corridor features dozens of trails to alpine lakes.

Keep an eye out for **moose** in the **Kawuneeche Valley**, which is bisected by the highest reaches of the Colorado River.

Hiking in Rocky Mountain National Park usually involves a water destination. Among the 355 miles (571 km) of hiking trails are more than 20 trails that lead to a lake, a dozen or more that reach waterfalls, and countless others that trace or cross rivers, creeks, or streams. Many of the most popular trails are nestled along the **Bear Lake Corridor**. If you take the **free shuttle bus**, you won't have to jockey for a spot at the trailhead parking lots, which are usually even more crowded than those at Trader Joe's.

Bear Lake itself is just 0.3 miles (0.5 km) from the parking lot, and the trail there is wheelchair-accessible all the way. It's just an *amuse bouche* to more than 30 other trails that depart from the same trailhead. **Dream Lake** (2.2 miles/4 km round-trip), is a charming walk through aspen groves and ponderosa pines. Keep walking around the north shore of Dream Lake for 1 more mile (1.6 km) to get to **Emerald Lake**, whose waters are actually more a shimmering shade of pale blue. Or trace Dream Lake's south shore and continue on to the boulder-strewn **Lake Haiyaha** (7 miles/11 km round-trip with 980 feet/299 meters of elevation gain).

Prefer waterfalls? Take the **Glacier Gorge Trail**. You'll come to **Alberta Falls** after 0.6 miles (1 km), **Glacier Falls** at the 2.2 mile (4 km) mark, and **Timberline Falls** 4 miles (6 km)

in, right below **Lake of Glass**. The trail ends half a mile (1 km) past the falls at **Sky Pond**. Many of these trails can be mixed and matched with routes to **The Loch, Mills Lake,** and **Black Lake**.

In September, the changing colors of the **quaking aspen trees** draw crowds. During the summer months, **afternoon thunderstorms** may arrive out of nowhere, often bearing the very real threat of lightning strikes (which are the cause of many a forest fire here). Hike in the morning if possible, and carry rain gear no matter what the weather looks like. Return to your car at the first sign of a storm. Failing that, shed all metal items, get as low to the ground as possible, and keep your head down.

Serious mountaineers, including a large contingent of

The changing colors of the quaking aspens are a big draw in September.

Nepali immigrants, visit Rocky Mountain Park to prepare for ascents of the world's tallest mountains. Locals sometimes joke that people climb Everest as a practice run for summiting **Longs Peak, the only 14,000-foot summit** (14,259 feet/4,346 m to be exact) in the park. Most times of year, this is a technical climb requiring equipment to navigate ice and snow. But when the snow melts (usually by late July, but sometimes not until mid-August), it's possible to make it to the summit in well-broken-in hiking boots, and about 10,000 people reach the summit every year. This walk in the park is no walk in the park, however. Even in the best weather, Longs Peak involves some Class 3 scrambling skill (climbing over rocks and boulders).

Afternoon thundershowers can result in stunning aftereffects in Rocky Mountain National Park.

Pikas look like a cross between a gerbil and a rabbit.

Wildlife is abundant throughout Rocky Mountain, on trails, on the sides of roads, sometimes even napping in the parking lots. Look for **elk** in places where meadows meet forest. **Sheep Lakes** is well-named; bighorn sheep frequent the area from May to mid-August. **Marmots** and **pikas** (gerbil-sized mammals that look a bit like tiny rabbits) favor rockpiles; you'll likely hear their sharp bark before you see them. From Trail Ridge Road, you can spot **Clark's nutcrackers, Steller's jays, golden eagles,** and **prairie falcons. American dippers** (a.k.a. water ouzels) are found along most streams.

More than 250 miles (402 km) of trails are open to horseback riding. Two stables within the park usually open around Memorial Day, inviting visitors to saddle up and ride around the ponderosa: **Glacier Creek Stables**: 970-586-3244; and **Moraine Park Stables**: 970-586-2327. There are also many other stables outside the park that have permission to bring riders onto the trails.

There are no lodgings within the park other than five campgrounds, with a total of 570 sites. Three (**Aspenglen, Glacier Basin,** and **Moraine Park**) can—and almost certainly must—be reserved in advance. **Longs Peak** and **Timber Creek Campgrounds** are first-come, first-served. Hotels and other accommodations are plentiful in **Estes Park** on the eastern side of the park, and in **Grand Lake** on the western side.

Sadly, Rocky Mountain is in danger of being loved to death. Crowds at popular hiking trails and picnic-worthy lakes threaten to overwhelm the park's resources. Traffic on Trail Ridge Road can come to a standstill on July weekends. To address the situation, the Park Service instituted a pilot timed-entry permit reservation system in 2021, limiting automobiles to no more than 85 percent of the total parking capacity. Tickets are released a month in advance (June 1 for dates in July, July 1 for dates in August, and so on). Two types of reservations are available, one that includes access to the popular **Bear Lake Road Corridor** (where most of the best hikes are), and one that doesn't.

The park's staff and volunteers also launched the **Rocky Pledge,** a public awareness campaign to enlist visitors in the park's preservation. Visitors who take the pledge vow "to preserve unimpaired for this and future generations the beauty, history, and wildness therein." That means never building fires outside campground or picnic area fire grates, driving only on paved roads and gravel parking areas, maintaining a safe distance from animals (and never feeding them), and taking nothing but photos and leaving nothing but footprints. Visitors are also encouraged to snap selfies while taking the pledge or doing things to protect the park, and then share them on social media with the hashtag **#rockypledge.**

Glacier National Park

Like its name suggests, Glacier National Park is home to an abundance of **glaciers**, more than 20 in all. Ironically, though, it's not necessarily the best place to see a glacier up close and in person, especially as climate change keeps causing them to melt. Most of the glaciers within the park require a hike, sometimes a strenuous one, and even then, some might be hard to distinguish from a snowfield. Two exceptions are the **Jackson Glacier**, visible from the helpfully named **Jackson Glacier Overlook**, and **Salamander Glacier**, which does in fact look like a salamander from the **Many Glacier park entrance** after the snow melts. Viewing **Sperry Glacier**, meanwhile, requires only a 1.3-mile (2-km) walk from the **Hidden Lake Overlook**, mostly on a boardwalk with stairs.

But while glaciers may be hard for the average visitor to see, viewing the **spectacular landscape** features they have left behind is easier than a Monday Sudoku. Very few roads intrude upon the pristine wilderness, and the ones that do are breathtaking. Primary among them is the **Going-to-the-Sun Road**, 50 miles (80 km) of two-lane blacktop wending its way through the park, from the West entrance near Whitefish, MT, to the St. Mary entrance on the Blackfeet Indian Reservation, which abuts the park's eastern edge. Because the road is itself a **national landmark**, you could be forgiven for doing nothing more than driving its length, so gorgeous is the mountain scenery of Glacier's five different ecosystems. Almost

Fast Facts

Established: 1910
Acreage: 1,013,324 (410,078 hectares)
Visitors (2019): 3,049,839
Visitor Centers: Apgar, St. Mary, Logan Pass
Nearest Major Airport: Missoula Intl. (MSO), Missoula, MT
Nearest Major Highways: I-15, US-2, US-89
Fees: $35/vehicle, $30/ motorcycle, $20/pedestrian or cyclist. All entry fees are valid for seven days. Additionally, a reservation ticket ($2, valid for seven days) is required from Memorial Day to Labor Day to visit the Going-to-the-Sun road corridor between the St. Mary and West entrances.
Accessibility: Varies by location. Improvements are being made every year, but the rugged nature of the park makes many sites challenging for visitors with disabilities. Visit www.nps. gov/glac/planyourvisit/ accessibility.htm for comprehensive information about access.
Contact Information: 406-888-7800 www.nps.gov/glac

all of Glacier's attractions are accessible from points along this main east-west road.

Going-to-the-Sun Road is only open for a short window, usually between late June and early October. The rest of the year, it's buried under several feet of snow, making it one of America's longest and most beautiful **cross-country ski trails**. (A variety of outfitters rent skis and snowshoes in the nearby town of Whitefish.) Summer is also when the great majority of people visit Glacier, so expect traffic. Indeed, between Memorial Day and Labor Day,

View from the East Tunnel, Going-to-the-Sun Road

125

In winter, Going-to-the-Sun Road becomes a very long cross-country ski/snowshoe trail.

all visitors must reserve a ticket ($2 at recreation.gov) to travel the park's main thoroughfare. The road is narrow and winding, with **no gas stations**, so fill up before entering the park. Vehicles longer than 21 feet (6.4 meters), higher than 10 feet (3 meters), or wider than 8 feet (2.4 meters) are not permitted; **bicycles** are not allowed between Apgar and Sprague Creek.

A **self-guided audio tour** of the road is available from the iTunes store. Android users can download it from the Glacier National Park website, which also features a series of short videos showing off the highlights at 15 different stops along the road. **Apgar Village** is where most people start their drive; **St. Mary Valley** is where they usually finish, often with a 1.6-mile (2.6-km) round-trip hike to **St. Mary's Falls**. A dozen or more other hikes in this valley range in length from the 3.2-mile (5.2-km) descent to **Virginia Falls**, to the 17-mile (27 km) climb to **Piegan**

Pass (with 2,650 feet/805 meters of elevation gain). The 6.6-mile (10-km) loop around **Beaver Pond** is a lovely half-day outing.

The **Lake McDonald** shuttle bus stop is the jumping off point for **boat tours** of the lake, **horseback riding trips**, and the historic **Lake McDonald Lodge** (a.k.a. Lewis Glacier Hotel). One of the few remaining Swiss

chalet-style hotels in the U.S., it's also a **National Historic Landmark**. Among the half-dozen hiking trails that leave from the lodge are the **Sperry Trail**, a 6.7-mile (11-km) climb to **Sperry Chalet**, one of two hike-in-only lodgings in the park. The other, **Granite Park Chalet**, is a bit easier to reach, via the 4-mile (6-km) **Loop**

Lake McDonald

The Many Glacier Hotel overlooks Swiftcurrent Lake.

The interior of the historic Many Glacier Hotel is almost as impressive as the location.

Trail ascent from **Logan Pass**. Accommodations in both chalets are primitive and rustic (no heat, no electricity, no running water) but include three meals daily; lunches are usually brown bagged so guests can take them with them on their outings.

For those who don't want to trek to their accommodations, Glacier is home to 13 different campgrounds with more than 1,000 tent sites. **Fish Creek**, overlooking Lake McDonald, is one of the most popular, and requires advance reservations. **Apgar** opens earliest (usually in late April) and closes latest (usually the first week in October). The season is shorter at most other campgrounds (approximately June 1 throught the second week of September).

The largest hotel in the park is the **Many Glacier Hotel**, another historic chalet-style lodge, built by the Great Northern Railway in 1914-15. Perched above **Swiftcurrent Lake**, the hotel can only be reached from the **Many Glacier** entrance on the east side of the park, 13 miles north of the St. Mary entrance. The first hotel built by the railway is **Glacier Park Lodge**, which still stands just outside the park in East Glacier Village, across the street from the railroad station that brought some of the earliest visitors to the park. Amtrak continues to offer service to this station along the **Great Northern Route** from Chicago to Seattle.

West Tunnel, The Loop, Triple Arch, and **East Tunnel** are four of the most visible feats of engineering that went into building Going-to-the-Sun Road. You don't need to be a transportation geek to appreciate the herculean labors of those who built this extraordinary road (some sections without any power tools). All you have to do is revel in the views of the surrounding valleys previously enjoyed only by birds and mountain goats. For the best views of **mountain goats**, watch the road near **Oberlin Bend**.

Logan Pass is the highest point of the drive (6,646 feet/2,025 meters), and often the high point of most visitors' trips to Glacier. The parking lot is usually full by 8:30 a.m., so taking the **shuttle bus** ($1) is always a good idea. Visit the Glacier National Park website to reserve your seats. From the back of the visitor center, an easy 1.5-mile (2.5-km) walk each

Watch for mountain goats throughout the park.

It's an easy walk to Hidden Lake from the Logan Pass Visitor Center.

way along a boardwalk leads to **Hidden Lake Overlook**, with tremendous views of **Mt. Reynolds**, **Clements Mountain**, and of course **Hidden Lake**. Logan Pass is also the spot for views of the **Garden Wall**, a massive sheer cliff face that marks the **Continental Divide**. The extremely popular **Highline Trail** allows visitors to walk along a ledge of the Garden Wall; hold the metal handrails bolted to the wall if you have a fear of heights. Keep an eye out for deer, marmots, and bighorn sheep. The trail doesn't become steep until about the 2-mile (3-km) mark.

The only north-south artery at Glacier is the **Continental Divide Trail**, a hiking path that extends for 110 miles (177 km) from its northern terminus at the delightfully named **Goat Haunt** to **Marias Pass** in the southeast corner of the park. About 36 miles (59 km) north of Marias Pass, the trail crests **Triple Divide Peak**, a rare hydrological apex where water may travel in any of three directions. To the northeast, the St. Mary River carries snowmelt all the way east to Canada's Hudson Bay. Points southeast of the Triple Divide flow ultimately to the Gulf of Mexico, while areas west of here eventually empty into the Columbia River on their way to the Pacific Ocean.

Glacier's northern limits abut **Canada's Waterton Lakes National Park**, designated by Canada in 1895. In 1932, the U.S. and Canada jointly designated the two parks, creating the world's first International Peace Park. Often referred to as "The Crown of the Continent," **Waterton-Glacier International Peace Park** commemorates the peace and goodwill between the two countries, and officially acknowledges that the parks' ecosystems do not stop at national borders. **Bears, moose, wolves**, and other wildlife routinely cross between countries at will, but the usual rules for humans still apply.

Visitors who wish to see both sides of the park must pay separate admission fees and clear immigration and customs at the international border (a passport or passport card is required). The only road between the two parks is the **Chief Mountain International Highway**, which clips the northeast corner of Glacier; the only hiking routes are the **Waterton Lake Trail** (which becomes the **Great Divide Trail** in Canada) and the **Mt. Richards Alternate Route**. The international checkpoint for either trail is at Goat Haunt Overlook on **Waterton Lake**.

The Iceberg Lake Trail delivers striking views of the Garden Wall's sheer cliff face.

MORE TO SEE IN THE ROCKY MOUNTAINS

COLORADO
Bent's Old Fort National Historic Site
Fast Facts

Established: 1960
Acreage: 799 (323 hectares)
Visitors (2019): 21,674
Nearest Major Airport: Denver Intl. (DEN), Denver, CO
Nearest Major Highways: US-50
Fees: The park charges a living history fee of $3/adult, $2/child aged 6–12 ($5/person during major events).
Accessibility: The second floor of the fort is inaccessible. A hand-held video player with a virtual tour is available.

Contact Information:
719-383-5010
www.nps.gov/beol

The fort, now completely reconstructed on its original footprint, was an important fur trading post on the Santa Fe Trail between 1833 and 1849, where trappers, traders, travelers, and the Cheyenne and Arapaho tribes exchanged furs for trade goods.

Black Canyon of the Gunnison National Park
Fast Facts
Established: 1933/1999

The Painted Wall at Black Canyon of the Gunnison National Park is Colorado's highest cliff.

Acreage: 30,750 (12,444 hectares)
Visitors (2019): 432,818
Nearest Major Airport: Denver Intl. (DEN), Denver, CO
Nearest Major Highways: US-50
Fees: $30/vehicle, $25/motorcycle, $15/cyclist or pedestrian. All entry fees valid for seven days.
Accessibility: The South Rim Visitor Center and Campground, as well as the Balanced Rock, Chasm View, Sunset View, and Tomichi Point Overlook are accessible to visitors with mobility impairments.
Contact Information:
970-641-2337
www.nps.gov/blca

Over the past two million years, the Gunnison River has sculpted this vertical wilderness of rock, water, and sky. The Painted Wall, a sheer drop of 2,250 feet, is the highest cliff in Colorado.

Colorado National Monument
Fast Facts
Established: 1911
Acreage: 20,536 (8,311 hectares)
Visitors (2019): 397,032
Nearest Major Airport: Denver Intl. (DEN), Denver, CO
Nearest Major Highways: I-70, US-50
Fees: $25/vehicle, $20/motorcycle, $15/cyclist or pedestrian. All entry fees valid for seven days.
Accessibility: Visit www.nps.gov/colm/planyourvisit/upload/SITEBULLETIN_Accessibility_2014.pdf for a brochure and map of accessible facilities.
Contact Information:
970-858-2800
www.nps.gov/colm

Sheer-walled canyons, towering monoliths, soaring arches, unusual formations, dinosaur fossils, and remains of prehistoric cultures reflect the environment and history of this colorful sandstone country.

Curecanti National Recreation Area
Fast Facts
Established: 1965
Acreage: 43,095 (17,440 hectares)

Visitors (2019): 836,034
Nearest Major Airport: Denver Intl. (DEN), Denver, CO
Nearest Major Highways: US-50
Fees: $0
Accessibility: The visitor center is accessible, as are several overlooks and the Cimarron, Elk Creek, Lake Fork, and Stevens Creek Campground.
Contact Information:
970-641-2337
www.nps.gov/cure

The three reservoirs along the once-wild Gunnison River that make up Curecanti National Recreation Area are a destination for water-based recreation high in the Rocky Mountains. Best known for salmon and trout fishing, Curecanti also offers opportunities for hiking, boating, camping, and bird watching.

Dinosaur National Monument
Fast Facts
Established: 1915
Acreage: 210,282 (85,098 hectares)
Visitors (2019): 298,965
Visitor Centers: Canyon, Quarry
Nearest Major Airport: Denver Intl. (DEN), Denver, CO
Nearest Major Highways: US-40, CO-318.
Fees: $25/vehicle, $20/motorcycle, $15/cyclist or pedestrian.
Accessibility: Varies by location. Visit www.nps.gov/dino/planyourvisit/accessibility.htm for location-specific information.

Dinosaur National Monument is a true Jurassic park.

Contact Information:
435-781-7700
www.nps.gov/dino
(Also in Utah)

Dinosaurs really did once roam here. The monument provides a remarkable window into the Late Jurassic world, while displaying the most complete geological record of any national park unit. The exceptionally diverse communities of plants and animals and thousands of years of human history in the monument result from its geographic locations at the hub of five major biophysical regions, including the lower 46 miles of the Yampa River, which is the last remaining large, free-flowing river in the entire Colorado River system.

Great Sand Dunes National Park is home to the tallest dunes in North America.

Florissant Fossil Beds National Monument
Fast Facts
Established: 1969
Acreage: 5,998 (2,427 hectares)
Visitors (2019): 77,340
Nearest Major Airport: Denver Intl. (DEN), Denver, CO
Nearest Major Highways: I-25, US-24, CO-42
Fees: $10/adult aged 16 and older.
Accessibility: Most of the monument is accessible, except when covered in snow.
Contact Information:
719-748-3253
www.nps.gov/flfo

Beneath a grassy mountain valley in central Colorado lies one of the richest and most diverse fossil deposits in the world. Petrified redwood stumps up to 14 feet (4 meters) wide and thousands of detailed fossils of insects and plants reveal the story of a very different, prehistoric Colorado of 34 million years ago.

Great Sand Dunes National Park and Preserve
Fast Facts
Established: 1932/2000
Acreage: National Park, 107,302 (43,424 hectares); National Preserve 41,686 (16,870 hectares)
Visitors (2019): 527,546

Nearest Major Airport: Denver Intl. (DEN), Denver, CO
Nearest Major Highways: US-160, CO-150, CO-159
Fees: $25/vehicle, $20/motorcycle, $15/cyclist or pedestrian. Valid for seven days.
Accessibility: A limited number of sand wheelchairs are available for loan at the visitor center.
Contact Information:
719-378-6395
www.nps.gov/grsa

The tallest dunes in North America developed as southwesterly winds blew ancient alluvial sediments from the San Luis Valley toward the Sangre de Cristo Mountains. The preserve, containing the entire surface watershed and primary topographic features interacting with the Great Sand Dunes, ranges in elevation from 8,000 to over 13,000 feet (2,438 to 3,962 meters) and includes life zones from desert to alpine tundra.

Hovenweep National Monument
Fast Facts
Established: 1923
Acreage: 785 (318 hectares)
Visitors (2019): 35,399
Nearest Major Airport: Denver Intl. (DEN), Denver, CO
Nearest Major Highways: US-160, US-491
Fees: $0

Hovenweep National Monument preserves ancestral Puebloan buildings.

Mesa Verde National Park is home to the best-preserved cliff dwellings in the U.S.

Accessibility: The visitor center, restrooms, and the Square Tower Group Trail to the first overlook are all accessible.

Contact Information:
970-562-4282
www.nps.gov/hove
(Also in Utah)

Once home to more than 2,500 people, Hovenweep includes six prehistoric villages built between 1200 and 1300 A.D. It preserves ancestral Puebloan towers, pueblos, and cliff dwellings spread over 26 miles (42 km) on the Utah-Colorado border. It was designated an International Dark Sky Park in 2014 for its exceptional stargazing opportunities.

Mesa Verde National Park
Fast Facts
Established: 1906
Acreage: 52,485 (21,240 hectares)
Visitors (2019): 556,203
Nearest Major Airport: Denver Intl. (DEN), Denver, CO
Nearest Major Highways: US-160
Fees: $30/vehicle May 1–Ocober 31, $20 the rest of the year; $25/motorcycle ($15 in winter), $15/cyclist or pedestrian ($10 in winter).
Accessibility: Largely inaccessible because of rugged terrain, steep cliffs, deep canyons, narrow trails, and high altitude.
Contact Information:
970-529-4465
www.nps.gov/meve

These world-famous cliff dwellings and other works of the Ancestral Pueblo people are some of the most notable and best preserved in the United States. The park protects the rich cultural heritage of 26 tribes and offers a spectacular window into the past. Designated a World Heritage Site Sept. 6, 1978.

Sand Creek Massacre National Historic Site
Fast Facts
Established: 2007
Acreage: 12,583 (5,092 hectares)
Visitors (2019): 5,701
Nearest Major Airport: Denver Intl. (DEN), Denver, CO
Nearest Major Highways: US-287, US-385, CO-96
Fees: $0
Accessibility: Varies by location. Visit www.nps.gov/sand/planyourvisit/accessibility.htm for location-specific information.
Contact Information:
719-438-5916
www.nps.gov/sand

On November 29, 1864, U.S. soldiers attacked a Cheyenne and Arapaho encampment along Sand Creek, killing more than 200 people, most of them women, children, or the elderly. The Sand Creek Massacre profoundly influenced U.S. relations with Native Americans and changed Cheyenne and Arapaho history, society, and culture. The site preserves the cultural and natural landscape and enhances public understanding of the tragedy.

Yucca House National Monument
Fast Facts
Established: 1919
Acreage: 34 (14 hectares)
Visitors (2019): NA
Nearest Major Airport: Denver Intl. (DEN), Denver, CO
Nearest Major Highways: US-160
Fees: $0
Accessibility: There are no federal facilities of any kind at the monument.
Contact Information:
970-529-4465
www.nps.gov/yuho

Preserves one of the largest archeological sites in southwest Colorado, largely untouched for the past 800 years. The unexcavated nature of the site preserves its integrity and beauty for future generations of scientists and visitors.

MONTANA
Big Hole National Battlefield
Fast Facts
Established: 1883/1910/1963
Acreage: 1,011 (409 hectares)
Visitors (2019): 45,861
Nearest Major Airport: Missoula Intl. (MSO), Missoula, MT
Nearest Major Highways: I-15, US-93, MT-43
Fees: $0
Accessibility: Largely accessible.
Contact Information:
406-689-3155
www.nps.gov/biho

Pays tribute to the battle between the Nez Perce Indians and the 7th U.S. Infantry forces with civilian volunteers on August 9–10, 1877. Ninety Nez Perce men, women, and children and 31 soldiers lost their lives. Added legislatively as a unit of Nez Perce National Historical Park in 1992.

Devil's Canyon overlooks Bighorn Canyon National Recreation Area.

Bighorn Canyon National Recreation Area
Fast Facts
Established: 1966
Acreage: 120,296 (48,682 hectares)
Visitors (2019): 249,659
Visitor Centers: Cal S. Taggart (Lovell, WY), Yellowtail Dam
Nearest Major Airport: Billings Logan Intl. (BIL), Billings, MT
Nearest Major Highways: MT-313
Fees: $0
Accessibility: The visitor centers and contact stations are accessible with some assistance. The park map is available in braille; audio descriptions of a dozen wayside areas are available.
Contact Information:
406-666-2412
www.nps.gov/bica
(Also in Wyoming)

This vast, wild landscape contains an astounding diversity of ecosystems, wildlife, and more than 10,000 years of human history. About one third of the area is within the Crow Indian Reservation.

Fort Union Trading Post National Historic Site
Fast Facts
Established: 1966
Acreage: 440 (178 hectares)
Visitors (2019): 12,967

Nearest Major Airport: Billings Logan Intl. (BIL), Billings, MT
Nearest Major Highways: I-94, US-2, MT-327
Fees: $0
Accessibility: In the pursuit of historical accuracy, many areas are inaccessible to wheelchairs. Visit www.nps.gov/fous/planyourvisit/physical-mobility.htm for location-specific information
Contact Information:
701-572-9083
www.nps.gov/fous
(Also in North Dakota)

The principal fur-trading post of the American Fur Company on the Upper Missouri River, Fort Union served the Assiniboine, Crow, Cree, Ojibway, and Blackfeet tribes. Between 1828 and 1867, more than 25,000 buffalo robes and $100,000 worth of cloth, guns, blankets, and beads were exchanged annually.

Grant-Kohrs Ranch National Historic Site
Fast Facts
Established: 1972
Acreage: 1,618 (655 hectares)
Visitors (2019): 25,043
Nearest Major Airport: Missoula Intl. (MSO), Missoula, MT
Nearest Major Highways: I-90, US-12
Fees: $0
Contact Information:
406-846-2070
www.nps.gov/grko

Once the headquarters of a 10-million-acre cattle empire, this site preserves the cowboy and other symbols of the American west and commemorates the role of cattlemen in American history.

Little Bighorn Battlefield National Monument
Fast Facts
Established: 1879/1946
Acreage: 765 (310 hectares)
Visitors (2019): 241,304
Nearest Major Airport: Billings Logan Intl. (BIL), Billings, MT
Nearest Major Highways: I-90, US-212

Colleen Cutschall's Spirit Warrior *sculpture memorializes the Battle of Little Big Horn.*

Fees: $25/vehicle, $20/motorcycle, $15/cyclist or pedestrian.
Contact Information:
406-638-3216
www.nps.gov/libi

Memorializes one of the last armed efforts of the Northern Plains people to preserve their way of life. On June 25-26, 1876, Lt. Col. George A. Custer and 262 other soldiers and attached personnel of the U.S. Army died fighting several thousand Lakota and Cheyenne warriors.

WYOMING
Devils Tower National Monument
Fast Facts
Established: 1906
Acreage: 1,347 (545 hectares)
Visitors (2019): 450,785
Nearest Major Airport: Rapid City Regional Airport (RAP), Rapid City, SD
Nearest Major Highways: I-90, US-24, WY-24.
Fees: $25/vehicle, $20/motorcycle, $15/cyclist or pedestrian. Entrance fees valid for seven days.
Accessibility: Largely accessible.
Contact Information:
307-467-5283
www.nps.gov/deto

The nation's first national monument is a high, isolated monolith of igneous rock, set upon a

Devils Tower was America's first National Monument.

pine-clad pedestal within a bend of the Belle Fourche River. It is considered sacred by Northern Plains people. Hundreds of parallel cracks make it one of the finest crack-climbing destinations in North America.

Fort Laramie National Historic Site
Fast Facts
Established: 1938/1960
Acreage: 867 (351 hectares)
Visitors (2019): 42,892
Nearest Major Airport: Denver Intl. (DEN), Denver, CO
Nearest Major Highways: I-25, US-26, WY-160
Fees: $0
Contact Information:
    307-837-2221
    www.nps.gov/fola

Originally established as a private fur trading fort in 1834, Fort Laramie evolved into the largest and best known military post on the Northern Plains before its abandonment in 1890. This "grand old post" witnessed the entire sweeping saga of America's western expansion and Native American resistance to encroachment on their territories.

Fossil Butte National Monument
Fast Facts
Established: 1972
Acreage: 8,198 (3,318 hectares)
Visitors (2019): 20,554
Nearest Major Airport: Salt Lake City, Intl. (SLC), Salt Lake City, UT
Nearest Major Highways: I-80, US-30, US-189
Fees: $0
Accessibility: Largely accessible.
Contact Information:
    307-877-4455
    www.nps.gov/fobu

Fossil insects, snails, turtles, birds, bats, and plant remains are found in the 50-million-year-old rock layers here. Fossil Butte is especially noted for its well-preserved Eocene fish.

John D. Rockefeller, Jr. Memorial Parkway
Fast Facts
Established: 1972
Acreage: 23,772 (9,622 hectares)
Visitors (2019): NA
Nearest Major Airport: Jackson Hole Airport (JAC), Jackson, WY
Nearest Major Highways: US-26, US-89
Fees: NA
Accessibility: NA
Contact Information:
    307-739-3399
    www.nps.gov/grte

This remote and largely uninhabited section of US-191 provides a natural link between Grand Teton and Yellowstone National Parks and contains features characteristic of each. The Tetons ramp down a gentle slope at the parkway's northern end, while rocks born of volcanic flows from Yellowstone line the Snake River and form outcroppings atop hills and ridges. Grand Teton National Park administers the parkway.

THE MIDWEST

Indiana Dunes National Park

The dunes are just the beginning at this relatively new National Park. In just 15 miles (24 km) of Lake Michigan shorefront, the park is home to an array of visitor experiences and the biodiversity of a region 10 times its size (you'll find more varieties of orchids here than in all of Hawaii, for example!). Birders, hikers, campers, kayakers, and sunbathers all find their own preferred corners of the beaches, bogs, marshes, swamps, and prairie remnants that make up the park.

The **West Beach hiking trails** are a terrific introduction to both the geologic history and the natural beauty of this area. That history began more than 11,000 years ago, when the Wisconsin glacier started receding, leaving behind the Great Lakes and their constantly fluctuating shorelines, wetlands, and rolling hills. **The Dune Succession Trail** (Loop 1) highlights the four major stages of dune development over a trail that's just 0.6-miles (1-km) long. There, you'll learn the difference between **foredunes** (covered in vegetation) and **blowout dunes** (Sahara-like terrain, caused by strong winds). For an even more detailed explanation of how dunes come into being, visit www.nps.gov/indu/learn/education/story-maps.htm

Fast Facts

Established: 1966/2019
Acreage: 15,347 (6,211 hectares)
Visitors (2019): 2,134,285
Visitor Centers: Dorothy Buell, Paul H. Douglas Center for Environmental Education.
Nearest Major Airport: O'Hare Intl. (ORD), Chicago, IL
Nearest Major Highways: I-94, US-12, US-20
Fees: $6/vehicle ($3 for seniors) daily between Memorial Day weekend and Labor Day weekend. Campsites are $25/night.
Accessibility: Many areas in the park are accessible, and a range of recreational wheelchairs can be borrowed for free. Visit www.nps.gov/indu/planyourvisit/accessibility.htm for details.
Contact Information: 219-395-1882 www.nps.gov/indu

The 270 steps along the Dune Succession Trail prevent people from trampling the dunes.

On a clear day, the Chicago skyline is visible from the dunes.

For some visitors, the spectacular views of Chicago and Lake Michigan are reason enough to climb the 270 stairs along the trail. To provide a little extra motivation, the Park Service started the **Diana Dunes Dare**, which encourages anyone who completes the route to share a selfie on social media (**#DianaDunesDare**) in exchange for a badge of honor at the visitor center. Diana's Dare is named for **Alice Mabel Gray**, who acquired the nickname Diana of the Dunes when she lived alone in a shanty on the dunes for more than nine years in the early 1900s.

Hardier hikers may choose to tack on two neighboring **loop trails** for a total of 3.4 miles (5.5 km) and 552 vertical feet (168 meters) over loose sand dotted with the occasional prickly pear cactus. Birders will enjoy looking for **waterfowl** from the **Long Lake viewing platform**. Use the hashtag **#3DuneChallenge** for your selfie if you complete all three loops and you'll get a **free bumper sticker** that attests to your accomplishment.

No climbing is necessary on the Portage **Lakefront and Riverfront Walk**, a 1-mile (1.6-km) stroll that's mostly wheelchair-accessible except for a short stairway down to the riverfront. Created on land formerly used for industrial purposes by a steel company, this trail is a successful model of **brownfield reclamation.** The 4.7-mile (7.5-km) **Cowles Bog Trail**, on the eastern side of the **Port of Indiana**, travels through the terrain (sometimes steeply) where Dr. Henry Cowles did pioneering work in the field of plant ecology. Cowles's dissertation demonstrated the importance of preserving the dunes; prior to that, glass companies like Ball Fruit and Pittsburgh Plate Glass ransacked the dunes and hauled away the sand in boxcars. The 1.3-mile (2-km) **Great Marsh Trail** is abundant with warblers, blackbirds, green herons, egrets, kingfishers, coots, mallards, and wood ducks.

Among the 60 historic structures within the park are five houses that were originally unveiled at the 1933 Chicago World's Fair. The fair was held in the midst of the Great Depression, yet its theme, "A Century of Progress," looked both backwards and forwards,

The park is home to five experimental homes from the 1933 Chicago World's Fair, including Robert Weed's Florida Tropical House.

celebrating the city's centennial, and heralding a future of innovation in science and technology. The architects who participated in the exposition were encouraged to create experimental buildings.

The **Armco Ferro House** is the only extant home that met the Fair Committee's design criteria: a residence that could be mass-produced and was affordable for the average American family. Its corrugated steel panels were the inspiration for the mass-produced houses developed by the Lustron Corporation after World War II. Murray Heatherington designed his **Cypress Log Cabin** to demonstrate the many ways cypress could be used in home construction. The bright pink color of Robert Law Weed's

Florida Tropical House evoked the tropics, and became an easily recognized landmark for mariners.

Defying the prevailing engineering wisdom at the time,

the solar heat captured through the wall of windows at George Keck's **House of Tomorrow** reduced the need for mechanical heating systems. (Unfortunately,

The dunes are constantly shifting.

The Little Calumet River Trail is a popular paddling destination.

The trail over the top of Mt. Baldy is short but steep.

the glass walls made the house too hot in summer, and were ultimately replaced by operable windows.) And the **Wieboldt-Rostone House** was clad in an experimental material called Rostone, a mix of shale and limestone that could be produced in a variety of colors and shapes. Rostone proved to be less durable than originally anticipated, and the house's exterior started deteriorating in 1950. The photos of the houses being moved across Lake Michigan on a barge to Indiana are worth the visit alone.

Then of course there are the beaches, all fronted by parking lots that fill up quickly on summer weekends and holidays. **West Beach** is the only one with lifeguards, so it tends to be favored by families with small children. **Dunbar Beach** is closest to the Century of Progress homes. **Smelt fishing** is permitted here, as well as at **Lake View Beach** and **Kemil Beach**. Lake View Beach is the one closest to **Dunewood**

Campground ($25/night). The trail over the 126-foot (38-meter) **Mt. Baldy** to the beach of the same name is accessible only via a ranger-led hike.

The **Calumet Bike Trail** (10-mile/16-km) links all of the beaches except for West Beach. Calumet is part of a 37-mile (59-km) **network of cycling trails** that ranges from the 3.6-mile (5.8-km) **Dunes Kankakee** loop to the **Prairie Duneland Trail**, 11 miles (17 km) of former railroad tracks mostly outside the park boundaries, linking the towns of Chesterton and Portage. From Memorial Day weekend to Labor Day (and select fall weekends), you can rent bikes at **Pedal Power** (www.pedalpowerrentals. com, 219-921-3085), located next to the visitor center.

Created in 2011, the **Lake Michigan Water Trail** traces the lakeshore from Wisconsin to Michigan, with public boat ramps, carry-in sites, parking and picnic areas, and restrooms available to paddlers at various locations along the way. The 75 miles (121 km) between Chicago and New Buffalo, MI, are managed by the Park Service as a National Recreational Water Trail. **Camp Stop General Store** (219-878-1382), across from the Dunewood Campground, rents kayaks and paddleboards.

Gateway Arch National Park

(formerly Jefferson National Expansion Memorial)

Fast Facts

Established: 1935/2018
Acreage: 192 (78 hectares)
Visitors (2019): 2,055,309
Visitor Centers: Gateway Arch
Nearest Major Airport: St. Louis Lambert Intl. (STL), St. Louis, MO
Nearest Major Highways: US-44, US-55, US-64
Fees: $3/adult. Children under age 16 are free. Admission includes entry to the Museum Under the Gateway Arch, but not the tram to the top, which costs $12–16 for adults; $8–12 for children ages 3–15; free for children age 2 and younger. Some fees depend on the day of the week.
Accessibility: The tram is not wheelchair-accessible. The rest of the complex and surrounding grounds are fully accessible. The upper floors of the Old Courthouse require climbing stairs.
Contact Information: 314-655-1600 www.nps.gov/jeff

Mention the name Jefferson National Expansion Memorial and you're likely to get blank stares. Say the words Gateway Arch, on the other hand, and most people immediately recognize the defining architectural feature of St. Louis. So when the Park Service received $380 million to renovate the National Memorial and make it into a National Park in 2018, it conceded to popular usage and changed the name to the one that people have been calling this place for more than 50 years.

Franklin D. Roosevelt first authorized the memorial in 1935 to commemorate Thomas Jefferson's 1803 purchase of the Louisiana Territory from France, which doubled the land area of the United States. In 1948, Finnish-American architect Eero Saarinen (a name beloved by crossword puzzle enthusiasts) floored the judges of the architectural competition to give the site a monument with a soaring, stainless steel ode to the pioneers of the American West. Construction on the arch didn't start for another 15 years (it was completed two years later for just $13 million).

The two trams that ferry visitors 630 feet (192 meters) from the ground to the apex of the parabola were added in 1967 and 1968. For most people, **riding the tram** is the highlight of a visit to Gateway Arch. The ride itself is just four minutes long, and most visitors spend 45–60 minutes at the top. On

Eero Saarinen's soaring stainless steel monument lights up the St. Louis skyline.

A 2018 renovation integrated the Arch and park into the rest of the city.

a clear day, the view extends east and west for up to 30 miles (48 km). Dense morning fog and afternoon haze, however, can reduce visibility to almost zero. There's usually a rush for the first (8 a.m.) tram, but by 9 a.m., it's much less crowded, especially on weekdays.

Each tram car fits just five people; passengers must be able to climb six flights of stairs and stand for up to an hour while waiting for your scheduled tram reservation. And there are no restrooms at the top, so plan accordingly.

The 2018 renovation did little to alter the tram ride experience, but made wholesale improvements to the surrounding landscape, integrating the national park with the city of St. Louis. Previously, six lanes of

traffic on Interstate 44 separated the arch from the rest of the city. That persuaded most visitors

to arrive by car, even those staying at hotels just across the freeway. Today, a new **pedestrian**

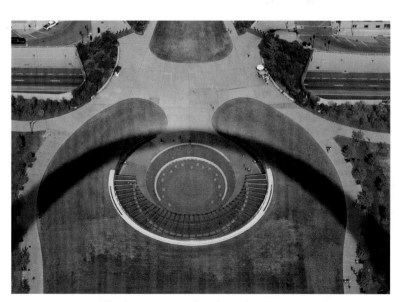

The lawn surrounding the subterranean museum entrance is a perfect picnic spot.

The Old Courthouse is part of the national park.

promenade and bell-shaped lawn (perfect for picnicking) on a land bridge atop the highway finally make the giant croquet wicket a focal point of the city.

The renovation also enhanced the beauty of **Dan Kiley's original landscape design**, which complements and echoes the shape of the arch. There's nary a straight line on the ground. Instead, sweeping walkways and amoeba-shaped ponds on either side reflect the catenary curve of the monument. So too does the anvil-shaped Grand Staircase on the back (eastern) side of the

monument, which leads to the levee on the Mississippi River.

The **Museum Under the Gateway Arch** also got a much-needed update, with a 21st-century perspective on westward expansion that is a lot more inclusive of indigenous peoples and women than the manifest destiny–heavy displays of its predecessor. The museum's six galleries tell the story of America, from colonial times to the monument's completion in 1965. Exhibits are high on interactive elements and touch factor, to engage younger visitors.

The other, often-overlooked attraction at the park is The **Old Courthouse,** a landmark with a checkered history two blocks west of the monument. Construction of the Greek revival building began in 1839 (but wasn't completed until 1862), with a cupola reminiscent of the U.S. Capitol and a façade similar to that of the White House. Auctions of enslaved men and women were staged on the courthouse steps here prior to the Civil War, a conflict hastened by the **Dred Scott case,** which was initially filed

Dred Scott and his wife, Harriet Robinson Scott, filed their historic lawsuit at the Old Courthouse.

here in 1847. Three years later, in the same courthouse, Scott and his wife Harriet won their freedom. But the U.S. Supreme Court overruled the decision in 1857, saying Black people had no constitutional right to American citizenship.

The 14th Amendment finally gave voting rights to Black men, but not to women, per the same St. Louis court's 1873 decision in the **Virginia Minor case.** The Supreme Court agreed unanimously a year later, with Chief Justice Morrison Waite writing, "the Constitution of the United States does not confer the right of suffrage upon anyone." The Old Courthouse hasn't seen a trial since 1930, and was incorporated into the park in 1940 after narrowly escaping bulldozers five years earlier.

The Courthouse closed in 2021 for a major renovation and was not expected to reopen until late 2023 or early 2024.

Cuyahoga Valley National Park

Cuyahoga Valley National Park is one of America's greatest environmental-recovery success stories. For the first half of the 20th century, the stretch of the **Cuyahoga River** between Akron and Cleveland was so filled with sewage and industrial pollution that it caught fire: not once, not twice, but 12 different times between 1868 and 1952. By the 13th time, in 1969, Ohioans (and Americans all over the country) had had enough. Media coverage of the fire sparked the first Earth Day celebration (in April 1970) and the creation of the Environmental Protection Agency eight months later.

Fifty years hence, this part of the river looks nothing like the ecological disaster area it once was. Removing several dams has restored the natural flow of water, and along with it, thriving schools of fish. Today, more than 40 piscine species swim in the Cuyahoga (up from zero in 1969), including **steelhead trout** and **northern pike**, which prosper only in clean water. Frogs and other amphibians feed on aquatic insects along the river's muddy banks.

Fast Facts

Established: 1975/2000
Acreage: 32,571 (13,181 hectares)
Visitors (2019): 2,237,997
Visitor Centers: Boston Mill, Canal Exploration Center, Hunt House
Nearest Major Airport: Cleveland Hopkins Intl. (CLE), Cleveland, OH
Nearest Major Highways: I-77, I-80, I-271
Fees: $0
Accessibility: Most attractions are fully accessible, except for a few steep hiking trails. The scenic railroad has a car with a lift for visitors with limited mobility.
Contact Information: 440-717-3890 www.nps.gov/cuva

The Everett Bridge spans the Cuyahoga River.

Bath Road Heronry is one of the best places to see . . . herons.

Great blue herons have built colonies with more than 100 nests. Healthy sycamore trees along the rivers and streams sustain **opossums**, **raccoons**, and **screech owls.** And in 2006, Cuyahoga County saw its first **bald eagle** in more than 70 years; a year later, the first bald eagle born in the park took flight from its nest. Through 2020, the park has seen a total of 17 eaglets fledged.

The best place to see bald eagles is in the **Pinery Narrows** area north of **Station Road Bridge Trailhead** (also visible from the **Towpath Trail**), or in the southern end of the park near **Beaver Marsh.** The easiest location for sighting great blue herons, meanwhile, is at **Bath Road Heronry**, just east of the river on W. Bath Road in the southern end of the park. The herons build their nests and raise their young from February through June.

The park has become increasingly popular with people as well. Half a million visitors came to see the cleanup work in progress in 1978. Today, more than 2 million people visit annually to bear witness to the valley's transformation; many

The accessible Towpath Trail is a popular route.

of them are frequent visitors, grateful to swap the urban settings of Cleveland or Akron for the great outdoors.

Most activities in the park trace the Cuyahoga River's meandering route. Perhaps the busiest corridor is the **Towpath Trail,** which follows the route originally constructed by the **Ohio & Erie Canal**. Dug between 1825 and 1832 to carry crops and other freight to markets, the canal opened rural Ohio to the commercial waterway of **Lake Erie**. The advent of the railroad made the canal obsolete by the turn of the 20th century, and today, the same thoroughfare handles much less urgent transportation: hiking, cycling, horseback riding, strolling, or running on a 20-mile

(32-km) **wheelchair-accessible recreational path** down the spine of the park. There are no horse rentals near the park, but you can rent bikes at **Century Cycles** near the **Lock 29 Trailhead**.

Riverview Road, also known as **County Road 9,** was designated a **National Scenic Byway** in 2000, meaning it's one of the prettiest drives in America. Most of the park's hiking trails, **waterfalls,** and picnic spots branch off from this central artery, so you're sure to travel some length of it no matter where you go. The **Cuyahoga River** itself is another freeway through the park, and, since 2019, an **Ohio Water Trail**. More than two dozen municipal and nonprofit agencies partner to maintain put-in locations and

trail markers and issue maps and brochures to make it easier for kayakers, canoers, and other paddlers to navigate the river. The closest canoe or kayak rental shops are in Akron.

An even more unexpected way to travel the park is by riding the rails. **The Cuyahoga Valley Scenic Railroad** bisects the park for its entire 26-mile (42-km) length, following the river as it carves its way through the surrounding valley. The train's large picture windows make it easy to spot **eagles, deer,** and **herons** in the surrounding wilderness. Tickets range from $15 for a standard coach seat to $35 for a coveted spot in the executive lounge car. A round-trip excursion takes 3.5 hours, but unless you're in a hurry, take

The Cuyahoga Valley Scenic Railway stops at eight different locations throughout the park.

Brandywine Falls is the most popular destination in the park.

time to dally at any of the eight stations along the way. Even better, use the train to shuttle you back to your car after a day of hiking, running, biking, or kayaking (but not canoeing) through the park. The cost to bring a kayak or bike on board ($5 for bikes, $10 for single kayaks, $15 for double kayaks) is well worth it.

The railway is a vestige from the 19th century, when trains carried coal to Cleveland, Akron, and Canton, and passengers from those cities into the countryside. Railfans will delight in the fleet of **vintage rail cars**, including **California Zephyrs** with skylight windows providing views in every direction. The railway also runs special excursions for beer lovers (Ales & Rails), oenophiles (Grape Escape), and murder mystery aficionados. For information on schedules, prices, and the historic cars in the railroad's fleet, visit www.cvsr.org.

Brandywine Falls is one of the few attractions that isn't on the main drag, but that doesn't stop it from being the most popular place in the park. The parking lot usually fills up by 10 a.m., so arrive early or plan to hike or bike from **Boston Mill Visitor Center** (5 miles/8 km round-trip).

Tinkers Creek Gorge is another worthwhile detour from the main road. The **gorge** is visible from the parking lot, while **Bridal Veil Falls** is less than 500 feet (152 meters) away, ensconced within a network of walking paths that also includes the **Buckeye Trail**, the 1,400-mile (2,2511-km) ribbon that encircles the entire state.

Camping is not allowed anywhere in the park, but it is possible to stay overnight in either of two **historic inns**. Built in 1848 as a private residence, the **Inn at Brandywine Falls** is now a bed and breakfast with four guest rooms and two luxurious suites, one located in the former granary and the other in the old carriage house. **Stanford House**, built in 1843, is less than ¾ miles (1 km) from the Boston Mill Visitor Center. With nine bedrooms, it sleeps up to 30, but must be rented in its entirety, making it popular for weddings, meetings, and other group events.

Cuyahoga Valley foliage

Mount Rushmore National Memorial

Mount Rushmore isn't close to anything. It's not really on the way to anything unless you're driving the northern route across the country on I-90. Some visitors walk away from the memorial nonplussed at how small the four presidential busts are in real life. And there isn't much to do here other than find the best vantage point to take a selfie with the 60-foot (18-meter) high faces of **George Washington**, **Thomas Jefferson**, **Theodore Roosevelt**, and **Abraham Lincoln** in the background.

None of that deters the nearly two million people who visit this remote part of South Dakota's **Black Hills National Forest** each year. Almost all of them come between May and September, and nearly half of the annual total arrive in July and August alone. The ambitious walk the 0.6-mile (1-km) **Presidential Trail** and climb 422 steps to reach a viewpoint that's about 400 feet (122 meters) closer than the main one by the visitor center. If you arrive on a summer evening, you can watch the lighting ceremony; the faces stay illuminated for two hours after sunset.

Conspiracy theorists and fans of the 2007 film *National Treasure: Book of Secrets* will be pleased to know there really is a **Hall of Records**, carved into a passageway behind Lincoln's head. In it are 16 porcelain enamel panels telling the story of how the memorial came to be, the people who created it, and why the four presidents were chosen. The Hall of Records is not open to the public.

There's an **audio tour** ($6) with interviews and historic recordings of the sculptors, workers, and Native Americans indigenous to the area. The **Mount Rushmore Self-Guided Multimedia Tour** ($8) uses a tablet computer to show photos and video at 29 stops throughout the memorial. Tours are also available in Spanish, German, French, and Lakota.

Among the nuggets of information is the story of how Mt. Rushmore got its name. Charles Rushmore was a lawyer who spent several weeks in the Black Hills securing tin mining

Fast Facts

Established: 1925
Acreage: 1,278 (517 hectares)
Visitors (2019): 1,963,540
Visitor Centers: The Lincoln Borglum Visitor Center is located beneath Grand View Terrace. There is also an information center at the park entrance.
Nearest Major Airport: Rapid City Regional Airport (RAP), Rapid City, SD; Denver Intl. (DEN), Denver, CO, is 392 miles (631 km) away.
Nearest Major Highways: I-90, US-16A, SD-244
Fees: $0. Parking fees are $10 ($5/seniors age 62 and older; free for active-duty members of the military).
Accessibility: Fully accessible, except for the Presidential Trail, which has 422 steps. Wheelchairs are available to check out from the Lincoln Borglum Visitor Center on a first-come, first-served basis.
Contact Information: 605-574-2523
www.nps.gov/moru

Mt. Rushmore's four presidents: George Washington, Thomas Jefferson, Theodore Roosevelt, and Abraham Lincoln.

The sculpture is smaller than some visitors expect.

rights. Enthralled by the granite mountain where the memorial now stands, Rushmore asked if it had a name. When the local prospectors said it did not, one of them serendipitously suggested they name it Rushmore Peak. The name stuck, perhaps aided by the fact that Rushmore donated $5,000 to the construction of the memorial.

For all of Mt. Rushmore's popularity, you'd think its sculptor would be a household name. And yet it isn't. Maybe it's because **Gutzon Borglum** doesn't exactly roll of the tongue. Or maybe it's because of his

Sculptor Gutzon Borglum at work on a scale model, which visitors can view in the Sculptor's Studio.

The Avenue of Flags includes one for each U.S. state, territory, and the District of Columbia.

association with the Ku Klux Klan. He denied being a member, but he was the original sculptor of Stone Mountain, the Atlanta-area memorial to the leaders of the Confederacy. In any event, the **Sculptor's Studio** where Borglum created his 1/12 scale model of Mount Rushmore is open from late May to mid-October. Park rangers deliver 15-minute presentations about the 400-plus workers who did the actual carving of the granite mountainside and the tools and techniques they used.

You can't help but walk through the **Avenue of Flags,** a colonnade of 56 banners—one for each state as well as the District of Columbia and the territories of American Samoa, Guam, the Northern Mariana Islands, Puerto Rico, and the U.S. Virgin Islands. The flags are arranged in alphabetical order, starting just past the gift shop and ending at **Grand View Terrace**. The avenue was established in 1976 as part of the U.S. Bicentennial celebration. A $14-million renovation in 2018 made it easier for visitors in wheelchairs to read the plaques identifying each flag.

MORE TO SEE IN THE MIDWEST

ILLINOIS
Lincoln Home National Historic Site
Fast Facts

Established: 1972
Acreage: 12.2 (4.9 hectares)
Visitors (2019): 197,816
Nearest Major Airport: St. Louis Lambert Intl. (STL), St. Louis, MO
Nearest Major Highways: I-55, I-72, IL-29
Fees: $0. Parking is $2/day.
Contact Information:
217-492-4241
www.nps.gov/liho

Preserves and protects the only home Abraham Lincoln ever owned. The future president lived here from 1844 until 1861, when he moved to the White House. The surrounding historic district preserves the 1860s environment in which the Lincoln family lived.

Mormon Pioneer National Trail
Fast Facts

Established: 1978
Length: 1,400 miles (2,251 km)
Visitors (2019): NA
Nearest Major Airport: Eastern end: O'Hare Intl. (ORD), Chicago, IL; Western end: Salt Lake City Intl. (SLC), Salt Lake City, UT
Nearest Major Highways: The trail runs approximately parallel to US-80 through six states.
Fees: $0
Contact Information:
773-660-2341
www.nps.gov/mopi
(Also in Iowa, Nebraska, Utah, and Wyoming)

Traces the route traveled by more than 500 families fleeing religious persecution in the Midwest to the Great Salt Lake Valley in 1846–47.

Pullman National Monument
Fast Facts

Established: 2015
Acreage: 0.4 (0.2 hectares)
Visitors (2019): NA
Visitor Center: Located at the Historic Pullman Foundation, 112th St. and S. Cottage Grove Ave.
Nearest Major Airport: O'Hare Intl. (ORD), Chicago, IL
Nearest Major Highways: I-94
Nearest Metro Station: 111th St. (Pullman)
Fees: $0
Accessibility: Mostly accessible, though the visitor center lacks automated doors.
Contact Information:
773-660-2341
www.nps.gov/pull

Preserves the integrated manufacturing complex and residential community built by railroad car magnate George Pullman south of Chicago in the 1880s. The town of Pullman's design and architecture still resonate with today's urban planners. The work opportunities that Pullman created attracted—and retained—a wide variety of European-American immigrants and formerly enslaved migrants from the South.

Pullman National Monument preserves the legacy of the 1880s town of Pullman, IL.

INDIANA
George Rogers Clark National Historical Park

Fast Facts

Established: 1966
Acreage: 26 (11 hectares)
Visitors (2019): 140,130
Nearest Major Airport: St. Louis Lambert Intl. (STL), St. Louis, MO
Nearest Major Highways: I-69, US-41, US-150,
Fees: $0
Contact Information:
812-882-1776
www.nps.gov/gero

Commemorates Lt. Col. George Rogers Clark's capture of Fort Sackville at Vincennes from the British on Feb. 25, 1779. A classical memorial building with seven large murals and a Hermon MacNeil statue of Lt. Col. Clark stands near the former location of the fort.

Lincoln Boyhood National Memorial

Fast Facts

Established: 1962
Acreage: 200 (81 hectares)
Visitors (2019): 138,714
Nearest Major Airport: Louisville Muhammad Ali Intl. (SDF), Louisville, KY
Nearest Major Highways: US-64, I-231, IN-62
Fees: $0
Accessibility: Mostly accessible, except for some hiking trails that may be too rocky or steep for wheelchairs.
Contact Information:
812-937-4541
www.nps.gov/libo

Abraham Lincoln lived on this southern Indiana farm from 1816 to 1830. During that time, he grew from a 7-year-old boy to a 21-year-old man. His mother, Nancy Hanks Lincoln, is buried here.

IOWA
Effigy Mounds National Monument

Fast Facts

Established: 1949

Acreage: 2,526 (1,022 hcctarcs)
Visitors (2019): 65,581
Nearest Major Airport: Rochester Intl. (RST), Rochester, MN
Nearest Major Highways: US-18, IA-76
Fees: $0
Accessibility: All buildings are wheelchair-accessible, but only three burial mounds can accommodate visitors with impaired mobility. The others involve hiking along steep trails.
Contact Information:
563-873-3491
www.nps.gov/efmo

Preserves 206 American Indian mound sites built along the Mississippi River between 450 B.C.E. and 1300 A.D., including 31 effigy mounds in the shapes of birds and bears. These mounds are examples of a significant phase of mound-building culture, commemorating the passing of loved ones and the sacred beliefs of these ancient peoples.

Herbert Hoover National Historic Site

Fast Facts

Established: 1965
Acreage: 187 (76 hectares)
Visitors (2019): 125,688
Nearest Major Airport: Des Moines Intl. (DSM), Des Moines, IA
Nearest Major Highways: I-80
Fees: $0
Accessibility: The historic nature of the site may present challenges to visitors with impaired mobility. Visit www.nps.gov/heho/planyourvisit/accessibility.htm for details about each building onsite.
Contact Information:
319-643-2541
www.nps.gov/heho

Commemorates the life of the 31st president. The site includes the cottage where Hoover was born, a blacksmith shop, the first West Branch schoolhouse, the Friends Meetinghouse where the Hoover family worshiped, the Hoover Presidential Library-Museum, and the graves of the president and his wife, Lou Henry Hoover.

KANSAS
Brown v. Board of Education National Historic Site
Fast Facts
Established: 1992
Acreage: 1.85 (0.74 hectares)
Visitors (2019): 21,413
Nearest Major Airport: Kansas City Intl. (MCI), Kansas City, MO
Nearest Major Highways: I-70, US-24, US-75
Fees: $0
Accessibility: Fully accessible.
Contact Information:
785-354-4273
www.nps.gov/brvb

Commemorates the landmark 1954 *Brown v. Board of Education of Topeka* decision, in which the U.S. Supreme Court held that "separate educational facilities are inherently unequal," ending legal racial segregation in public schools. The site is located in the former Monroe Elementary School, which was once one of four segregated schools for Black children in Topeka.

Fort Larned National Historic Site
Fast Facts
Established: 1964
Acreage: 718 (291 hectares)
Visitors (2019): 26,958
Nearest Major Airport: Wichita Dwight D. Eisenhower National (ICT), Wichita, KS
Nearest Major Highways: I-70, US-156, US-183
Fees: $0
Accessibility: Most buildings are wheelchair-accessible, except after a heavy rain or snowmelt.
Contact Information:
620-285-6911
www.nps.gov/fols

Preserves one of the most authentic and intact examples of a frontier military post. Established along the Santa Fe Trail in 1859, Fort Larned served as an agency for the Indian Bureau and was a key military base of operations during the Indian War of 1867–69. Troops stationed here escorted mail coaches, protected wagon trains, and patrolled the region. It was deactivated in 1878 after railroad service replaced the trail.

Fort Scott National Historic Site
Fast Facts
Established: 1978
Acreage: 17 (7 hectares)
Visitors (2019): 24,068
Nearest Major Airport: Kansas City Intl. (MCI), Kansas City, MO
Nearest Major Highways: I-49, US-54, US-69
Fees: $0
Accessibility: Varies. Visit www.nps.gov/fosc/planyourvisit/physical-mobility.htm for detailed information about which buildings are wheelchair-accessible.
Contact Information:
620-223-0310
www.nps.gov/fosc

Preserves an 1842 fort that witnessed multiple chapters of American history. Fort Scott soldiers fought in the U.S.-Mexican War (1846–48), provided armed escort along the Santa Fe and Oregon trails, surveyed unmapped country, and managed white contact with Plains Indians. After the post closed in 1853, the civilian town of Fort Scott became a center of violent conflicts over whether "Bleeding Kansas" would be a free or slave state. Union troops fortified the town during the Civil War and the first Black regiment to serve in combat was organized here.

Nicodemus National Historic Site
Fast Facts
Established: 1996
Acreage: 4.59 (1.86 hectares)
Visitors (2019): 3,540
Nearest Major Airport: Wichita Dwight D. Eisenhower National (ICT), Wichita, KS
Nearest Major Highways: I-70, US-24
Fees: $0
Accessibility: The restrooms are up a flight of six stairs (with handrails). Wheelchair-accessible mobile toilets are available outside the visitor center.
Contact Information:
785-839-4233
www.nps.gov/nico

Preserves the only remaining western town established by formerly enslaved African Americans during the post-Civil War Reconstruction period. The town symbolizes the pioneer spirit of

African-Americans seeking personal freedom in the American west.

Tallgrass Prairie National Preserve
Fast Facts
Established: 1996
Acreage: 10,893 (4,408 hectares)
Visitors (2019): 33,750
Nearest Major Airport: Kansas City Intl. (MCI), Kansas City, MO
Nearest Major Highways: I-35, US-50
Fees: $0
Accessibility: Mostly accessible. All 40 miles (64 km) of hiking are accessible to visitors with visual impairments with the use of a hand-held audio describing device.
Contact Information:
620-273-8494x270
www.nps.gov/tapr

Preserves a nationally significant example of the once vast tallgrass prairie ecosystem, and includes historic buildings and cultural resources of the Spring Hill Ranch in the Flint Hills region. The Nature Conservancy owns most of the land and manages it in cooperation with the National Park Service.

Bison roam Kansas's Tallgrass Prairie National Preserve.

KENTUCKY
Abraham Lincoln Birthplace National Historical Park
Fast Facts
Established: 1916/1933/1939/1959/2009
Acreage: 345 (140 hectares)
Visitors (2019): 238,226
Nearest Major Airport: Louisville Muhammad Ali Intl. (SDF), Louisville, KY
Nearest Major Highways: I-65, US-31E
Fees: $0
Accessibility: Mostly accessible. Visit www.nps.gov/abli/planyourvisit/accessibility.htm for details.
Contact Information:
270-358-3137
www.nps.gov/abli

The "First Lincoln Memorial" commemorates the rural beginnings of the nation's 16th president. The memorial includes a replica of the one-room log cabin where Lincoln was born. This park includes Lincoln's boyhood home at Knob Creek, 10 miles (16 km) to the northeast.

Camp Nelson National Monument
Fast Facts
Established: 2018
Acreage: 380 (154 hectares)
Visitors (2019): NA
Nearest Major Airport: Louisville Muhammad Ali Intl. (SDF), Louisville, KY
Nearest Major Highways: I-75, US-27
Fees: $0
Accessibility: Mostly accessible. Trails closest to the forts may be navigable by the sturdiest wheelchairs.
Contact Information:
859-881-5716
www.nps.gov/cane

Established as a Union Army supply depot and hospital during the Civil War, Camp Nelson became a large recruitment and training center for Black soldiers and a refugee camp for their wives and children. Thousands of enslaved people escaped to Camp Nelson with the hope of securing freedom and ultimately controlling their futures by aiding in the destruction of slavery.

At 350 miles (563 km), Mammoth Cave is the world's longest cave system.

Cumberland Gap National Historical Park

Fast Facts

Established: 1940
Acreage: 24,547 (9,934 hectares)
Visitors (2019): 704,598
Nearest Major Airport: Louisville Muhammad Ali Intl. (SDF), Louisville, KY
Nearest Major Highways: I-75, US-25E, US-58
Fees: $0
Accessibility: Fully accessible.
Contact Information:
   606-248-2817
   www.nps.gov/cuga
(Also in Tennessee and Virginia)

This mountain pass on the Wilderness Road, explored by Daniel Boone, was the first great gateway across the Allegheny Mountains into the west. It was an important military objective during the Civil War.

Mammoth Cave National Park

Fast Facts

Established: 1941
Acreage: 52,830 (21,380 hectares)
Visitors (2019): 551,590
Nearest Major Airport: Louisville Muhammad Ali Intl. (SDF), Louisville, KY
Nearest Major Highways: I-35, US-31W
Fees: Tours of the cave range from $8 (for the half-hour-long self-guided Discovery Tour) to $66. The most-expensive, the Wild Cave Tour, is a six-hour excursion with 500 stairs and extensive segments requiring visitors to climb and/or crawl through tight spaces. Sturdy lace-up hiking boots that cover the ankle are required; no exceptions.
Accessibility: Several cave tours are designed expressly for visitors in wheelchairs.
Contact Information:
   270-758-2180
   www.nps.gov/maca

Preserves the world's longest known cave system (more than 350 miles/563 km) as well as the surrounding river valleys of the Green and Nolin rivers. Organized tours began in 1816. UNESCO designated Mammoth Cave a World Heritage Site in 1981, and a Biosphere Region in 1990.

Mill Springs Battlefield National Monument

Fast Facts

Established: 2019
Acreage: 1,459 (590 hectares)
Visitors (2019): NA
Nearest Major Airport: Louisville Muhammad Ali Intl. (SDF), Louisville, KY
Nearest Major Highways: I-75, US-27, KY-80
Fees: $0
Accessibility: Mostly accessible. The Ravine Trail can be difficult for visitors with impaired mobility.
Contact Information:
606-636-4045
www.nps.gov/misp

Preserves the location where the Union won its first major victory during the Civil War. The decisive triumph allowed the Union to retain control of Kentucky throughout the war.

MICHIGAN
Isle Royale National Park

Fast Facts

Established: 1931
Acreage: 571,790 (231,395 hectares)
Visitors (2019): 26,410
Visitor Centers: Houghton, Rock Harbor, Windigo
Nearest Major Airport: Minneapolis-St. Paul Intl. (MSP), MN
Nearest Major Highways: US-41, US-61. Access to the park is by passenger ferry, seaplane, or private boat from the towns of Cooper Harbor, MI: Houghton, MI: Grand Marais, MN: and Grand Portage, MN.
Fees: $7/per person per day. Season pass is $60 and covers up to four adults.
Accessibility: Mostly accessible with a few exceptions. Visit www.nps.gov/isro/planyourvisit/accessibility.htm for details.

Contact Information:
906-482-0984
www.nps.gov/isro

The largest island in Lake Superior is distinguished by its forested wilderness, timber wolves, moose herd, and pre-Columbian copper mines. There are no roads on the island; wheeled vehicles—even bicycles—are not permitted (except for wheelchairs). The park is open only from April 16 through October 31.

Keweenaw National Historical Park

Fast Facts

Established: 1992
Acreage: 1,869 (756 hectares)
Visitors (2019): 20,535
Visitor Center: A visitor center in Calumet is open seasonally. Call in advance.
Nearest Major Airport: Sawyer Intl. (MQT), Marquette, MI
Nearest Major Highway: US-41
Fees: $0
Contact Information:
906-337-3168
www.nps.gov/kewe

Interprets the history of copper mining on the Keweenaw Peninsula, beginning with prehistoric activity nearly 7,000 years ago through large-scale industrial mining in the 1800s and 1900s. The park's Keweenaw Heritage Sites partners operate most visitor facilities, providing diverse experiences and views of the industry and its participants.

Rock Harbor Lighthouse at Michigan's Isle Royale National Park

Pictured Rocks National Lakeshore

Fast Facts
Established: 1966
Acreage: 73,236 (29,638 hectares)
Visitors (2019): 858,715
Visitor Centers: Grand Sable, Munising Falls
Nearest Major Airport: Sawyer Intl. (MQT), Marquette, MI
Nearest Major Highways: MI-77
Fees: $0. Campsite fees are $20/night, May-October; $15/night the rest of the year. Reservations required.
Accessibility: Varies. Visit www.nps.gov/piro/planyourvisit/accessibility.htm for details about specific areas.
Contact Information:
906-387-3700
www.nps.gov/piro

Multicolored sandstone cliffs, long beach strands, towering sand dunes, waterfalls, inland lakes, wetlands, hardwood and coniferous forests, and a variety of wildlife compose this scenic area on Michigan's Upper Peninsula. The power of Lake Superior shapes the park's coastal features and affects every ecosystem, creating a unique landscape.

River Raisin National Battlefield Park

Fast Facts
Established: 2010
Acreage: 42 (17 hectares)
Visitors (2019): 226,354
Nearest Major Airport: Detroit Metropolitan Wayne County (DTW), Detroit, MI
Nearest Major Highways: I-75, US-24
Fees: $0. Viewings of the park film cost $3/person, $5/couple, or $10/family.
Accessibility: Fully accessible.
Contact Information:
734-243-7136
www.nps.gov/rira

Lover's Leap Arch at Pictured Rocks National Lakeshore on Lake Superior

Commemorates and interprets the January 1813 battles of the War of 1812 and their aftermath in Monroe and Wayne counties in Southeast Michigan. The Battles of the River Raisin resulted in the greatest victory for Shawnee leader Tecumseh's American Indian Confederation and the greatest defeat for the United States during the war. The resulting battle cry, "Remember the Raisin!" spurred American support for the rest of the war.

Sleeping Bear Dunes National Lakeshore

Fast Facts

Established: 1970
Acreage: 71,210 (28,818 hectares)
Visitors (2019): 1,570,001
Nearest Major Airport: Gerald R. Ford Intl. (GRR), Grand Rapids, MI
Nearest Major Highways: US-31
Fees: $25/vehicle, $20/motorcycle, $15/cyclist or pedestrian. All admission fees are valid for 7 days.
Accessibility: Because the lakeshore is designated as primitive wilderness, it may present extra obstacles for visitors with impaired mobility. Visit www.nps.gov/slbe/planyourvisit/physical-mobility-needs.htm for details.
Contact Information:
    231-326-4700
    www.nps.gov/slbe

Preserves a diverse landscape with quiet rivers, sandy beaches, beech-maple forests, clear lakes, and massive "perched" sand dunes towering up to 460 feet (140 meters) above Lake Michigan. Two wilderness islands offer tranquility and seclusion. The many historic sites include a lighthouse, life-saving service stations, and agricultural landscapes.

MINNESOTA
Grand Portage National Monument

Fast Facts

Established: 1951/1958
Acreage: 710 (287 hectares)
Visitors (2019): 94,985
Nearest Major Airport: Minneapolis-St. Paul Intl. (MSP), MN
Nearest Major Highways: US-61
Fees: $0

Accessibility: Mostly accessible except for the path to the Voyageurs , the Grand Portage footpath, and the Mount Rose Trail.
Contact Information:
    218-475-0123
    www.nps.gov/grpo

This 9-mile (14-km) portage was a vital link on one of the principal routes for Native Americans, explorers, missionaries, and fur traders heading for the Northwest. Includes a reconstruction of the Grand Portage post established by the North West Company, a Canada-based fur-trading business.

Mississippi National River and Recreation Area

Fast Facts

Established: 1988
Acreage: 53,775 (21,762 hectares)
Visitors (2019): 374,682
Visitor Centers: Mississippi River, St. Anthony's Falls
Nearest Major Airport: Minneapolis-St. Paul Intl. (MSP), MN
Nearest Major Highways: I-94, I-494, US-61
Fees: $0
Accessibility: Varies. Some segments of the park are managed by local, regional, or state agencies. In general, buildings are accessible, but trails may not be.
Contact Information:
    651-293-0200
    www.nps.gov/miss

Encompassing 72 miles (116 km) of the Mississippi River corridor through the Twin Cities, the area features a wealth of significant natural, cultural, historic, economic, and scientific resources, as well as quiet stretches for fishing, paddling, birdwatching, bicycling, and hiking.

Pipestone National Monument

Fast Facts

Established: 1937
Acreage: 282 (114 hectares)
Visitors (2019): 77,508
Nearest Major Airport: Sioux Falls Regional (FSD), Sioux Falls, SD
Nearest Major Highways: I-90, US-75, MN-23

Minnesota's Voyageurs National Park is a spectacular place to see the Northern Lights.

Fees: $3/person
Accessibility: The trail does not meet ADA
  accessibility standards.
Contact Information:
  507-825-5464x214
  www.nps.gov/pipe

For centuries, American Indians have quarried
red pipestone from these ancient quarries. Pipes
made from this stone are considered sacred and are
important spiritual objects for American Indians.
Recognizing this cultural activity, the monument's
enabling legislation allows quarrying to continue
today.

Voyageurs National Park
Fast Facts
Established: 1975

Acreage: 218,200 (88,302 hectares)
Visitors (2019): 232,974
Visitor Centers: Rainy Lake (year-round), Ash
  River (May-Sept. only), Kabetogama Lake (May-
  Sept. only)
Nearest Major Airport: Minneapolis-St. Paul Intl.
  (MSP), MN
Nearest Major Highways: US-53, MN-11
Fees: $0
Accessibility: All three visitor centers are
  wheelchair-accessible.
Contact Information:
  218-283-6600
  www.nps.gov/voya

This waterway of four large lakes (Rainy, Kabetogama,
Namakan, and Sand Point) connected by narrows
was once the route of the French-Canadian voyageurs,
who opened the Great Northwest for fur trading with

Europeans more than 250 years ago. With over 500 islands, the lakes surround the boreal forest of the Kabetogama Peninsula.

MISSOURI
George Washington Carver National Monument
Fast Facts

Established: 1943
Acreage: 210 (85 hectares)
Visitors (2019): 49,553
Nearest Major Airport: Kansas City Intl. (MCI), Kansas City, MO
Nearest Major Highways: I-44, I-49, MO-59
Fees: $0
Contact Information:
 417-325-4151
 www.nps.gov/gwca

Preserves the birthplace and childhood home of George Washington Carver, African American agronomist, educator, and humanitarian. The site includes a museum, interactive exhibits, a theater, a store, a cemetery, and the restored 1881 Moses Carver House.

Harry S Truman National Historic Site
Fast Facts

Established: 1983
Acreage: 13 (5 hectares)
Visitors (2019): 30,746
Nearest Major Airport: Kansas City Intl. (MCI), Kansas City, MO
Nearest Major Highways: I-435, MO-350
Fees: $0. Free tickets are required.
Accessibility: Only the first floor of the home is accessible.
Contact Information:
 816-254-2720
 www.nps.gov/hstr

Preserves the stomping grounds of the 33rd U.S. president. The Truman Home, his residence in Independence, MO, from 1919 to 1972, was called the Summer White House during his administration. The surrounding Landmark District includes his Uncle and Aunt Noland's home (next to his), the

homes of Bess Truman's two brothers (not open to the public), and the Truman Presidential Library and Museum, the first-ever presidential library, four blocks away. The Truman Farm Home is located 20 miles (32 km) south in Grandview, MO.

Ozark National Scenic Riverways
Fast Facts

Established: 1972
Acreage: 80,785 (32,693 hectares)
Visitors (2019): 1,221,489
Visitor Centers: Headquarters (Van Buren, MO), Alley Mill General Store, Round Spring Cave
Nearest Major Airport: St. Louis Lambert Intl. (STL), St. Louis, MO
Nearest Major Highways: I-44, US-60
Fees: $0
Accessibility: The headquarters visitor center is accessible. The access trail at Big Spring, the Slough Trail at Big Spring, and the trail to the Round Spring are level and paved with gravel, and may be accessible to some visitors with mobility impairments.
Contact Information:
 573-323-4236
 www.nps.gov/ozar

America's first National Scenic River extends for 134 miles (216 km) along the Current and Jacks Fork rivers in the Ozark Highlands. Over 300 springs pour thousands of gallons of clear, cold water into the streams, creating excellent opportunities for canoeing, tubing, fishing, swimming, and birdwatching.

Ste. Genevieve National Historical Park
Fast Facts

Established: 2018
Acreage: 17 (7 hectares)
Visitors (2019): NA
Nearest Major Airport: St. Louis Lambert Intl. (STL), St. Louis, MO
Nearest Major Highways: I-55, US-61
Fees: $0
Accessibility: The historic Amoureux House is not wheelchair-accessible.

Contact Information:
573-880-7189
www.nps.gov/stge

Established by 1750, Ste. Geneviève was the first permanent European settlement in Missouri. Early French Canadian settlers were drawn here by the rich agricultural land known as Le Grand Champ (the Big Field). After the flood of 1785, the town relocated to its present location on higher ground, approximately 3 miles (5 km) to the northwest of its original site.

Ulysses S. Grant National Historic Site

Fast Facts

Established: 1989
Acreage: 10 (4 hectares)
Visitors (2019): 39,449
Nearest Major Airport: St. Louis Lambert Intl. (STL), St. Louis, MO
Nearest Major Highways: I-44, I-55, MO-30
Fees: $0
Accessibility: Only the first floor of the home is accessible. All outbuildings are fully accessible.
Contact Information:
314-842-1867
www.nps.gov/ulsg

Before he became the 18th U.S. president and before Abraham Lincoln appointed him General of all Union Armies during the Civil War, Ulysses S. Grant (then a captain) lived with his wife, Julia Dent Grant, and their four children at White Haven, the Dent family home and a plantation worked by enslaved people.

Wilson's Creek National Battlefield

Fast Facts

Established: 1960/1970
Acreage: 2,368 (958 hectares)
Visitors (2019): 232,838
Nearest Major Airport: Kansas City Intl. (MCI), Kansas City, MO
Nearest Major Highways: I-44, US-60, US-160, MO-115
Fees: $20/vehicle, $15/motorcycle, $10 pedestrian or cyclist. Admission fees are valid for seven days.
Accessibility: Fully accessible except for the interpretive trails off the Tour Road.

Contact Information:
417-732-2662x227
www.nps.gov/wicr

Commemorates and interprets the field where the Confederacy won the first major battle west of the Mississippi River, but failed to pry Missouri from Union hands. Major features include a 5-mile (8-km) vehicle tour road, the restored 1852 Ray House, Bloody Hill, and the Trans-Mississippi museum and library.

NEBRASKA
Agate Fossil Beds National Monument

Fast Facts

Established: 1997
Acreage: 3,058 (1,238 hectares)
Visitors (2019): 16,657
Nearest Major Airport: Denver Intl. (DIA), Denver, CO
Nearest Major Highways: US-20, NE-29
Fees: $0
Accessibility: The visitor center is wheelchair-accessible and features a touch-screen interactive presentation with video of two mostly accessible hiking trails in the monument.
Contact Information:
308-665-4113
www.nps.gov/agfo

Protects the quarries where, in the early 1900s, paleontologists found full skeletons of extinct Miocene-Epoch mammals—species previously only known through fragments. Cattle rancher James Cook, who owned the land, and Chief Red Cloud of the Lakota maintained a relationship from the late 1880s on, with the venerable chief gifting Cook a number of Plains Indian artifacts, now included in the collection of the park's museum.

Homestead National Historic Monument

Fast Facts

Established: 1936
Acreage: 211 (85 hectares)
Visitors (2019): 61,636
Visitor Centers: Heritage Center, Homestead Education Center

Nearest Major Airport: Eppley Airfield (OMA), Omaha, NE
Nearest Major Highways: I-80, US-77, US-136
Fees: $0
Accessibility: The Heritage Center and Education Center buildings are fully accessible. The monument has won awards for its innovations in making exhibits accessible to the visually impaired.
Contact Information:
    402-223-3514
    www.nps.gov/home

The Homestead Act of 1862 had an immediate and enduring effect upon America and the world that is still felt today. This park includes the 160-acre (65-hectare) Daniel Freeman Claim, the National Museum on Homesteading, historic buildings and agricultural equipment, genealogy research opportunities, and an education center.

Missouri National Recreational River
Fast Facts
Established: 1978/1991
Acreage: 48,457 (19,610 hectares)
Visitors (2019): 129,280
Visitor Center: National Recreational River headquarters are in Yankton, SD.
Nearest Major Airport: Sioux Falls Regional (FSD), Sioux Falls, SD
Nearest Major Highways: I-29, US-81
Fees: $0
Accessibility: Limited accessibility. The Lewis & Clark Visitor Center on the South Dakota side is wheelchair-accessible.
Contact Information:
    605-665-0209 x28
    www.nps.gov/mnrr
(Also in South Dakota)

Protects more than 100 miles (161 km) of America's longest river system. The 59-mile (94-km) portion originally set aside in 1978 (from Yankton, SD to Ponca, NE) still exhibits the river's untamed, dynamic character in its islands, bars, chutes, and snags. A separate 39-mile (68-km) stretch was added in 1991 from Fort Randall, SD to Niobrara, NE. It features native floodplain forest, tallgrass and mixed-grass prairies, and habitats for several endangered species.

Lewis & Clark National Historic Trail
Fast Facts
Established: 1978
Length: 4,900 miles (7,880 km)
Visitors (2019): NA
Visitor Centers: Trail headquarters is in Omaha, NE.
Nearest Major Airport: Eastern end: Pittsburgh Intl. (PIT), Pittsburgh, PA; Western end: Portland Intl. (PDX), Portland, OR.
Nearest Major Highways: NA
Fees: $0
Accessibility: The main visitor center is wheelchair-accessible.
Contact Information:
    402-661-1804
    www.nps.gov/lecl
(Also in 15 other states)

Traces the inbound and outbound routes of the Lewis & Clark expedition through Louisiana Purchase territory and the Pacific Northwest from 1804 to 1806. The trail crosses through 16 states on its way from Pittsburgh, PA, to the mouth of the Columbia River near Astoria, OR.

Niobrara National Scenic River
Fast Facts
Established: 1991
Acreage: 29,101 (11,777 hectares)
Visitors (2019): 60,812
Nearest Major Airport: Sioux Falls Regional (FSD), Sioux Falls, SD
Nearest Major Highways: US-20, US-83
Fees: $0
Accessibility: Limited accessibility.
Contact Information:
    402-376-1901
    www.nps.gov/niob

This 104-mile (167-km) section of the Niobrara River protects an unusual area where many species and ecosystems overlap. The Niobrara supports Boreal, Eastern Woodland, and Rocky Mountain forest types, and multiple prairie ecosystems including Tallgrass, Sandhills, and Mixed-Grass Prairies. The river is rated as one of America's top canoeing adventures; kayaking and tubing are also popular.

Scotts Bluff National Monument

Fast Facts
Established: 1919
Acreage: 3,004 (1,216 hectares)
Visitors (2019): 166,007
Nearest Major Airport: Denver Intl. (DIA), Denver, CO
Nearest Major Highways: US-26, NE-71, NE-92
Fees: $0
Accessibility: The visitor center is fully accessible. Trails are paved, but all feature at least some portion that is too steep for wheelchairs.
Contact Information:
308-436-9700
www.nps.gov/scbl

Rising 800 feet (244 meters) above the North Platte River, this massive promontory was a landmark for native peoples as well as to westward-migrating travelers on the Oregon, California, and Mormon Trails.

NORTH DAKOTA
Knife River Indian Villages National Historic Site

Fast Facts
Established: 1974
Acreage: 1,749 (708 hectares)
Visitors (2019): 10,354
Nearest Major Airport: Bismarck Municipal (BIS), Bismarck, ND
Nearest Major Highways: I-94, ND-200
Fees: $0
Accessibility: Trails may be difficult to navigate in wheelchairs.
Contact Information:
701-745-3300
www.nps.gov/knri

Preserves and interprets archeological and historic remnants of the Plains Indian culture and agricultural way of life. This site was a major Native American trade center for hundreds of years before becoming a marketplace for fur traders in the second half of the 18th century.

North Country National Scenic Trail

Fast Facts
Established: 1980
Length: 4,600 miles (7,397 km)
Visitors (2019): NA
Nearest Major Airport: Eastern end: Burlington Intl. (BTV), Burlington, VT; Western end: Bismarck Municipal (BIS), Bismarck, ND
Nearest Major Highways: NA
Fees: $0
Accessibility: Some segments of the trail are too narrow for a wheelchair.
Contact Information:
619-319-7906
www.nps.gov/noco
(Also in seven other states from Vermont to North Dakota.)

America's longest National Scenic Trail is more than twice the length of the Appalachian Trail. It starts in the Green Mountain National Forest near Hancock, VT, and ends at Lake Sakakawea State Park, ND. Clear-flowing lakes and rivers, open prairies, and rugged mountains paint the land. Historic sites along the way tell how America grew as a nation.

Theodore Roosevelt National Park

Fast Facts
Established: 1947/1978
Acreage: 70,447 (28,509 hectares)
Visitors (2019): 691,658
Visitor Centers: South Unit (park headquarters), North Unit, Painted Canyon
Nearest Major Airport: Bismarck Municipal (BIS), Bismarck, ND
Nearest Major Highways: I-94, US-85
Fees: $30/vehicle, $25/motorcycle, $15/cyclist or pedestrian. All admission fees are valid for 7 days.
Accessibility: All three visitor centers are wheelchair-accessible, as is the Maltese Cross Cabin. Many campgrounds and vista points are also accessible.
Contact Information:
701-623-4466
www.nps.gov/thro

Preserves and protects three separate units along the Little Missouri River where a young Theodore Roosevelt developed a love for the outdoors and a lifelong devotion to conservation. The South Unit is closest to the highway, and the most popular; the North Unit is remote and consequently less visited. In between is the Elkhorn Ranch Unit, which

Hoodoos at Theodore Roosevelt National Park in North Dakota

Roosevelt chose for his home ranch after the deaths of his wife and his mother. There are no visitor facilities in the Elkhorn Ranch Unit.

OHIO
Charles Young Buffalo Soldiers National Monument

Fast Facts

Established: 2013
Acreage: 60 (24 hectares)
Visitors (2019): 14,106
Nearest Major Airport: John Glenn Columbus Intl. (CMH), Columbus, OH
Nearest Major Highways: US-42, US-68
Fees: $0
Contact Information:
  937-352-6757
  www.nps.gov/chyo

Preserves the home of Col. Charles Young, a soldier, diplomat, and civil rights leader, who overcame racism and stifling inequality to become a leading figure in the years after the Civil War when the

U.S. emerged as a world power. In 1903, he led a company of all-Black regiments (a.k.a. Buffalo Soldiers) in building roads and other infrastructure improvements at Sequoia and Kings Canyon National Parks.

Dayton Aviation Heritage National Historical Park

Fast Facts

Established: 1992
Acreage: 111 (45 hectares)
Visitors (2019): 94,709
Visitor Centers: Wright-Dunbar, Huffman Prairie
Nearest Major Airport: John Glenn Columbus Intl. (CMH), Columbus, OH
Nearest Major Highways: I-75, US 35, OH-4
Fees: $0
Contact Information:
  937-225-7705
  www.nps.gov/daav

Preserves sites associated with Wilbur and Orville Wright and the early development of aviation. It also honors the life and work of Black poet Paul Laurence Dunbar, classmate and business associate of Orville Wright. The park includes a bicycle and printing shop, the 1905 Wright Flyer III, the flying field where the brothers perfected their airplane, and the Paul Laurence Dunbar House State Memorial.

First Ladies National Historic Site

Fast Facts

Established: 2000
Acreage: 0.46 (0.19 hectares)
Visitors (2019): 10,913
Nearest Major Airport: Cleveland Hopkins Intl. (CLE), Cleveland, OH
Nearest Major Highways: I-77, US-30, US-62
Fees: $0. A guided tour of the Saxton House is $7/adult, $6/senior, $5/children aged 17 and younger. Tours are limited to five people and leave from the Education Center daily at 10 a.m., noon, and 2 p.m.
Accessibility: Many accommodations have been made to welcome visitors with impaired mobility.
Contact Information:
330-452-0876
www.nps.gov/fila

Interprets the role, impact, and history of first ladies and other notable women in American history. There is an electronic virtual library and a complete annotated bibliography of every first lady, updated annually. Costumed docents conduct tours. The National First Ladies' Library and the National Park Service cooperatively manage the site, part of which occupies the former home of Ida Saxton-McKinley, first lady to William McKinley, the 25th president.

Hopewell Culture National Historical Park

Fast Facts

Established: 1923/1992
Acreage: 1,766 (715 hectares)
Visitors (2019): 60,338
Nearest Major Airport: John Glenn Columbus Intl. (CMH), Columbus, OH
Nearest Major Highways: I-71, US-23, OH-116
Fees: $0
Accessibility: The visitor center is wheelchair-accessible, but some of the trails around the

earthworks may be muddy, uneven, or too steep for visitors with impaired mobility.
Contact Information:
740-774-1126
www.nps.gov/hocu

Preserves and interprets multiple significant archeological resources—including large earthwork and mound complexes—that provide an insight into the social, ceremonial, political, and economic life of the Hopewell people. The term Hopewell describes a broad network of beliefs and practices among different Native American groups over a large portion of eastern North America between 200 BCE to 500 CE. The most striking sites contain earthworks in the form of squares, circles, and other geometric shapes.

James A. Garfield National Historic Site

Fast Facts

Established: 1996
Acreage: 7.82 (3.16 hectares)
Visitors (2019): 41,305
Nearest Major Airport: Cleveland Hopkins Intl. (CLE), Cleveland, OH
Nearest Major Highways: I-90, OH-2
Fees: $10/adult; children aged 15 and under are free. Admission includes a guided tour of the home; tours are limited to seven people and leave every hour from 10:15 a.m. to 4:15 p.m.
Accessibility: Mostly accessible.
Contact Information:
440-255-8722
www.nps.gov/jaga

Preserves the artifacts and family home where the 20th president launched his "Front Porch" campaign after his selection as the 1880 Republican nominee. Exhibits and tours introduce Garfield's humble upbringing and family life.

Perry's Victory and International Peace Memorial

Fast Facts

Established: 1936/1972
Acreage: 25 (10 hectares)
Visitors (2019): 121,325

Nearest Major Airport: Cleveland Hopkins Intl. (CLE), Cleveland, OH
Nearest Major Highways: I-80/90, US-250, OH-2. The memorial is on an island; access is via ferry boat or small plane from the town of Port Clinton.
Fees: Visitor center admission is free to all. $10/adult, to visit the observation deck, children aged 15 or younger are free.
Accessibility: The visitor center is fully accessible, but the memorial itself is not.
Contact Information:
419-285-2184
www.nps.gov/pevi

Commemorates a pivotal U.S. naval victory in the War of 1812 and the lasting peace with Great Britain and Canada since. The memorial consists of a 352-foot (107-meter) high column on South Bass Island in Lake Erie surrounded by 25 acres (10 hectares) of landscaped grounds.

William Howard Taft National Historic Site
Fast Facts
Established: 1969
Acreage: 3.64 (1.47 hectares)
Visitors (2019): 32,396
Nearest Major Airport: Cincinnati/Northern Kentucky Intl. (CVG), Covington, KY
Nearest Major Highways: I-71, US-22, US-42
Fees: $0
Accessibility: Mostly accessible.
Contact Information:
513-684-3262
www.nps.gov/wiho

Preserves the birthplace and childhood home of the only man to serve as both president (1909–13) and chief justice of the United States Supreme Court (1921–30). The Taft education center offers an orientation video and interactive exhibits on the Taft family.

OKLAHOMA
Chickasaw National Recreation Area
Fast Facts
Established: 1902/1906/1976
Acreage: 9,899 (4,006 hectares)

Visitors (2019): 1,422,612
Nearest Major Airport: Will Rogers World Airport (OKC), Oklahoma City, OK
Nearest Major Highways: I-35, US-177, OK-7
Fees: $0
Accessibility: Buildings, docks, campgrounds, and restrooms are wheelchair-accessible. Some trails may not be.
Contact Information:
580-622-7234
www.nps.gov/chic

Honors the Chickasaw Nation, original occupants of this land of forested hills, natural springs, streams, and lakes. Swimming, boating, fishing, camping, and hiking are all popular activities.

Oklahoma City National Memorial
Fast Facts
Established: 1997
Acreage: 3.3 (1.3 hectares)
Visitors (2019): NA
Nearest Major Airport: Will Rogers World Airport (OKC), Oklahoma City, OK
Nearest Major Highways: I-40, I-235
Fees: $0 for the outdoor symbolic memorial. $15/person to enter the museum.
Accessibility: Fully accessible.
Contact Information:
405-609-8859
www.nps.gov/okci

The Oklahoma City National Memorial honors the victims, survivors, and rescuers involved in the 1995 bombing.

Honors the victims, survivors, and rescuers involved in the April 19, 1995 bombing of the Alfred P. Murrah Federal Building. The 168 empty chairs in the field where the building once stood represent the lives lost that day. The memorial consists of an outdoor memorial and an indoor museum. It is run in partnership with the non-profit Oklahoma City National Memorial Foundation.

Washita Battlefield National Historic Site
Fast Facts
Established: 1966
Acreage: 315 (127 hectares)
Visitors (2019): 9,119
Nearest Major Airport: Will Rogers World Airport (OKC), Oklahoma City, OK
Nearest Major Highways: I-40, US-283
Fees: $0
Accessibility: The self-guided trail is not fully accessible. The visitor center is fully accessible.
Contact Information:
580-497-2742
www.nps.gov/waba

Commemorates the November 27, 1868, attack during which the 7th U.S. Cavalry under Lt. Col. George A. Custer destroyed Southern Cheyenne leader Black Kettle's village on the Washita River, killing the chief, his wife, and dozens of Cheyenne civilians and warriors. The controversial attack has been described as both a battle and a massacre.

SOUTH DAKOTA
Badlands National Park
Fast Facts
Established: 1939/1978
Acreage: 233,809 (94,619 hectares)
Visitors (2019): 970,998
Visitor Centers: Ben Reifel (headquarters), White River (Memorial Day-October 1 only)
Nearest Major Airport: Rapid City Regional Airport (RAP), Rapid City, SD; Denver Intl. (DEN), Denver, CO
Nearest Major Highways: I-90, SD-240
Fees: $30/vehicle, $25/motorcycle, $15/cyclist or pedestrian. All admission fees are valid for 7 days.

Accessibility: Both visitor centers are fully accessible, as are two campgrounds and most scenic overlooks.
Contact Information:
605-433-5361
www.nps.gov/badl

Carved by erosion, this dramatic landscape contains animal fossils (including ancestors of rhinos) from 26 to 37 million years ago. Prairie grasslands support bison, bighorn sheep, deer, pronghorn antelope, swift fox, and black-footed ferrets. Approximately half of the park (133,300 acres/53,945 hectares) is on the Pine Ridge Indian Reservation, home of the Oglala Lakota Tribe.

Jewel Cave National Monument
Fast Facts
Established: 1908
Acreage: 1,274 (516 hectares)
Visitors (2019): 123,489
Nearest Major Airport: Rapid City Regional Airport (RAP), Rapid City, SD; Denver Intl. (DEN), Denver, CO
Nearest Major Highways: I-90, US-16
Fees: The Scenic Tour and the Historic Lantern Tour both cost $12/adult, $8/children aged 6–16, free for children aged 5 and under. The Wind Caving tour is $31 and is limited to visitors 16 and older.
Accessibility: None of the trails are wheelchair-accessible, though most of the facilities are.
Contact Information:
605-673-8300
www.nps.gov/jeca

Preserves an underground wilderness: a three-dimensional maze of passages, with a layer of calcite spar covering most of the cave surfaces. The cave is the third-longest in the world, with over 200 miles (322 km) of mapped passages.

Minuteman Missile National Historic Site
Fast Facts
Established: 1999
Acreage: 44 (18 hectares)
Visitors (2019): 125,776

Nearest Major Airport: Rapid City Regional Airport (RAP), Rapid City, SD; Denver Intl. (DEN), Denver, CO

Nearest Major Highways: I-90, SD-240

Fees: $0. The ranger-led Delta-01 Tour costs $12 for adults, $8 for children aged 6–16. Each 45-minute tour is limited to six participants, and advance reservations are required and can be made online or by phone at 866-601-5129.

Accessibility: The historic compound, built to execute nuclear war, cannot be made fully accessible.

Contact Information:
605-433-5552
www.nps.gov/mimi

By preserving elements of the Minuteman II Intercontinental Ballistic Missile System, the park interprets the deterrent value of the land-based portion of America's nuclear arsenal during the Cold War. Resources feature the Delta-09 Launch Facility, where a Minuteman missile is housed in its underground silo, and the Delta-01 Launch Control Facility, where Air Force personnel controlled and maintained 10 of the 150 nuclear missiles located in South Dakota.

Wind Cave National Park
Fast Facts

Established: 1903 (Wind Cave National Game Preserve, est. 1912, was added to the park in 1935.)

Acreage: 33,924 (13,729 hectares)

Visitors (2019): 615,350

Nearest Major Airport: Rapid City Regional Airport (RAP), Rapid City, SD; Denver Intl. (DEN), Denver, CO

Nearest Major Highways: I-90, US-385

Fees: $0. Tours of the cave are $10–$30, depending on tour length. Seniors and children aged 6–16 are half-price. Children aged 5 and under are free. Reserve in advance for the Candlelight Cave Tour ($12, no children under 8 years old) or the Wind Cave tour ($30, no children under 17).

Accessibility: An accessible cave tour ($5 for adults, $2.50 for seniors and children aged 6–16) is available for visitors with limited mobility. Call in advance to schedule.

Contact Information:
605-745-4600
www.nps.gov/wica

Named for the barometric winds at its entrance, this limestone cave in the scenic Black Hills is decorated by beautiful boxwork, a unique formation rarely found elsewhere. The mixed-grass prairie above the cave is home to an unexpected variety of wildlife for such a small park: bison, elk, pronghorns, and prairie dogs.

WISCONSIN
Apostle Islands National Lakeshore
Fast Facts

Established: 1970

Acreage: 69,377 (28,076 hectares)

Visitors (2019): 240,613

Visitor Centers: Bayfield, Little Sand Bay (June through Labor Day only), Stockton Island (June through Labor Day only), David R. Obey Northern Great Lakes,

Nearest Major Airport: Minneapolis-St. Paul Intl. (MSP), MN

Nearest Major Highways: I-35, US-2, WI-13

Fees: $0

Accessibility: Mostly accessible, with more accommodations continually introduced.

Contact Information:
715-779-3397
www.nps.gov/apis

This wild archipelago park consists of 21 islands, 12 miles (19 km) of mainland shore, a detached lighthouse, and the beautiful but challenging Lake Superior waters. Its picturesque sea caves, pristine beaches, and remote campsites and docks make it a haven for sailors, boaters, and sea kayakers. The park's rich matrix of human stories includes the homeland of the Ojibwe people and the largest number of historic light stations (seven) in the NPS. Old growth forests, black bears, timber wolves, and endangered piping plovers also thrive here.

Ice Age National Scenic Trail
Fast Facts

Established: 1980

Length: 1,200 miles (1,930 km)

Visitors (2019): NA

Nearest Major Airport: Eastern end: Milwaukee Mitchell Intl. (MKE); Western end: Minneapolis-St. Paul Intl. (MSP), MN

Nearest Major Highways: Eastern end: I-43, WI-42; Western end: I-35, WI-35.

Fees: $0

Accessibility: The Ahnapee, Sugar River, Kewaunee River, Badger State, and Mountain-Bay Trails all overlay former railways, and are thus more accessible than other sections of the route.

Contact Information:
608-798-8700
www.nps.gov/iatr

Traces the edge of a huge glacier that covered much of North America as recently as 15,000 years ago, when mammoths, sabre-tooth cats, and cave lions roamed. Some of the best evidence of this glacier is found in Wisconsin's many lakes, river valleys, gently rolling hills, and ridges. The eastern end is in Potawatomi Park on Green Bay; the western terminus is at Interstate State Park on the St. Croix River in Polk County.

Saint Croix National Scenic Riverway
Fast Facts

Established: 1968

Acreage: 67,469 (27,303 hectares)

Visitors (2019): 638,258

Visitor Centers: Namakegon River, St. Croix River. Both visitor centers are open only in summer.

Nearest Major Airport: Minneapolis-St. Paul Intl. (MSP), MN

Nearest Major Highways: US-63 parallels the eastern section of the river, which begins at Namakegon Dam. I-94 and US-12 are the closest highways to the western terminus in Prescott.

Fees: $0

Accessibility: Both visitor centers are fully accessible, as are several picnic areas.

Contact Information:
715-483-2274
www.nps.gov/sacn
(Also in Minnesota)

The St. Croix and Namekagon rivers flow for 252 miles (405 km) through some of the most undeveloped country in the upper Midwest. Visitors canoe, boat, camp, fish, hike, and view wildlife amid the spectacular scenery. The states of Minnesota and Wisconsin manage the lower 25 miles (40 km) of the St. Croix River to its confluence with the Mississippi River.

Sea caves along Lake Superior, Apostle Islands National Lakeshore

THE SOUTH

Great Smoky Mountains National Park

Fast Facts

Established: 1930
Acreage: 522,427 (211,419 hectares)
Visitors (2019): 12,547,743
Visitor Centers: Cades Cove, Clingmans Dome, Gatlinburg Welcome Center, Oconaluftee, Sugarlands.
Nearest Major Airport: Charlotte-Douglas Intl. (CLT), Charlotte, NC; Nashville Intl. (BNA), Nashville, TN
Nearest Major Highways: I-40, I-75, I-81, US-19, US-74, US-129, US-321, US-441
Fees: $0
Accessibility: Most parking lots and buildings are accessible to people with disabilities.
Contact Information: 865-436-1200 www.nps.gov/grsm

America's most-visited National Park straddles the North Carolina-Tennessee border, from Asheville, NC, to Chattanooga, TN. The **Appalachian Trail** cuts a diagonal through the Smoky Mountains, bisecting the park for 72 miles (116 km), while managing to cross only one road. The **Blue Ridge Parkway** begins (or ends) here, linking the park to Shenandoah National Park in Virginia. The gateway town of Pigeon Forge, TN, is home to Dollywood and Dollywood's Splash Country

theme parks, a branch of the Hollywood Wax Museum, and a half-scale *Titanic* museum.

Yet despite everything going on nearby, Great Smoky Mountains still manages to feel pristine, truly like a National Park and not an amusement park. It's crowded, for sure, especially in summer and fall foliage season. But like so many other national parks, the crowds thin as you branch out from the most popular attractions.

Many of the park's gems are accessible by car. The 34-mile

Sunset over Great Smoky Mountains National Park

The Appalachian Trail bisects Great Smoky Mountains National Park for 72 miles (116 km).

(55-km) route between Cherokee, NC, and Gatlinburg, TN, follows US-441 over **Newfound Gap**, the pass with the lowest elevation (5,046 feet/1,538 m) in the park.

Hardwood forests line the road at lower elevations, giving way to evergreen spruce and firs at the top of the pass. At certain times of year, the trip over the pass may feel like driving through all four seasons.

Clingmans Dome, on the other hand, is the highest point in the park and the highest point in all of Tennessee. The access road to the summit (closed in winter) starts just south of the Newfound Gap Road and more or less parallels the Appalachian Trail for 7 miles (11 km) into coniferous rainforest and a large parking area. The half-mile (1-km) walking trail to the **observation tower** at the summit is paved but likely too steep for wheelchairs. On a clear day, views from the tower extend for more than 100 miles (161 km). Unfortunately, air pollution often reduces visibility to 20 miles (32 km) or less. If, in your rush to get to Clingmans Dome, you raced past the overlooks at **Mt. Weaver, Beech Flats, Luftee Gap, Big Slick Ridge, Noland**

On a clear day, views from Clingmans Dome Observation Tower extend for more than 100 miles (160 km).

Just a few of the cascades at the Place of a Thousand Drips

Divide, and **Forney Ridge**, be sure to check them out on your way back down.

The **Roaring Fork Motor Nature Trail** is a narrow, winding 5.5-mile (8.9-km) one-way loop near the Gatlinburg entrance that traces mountain streams through old-growth forest, log cabins and other historic buildings, and several trailheads that lead to **waterfalls**. The popular **Rainbow Falls trail**, at the beginning of the motor trail, is 2.7 miles (4.3 km) from the road, with an elevation gain of 1,500 feet (457 m). **Grotto Falls**, in the middle of the drive, only requires hiking 1.3 miles (2.1 km) each way along the **Trillium Gap Trail**. Grotto

Falls is the only place in the park where visitors can stand behind the rush of cascading water. **Place of a Thousand Drips**, at the far end of the driving tour, doesn't even require getting out of the car. It may not even look like a waterfall in dry seasons. But if there's been a recent rain, the water doesn't so much fall as find dozens of pathways to ooze down the rocky hillside.

Ramsey Cascades is the tallest waterfall in the park, accessed by a strenuous 4-mile (6-km) hike through tulip trees and silver birches. **Abrams Falls** is only 20 feet (6 m) high, but it makes up in volume what it lacks in height. The **Lynn Camp Prong**

Cascades feature multiple drops along a short, easy walk on an old logging road that's festooned with wildflowers in spring and summer. Closer to the southern entrance, cataracts with curious names like **Mingo Falls, Juney Whank Falls**, and **Twentymile Creek Cascade** require hikes of less than 1 mile (1.6 km) each way.

Wildlife is abundant in the Smokies but isn't easy to see for the thickly wooded forest. Animals also tend to avoid humans, of whom there are many in the park in spring, summer, and fall. The best wildlife viewing is usually early in the morning or at dusk, when nocturnal animals

Looks like somebody's been sleeping in their bed.

are active, and in winter, when the leaves have fallen from the trees.

In 2001, elk were reintroduced to the **Cataloochee Valley,** at the eastern edge of the park. **Cataloochee Creek** is known for its outstanding trout fishing. Two long, but popular hikes leave from the **Cataloochee Campground**: The moderate **Little Cataloochee Trail** (10 miles/16 km), and the shorter but more difficult **Boogerman Loop** (7 miles/11 km). Note that the gravel road to Cataloochee is narrow with steep drop-offs and no guardrails.

White-tailed deer are frequent visitors to **Cades Cove,** in the northwestern corner of the park, as are the occasional black bear, coyote, and wild turkey. That makes **Cades Cove Campground** fill up quickly and **Cades Cove Loop Road** a slow, but extremely

Barns, log cabins, and a working grist mill are among the numerous historic structures along Cades Cove Loop Road.

Elk and other wildlife are easier to spot in winter, when deciduous trees shed their leaves.

scenic drive. Bicyclists and pedestrians have the loop road to themselves every Wednesday, when cars are prohibited.

Cherokee people hunted in Cades Cove for hundreds of years; Europeans arrived in the early 19th century. Numerous **historic structures** are scattered along the loop road, including a working grist mill, barns, and log cabins. From Cades Cove Campground, an all-day (14 miles/22 km round-trip) hike follows **Anthony Creek** to the Appalachian Trail and on to **Rocky Top,** the mountain peak name-checked in the University of Tennessee's unofficial fight song.

In autumn, New England has nothing on the Smokies when it comes to **foliage viewing**. The park's amazing diversity of trees—more than 100 native species—burst into brilliant vermilion, crimson, and persimmon colors every October. Cars travel a little more slowly along the Roaring Fork Motor Nature Trail and the Blue Ridge Parkway in autumn because of all the leaf peepers. The **Alum Cave Trail** to **Inspiration Point, Oconaluftee River Trail**, and **Look Rock Tower Trail** are all popular foliage hikes less than 3 miles (5 km) long.

The diversity of trees in the park makes for spectacular drives and hikes as the leaves change seasonally.

Hot Springs National Park

Fast Facts

Established: 1832/1921
Acreage: 5,549 (2,246 hectares)
Visitors (2019): 1,467,153
Visitor Center: Fordyce Bathhouse
Nearest Major Airport: Bill and Hillary Clinton National Airport (LIT), Little Rock, AR
Nearest Major Highways: I-30, US-70, US-270, AR-7
Fees: $0
Accessibility: Most buildings are wheelchair-accessible.
Contact Information: 501-623-2824 www.nps.gov/hosp

Originally set aside by President Andrew Jackson in 1832 "for the future disposal of the United States," the area now known as Hot Springs National Park was federally protected for 40 years before Ulysses S. Grant established Yellowstone. And the springs themselves have been attracting visitors since the U.S. acquired the Louisiana Territory in 1803. Today, the park is cherished not only for its ancient thermal waters but also for the grand architecture of the historic bathhouses that, er, sprung up to create America's first spa. The natural setting that produced the springs is also responsible for views of the **Zig Zag** range of the **Ouachita Mountains**, incredible geology, and hikes along creeks through the surrounding forest.

Any visit to Hot Springs begins at **Bathhouse Row**, a National Historic Landmark itself, where eight grand buildings, all built between 1892 and 1937, stand shoulder to shoulder along the east side of Central Avenue. (The usual assortment of eateries, souvenir shops, and recreation outfitters line the west side of the street.)

Only two of the buildings continue to operate as bathhouses: **Buckstaff,** a stately

Steam rises off the spring near Hot Springs National Park.

Historic Bathhouse Row

Edwardian brick building with Colorado marble throughout its interior, and the Spanish Colonial Revival **Qapaw,** with its exquisitely mosaic-tiled dome. Both offer thermal baths filled with water piped in from the hot springs (and cooled from the 143°F/62°C source temperature), as well as all the traditional massaging and pampering you'd expect from a full-service spa. Buckstaff is the oldest continuously operating spa in the park, in business since 1912. Qapaw, named for a local Native American tribe, has a public thermal pool (swimsuits required), a steam cave, and a café where you can relax after a facial, eyebrow waxing, or blow out.

    Lamar Bathhouse, a white brick and stone building built in 1923, is now home to **Bathhouse**

You can't soak in this pool, but you can get a free facial.

A public thermal pool (swimsuits required), a steam cave, and a licensed café are among the options beneath the mosaic-tiled dome at Qapaw Bathhouse.

Row Emporium, the park store. It sells more spa-related products than the typical National Park gift shop, in addition to the usual souvenirs, postcards, and passes. **Ozark Bathhouse**, completed in 1922 and renovated in 1942, originally catered to budget-minded soakers. Today it's home to the **Hot Springs National Park Cultural Center,** a free museum that displays artwork from the park's **Artist-in-Residence Program**.

The three-story **Fordyce Bathhouse** is the largest on the row. Built in 1915 and extensively restored in 1989, it currently serves as the park's lone **Visitor Center**. The **Maurice Bathhouse** is nearly as large; for many years, it was the only spa with a pool. It closed in 1974 and remains vacant today.

The **Hale Bathhouse** is the oldest structure, dating back to 1892. It has been converted to the **Hotel Hale,** a historic lodging that

preserves many of the spa's original brick, marble, and hardwood finishes. Every room features a full-size soaking tub, with water piped in from the local hot spring, just like the bathhouses. It's the only place you can soak in the spring water without leaving your hotel room. The spa's original skylight ceiling allows sunlight to pour down on the wall of plants at the hotel's restaurant, **Eden.**

The smallest bathhouse, **Superior,** at the north end

A vintage bath with a patient lift, one of the items on display at Fordyce Bathhouse.

of the row, was also the least expensive. Today, after lying vacant for 30 years, it has been lovingly converted into **Superior Bathhouse Brewery**, the only brewery located in a National Park. The 18 beers and ales on tap are all brewed using the hot springs water. The **Beer Bath** allows diners to sample a flight of all 18 varieties for $35.

The water from the springs doesn't just make for good beer. It's also delicious straight. There are seven **fountains** throughout the park where visitors can "quaff the elixir" straight from the source. Two fountains on Reserve Street and one just outside the park at **Hill Wheatley Plaza** allow anyone to fill up a jug, as long as they don't sell the water. There are also two cold spring fountains, whose water comes from different springs. **Whittington Spring** flows out

of West Mountain, while **Happy Hollow Spring** cascades down from North Mountain.

Although there's no place to soak in the springs outdoors, there are some small pools where the water has cooled enough to dip a toe into: **Display Spring**, right behind Maurice Bathhouse, and **Hot Water Cascade**, at **Arlington Lawn** just north of Bathhouse Row. **Gulpha Gorge Campground** isn't on a spring, but 40 tent or RV sites there overlook **Gulpha Gorge Creek**. Its location in the midst of the park's 26 miles (42 km) of hiking trails make it a popular getaway spot. Most of the trails are 2 miles (3 km) or less, but can be combined into longer walks. An exception is the **Sunset Trail**, which travels 10 miles (16 km) through the most remote sections of the park. The steep terrain along many

sections of this trail makes it easy to understand how the Zig Zag range got its name.

Most of the trails are excellent birding venues, but it isn't necessary to go deep into the woods to sight the 113 different avian species that have been recorded here. Because it is lined with both evergreen and deciduous trees, the **Grand Promenade**, right behind Bathhouse Row, attracts a great variety of birds. Herons, geese, vultures, owls, hummingbirds, kingfishers, and woodpeckers are just a few of the species that have been sighted. As its name suggests, Grand Promenade is a broad strolling lane, paved with stone pavers and accessible to wheelchairs by a ramp behind the visitor center.

Gulf Islands National Seashore

This collection of 12 different recreation areas ranges from Cat Island, Mississippi, eastward to the Okaloosa Area east of Fort Walton Beach, Florida. It is an area of sparkling blue-green gulf waters, powdery white sand beaches, historic fortifications, and nature trails.

The seashore is divided into two different sections: one in Florida and the other in Mississippi. The islands in the Florida section are accessible by car, via bridges across the Gulf Intracoastal Waterway in Destin, Fort Walton Beach, Pensacola, and Perdido Key. The Mississippi section, save for a small portion on the mainland, can only be reached by boat. If you don't have your own vessel, you can catch a ride from a large variety of commercial operators, many of whom also offer fishing charters, guided backpacking tours, and kayak and paddleboard rentals.

The primary draw of both sections, is, of course, the beach, 160 miles (257 km) of it in all, mostly on barrier islands. *USA Today* readers routinely rank the National Seashore among the best beaches in the U.S., naming it Best Naturally Preserved Shoreline in 2015 and Best East Coach Beach

Fast Facts

Established: 1971
Acreage: 138,306 (55,970 hectares)
Visitors (2019): 5,600,240
Visitor Centers: Florida: Fort Barranca, Fort Pickens, Naval Live Oaks; Mississippi: William M. Colmer
Nearest Major Airports: Pensacola Intl. (PNS), Pensacola, FL; Gulfport-Biloxi Intl. (GPT), Gulfport, MS
Nearest Major Highways: Florida: I-10, I-110, US-98; Mississippi: I-10, US-90
Fees: $15/person, $20/motorcycle, $25/vehicle at Fort Barrancas, Fort Pickens, Okaloosa, Opal Beach, and Perdido Key.
Accessibility: Varies by location.
Contact Information: 850-934-2600 www.nps.gov/guis

Miles of beaches are the principal attraction at Gulf Islands National Seashore.

The powdery white sand gives Opal Beach its name.

the year after. Lifeguards are on duty from May through August at Florida's **Johnson Beach** (on Perdido Key), **Langdon Beach** (near Fort Pickens), and **Opal Beach** (in the Santa Rosa Area), and on Mississippi's **Ship Island**. Ship Island is the only Mississippi island with any public facilities (picnic pavilions, restrooms, snack bar, and chair and umbrella rentals).

Mississippi's **Horn Island** and **Petit Bois Island**, meanwhile, are completely undeveloped, thanks to their status as designated wilderness areas. That not only preserves the natural conditions on the islands, it makes them prime viewing areas for birds, animals, and marine life. Birders and anglers seeking solitude flock to both islands for the opportunity to spot alligators, raccoons, frogs, and turtles amid the live oaks and pine trees. Unfortunately, the ecological bounty of both islands is threatened by rising sea level and by garbage and fertilizer runoff from the Mississippi River. Tread lightly.

Five of the world's seven species of **sea turtles** (Loggerhead, Green, Kemps's Ridley, Leatherback, and Hawksbill) are found within the Gulf Islands National Seashore. All five are designated as either endangered or threatened species. **Loggerhead Sea Turtles**, which grow up to about 350 pounds (159 kg), are the only one of the five species that regularly nest on the sands here. Every year between May and September they come ashore to lay their eggs.

The **Kemp's Ridley Sea Turtle** is the rarest turtle species in the world. In 2016, the Park Service discovered two Kemp's Ridley nests in the National Seashore sands. Usually, however, they're found only in the coastal waters. That's also the case with **Hawksbills,** which can grow to 3 feet (1 m) long and weigh up to 150 pounds (68 kg); **Green Sea Turtles** (3 feet/1 m long, 500 pounds/228 kg); and **Leatherbacks,** (12 feet/5 m long, 2,000 pounds/907 kg). As with all wild animals (even slow-moving ones), keep a safe distance and don't shine flashlights on nesting turtles. To see turtles in the water, rent **snorkel or scuba** gear and explore the south side of **Santa Rosa Island**, the 1906 **wreck of the tugboat *Sport*** (0.9 miles/1.5 km east of the Fort Pickens Ranger Station on the bayside) or the **sunken *USS Massachusetts* battleship** (1.5 miles/2 km outside Pensacola Pass).

Because it is so close to Pensacola, Fort Pickens is one of the most visited areas of the

Loggerhead turtles come ashore every summer to lay their eggs in the sand.

A historic cannon remains at Fort Pickens.

Seashore. Even if you bring your car, you might be tempted to leave it in the parking lot and get around on the free, seasonal **Fort Pickens Tram Service**. It runs on the same schedule as the **ferry boats** arriving from Pensacola, and stops at the Ferry Plaza (home to the historic fort, the National Park Bookstore, and a snack bar), the campgrounds, and Langdon Beach, the popular swimming spot.

Where there are beaches, there is usually flat ground perfect for **cycling**, and the Emerald Coast (the unofficial name for this region, when it's not being affectionately called the Redneck Riviera) is no exception. The 15-mile (24-km) **Live Oaks Bicycle Route**, on the mainland Mississippi portion of the Seashore, connects the **Davis**

Great blue herons are among the Gulf Islands' appeals for birders.

The U.S. Navy's Blue Angels practice maneuvers above their homebase in nearby Pensacola.

Bayou area to the town of **Ocean Springs**. Follow the **green-and-white bike route signs** or pick up a map at the Visitor Center. The Florida section boasts 4 miles (6 km) of bike lanes in the Fort Pickens Area, 7 miles (11 km) along **J. Earle Bowden Way** in the Santa Rosa Area, and a multi-use trail adjacent to US-98 in the Naval Live Oaks Area. Cyclists also share the road through the dunes at Johnson Beach on Perdido Key.

Flatland Florida doesn't have much in the way of true hiking, but the **Naval Live Oaks Area** on Pensacola Beach does have a total of 7.5 miles (12 km) of walking paths, including a 0.8-mile (1.1-km) **Brackenridge Nature Trail** that is fully accessible to visitors using wheelchairs or strollers. Fort Pickens is also the western terminus of the **Florida National Scenic Trail** (a.k.a. the Florida Trail), 1,300 miles (2,080 km) of pathways for

non-motorized recreation that goes all the way to Big Cypress National Preserve. More than 375,000 people walk some portion of the Florida Trail each year, usually during the cooler, dry season between October and May. The portion from Fort Pickens to **Navarre Beach Marine Park** runs mostly parallel to Gulf Boulevard (FL-399) for 26 miles (42 km).

That noise you hear overhead isn't the sound of planes full of tourists landing at the nearby airport. It's the **Blue Angels**, the U.S. Navy's storied Flight Demonstration Squad. The squad is headquartered in Pensacola, and from November to March, you can watch them practice the tight-formation **aerial maneuvers** they use in air shows around the country. There are also two shows a year in the Pensacola area, but the National Seashore isn't the best place to watch from.

Hotels and motels are plentiful in the nearby communities of Pensacola and Pensacola Beach and in Gulfport-Biloxi, but there are **no indoor lodgings** anywhere within the seashore boundaries. That makes for an experience that's even more removed from civilization. The Fort Pickens Area is home to more than 200 **campsites**, most with electric hookups and all with laundry facilities, potable water, flush toilets, and hot showers year-round. The only drive-in campgrounds in the Mississippi section are at a small mainland portion of the seashore north of **Davis Bayou**. But there are several boat-in camping areas that are inaccessible by car: Florida's **Perdido Key** or Mississippi's **Petit Bois**, **West Petit Bois**, **Horn Island**, and **Cat Island**. No permit is required to pitch a tent in any of these remote, backcountry sites.

Chattahoochee River National Recreation Area

Fast Facts

Established: 1978
Acreage: 9,798 (3,965 hectares)
Visitors (2019): 3,393,133
Visitor Centers: Island Ford (in Hewlett Lodge)
Nearest Major Airport: Hartsfield-Jackson Atlanta Intl. (ATL), Atlanta, GA
Nearest Major Highways:
Fees: $5/vehicle per day. $40 annual pass.
Accessibility: The visitor center and restrooms are wheelchair-accessible.
Contact Information: 678-538-1200 www.nps.gov/chat

The 434-mile (694-km) Chattahoochee River starts in the southern Appalachian Mountains (not far from the Appalachian Trail), and travels the length of Georgia and halfway down Florida before terminating in Lake Seminole. But it's the 48 miles (77 km) closest to Atlanta's suburbs and exurbs that receive the most attention (and consequently the most need for federal protection). The river and its surroundings are a welcome respite from the big city, with a variety of opportunities for recreation. Think of this park as Atlanta's biggest backyard.

The river itself is a hit with **anglers.** Unlike many other waterways this far south, the Chattahoochee rarely gets above 50°F (10°C), making it a haven for **trout fishing**. The Georgia Dept. of Natural Resources stocks the Chattahoochee with brown and rainbow trout just below **Buford Dam**, at the far northern end of the park. The waters near the hatchery are a good place to cast a line (fly fishing only; no bait allowed). Just beware of how and when releases from the dam will affect the water levels of the river. Check spatialdata. sam.usace.army.mil/hydropower/ default.aspx for an hour-by-hour

The Chattahoochee River travels nearly the entire length of Georgia.

The waters just below Buford Dam are stocked with rainbow and brown trout.

schedule of how much water is released. A Georgia fishing license and a trout stamp are required, even if you're fishing for species other than trout.

Opportunities for **canoeing**, **kayaking**, **stand-up paddling**, and **rafting** are also plentiful up and down the river. And when the dam is not releasing water, the current can be calm enough to plop onto an inner tube, inflatable pool toy, or any other flotation device and simply drift downriver. The National Park Service doesn't rent boats or floats, but numerous authorized

Canoeing, kayaking, stand-up paddling, and rafting are all popular ways of traveling the slow-moving river.

Hiking trails in the Sope Creek section pass by ruins dating to the Civil War era.

be the Confederate Mint during the Civil War. Though those claims were never substantiated, the Union Army burned it in 1864. It was rebuilt a second time less than a decade later, after another fire in 1870. For a longer walk, take the multi-use trail that connects the Sope Creek area to the **Cochran Shoals** network of trails farther south, which welcome walkers, runners, and mountain bikers.

The **Vickery Creek Trail** follows a tributary of the Chattahoochee to carve out a 5-mile (8-km) loop across a covered bridge and past the ruins of **Roswell Mill**. During the Civil War, the mill produced cotton and wool, including a blend known as "Roswell Gray," used to make Confederate uniforms. The adjacent spillway that powered the mill is a relaxing spot to have lunch while watching for heron, geese, and other wildlife.

outfitters in surrounding towns do, and many will arrange to pick you up at the end of your trip.

The park website has a handy chart of distances and float times between prominent points along the river. The longest (but also coldest) stretch, between **Buford Dam** and **Abbotts Bridge**, is about 13 miles (21 km), which translates into a 6–8 hour canoe trip or 10 hours of floating. Closer to Atlanta, the 3 miles (5 km) between **Powers Island** and **Paces Mill** takes an hour or two if you paddle, and three hours or so if you don't. Small motorboats are also permitted on the river, but Jet Skis are not.

The riparian zones on either side of the river are prime **day hiking** territory. None of these walks through the woods are rated more than moderate, and none involve an elevation gain of more than 672 feet (204 m). The 3.3-mile (5.3-km) **East Palisades Trail** loop is one of the closest to downtown Atlanta, and therefore one of the most trafficked. It features a variety of riverside and cliff views, and includes an option to extend the walk another

half-mile (1 km) each way to a bamboo forest.

Farther north, half a dozen trails leave from the **Sope Creek** parking area on Paper Mill Road. The longest loop is a little more than 3 miles (5 km), passing by the stone wall ruins of the **Marietta Paper Mill**. Built in 1853, the mill was rumored to

The spillway below the old Roswell Mill is a pleasant spot for lunch along the 5-mile (8-km) round-trip Vickery Creek Trail.

Natchez Trace Parkway

Imagining the Natchez Trace as just a parkway is like thinking of a multi-island Caribbean cruise as just a boat ride. The 444-mile (715-km) road is indeed a leisurely, scenic, historic road trip through Mississippi, Alabama, and Tennessee. But it is chockablock with recreational opportunities. And the sights you see from behind the windshield are only a small portion of those you'll discover when you get out of the car.

Whether you motor just a few miles or drive the entire length, you'll be following in the footsteps of the **Choctaw**, **Chickasaw**, and **Natchez peoples**, who walked these trails for millennia before European settlers arrived. At several different locations, the Trace also crosses parts of the "Trail of Tears" routes, taken when the Cherokee people were forced westward from their homelands across the south. Look for markers at milepost 328.7 (the **Water Route**), milepost 370 (the **Bell Route**), and milepost 400.2 (the **Benge Route**).

In the 1800s, boatmen known as "**Kaintucks**" floated goods down the Ohio and Mississippi Rivers from states throughout the

Fast Facts

Established: 1938/1961
Acreage: 52,302 (21,166 hectares)
Visitors (2019): 6,296,041
Visitor Centers: Mount Locust Information Center (Milepost 15.5); Parkway Information Cabin (Milepost 102.4); Parkway [*Main Visitor Center*] (Milepost 266); Meriwether Lewis (Milepost 385.9)
Nearest Major Airport: Nashville Intl. (BNA), Nashville, TN; Jackson-Medgar Wiley Evers Intl. (JAN), Jackson, MS
Nearest Major Highways: I-20, I-55, I-40, I-65
Fees: $0
Accessibility: Visit www.nps.gov/natr/planyourvisit/accessibility.htm for a detailed chart of accessible services along the route.
Contact Information: 662-680-4025 www.nps.gov/natr

The Natchez Trace Parkway Bridge welcomes travelers heading southbound from Nashville.

The Parkway travels through forest and cotton fields alike.

Ohio River valley to markets in Natchez and New Orleans. Once the merchandise was unloaded, the boats themselves were often dismantled and sold as lumber, since there was no practical way to send them back north. That meant the boatmen had to walk back home (or ride a horse if they were lucky). In 1810 alone, more than 10,000 Kaintucks traveled the Old Natchez Trace.

Explorer **Meriwether Lewis** (of "Lewis and Clark" expedition fame) died while traveling the Old Trace in 1809; a monument at milepost 385.9 marks his burial site. Maj. Gen. (and future president) Andrew Jackson earned the nickname "Old Hickory" for his sturdy determination in leading his troops along the trail from Nashville to Natchez and back during the War of 1812.

Autumn along the Parkway is prime time for leaf-peeping. Starting in mid-October, maple, hickory, and oak trees along the roadside begin their annual

transformation. Some of the choicest sections for foliage viewing include the **Little Mountain Overlook in Jeff Busby Campground** (milepost

Thousands of years of traffic along easily-eroding soil have carved long portions of the Natchez Trace Trail into a chute.

The Natchez Trace Trail parallels the Parkway in five discrete areas, including this one near Tupelo, MS.

193.1), **Freedom Hills Overlook** (milepost 317), **Old Trace Drive** (milepost 375.8), **Metal Ford** (milepost 382.8), and **Swan View Overlook** (milepost 392.5).

Getting out of your car and into the forest is an even better way to soak up fall color. No hiking shoes are required for the short walk into the woods at **Rock Spring Nature Trail** (milepost 330) or **Fall Hollow** (milepost 391.9). For a longer outing, spend a few hours (or all day) hiking a portion of the **Natchez Trace National Scenic Trail**. The trail is comprised of five noncontiguous areas, ranging in length from the 3-mile (5-km) **Potkopinu** section (milepost 17-20) to the 26-mile (42-km) **Yockanookany** section just north of Jackson (milepost 107.9 to milepost 130.9). Yockanookany traces the shore of

the **Ross Barnett Reservoir** for 8 miles (13 km).

The Potkopinu section contains the longest stretch of the "sunken" Trace, so nicknamed because thousands of years of traffic along the trail's easily-eroding soil have carved the trail into a chute. Indeed, Potkopinu means "little valley" in the Natchez language.

Because it is so close to Nashville, the 20-mile (32 km) long **Highland Rim** section (milepost 407.9-427.4) is the most popular part of the trail, both with hikers and equestrians. Horses are permitted in all sections of the trail except Potkopinu. Most folks start at the northern terminus at **Garrison Creek**, where there are restrooms, picnic tables, and hitching posts. For a short walk, take the 1.3-mile (2-km) **Garrison**

Creek Loop Trail, unless it has been raining, in which case the trail can be muddy. For a longer hike, head south past the **War of 1812 Memorial** (milepost 426.3) to the **Tennessee Valley Divide** (milepost 423.9) before turning around. The hardy can take the trail all the way to **Jackson Falls** (24 miles/38 km), though this route involves multiple road crossings.

Jackson Falls (milepost 404.7), named for the first president from Tennessee, is one of two **waterfalls** along the parkway, accessed via a paved path. **Fall Hollow**, the louder and more impressive of the two, is conveniently located just 13 miles (22 km) south (milepost 391.9). A short trail leads to a viewing platform

Cyclists love the parkway for myriad reasons. You don't

The entirety of the Natchez Trace Parkway is a designated bike route.

have to bike the entire length (although thousands of people do every year) to understand why. The Park Service has designated the entire parkway a **bike route**, and numerous signs remind cars to share the road. The speed limit on the parkway is 50 mph, and commercial vehicles are prohibited, so there's no chance of a fast-moving 18-wheeler crowding you onto the shoulder. And it's relatively flat: the total net elevation gain from Natchez to Nashville is only 550 feet (168 m), or about 15 inches per mile (0.2 m/km). Of course, every hill is harder on two wheels.

In addition to three general-use **campgrounds** along the parkway, there are five **bicycle-only primitive campsites** with picnic tables and fire grates. The longest distance between campgrounds is the 106 miles between **Rocky Springs** (milepost 54) and **Kosciusko bicycle-only camp** (milepost 160). If that's too long a ride for one day, the city of **Jackson,**

MS, lies about halfway between the two camps, with plenty of lodging options. The **Chisha Foka Multi-Use Trail** parallels the parkway for 10 miles (16 km) through downtown Jackson, giving cyclists a less-trafficked alternative during rush hour.

The Chisha-Foka trail (Choctaw for "among the post oaks") is also popular among recreational cyclists who don't plan to be out for more than a few hours, as well as with joggers, walkers, and nature enthusiasts.

The Parkway passes by seven sites where you can still see **Indian mounds**. The Mississippian people built the earliest of these around 2,100 years ago. The tallest (35 feet/11 m) of the seven, **Emerald Mound** (milepost 10.3), is surpassed in height only by Monk's Mound in Illinois. The oldest, **Bynum Mounds** (milepost 232.4), was originally built between 100 B.C.E. and 100 C.E. and rebuilt in the 1940s after National Park Service archeologists excavated five of the six, uncovering trade goods and other precious artifacts from the era. **Pharr Mounds** (milepost 286.7) consists of eight mounds spread over 90 acres (36 hectares), surrounding what was once a sizable village.

Emerald Mound is the tallest of seven ceremonial mounds along the Parkway's length.

MORE TO SEE IN THE SOUTH

ALABAMA
Birmingham Civil Rights National Monument

Fast Facts

Established: 2017
Acreage: 18 (7 hectares)
Visitors (2019): NA
Nearest Major Airport: Birmingham-Shuttlesworth Intl. (BHM), Birmingham, AL
Nearest Major Highways: I-20, I-65
Fees: NA
Accessibility: NA
Contact Information:
    205-568-3963
    www.nps.gov/bicr

Encompasses roughly four city blocks in downtown Birmingham. The site includes the A.G. Gaston Motel, where civil rights leaders like Rev. Dr. Martin Luther King Jr. and Ralph Abernathy orchestrated their nonviolent protests against segregation in Birmingham. There were no visitor services at the park as of 2021.

Freedom Riders National Monument

Fast Facts

Established: 2017
Acreage: 8 (3 hectares)
Visitors (2019): NA
Nearest Major Airport: Birmingham-Shuttlesworth Intl. (BHM), Birmingham, AL Nearest Major Highways: I-20, US 431, AL-21
Fees: NA
Contact Information:
    (256) 237-3536
    www.nps.gov/frri

Includes the former Greyhound Bus Station in Anniston, Alabama, where segregationists attacked a bus carrying Freedom Riders in May of 1961, and the spot 6 miles (10 km) away on the side of the highway where the segregationists firebombed the hobbled bus and attempted to trap the Freedom

A statue at the Birmingham Civil Rights National Monument recalls the violent attacks on protesters.

Riders inside it. There were no visitor services at the park as of 2021.

Horseshoe Bend National Military Park

Fast Facts

Established: 1956
Acreage: 2,040 (826 hectares)
Visitors (2019): 45,372

Nearest Major Airport: Birmingham-Shuttlesworth Intl. (BHM), Birmingham, AL
Nearest Major Highways: US-280, I-20
Fees: $0
Contact Information:
256-234-7111
www.nps.gov/hobe

Commemorates the battle that began Maj. Gen. Andrew Jackson's rise to prominence. On March 27, 1814, Jackson's army of 3,300 men attacked Chief Menawa's 1,000 Muscogee (Creek) "Red Stick" warriors, who were fortified in a horseshoe-shaped bend of the Tallapoosa River. Over 800 of Menawa's forces died that day. The battle ended the Creek War and opened 23 million acres (9.3 million hectares) of Alabama and Georgia to takeover.

Little River Canyon National Preserve
Fast Facts
Established: 1992
Acreage: 15,288 (6,187 hectares)
Visitors (2019): 649,986
Visitor Centers: Canyon Mouth Park, Jacksonville State University Little River Canyon Center
Nearest Major Airport: Birmingham-Shuttlesworth Intl. (BHM), Birmingham, AL
Nearest Major Highways: I-59, AL-35
Fees: $0
Contact Information:
256-845-9605
www.nps.gov/liri

Protects the natural, recreational, and cultural resources of the Little River Canyon of northeast Alabama. Rock expanses, benches, and bluffs create a unique environment for several threatened and endangered species and for recreational pursuits, including kayaking and rock climbing. Hunting, fishing, and trapping are permitted, in accordance with local regulations.

Russell Cave National Monument
Fast Facts
Established: 1961
Acreage: 310 (125 hectares)
Visitors (2019): 16,642
Nearest Major Airport: Birmingham-Shuttlesworth Intl. (BHM), Birmingham, AL

Nearest Major Highways: I-24, US-72
Fees: $0
Accessibility: The Visitor Center and the trail to the cave are wheelchair-accessible. The trail in the cave is not.
Contact Information:
205-495-2672
www.nps.gov/ruca

Preserves an archaeological site with one of the most complete records of prehistoric cultures in the Southeast. Discovered in the 1950s, the cave is an almost continuous archeological record of human habitation from at least 9000 BCE to about 1650 CE (the Transitional Paleo to Mississippian cultural periods). Today, Russell Cave National Monument helps bring to light many human cultural developments.

Selma to Montgomery National Historic Trail
Fast Facts
Established: 1966
Acreage: NA
Visitors (2019): NA
Visitor Centers: Interpretive Centers are located in Montgomery, Lowndes, and Selma
Nearest Major Airport: Birmingham-Shuttlesworth Intl. (BHM), Birmingham, AL
Nearest Major Highways: I-65, US-80, AL-41
Fees: $0
Contact Information:
334-877-1983
www.nps.gov/semo

Commemorates the people, events, and route of the 1965 Voting Rights March led by Rev. Dr. Martin Luther King Jr. and John Lewis.

Tuskegee Airmen National Historic Site
Fast Facts
Established: 1998
Acreage: 90 (36 hectares)
Visitors (2019): 30,097
Nearest Major Airport: Birmingham-Shuttlesworth Intl. (BHM), Birmingham, AL
Nearest Major Highways: I-85
Fees: $0

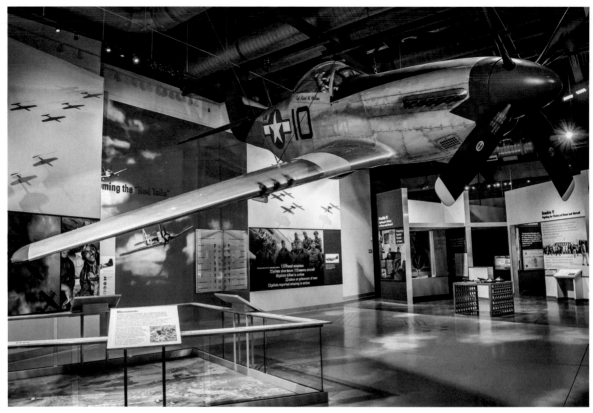

A full-sized Redtail P-51 Mustang hangs above the other exhibits at Tuskegee Airmen National Historic Site.

Contact Information:
334-724-0922
www.nps.gov/tuai

Preserves the airfield, hangar, and other buildings at Moton Field, where Black American pilots known as the Tuskegee Airmen received their initial flight training during World War II.

Booker T. Washington founded this college for Black students in 1881. Preserved here are the brick buildings the students constructed themselves, Washington's home, and the George Washington Carver Museum, which serves as the visitor center. Tuskegee University, an active educational institution with nearly 3,000 students enrolled annually, owns most of the property within the national historic site.

Tuskegee Institute National Historic Site
Fast Facts
Established: 1974
Acreage: 58 (23 hectares)
Visitors (2019): 36,395
Nearest Major Airport: Birmingham-Shuttlesworth Intl. (BHM), Birmingham, AL
Nearest Major Highways: I-85
Fees: $0
Accessibility: Fully accessible.
Contact Information:
334-727-3200
www.nps.gov/tuin

ARKANSAS
Arkansas Post National Memorial
Fast Facts
Established: 1960
Acreage: 756 (306 hectares)
Visitors (2019): 28,519
Nearest Major Airport: Bill and Hillary Clinton National Airport (LIT), Little Rock, AR
Nearest Major Highways: US-165
Fees: $0
Accessibility: Fully accessible. Three wheelchairs are available for loan.

Contact Information:
870-548-2207
www.nps.gov/arpo

Commemorates four key events that occurred here or near here: the first semi-permanent European settlement in the Lower Mississippi Valley (1686), a Revolutionary War skirmish (1783), the first territorial capital of Arkansas (1819–1821), and the Civil War Battle of Arkansas Post (1863).

Buffalo National River
Fast Facts
Established: 1972
Acreage: 94,293 (38,159 hectares)
Visitors (2019): 1,326,282
Visitor Centers: Buffalo Point, Tyler Bend, Still Creek Ranger Station.
Nearest Major Airport: Bill and Hillary Clinton National Airport (LIT), Little Rock, AR
Nearest Major Highways: US-65, AR-14
Fees: $0
Contact Information:
870-365-2700
www.nps.gov/buff

The nation's first national river winds its way for 135 miles (216 km) through the Arkansas Ozarks, past towering bluffs, running rapids, quiet pools, and numerous springs, caves, and waterfalls. The river and adjacent lands include three wilderness areas, providing plentiful recreational and educational opportunities, including canoeing, hiking, and exploring Boxley Mill, a 19th-century mining town.

Fort Smith National Historic Site
Fast Facts
Established: 1961
Acreage: 75 (30 hectares)
Visitors (2019): 125,500
Nearest Major Airport: Bill and Hillary Clinton National Airport (LIT), Little Rock, AR
Nearest Major Highways: I-40, US-64, US-71B
Fees: $10/person to see the exhibits inside the Visitor Center building. The grounds are free of charge.
Contact Information:
479-783-3961
www.nps.gov/fosm
(Also in Oklahoma)

This fortress on the east bank of the Arkansas River commemorates the forced removal of the five southeastern tribes from their homelands to Indian Territory (present-day Oklahoma). A stop on the Trail of Tears National Historic Trail, Fort Smith preserves almost 80 years of frontier history, from the establishment of the first Fort Smith on December 25, 1817, to the final days of Judge Isaac C. Parker's jurisdiction over Indian Territory in 1896.

Little Rock Central High School National Historic Site
Fast Facts
Established: 1998
Acreage: 27 (11 hectares)
Visitors (2019): 168,918
Nearest Major Airport: Bill and Hillary Clinton National Airport (LIT), Little Rock, AR
Nearest Major Highways: I-630, US-78
Fees: $0
Accessibility: Fully accessible.
Contact Information:
501-374-1957
www.nps.gov/chsc

Commemorates the struggle to desegregate Central High School in the wake of the U.S. Supreme Court's *Brown v. Board of Education* rulings, and how the events at Central High served as a catalyst for the Civil Rights Movement.

Pea Ridge National Military Park
Fast Facts
Established: 1956
Acreage: 4,300 (1,740 hectares)
Visitors (2019): 102,753
Nearest Major Airport: Bill and Hillary Clinton National Airport (LIT), Little Rock, AR
Nearest Major Highways: I-49, US-62
Fees: $0
Contact Information:
479-451-8122
www.nps.gov/peri

In the most pivotal Civil War battle west of the Mississippi River, victory by the Union here in 1862 allowed it to maintain control of the state of Missouri. The site remains one of the most intact Civil War battlefields in the country. Among the

Confederate ranks at Pea Ridge were about 1,000 Cherokee and Choctaw-Chickasaw troops.

President William Jefferson Clinton Birthplace Home National Historic Site
Fast Facts
Established: 2009
Acreage: 0.68 (0.28 hectares)
Visitors (2019): 8,758
Nearest Major Airport: Bill and Hillary Clinton National Airport (LIT), Little Rock, AR
Nearest Major Highways: I-30, US-67, US-278
Fees: $0
Contact Information:
870-777-4455
www.nps.gov/wicl

On August 19, 1946, Virginia Blythe gave birth to her son, William Jefferson Blythe III. Named for his father who died before he was born, he grew up to become the 42nd president of the United States. In this house, in a town called Hope, he learned many of the early lessons that defined his life and presidency.

Trail of Tears National Historic Trail
Fast Facts
Established: 1987
Length: 5,043 miles (8,069 km)
Visitors (2019): NA
Nearest Major Airport: NA
Nearest Major Highways: NA
Fees: $0
Contact Information:
870-777-4455
www.nps.gov/trte

Commemorates the forced removal of Cherokee people from their homelands; the paths that 17 detachments followed westward; and the enduring survival of the Cherokee Nation. The trail stretches across nine states (Alabama, Arkansas, Georgia, Illinois, Kentucky, Missouri, North Carolina, Oklahoma, and Tennessee). Together, the sites along these paths tell stories of suffering and intolerance, as well as survival, compassion, and understanding.

FLORIDA
Big Cypress National Preserve
Fast Facts
Established: 1974
Acreage: 720,564 (291,601 hectares)
Visitors (2019): 1,007,471
Visitor Centers: Big Cypress Swamp Welcome Center, Oasis, Nathaniel Reed.
Nearest Major Airport: Miami Intl. (MIA), Miami, FL
Nearest Major Highways: I-75, US-41, FL-29
Fees: $0
Contact Information:
239-695-2000
www.nps.gov/bicy

Protects the watershed for South Florida's threatened ecosystem. Subtropical plant and animal life abounds in a park that is home to endangered species like the Florida panther and the red-cockaded woodpecker.

Biscayne National Park
Fast Facts
Established: 1968/1980
Acreage: 172,971 (69,999 hectares)
Visitors (2019): 708,522
Nearest Major Airport: Miami Intl. (MIA), Miami, FL
Nearest Major Highways: US-1
Fees: $0
Accessibility: Most of the park is accessible only by boat.

Miles of undeveloped barrier island preserve the marsh and lagoon habitats for countless bird species at Canaveral National Seashore.

Contact Information:
305-230-1140
www.nps.gov/bisc

Subtropical islands form a north-south chain between Biscayne Bay and the Atlantic. The park protects the longest stretch of mangrove forest on Florida's east coast; the clear, shallow waters of Biscayne Bay; the northernmost Florida Keys; and 10,000 years of human history.

Canaveral National Seashore
Fast Facts
Established: 1975
Acreage: 57,662 (23,335 hectares)
Visitors (2019): 1,884,122
Nearest Major Airport: Orlando Intl. (MCO), Orlando, FL
Nearest Major Highways: I-95, FL-A1A
Fees: $20/vehicle; $15/motorcycle; $10/bicycle or pedestrian.
Accessibility: A beach wheelchair is available at Apollo Beach but not at Playalinda Beach.
Contact Information:
321-267-1110
www.nps.gov/cana

Twenty-five miles (40 km) of undeveloped barrier island preserve the natural beach, dune, marsh, and lagoon habitats for many species of birds. Because the Kennedy Space Center occupies the southern end of the island, some portions of the seashore are closed during spacecraft launch-related activities.

Castillo de San Marcos National Monument
Fast Facts
Established: 1924/1942
Acreage: 19 (8 hectares)
Visitors (2019): 673,395
Nearest Major Airport: Jacksonville Intl. (JAX), Jacksonville, FL
Nearest Major Highways: I-95, US-1, FL-A1A
Fees: $15/visitor age 16 or over. Children under 16 years old are free.
Accessibility: Mostly accessible except for pedestrian walkways within the moat. The gun deck can only be reached via stairs.

Contact Information:
904-829-6506
www.nps.gov/casa

Construction of the oldest masonry fort in the continental United States was started in 1672 by the Spanish to protect St. Augustine, the first permanent settlement by Europeans in the continental United States. The current floor plan is the result of modernization work done in the 1700s.

De Soto National Memorial
Fast Facts
Established: 1948
Acreage: 30 (12 hectares)
Visitors (2019): 187,880
Nearest Major Airport: Tampa Intl. (TPA), Tampa, FL
Nearest Major Highways: I-75
Fees: $0
Accessibility: Fully accessible.
Contact Information:
941-792-0458
www.nps.gov/deso

Commemorates the landing of Spanish explorer Hernando de Soto in Florida in 1539 and the first extensive organized exploration by Europeans of what is now the southern United States.

Dry Tortugas National Park
Fast Facts
Established:
Acreage: 64,701 (26,184 hectares) mostly in the Gulf of Mexico

Most of the appeal of Dry Tortugas National Park lies in the reefs and waters surrounding Fort Jefferson.

Visitors (2019): 79,200
Visitor Centers: Florida Keys Discovery Center, Garden Key
Nearest Major Airport: Miami Intl. (MIA), Miami, FL
Nearest Major Highways: US-1 in Key West, 70 miles (113 km) away by boat or seaplane.
Fees: $15/visitor age 16 or over. Children under 16 years old are free. Access to the park is only by boat. Visit www.drytortugas.com for information about ferry trips from Key West.
Accessibility: Call 1-800-634-0939 ahead of time to ensure ramps are at the ferry dock.
Contact Information:
305-242-7700
www.nps.gov/drto

Fort Jefferson, the largest all-masonry fortification in the Western world, was built here between 1846 and 1866 to help control the Florida Straits. The park is mostly water, with seven small islands that provide refuge to a vast assortment of birds. Coral reefs sustain a rich variety of marine life.

Everglades National Park
Fast Facts
Established: 1947
Acreage: 1,508,976 (610,661 hectares)
Visitors (2019): 1,118,300
Visitor Centers: Ernest Coe, Flamingo, Gulf Coast, Shark Valley
Nearest Major Airport: Miami Intl. (MIA), Miami, FL
Nearest Major Highways: US-1, US-41, FL-9336
Fees: $30/vehicle; $25/motorcycle; $15/pedestrian or cyclist.

Baby alligators face off in Everglades National Park.

Contact Information:
305-242-7700
www.nps.gov/ever

This largest remaining subtropical wilderness in the contiguous United States has extensive fresh water and salt water areas, open sawgrass prairies, and mangrove forests. Abundant wildlife includes rare and colorful birds.

Fort Caroline National Memorial
Fast Facts
Established: 1950
Acreage: 138 (56 hectares)
Visitors (2019): 187,658
Nearest Major Airport: Jacksonville Intl. (JAX), Jacksonville, FL
Nearest Major Highways: I-295, FL-A1A
Fees: $0
Accessibility: Most of the memorial is accessible; call ahead with questions about visiting the Theodore Roosevelt Area.
Contact Information:
904-641-7155
www.nps.gov/timu/learn/historyculture/foca.htm

Part of Timucuan Ecological and Historic Preserve, Fort Caroline memorializes the short French presence in 16th-century Florida, beginning two centuries of colonial rivalry with the Spanish in North America.

Fort Matanzas National Monument
Fast Facts
Established: 1924
Acreage: 300 (121 hectares)
Visitors (2019): 593,788
Nearest Major Airport: Jacksonville Intl. (JAX), Jacksonville, FL
Nearest Major Highways: I-295, FL-A1A
Fees: $0
Accessibility: Download the NPS Fort Matanzas National Monument App for the most up-to-date information on accessibility modifications to the 280-year-old fort.
Contact Information:
904-471-0116
www.nps.gov/foma

Preserves the watchtower built by Spanish settlers, 1740–42, to defend St. Augustine against approaches from the south.

Timucuan Ecological and Historic Preserve

Fast Facts

Established: 1988
Acreage: 46,263 (18,721 hectares)
Visitors (2019): 1,205,065
Visitor Center: Fort Caroline National Memorial serves as the Visitor Center.
Nearest Major Airport: Jacksonville Intl. (JAX), Jacksonville, FL
Nearest Major Highways: I-295, FL-A1A
Fees: $0
Accessibility: Most of the park is accessible; call ahead with questions about visiting Cedar Point or the Theodore Roosevelt Area of Fort Caroline National Memorial.
Contact Information:
904-641-7155
www.nps.gov/timu

Named for the native tribes who lived here for 4,000 years, the preserve encompasses Atlantic coastal marshes, islands, tidal creeks, and the estuaries of the St. Johns and Nassau rivers. Besides traces of indigenous life, remains of Spanish, French, and English colonial ventures can be found, as well as plantation life and military activities in the 1800s.

GEORGIA
Andersonville National Historic Site

Fast Facts

Established: 1970
Acreage: 515 (208 hectares)
Visitors (2019): 103,635
Nearest Major Airport: Hartsfield-Jackson Atlanta Intl. (ATL), Atlanta, GA
Nearest Major Highways: I-75, US-19
Fees: $0
Accessibility: Some portions of the historic prison are on uneven terrain.
Contact Information:
229-924-0343
www.nps.gov/ande

Protects the site of the Civil War prisoner-of-war camp used from 1864–1865. The site includes the National Prisoner of War Museum, which is dedicated to the stories of all American POWs, and Andersonville National Cemetery. The cemetery began as the burial grounds for almost 13,000 Union POWs but continues as an active national cemetery, with more than 21,000 military personnel and their dependents interred here.

Chickamauga and Chattanooga National Military Park

Fast Facts

Established: 1890
Acreage: 9,078 (3,674 hectares)
Visitors (2019): 977,158
Visitor Centers: Chickamauga Battlefield, Lookout Mountain Battlefield
Nearest Major Airport: Hartsfield-Jackson Atlanta Intl. (ATL), Atlanta, GA
Nearest Major Highways: I-24, US-11, US-41
Fees: $0. There is a $10 entrance fee to Point Park (Lookout Mountain Battlefield) for visitors ages 16 or older.
Accessibility: Varies by location. Visit www.nps.gov/chch/planyourvisit/physical-mobility.htm for specific information about each site within the park.
Contact Information:
706-866-9241
www.nps.gov/chch
(Also in Tennessee)

The nation's first military park commemorates

A monument to the 13th Michigan Infantry Regiment on the Chickamauga Battlefield.

what one Civil War soldier called "the death knell of the Confederacy." A Confederate victory on Chickamauga Creek, Georgia, September 18–20, 1863, was countered by Union victories at Orchard Knob, Lookout Mountain, and Missionary Ridge just across the state line in Chattanooga, Tennessee, November 23–25, 1863.

Cumberland Island National Seashore
Fast Facts
Established: 1972
Acreage: 36,347 (14,709 hectares)
Visitors (2019): 53,904
Visitor Centers: The Visitor Center and a museum are on the mainland at St. Mary's, GA. Ranger station at Sea Camp.
Nearest Major Airport: Jacksonville Intl. (JAX), Jacksonville, FL
Nearest Major Highways: I-95, GA-40
Fees: $10/adults ages 16 and over. Ferry (round trip) from St. Mary's: $30/adults ages 16–61, $28/seniors (ages 62 and older), $20/children ages 6-15. $20/bike. Georgia sales tax not included in ferry admission. Fees for campgrounds range from $9 (Hickory Hill and Brickhill Bluff) to $22 (Sea Camp).
Contact Information:
912-882-4335
www.nps.gov/cuis

Accessible only by a 45-minute tour boat ride from the mainland, the largest of Georgia's Golden Isles is comprised of magnificent and unspoiled beaches and dunes, marshes, and freshwater lakes, along with historic sites.

Fort Frederica National Monument
Fast Facts
Established: 1936
Acreage: 284 (115 hectares)
Visitors (2019): 212,330
Nearest Major Airport: Jacksonville Intl. (JAX), Jacksonville, FL
Nearest Major Highways: I-95, US-17
Fees: $0
Contact Information:
912-638-3639
www.nps.gov/fofr

Gen. James E. Oglethorpe built this British town and fort in 1736–48 during the Anglo-Spanish struggle for control of what is now the southeastern United States.

Fort Pulaski National Monument
Fast Facts
Established: 1924
Acreage: 5623 (2,276 hectares)
Visitors (2019): 374,290
Nearest Major Airport: Savannah/Hilton Head Intl. (SAV), Savannah, GA
Nearest Major Highways: I-16, US-80
Fees: $10/visitor age 16 or over. Children under 16 years old are free.
Accessibility: The lower level of the fort is accessible, as are the visitor center parking lot, restrooms, and exhibits.
Contact Information:
912-786-5787
www.nps.gov/fopu

Fort Pulaski took 18 years and 25 million bricks to build, but only 30 hours in 1862 to fall to bombardment by Union troops, armed with new experimental rifled cannons. The strategy of warfare and the role of fortifications were changed forever.

Jimmy Carter National Historic Site
Fast Facts
Established: 1987
Acreage: 72 (29 hectares)
Visitors (2019): 50,789

Carter family store, on display at the Jimmy Carter National Historic Site

Visitor Centers: Jimmy Carter Boyhood Farm, Plains Depot-1976 Presidential Campaign Headquarters, Plains High School (main visitor center and museum)
Nearest Major Airport: Hartsfield-Jackson Atlanta Intl. (ATL), Atlanta, GA
Nearest Major Highways: I-75, US-19, US-280
Fees: $0
Accessibility: Visit www.nps.gov/jica/planyourvisit/ accessibility.htm for detailed information about various accessibility issues in the site's three distinct units.
Contact Information:
229-824-4104
www.nps.gov/jica

The rural southern culture of Plains, Georgia, had a large influence in molding the character and in shaping the political policies of America's 39th president. The site includes President Carter's boyhood home, Plains High School (which serves as the park visitor center), and Plains Depot, which served as Carter's campaign headquarters during the 1976 election. The Carter home and compound are protected by the Secret Service, and closed to the public. No attempt should be made to enter.

Kennesaw Mountain National Battlefield Park

Fast Facts
Established: 1917/1935
Acreage: 2,824 (1,143 hectares)
Visitors (2019): 2,621,050
Nearest Major Airport: Hartsfield-Jackson Atlanta Intl. (ATL), Atlanta, GA
Nearest Major Highways: I-75, US-41, GA-120
Fees: $5/vehicle per day.
Accessibility: Some of the historic trails are inaccessible to wheelchairs.
Contact Information:
770-427-4686
www.nps.gov/kemo

Preserves 11 miles (17 km) of Union and Confederate earthworks. At the battles of Kolb's Farm (June 22, 1864) and Kennesaw Mountain (June 27, 1864), Confederate Gen. Joseph T. Johnston temporarily halted Gen. William Tecumseh Sherman's southward march to the sea.

A mural at the Martin Luther King Jr. National Historic Site

Martin Luther King Jr. National Historic Site

Fast Facts
Established: 1980
Acreage: 39 (16 hectares)
Visitors (2019): 761,650
Nearest Major Airport: Hartsfield-Jackson Atlanta Intl. (ATL), Atlanta, GA
Nearest Major Highways: I-75/85
Fees: $0
Accessibility: An elevator provides access to the second floor of Dr. King's birth home.
Contact Information:
404-331-5190
www.nps.gov/malu

Preserves the birthplace and gravesite of Martin Luther King Jr., as well as historic Ebenezer Baptist Church, where he and his father were co-pastors, 1960–68. Ebenezer's new Horizon Sanctuary, where religious services are held Sunday mornings and Wednesday evenings, welcomes all visitors. The park visitor center has exhibits and films on Dr. King. The surrounding preservation district includes Sweet Auburn, the economic and cultural center of Atlanta's Black community for most of the 20th century.

Ocmulgee Mounds National Monument

Fast Facts
Established: 1936
Acreage: 703 (284 hectares)

Visitors (2019): 146,925
Nearest Major Airport: Hartsfield-Jackson Atlanta Intl. (ATL), Atlanta, GA
Nearest Major Highways: I-16, US-23, US-80
Fees: $0
Accessibility: The entrance to the Earth Lodge is too narrow for wheelchairs. There are 80 steps to the top of the mounds.
Contact Information:
478-752-8257
www.nps.gov/ocmu

Preserves traces of 17,000 years of continuous human habitation in this part of North America. Indigenous people first came here during the Paleo-Indian period to hunt Ice Age mammals. The temple mounds date to the year 900, when the Mississippian people settled the area.

The Ocmulgee temple mounds date back to the year 900 CE.

LOUISIANA
Cane River Creole National Historical Park
Fast Facts
Established: 1994
Acreage: 205 (83 hectares)
Visitors (2019): 29,922
Visitor Centers: Oakland Plantation Store (main visitor center), Magnolia Plantation Store
Nearest Major Airport: George Bush Intercontinental (IAH), Houston, TX
Nearest Major Highways: I-49, LA-119, LA-494
Fees: $0
Accessibility: Limited access due to the historic nature of the buildings and terrain.

Contact Information:
318-352-0383
www.nps.gov/cari

This historical park is part of the 116,000-acre (46,944-hectare) Cane River National Heritage Area. It consists of Oakland Plantation and portions of Magnolia Plantation. Both demonstrate the history of colonization, frontier influences, Creole architecture and culture, cotton agriculture, slavery, and social practices over the course of 200 years.

Jean Lafitte National Historical Park and Preserve
Fast Facts
Established: 1907/1939/1978
Acreage: 22,420 (9,073 hectares)
Visitors (2019): 590,329
Visitor Centers: Acadian Cultural Center, Barataria Preserve, French Quarter, Prairie Acadian Cultural Center, Wetlands Acadian Cultural Center, Chalmette Battlefield and National Cemetery
Nearest Major Airport: Louis Armstrong New Orleans Intl. (MSY), Kenner, LA
Nearest Major Highways: I-10, US-90
Fees: $0
Accessibility: Fully accessible. Special programs are available by reservation only for visitors with hearing or sight impairments.
Contact Information:
504-589-3882
www.nps.gov/jela

An aggregation of six different sites, Lafitte National Historical Park and Preserve incorporates representative examples of southern Louisiana resources and culture. The Acadian Cultural Center in Lafayette, the Prairie Acadian Cultural Center in Eunice, and the Wetlands Acadian Cultural Center in Thibodaux interpret Cajun culture and history. The Barataria Preserve, south of New Orleans, offers trails and waterways through bottomland forests, swamp, and marsh. The Chalmette unit, east of New Orleans, was the site of the Battle of New Orleans during the War of 1812, and contains the Chalmette National Cemetery. The French Quarter unit interprets the diverse cultures of New Orleans.

Second Line parades are practically a feature of New Orleans Jazz National Historical Park.

New Orleans Jazz National Historical Park

Fast Facts

Established: 1994
Acreage: 5 (2 hectares)
Visitors (2019): 41,049
Nearest Major Airport: Louis Armstrong New Orleans Intl. (MSY), Kenner, LA
Nearest Major Highways: I-10, US-90
Fees: $0
Contact Information:
    504-589-4806
    www.nps.gov/jazz

Preserves and perpetuates knowledge and understanding of jazz from its origins in New Orleans through its continued evolution. The park provides education and interpretation with an emphasis on jazz performance and assists organizations involved with jazz and its history.

Poverty Point National Monument

Fast Facts

Established: NA
Acreage: 911 (369 hectares)
Visitors (2019): NA
Nearest Major Airport: Jackson-Medgar Wiley Evers Intl. (JAN), Jackson, MS
Nearest Major Highways: I-20, LA-17
Fees: $4/adults. $0/seniors and children age 12 and under.
Contact Information:
    318-926-5492
    www.nps.gov/popo

Commemorates a culture that thrived from 4,000 to 3,000 years ago. Also designated as a World Heritage Site, the monument has some of the largest prehistoric earthworks in North America. Poverty Point is managed by the state of Louisiana. State park facilities are open to the public, but there are no federal facilities.

MISSISSIPPI
Brices Cross Roads National Battlefield Site

Fast Facts

Established: 1929
Acreage: 1.0 (0.4 hectares)
Visitors (2019): NA
Visitor Center: No visitor facilities at Battlefield site. Parkway Visitor Center, at milepost 266 of the Natchez Trace Parkway, has information about the battlefield.
Nearest Major Airport: Memphis Intl. (MEM), Memphis, TN
Nearest Major Highways: I-22, US-45
Fees: $0
Contact Information:
    662-680-4025
    www.nps.gov/brcr

Despite a decisive tactical victory over a larger Union force on June 10, 1864, Maj. Gen. Nathan Bedford Forrest's Confederate troops ultimately failed to disrupt Union supply lines critical to Brig. Gen. William Tecumseh Sherman's Atlanta campaign. United States Colored Troops (USCT) played a crucial role in the battle.

Medgar & Myrlie Evers Home National Monument

Fast Facts

Established: 2020
Acreage: NA
Visitors (2019): NA
Nearest Major Airport: Jackson-Medgar Wiley Evers Intl. (JAN), Jackson, MS
Nearest Major Highways: I-20, I-55
Fees: $0
Contact Information:
    601-345-7211
    www.nps.gov/memy

Preserves the Jackson, Mississippi, home of civil rights leaders Myrlie and Medgar Evers, the latter of whom was assassinated in its carport on June 12, 1963. The assassination catalyzed the civil rights movement in the U.S. and led to the passage of the Civil Rights Act of 1964. Built in 1956, the home was designed without a front door with the hope that a side entrance through the carport would increase security.

Natchez National Historical Park
Fast Facts
Established: 1988
Acreage: 108 (44 hectares)
Visitors (2019): 182,123
Visitor Center: The Natchez Visitor Reception Center is also the southern terminus and welcome center for the Natchez Trace Parkway.
Nearest Major Airport: Jackson-Medgar Wiley Evers Intl. (JAN), Jackson, MS
Nearest Major Highways: US-64, US-81
Fees: $10/adults age 18 and older, $0 for all others. Entry fee includes a 30-minute ranger-led tour of the Melrose mansion.
Accessibility: The historic nature of the park makes some facilities inaccessible. Visit website for more information.
Contact Information:
601-446-5790
www.nps.gov/natc

Before the Civil War, Natchez was a commercial, cultural, and social center of the South's cotton belt. The city today represents one of the best-preserved concentrations of significant antebellum properties in the U.S. Within the park are Melrose, an excellent example of a planter's home, and the home of William Johnson, a prominent free Black man.

Natchez Trace National Scenic Trail
Fast Facts
Established: 1983
Acreage: 10,995 (4,450 hectares)
Visitors (2019): NA
Visitor Center: Parkway Visitor Center, milepost 266 of the Natchez Trace Parkway
Nearest Major Airport: Nashville Intl. (BNA), Nashville, TN; Jackson-Medgar Wiley Evers Intl. (JAN), Jackson, MS

Nearest Major Highways: I-20, I-40, I-55, I-840
Fees: $0
Accessibility: The multi-use trail in Ridgeland, Mississippi, and the Beech Springs Trail in Tupelo, Mississippi, are fully accessible. The others feature steep grades, varying terrain, and uneven surfaces.
Contact Information:
662-680-4025
www.nps.gov/natt
(Also in Tennessee)

This trail consists of five noncontiguous sections, each running alongside the Natchez Trace Parkway near Natchez, Port Gibson, Ridgeland, and Tupelo, Mississippi and in Leipers Fork, Tennessee. The trail provides visitors an opportunity to experience the unique cultural and natural aspects of the Natchez Trace.

Tupelo National Battlefield
Fast Facts
Established: 1929/1961
Acreage: 1 (0.4 hectares)
Visitors (2019): NA
Visitor Center: No visitor facilities at Battlefield site. Parkway Visitor Center, at milepost 266 of the Natchez Trace Parkway, has information about the battlefield.
Nearest Major Airport: Memphis Intl. (MEM), Memphis, TN
Nearest Major Highways: I-22, US-45
Fees: $0
Accessibility: A paved trail around the monument provides access.
Contact Information:
662-680-4025
www.nps.gov/tupe

Confederates under Maj. Gen. Nathan Bedford Forrest could not overpower Union forces in the Battle of Tupelo, July 13–14, 1864. Critical Union supply lines remained open to support Brig. Gen. William Tecumseh Sherman's Atlanta campaign.

Vicksburg National Military Park
Fast Facts
Established: 1899
Acreage: 1,802 (729 hectares). Cemetery acreage: 116 (47 hectares)

Visitors (2019): 576,456
Nearest Major Airport: Jackson-Medgar Wiley Evers Intl. (JAN), Jackson, MS
Nearest Major Highways: I-20, US-61
Fees: $20/vehicle; $15/motorcycle; $10 pedestrian or cyclist
Contact Information:
   601-636-0583
   www.nps.gov/vick
(Also in Louisiana)

Reconstructed forts and trenches evoke the 47-day siege that ended in the surrender of the city on July 4, 1863, giving the North control of the Mississippi River. The Civil War ironclad gunboat USS *Cairo* is on display. More than 17,000 soldiers, 13,000 of them unidentified, are buried at Vicksburg National Cemetery within the park.

NORTH CAROLINA
Blue Ridge Parkway

See full listing in The Capital Region on page 273.

Cape Hatteras National Seashore
Fast Facts
Established: 1953
Acreage: 30,351 (12,283 hectares)
Visitors (2019): 2,606,632
Visitor Centers: Bodie Island, Hatteras Island, Museum of the Sea, Ocracoke Island, Whalebone Junction
Nearest Major Airport: Norfolk Intl. (ORF), Norfolk, VA
Nearest Major Highways: US-64, NC-12
Fees: $0

The Blue Ridge Parkway curves around Grandfather Mountain in North Carolina.

Contact Information:
   252-473-2111
   www.nps.gov/caha

The nation's first national seashore is home to beaches, migratory waterfowl, fishing, surfing, and points of historical interest. Its lands include the 5,915-acre (2,394-hectare) Pea Island National Wildlife Refuge, administered by the U.S. Fish and Wildlife Service.

Cape Lookout National Seashore
Fast Facts
Established: 1966
Acreage: 28 243 (11,430 hectares)
Visitors (2019): 455,526
Visitor Centers: Beaufort, Harkers Island, Light Station, Portsmouth, Great Island Cabin Office. The Shell Point area of Harkers Island is the only part of the park accessible by vehicle. All other sections must be accessed by boat. Visit the website for a list of authorized ferry services.
Nearest Major Airport: Norfolk Intl. (ORF), Norfolk, VA
Nearest Major Highways: US-70
Fees: $0
Contact Information:
   252-728-2250
   www.nps.gov/calo

These undeveloped barrier islands extend 56 miles (90 km) along the lower Outer Banks embracing beaches, dunes, two historic villages, and Cape Lookout Lighthouse.

Carl Sandburg Home National Historic Site
Fast Facts
Established: 1972
Acreage: 264 (107 hectares)
Visitors (2019): 78,144
Nearest Major Airport: Charlotte Douglas Intl. (CLT), Charlotte, NC
Nearest Major Highways: I-26, US-25
Fees: $0. House tours: $10/adults age 16-61; $6/ seniors age 62 and over; free for children age 15 and under.
Accessibility: Uneven ground limits accessibility to trails. The third floor of the house is inaccessible to wheelchairs.

Connemara was the farm home of the noted poet, Lincoln biographer, and activist for the last 22 years of his life. The site includes four short walking trails.

Fort Raleigh National Historic Site
Fast Facts
Established: 1941
Acreage: 513 (208 hectares)
Visitors (2019): 248,139
Nearest Major Airport: Norfolk Intl. (ORF), Norfolk, VA
Nearest Major Highways: US-64, NC-12
Fees: $0
Contact Information:
252-473-5772
www.nps.gov/fora

Preserves Roanoke Island, where Sir Walter Raleigh led England's first attempt to colonize North America (1584–87). The fate of the so-called Lost Colony remains a mystery. The site also preserves the cultural heritage of the native people who preceded European arrivals.

Guilford Courthouse National Military Park
Fast Facts
Established: 1917
Acreage: 251 (102 hectares)
Visitors (2019): 223,900
Nearest Major Airport: Piedmont Triad Intl. (GSO), Greensboro, NC
Nearest Major Highways: I-40, I-73, US-220
Fees: $0
Accessibility: A tactile tabletop display with audio description is available to help the visually impaired understand what happened during the battle.
Contact Information:
336-288-1776
www.nps.gov/guco

The battle fought here on March 15, 1781, opened the campaign that led to American victory in the

Revolutionary War. The British lost a substantial number of troops at the battle, a factor in their surrender at Yorktown seven months later.

Moores Creek National Battlefield
Fast Facts
Established: 1926/1980
Acreage: 88 (36 hectares)
Visitors (2019): 77,006
Nearest Major Airport: Charlotte Douglas Intl. (CLT), Charlotte, NC
Nearest Major Highways: US-421
Fees: $0
Contact Information:
910-283-5591
www.nps.gov/mocr

Commemorates the February 27, 1776, battle between North Carolina Patriots and British Loyalists. It was the Patriots' first significant victory of the American Revolution.

Overmountain Victory National Historic Trail
Fast Facts
Established: 1980
Length: 330 miles (528 km)
Visitors: NA
Visitor Centers: The trail passes through North Carolina, South Carolina, Tennessee, and Virginia. The nearest visitor centers are Cowpens and Kings Mountain, both in South Carolina.
Nearest Major Airport: Charlotte Douglas Intl. (CLT), Charlotte, NC
Nearest Major Highways: US-19E, US-64, NC-268
Fees: $0
Contact Information:
864-461-2828
www.nps.gov/ovvi

Traces the route used by patriot militia during the pivotal Kings Mountain campaign of 1780. Visitors can follow the campaign by utilizing a Commemorative Motor Route, which uses existing state highways marked with the distinctive trail logo, or walk 87 miles (139 km) of trails.

Wright Brothers National Memorial commemorates the first airplane flight in 1903.

Wright Brothers National Memorial
Fast Facts
Established: 1927/1953
Acreage: 428 (173 hectares)
Visitors (2019): 400,135
Nearest Major Airport: Norfolk Intl. (ORF), Norfolk, VA
Nearest Major Highways: US-64, US-158, NC-12
Fees: $10/visitors age 16 or older; free for all others.
Contact Information:
  252-441-7430
  www.nps.gov/wrbr

Preserves the site where Wilbur and Orville Wright achieved the first successful airplane flight on December 17, 1903.

SOUTH CAROLINA
Charles Pinckney National Historic Site
Fast Facts
Established: 1988
Acreage: 28 (11 hectares)
Visitors (2019): 35,495
Nearest Major Airport: Charleston Intl. (CHS), Charleston, SC
Nearest Major Highways: I-526, US-17
Fees: $0
Contact Information:
  843-883-3123
  www.nps.gov/chpi

Commemorates Charles Pinckney's contribution as a principal author and signer of the U.S. Constitution. The site preserves a portion of Pinckney's coastal plantation to tell the story of the four-term governor and "forgotten founder," and of how enslaved African Americans influenced Pinckney, himself a slaveholder.

Congaree National Park
Fast Facts
Established: 1976/2003
Acreage: 26,276 (10,634 hectares)
Visitors (2019): 159,445
Nearest Major Airport: Charleston Intl. (CHS), Charleston, SC
Nearest Major Highways: I-26, US-21, SC-768
Fees: $0
Accessibility: There are no roads in the park, so all activities require walking uneven terrain. Only the area around the Harry Hampton Visitor Center is accessible to all visitors.
Contact Information:
  803-776-4396
  www.nps.gov/cong

Protects the last significant tract of southern bottomland hardwood forest in the U.S. It is home to a rich diversity of plant and animal species associated with an alluvial floodplain. Several national- and state-record trees are in the park.

Cowpens National Battlefield
Fast Facts
Established: 1929/1972
Acreage: 842 (341 hectares)
Visitors (2019): 223,413
Nearest Major Airport: Charlotte Douglas Intl. (CLT), Charlotte, NC
Nearest Major Highways: I-85, US-221
Fees: $0
Contact Information:
  864-461-2828
  www.nps.gov/cowp

Commemorates the site where Brig. Gen. Daniel Morgan won a decisive Revolutionary War victory here over British Lt. Col. Banastre Tarleton on January 17, 1781.

Fort Sumter is accessible only by ferry.

Fort Sumter and Fort Moultrie National Historical Park
Fast Facts
Established: 1948/2019
Acreage: 235 (95 hectares)
Visitors (2019): 877,894
Visitor Center: Fort Sumter is accessible only by boat. The Fort Sumter Visitor Education Center is on the mainland in Charleston. Fort Moultrie Visitor Center is accessible by car.
Nearest Major Airport: Charleston Intl. (CHS), Charleston, SC
Nearest Major Highways: I-26, US-17
Fees: Ferries ($30/adults; $28/seniors; $18/children ages 4–11) leave from Fort Sumter Visitor Education Center in Charleston or from Patriots Point in Mt. Pleasant. Visit www.fortsumtertours.com for schedule. Admission to Fort Moultrie is $10/adult; free for all others.
Accessibility: Fort Sumter is inaccessible to visitors in wheelchairs. Fort Moultrie is largely accessible.
Contact Information:
143-883-3123
www.nps.gov/fosu

The first military engagement of the Civil War took place here on April 12, 1861. The park also includes Fort Moultrie, scene of the patriot victory of June 28, 1776—one of the early defeats of the British in the American Revolution. Together, the two forts reflect 171 years of seacoast defense.

Kings Mountain National Military Park
Fast Facts
Established: 1931
Acreage: 3,945 (1,596 hectares)
Visitors (2019): 262,031
Nearest Major Airport: Charlotte Douglas Intl. (CLT), Charlotte, NC
Nearest Major Highways: I-85, US-29, SC-216
Fees: $0
Contact Information:
864-936-7921
www.nps.gov/kimo

American frontiersmen defeated the British here on October 7, 1780, at a critical point during the American Revolution.

Ninety Six National Historic Site
Fast Facts
Established: 1976
Acreage: 1,022 (413 hectares)
Visitors (2019): 97,295
Nearest Major Airport: Charlotte Douglas Intl. (CLT), Charlotte, NC
Nearest Major Highways: I-26, US-178, SC-248
Fees: $0
Contact Information:
864-543-4068
www.nps.gov/nisi

Named for the distance (in miles) Charleston traders thought it was from the Cherokee village of Keowee during the 1700s, Ninety Six Historical Site is an area of both historical and archaeological importance. Europeans who settled here in the 1700s built Fort Ninety Six as a defense against Cherokee attempts to reclaim their land. In 1781, Maj. Gen. Nathanael Greene's patriot troops staged the longest field siege of the Revolutionary War against 550 loyalists who had occupied the strategically located fortress. The site also contains the remains of two historic villages and a colonial plantation complex.

Reconstruction Era National Historical Park
Fast Facts
Established: 2017/2019
Acreage: 65 (26 hectares)

Visitors (2019): NA
Visitor Center: There are currently no visitor services at the park.
Nearest Major Airport: Savannah/Hilton Head Intl. (SAV), Savannah, GA
Nearest Major Highways: I-95, US-21
Fees: $0
Contact Information:
 (843) 962-0039
 www.nps.gov/reer

Tells the story of Reconstruction (1861–1900), when the U.S. struggled with questions of how to integrate millions of formerly enslaved Americans into existing political, social and economic systems. Includes the Brick Baptist Church, Darrah Hall, Camp Saxton, and the Old Beaufort Firehouse.

TENNESSEE
Andrew Johnson National Historic Site
Fast Facts
Established: 1935/1963
Acreage: 17 (7 hectares)
Visitors (2019): 51,189
Nearest Major Airport: Charlotte Douglas Intl. (CLT), Charlotte, NC
Nearest Major Highways: I-81, US-321
Fees: $0
Contact Information:
 423-639-3711
 www.nps.gov/anjo

Includes two homes, a tailor shop, and the burial place of the 17th president.

Big South Fork National River and Recreation Area
Fast Facts
Established: 1974/1991
Acreage: 123,679 (50,051 hectares)
Visitors (2019): 750,494
Visitor Centers: Bandy Creek, Crossville, Helenwood, Rugby, Stearns Visitor Contact Station
Nearest Major Airport: Nashville Intl. (BNA), Nashville, TN
Nearest Major Highways: US-27, TN-52, TN-297
Fees: $0

Contact Information:
 423-569-9778
 www.nps.gov/biso
(Also in Kentucky)

Protects the free-flowing Big South Fork of the Cumberland River from Yahoo Falls, in Kentucky, to Rugby, Tennessee. This was the first park designated as both a national river and a national recreation area.

Fort Donelson National Battlefield
Fast Facts
Established: 1928
Acreage: 1,309 (530 hectares). Cemetery acreage: 15 (6 hectares)
Visitors (2019): 254,431
Visitor Center: The Visitor Center and the National Cemetery are in the Tennessee portion of the park. A separate section sits across the Cumberland River in Kentucky.
Nearest Major Airport: Nashville Intl. (BNA), Nashville, TN
Nearest Major Highways: I-24, US-79, TN-49
Fees: $0
Contact Information:
 931-232-5706
 www.nps.gov/fodo
(Also in Kentucky)

Union Gen. Ulysses S. Grant captured three forts, opened two rivers, and received national recognition for his Civil War victories here in February 1862. The National Cemetery, on the Tennessee side, is the burial site of 670 Union dead.

Manhattan Project National Historical Park
Fast Facts
Established: 2015
Acreage: Not yet established
Visitors (2019): 30,123
Visitor Center: The Oak Ridge unit visitor center is located within the Children's Museum of Oak Ridge
Nearest Major Airport: Nashville Intl. (BNA), Nashville, TN
Nearest Major Highways: I-40, TN-62
Fees: $0.

Accessibility: The Visitor Center is accessible. Guided tours of sites can be accessible to wheelchairs with two days' advance notice.

Contact Information:
865-482-1942
www.nps.gov/mapr
(Also in New Mexico and Washington)

The Oak Ridge unit of this tripartite park commemorates the contributions of thousands of workers who played a part in the top-secret atomic weapons program starting in 1942. Oak Ridge was home to several massive facilities enriching uranium for use in the world's first atomic bomb. Several highly-secured nuclear research facilities still exist in the community and the city is home to a wealth of historic sites.

Obed Wild and Scenic River
Fast Facts
Established: 1976
Acreage: 5,073 (2,053 hectares)

Visitors (2019): 221,301
Nearest Major Airport: Nashville Intl. (BNA), Nashville, TN
Nearest Major Highways: I-40, TN-62
Fees: $0
Contact Information:
423-346-6294
www.nps.gov/obed

Protects 45 miles (72 km) of free-flowing streams, varied wildlife and plant resources, and the rugged character of this area on the Cumberland Plateau. The river was designated for outstandingly remarkable aesthetics, wildlife, fish, and recreational, cultural, ecological, geological, and aquatic values.

Shiloh National Military Park
Fast Facts
Established: 1894
Acreage: 6,720 (2,719 hectares). Cemetery acreage: 10 (4 hectares)
Visitors (2019): 360,989

The Obed Wild and Scenic River

Visitor Center: Shiloh Battlefield. The Corinth Civil War Interpretive Center is located at the separate Corinth, Mississippi, section of the park.
Nearest Major Airport: Memphis Intl. (MEM), Memphis, TN
Nearest Major Highways: I-40, US-64, TN-128
Fees: $0
Contact Information:
  731-689-5275
  www.nps.gov/shil
(Also in Mississippi)

Preserves the location of the first major battle in the Western theater of the Civil War on April 6–7, 1862. Nearly 110,000 troops clashed in a bloody contest that resulted in more casualties (23,476) than in all of America's previous wars combined. The decisive victory enabled Union forces to seize control of the strategic Confederate railway junction at Corinth, Mississippi, on May 30, 1862.

Stones River National Battlefield
Fast Facts
Established: 1933/1960
Acreage: 709 (287 hectares). Cemetery acreage: 20 (8 hectares)
Visitors (2019): 284,516
Nearest Major Airport: Nashville Intl. (BNA), Nashville, TN
Nearest Major Highways: I-24, I-840, US-41
Fees: $0
Contact Information:
  615-893-9501
  www.nps.gov/stri

Preserves the location of a fierce midwinter battle, December 31, 1862 to January 2, 1863. Confederate forces withdrew after the battle and ceded middle Tennessee to Union control. Stones River National Cemetery—6,850 interments, 2,562 unidentified—is within the park.

WEST VIRGINIA
Bluestone National Scenic River
Fast Facts
Established: 1988
Acreage: 4310 (1,744 hectares)
Visitors (2019): 37,663

Visitor Center: No federal facilities. The nearest visitor center is Sandstone in New River Gorge National Park and Preserve.
Nearest Major Airport: Richmond Intl. (RIC), Richmond, VA
Nearest Major Highways: I-77, WV-3
Fees: $0
Contact Information:
  304-465-0508
  www.nps.gov/blue

Preserves the remarkable scenery, wildlife, and other natural and historic features of the Appalachian plateau. In its 10 miles (16 km), the lower Bluestone River offers fishing, hiking, boating, and scenery.

Gauley River National Recreation Area
Fast Facts
Established: 1988
Acreage: 11,606 (4,697 hectares)
Visitors (2019): 119,282
Visitor Center: Limited federal facilities. The nearest Visitor Center is at Canyon Rim in New River Gorge National Park and Preserve.
Nearest Major Airport: Richmond Intl. (RIC), Richmond, VA
Nearest Major Highways: I-64/77, US-19, WV-129
Fees: $0
Contact Information:
  304-465-0508
  www.nps.gov/gari

The 25 miles (41 km) of free-flowing Gauley River and the 6 miles (10 km) of the Meadow River pass through scenic gorges and valleys containing a wide variety of natural and cultural features. The Gauley River contains several Class V+ rapids, making it one of the most adventurous whitewater boating rivers in the eastern U.S. Both rivers also provide excellent fishing opportunities.

Harpers Ferry National Historical Park
Fast Facts
Established: 1944/1963
Acreage: 3,669 (1,485 hectares)
Visitors (2019): 299,577
Visitor Center: Harpers Ferry, Lower Town Information Center

Historic buildings and shops line High Street in Harpers Ferry National Historical Park.

Nearest Major Airport: Washington Dulles Intl. (IAD), Dulles, VA

Nearest Major Highways: US-340, WV-230

Fees: $20/vehicle, $15/motorcycle, $10/pedestrian or cyclist. Entry fees are valid for three consecutive days.

Accessibility: Some historic sites may not be completely wheelchair-accessible.

Contact Information:
304-535-6029
www.nps.gov/hafe
(Also in Maryland and Virginia)

The town of Harpers Ferry witnessed the arrival of the first successful American railroad, the first successful application of interchangeable parts, John Brown's attack on slavery, the largest surrender of federal troops during the Civil War, education of formerly enslaved Americans, and the beginning of the modern civil rights movement.

New River Gorge National Park and Preserve

Fast Facts

Established: 1978

Acreage: 72 (29 hectares)

Visitors (2019): 1,195,721

Visitor Center: Canyon Rim, Grandview, Sandstone, Thurmond Depot

Nearest Major Airport: Richmond Intl. (RIC), Richmond, VA

Nearest Major Highways: I-64, US-19, WV-7, WV-20

Fees: $0

Accessibility: All four visitor centers are wheelchair-accessible. Canyon Rim and Sandstone have accessible trails.

Contact Information:
304-465-0508
www.nps.gov/neri

A rugged, whitewater river flowing northward through deep canyons, the New River is, ironically, among the oldest rivers on the continent. The free-flowing, 53-mile (85-km) section from Hinton to Hawks Nest State Park is abundant in natural, scenic, historic, and recreational features.

THE NORTHEAST

Acadia National Park

Acadia is the only National Park in the northeastern United States, tucked away on the Maine coast about halfway between New Hampshire and the Canadian border, far from the teeming metropolises of New York and Boston. The Park occupies much of **Mt. Desert Island** as well as smaller portions of nearby **Isle Au Haut** and the **Schoodic Peninsula**.

On Mt. Desert Island, land and water don't so much meet as establish an uneasy truce. That makes for hundreds of uncrowded coves, harbors, rocky coasts, lagoons, and simple undiscovered places that nobody has bothered to name because there are so many of them. From one of these inlets, it's easier to fathom how Maine has more miles of jagged coastline than California.

The tranquil, deep waters of **Somes Sound** divide the eastern and western halves of Mount Desert Island. Local lore claims Somes Sound is the only fjord in North America, but geologists say it's more like a fjard, lacking the anoxic sediments of a true fjord. Either way, it's a transfixing sight from either half of the island. Most of Acadia's attractions are concentrated on the northeastern half, close to **Bar Harbor**, the charming gateway town just outside the main entrance. That makes for even more remote solitude on the southwestern lobe.

The main (pardon the pun) attractions at Acadia are the 45 miles (72 km) of rustic **carriage roads**, built between 1913 and 1940 by John D. Rockefeller Jr. on his 11,000 acres (4,451 hectares) of land. He connected the trails with 16 magnificent **hand-cut stone bridges** spanning streams, waterfalls, roads, and cliff sides. Then he gave the land to the government, which in 1919 made it the first National Park east of the Mississippi River. The carriage roads are closed to motorized vehicles, making them oases for walking, **horseback riding, bicycling,** or **cross-country skiing** and **snowshoeing** in winter. The 6-mile (10-km) loop around **Eagle Lake** is one of the most popular circuits, as is the 8.6-mile (13.8-km) **Jordan Pond Loop**. The two circles meet at **Bubble Pond Bridge**, making it possible to connect the two for a longer outing.

Cadillac Mountain is where mornings begin at Acadia (and

Fast Facts

Established: 1916/1919
Acreage: 48,996 (19,828 hectares)
Visitors (2019): 3,437,286
Visitor Centers: Hulls Cove, Rockefeller Welcome Center, Schoodic Woods Campground Ranger Station, Sieur de Monts Nature Center, Thompson Island Information Center, Village Green Information Center.
Nearest Major Airport: Portland Intl. (PWM), Portland, ME; Boston Logan Intl. (BOS), Boston, MA
Nearest Major Highways: ME-3, US-1, US-1A,
Fees: $30/car; $15/individual
Accessibility: Two carriage roads and parts of four walking trails are accessible. Visit www.nps.gov/acad/planyourvisit/upload/AccessibilityGuide.pdf for a complete list of Acadia's accessible areas and other information for the disabled.
Contact Information: 207-288-3338 www.nps.gov/acad

Thousands of coves and inlets make Maine's coastline longer than California's.

The 45 miles (72 km) of carriage roads are among Acadia's most popular attractions.

everywhere else in the U.S. between October and March) because its summit is the first place in the country to see the **sunrise**. Each day, hundreds of visitors wake before dawn and drive the 3.5 miles (5.6 km) from the main park road to the 1,530-ft (466-m) peak. Advance reservations are required for vehicles from May 26 to October 19. The hour before sunrise is the busiest time to head for the mountaintop, but the views are stunning all day. Several hiking trails lead to the summit, including the **Cadillac North Ridge Trail** (4.4 miles/7.1 km round-trip) and the **Cadillac South Ridge Trail** (7.1 miles/ 11.4 km round-trip).

Acadia abounds with flatter options for hiking, walking, and birdwatching. And unlike the trails in most National Parks, many are open to **leashed dogs**. The 3.4-mile (5.5 km) **Jordan Pond Loop Trail** hugs the lakeshore more closely than the carriage road of the same name. It's immensely popular, especially during fall foliage season, in large part because it begins and ends at the Jordan Pond House, the only

Sixteen hand-cut stone bridges link Acadia's carriage roads.

221

From October to March, Cadillac Mountain is the first place in the U.S. to see the sunrise.

full-service restaurant in the park. Stopping in for a pre- or post-hike snack of **tea and popovers** has been a tradition at Jordan Pond House since the 19th century.

At low tide, a half-mile-long (1-km) gravel sand bar links Mt. Desert Island to 2 miles (3 km) of trails that poke around neighboring **Bar Island**, offering unexpected views of Bar Harbor and **Frenchman Bay**. **Ocean Path** traces Acadia's rocky southeastern shore for 2.2 miles (3.5 km) from **Otter Point** past **Thunder Hole** (so named for the sound produced when waves crash into the a sea cave) to the more prosaically named **Sand Beach**, the park's only sandy ocean beach. The frigid ocean temperatures seldom climb above 60°F (16°C), but that doesn't

deter the hardy from dipping a toe, or even their entire bodies into the chilly surf. There are even lifeguards here. The only other spots for swimming (both with equally brisk waters) are at

Echo Lake Beach and the pond at **Lake Wood**.

Canoeing and kayaking offer visitors a way to test the waters at Acadia without risking hypothermia. Outfitters in Bar

Jordan Pond House is the only restaurant in Acadia National Park.

Acadia is one of the most dog-friendly National Parks.

Harbor and Southwest Harbor rent both kayaks and canoes and can offer advice on guided tours or self-guided itineraries ranging from a half-day paddle on poky **Northeast Creek** to a week-long camping circuit of Mt. Desert Island. Keep an eye out for **river otters, whitetail deer, loons, great blue herons,** and **eagles.**

Almost all of Acadia is prime birding territory. The park is home to 308 different avian species, including 20 different kinds of warblers. Famed ornithologist Roger Tory Peterson once dubbed Mt. Desert Island the "warbler capital of the world." The carriage roads, **Otter Point**, **Jordan Pond**, and Cadillac Mountain are all excellent, albeit crowded, birdwatching sites. For a more secluded experience, head to **Wonderland** (on the southwestern half of the island), **Thomson Island** (underneath the road bridge to the mainland), or the **Schoodic Peninsula** on the other side of **Eastern Bay**.

No visit to Maine is complete without a lobster lunch or dinner, and there may be no better place to do it than on Mt. Desert Island. Seafood restaurants here offer views not only of the National Park, but also the very waters where the crustaceans were caught, sometimes earlier that morning. For the complete Maine experience, order the "meal deal" (a variation on what is also known as the Shore Dinner) if it's on the menu. It usually includes a cup of New England clam chowder, whole lobster with corn on the cob and new potatoes, and finished with Maine blueberry pie.

Autumn in Acadia

Boston National Historical Park

Fast Facts

Established: 1974
Acreage: 44 (18 hectares)
Visitors (2019): 3,201,834
Visitor Centers: Faneuil Hall, Charlestown Navy Yard
Nearest Major Airport: Boston Logan Intl. (BOS), Boston, MA
Nearest Major Highways: I-90, I-93
Fees: $0 at federal, state, or local historic sites.
Old South Meeting House: $6/adult, $5/seniors and college students, $1/children aged 5–17. Old State House: $12/adult, $10/seniors and college students, free for children aged 18 and under. Paul Revere House: $6/adults, $5.50/seniors and college students, $1/children aged 5–17. Old North Church: $8/adults, $6 seniors and college students, $4 children 6–17.
Accessibility: Varies by location. Visit www.nps.gov/bost/planyourvisit/accessibility.htm for information about each site.
Contact Information:
617-242-5601
www.nps.gov/bost

The American Revolution comes to life in the streets of the city known as the "cradle of liberty." Boston National Historical Park largely overlaps the **Freedom Trail**, a 2.5-mile (4-km) route that connects 16 key sites from the Revolutionary War. But it also includes sites beyond the trail that complete the picture of 18th-century life in Massachusetts.

Walking the Freedom Trail is a terrific introduction to not only the colonial town of Boston, but also the 21st-century version, a modern metropolis where 400 years of history are merely the backdrop. It's also a whole lot more enjoyable than driving the traffic-clogged, narrow, one-way streets. As with every other National Park, getting out of the car opens worlds you could never see from behind the wheel.

National Park Service rangers lead a variety of **themed tours and talks** at different locations throughout the Park. "**Meetings, Mobs & Martyrs**" hits the highlights, including Faneuil Hall, The Old State House, the Boston Massacre Site, and Old South Meeting House. "**Enemies to this Country**" looks at the events of the revolution in a somewhat different light. Rangers dressed in period costumes give a detailed history of the Battle of Bunker Hill in

Walking the Freedom Trail is a terrific introduction to both the colonial town of Boston and the 21st-century city.

The Freedom Trail follows the red brick road in the sidewalk.

"**Muskets, Men, and Liberty**." You can also witness re-created town meetings where period dress characters debate the Boston Massacre ("**Vengeance or Justice?**"), abolition ("**Rocking the Cradle**"), or women's suffrage ("**The Woman's Tea Party**").

The Freedom Trail Foundation, the nonprofit organization charged with preserving the trail, also leads guided tours that depart from the **Freedom Trail Visitor Information Booth** on Tremont Street. Opt for the standard "**Walk Into History**," or choose from a range of themed tours, including ones focused on **Revolutionary Women**, **African American Patriots**, or **Pirates**. Reserve ahead of time for the private **Historic Pub Crawl** (minimum 6 people).

To walk the trail without a guide, just follow the red bricks (or painted lines) in the sidewalk. **Boston Common** is America's oldest public park, dating back to 1634. Its 44 acres (18 hectares) of green space are an oasis of calm in downtown Boston. The Common's lush lawns are as pleasant a place for a picnic today as they were 350 years ago.

Up the hill is the gold-domed **Massachusetts State House**. Built by architect Charles Bulfinch in 1789 on the former site of the Hancock family mansion—Samuel Adams laid the cornerstone—it's sometimes called the "new" state house to avoid confusion with the Old State House, erected 85 years

The Declaration of Independence was first read aloud in front of the Old State House in 1776.

earlier. The Massachusetts Legislature still meets here.

Park Street Church, at the corner of Tremont Street, became known as "Brimstone Corner" during the War of 1812, when it was used to store gunpowder. The nickname later took on a more metaphorical meaning after abolitionist William Lloyd Garrison delivered his first anti-slavery speech here in 1829.

Next door is the **Granary Burying Ground**, the first (and best) of the urban cemeteries on the trail. Built in 1660, it got its name for the adjacent grain storage facility that was once next door. The roster of people buried here reads like a Who's Who of American history. Paul Revere, Samuel Adams, Peter Faneuil, John Hancock, and the Boston Massacre victims are among the colonial-era Americans commemorated with gravestones here. The oversized obelisk in the center marks the burial plot of Ben Franklin's parents. The bodies aren't actually buried beneath the headstones that bear their names—the stones have been rearranged since their burials into neat, orderly rows to accommodate lawn mowers.

King's Chapel was the first Anglican church in New England (1686) and still houses the oldest American pulpit still in existence; the bell was recast by Paul Revere in 1816 and still rings today. The adjacent **King's Chapel Burying Ground** predates the church by 66 years; it's home to the gravesite of John Winthrop, Massachusetts' first governor.

School Street gets its name from **Boston Latin School**, founded on this site in 1635. A statue of Benjamin Franklin, the school's most famous dropout (at age 9) marks the spot where the institution once stood (it

Samuel Adams, John Hancock, and the Boston Massacre victims are among thousands commemorated with gravestones at Old Granary Burying Ground.

moved to its current location near the Museum of Fine Arts in 1922). Other famous alumni include founding fathers Samuel Adams and John Hancock, as well as more recent graduates like poet Ralph Waldo Emerson, conductor Leonard Bernstein, and media magnate Sumner Redstone.

At the end of School Street is the site of the **Old Corner Book Store**. All of literary Boston once flocked here for the latest works by Hawthorne, Thoreau, and Julia Ward Howe. The building was saved from demolition in 1960, and today, lines snake out the door for the latest works by the employees at Chipotle.

The **Old South Meeting House** is best known for the December 16, 1773, assembly that began the Boston Tea Party. An admission fee is required to tour the inside of the building. A ring of stones in front of the **Old State House** marks the site of the 1770 Boston Massacre, where British soldiers killed Crispus Attucks and four other colonists. The building dates back to 1713; the Declaration of Independence was first read aloud here in 1776, and is recited again every July 4th.

Faneuil Hall is where colonists first openly protested the Sugar Act and Stamp Act in 1764. Today, it's the centerpiece of the Faneuil Hall Marketplace, a shopping and dining complex that incorporates the adjacent **Quincy Market**.

The Trail heads into the **North End**, a historically Italian-American neighborhood with pizzerias and other restaurants lining **Hanover St.**, the main drag. The **Paul Revere House** is a highlight of the trail, and the $6 admission ($5.50 for seniors and college students, $1 for kids 5–17) is worth it, if even just for the air conditioning on hot days.

Revere's famous midnight ride began April 18, 1775, at **Old North Church**, where the two lanterns that shone here signaled that the British were coming by sea. Few recognizable names are interred at **Copp's Hill Burying Ground**, but its view of **Boston Harbor** makes it worth a stop.

It's nearly a 1-mile (1.45 km) walk across the Charlestown Bridge to the last two stops, a distance that persuades many

Quincy Market at Faneuil Hall Marketplace

Old North Church (in background) was the departure point for Paul Revere's famous ride.

The USS Constitution, *a.k.a. Old Ironsides*

visitors to retrace their steps to Hanover St. for a gelato or a glass of chianti. Launched in 1797, the **USS *Constitution*** earned its nickname, "Old Ironsides," not during the Revolution but during the War of 1812, when British cannonballs bounced off the ship's oak hull. The U.S. Navy administers this site, while the National Park Service oversees the adjacent **USS *Cassin Young***, a World War II-era destroyer. The *Cassin Young* wasn't constructed in Boston, but dozens of similar vessels were built, repaired, modernized, and resupplied at the **Charlestown Navy Yard** between 1800 and 1974. The efforts of the men and women who worked at

Col. William Prescott guards the entrance to the Bunker Hill Monument.

the Navy Yard were key to America's victory in World War II. Admission to the Navy Yard, now a museum, is free.

The final stop, the **Bunker Hill Monument**, commemorates the first battle of the Revolution (at nearby Breed's Hill). It's 294 steps to the top of the obelisk, built in 1842. To avoid the long walk back to downtown Boston, take a **water taxi** from the **Charlestown Navy Yard** (behind the USS *Constitution* Museum). On a clear day, the views from the water are well worth the $3.70 starting ticket price ($1.85 for seniors, free for kids under 12).

Boston National Historical Park also includes the **Boston African American National Historic Site**. The **Black Heritage Trail** links 10 of the attractions by a separate 1.6-mile (3-km) walking tour. **The Massachusetts 54th Regiment Memorial** commemorates one of the first Black regiments to serve in the Civil War. Their exploits were the basis for the 1989 film *Glory*, starring Denzel Washington and Matthew Broderick.

The Massachusetts 54th Regiment Memorial, near the state capitol building, honors the Union Army's pioneering Black regiments.

Cape Cod National Seashore

Nearly all of Cape Cod's Atlantic Ocean beaches, as well as a few on the bay side, are encompassed within the Cape Cod National Seashore. Its 40 miles (64 km) of pristine sands begin at Nauset Beach Dunes south of Chatham and extend all the way around the tip of Provincetown, at the Cape's far end.

Between May and October, the main attraction is, of course, **the beach** itself. Cape Cod is where many New Englanders go to escape the heat, often returning to the same homes, hotels, cottages, or cabins year after year. In addition to the six National Park Service beaches detailed below, several towns up and down the cape operate their own town beaches.

Coast Guard Beach in Eastham is usually one of the most popular strands—so popular, in fact, that parking is restricted to Eastham residents and vehicles with handicap placards. All other visitors arriving in vehicles must decamp at Little Creek parking lot and take a shuttle bus to the beach. Coast Guard Beach is where *Mayflower* captain Christopher Jones Jr. first spotted the New World coast in November 1620. But strong winds and rough shoals deterred him from making landfall here; a change in the wind allowed the captain to reach Provincetown Harbor safely two days later.

For a beach so popular with humans, there's a surprising

Fast Facts

Established: 1966
Acreage: 43,607 (17,647 hectares)
Visitors (2019): 4,096,104
Visitor Centers: Salt Pond (Eastham), Province Lands (Provincetown)
Nearest Major Airport: Boston Logan Intl. (BOS), Boston, MA
Nearest Major Highways: US-6, I-195, I-495
Fees: $25/vehicle or $15/ pedestrian or cyclist per day at six national seashore beaches between May and September: Coast Guard and Nauset Light in Eastham, Marconi in Wellfleet, Head of the Meadow in Truro, and Race Point and Herring Cove in Provincetown.
Accessibility: Visit www.nps .gov/caco/planyourvisit /accessibility.htm for detailed information about accessible areas.
Contact Information: 508-771-2144 www.nps.gov/caco

Sandy Point

Shorebirds are a common sight on all Cape Cod beaches.

amount of **wildlife** here. Shorebirds work the tidal flats of nearby Nauset marsh, plovers and terns dodge waves in spring, and harbor seals by the dozen relax on sandbars. Keep at least 150 feet (46 m) away from seals, and a safe distance from endangered plovers.

Nauset Light beach, just a mile north, is more dramatic, with cliffs nearly 100 feet (30 m) high towering over the broad, sandy beach. It's popular not only with beachgoers, but also lighthouse lovers. **Nauset Lighthouse** is the one that gives the beach its name; the trio of towers farther inland are known as the **Three Sisters** because from the sea, they looked like women in white dresses with black hats.

On January 18, 1903, Guglielmo Marconi successfully transmitted the first two-way transatlantic radio communication from the bluffs

Three Sisters Lighthouse

high above what is now known as **Marconi Beach.** Today, the area is popular for its unspoiled view of ocean to the east and dunes to the east.

The three northernmost beaches—Head of the Meadow in Truro, and Race Point and Herring Cove in

Provincetown—are too far from Boston for all but the most dedicated day-trippers. As a result, they have a more wild feeling about them. **Herring Cove**, on the western-facing bay side of the Cape, is one of the best places to catch the sunset. Parents of young children like

231

Marconi Beach, named for radio pioneer Guglielmo Marconi

it because it lacks the pounding waves of many Atlantic beaches. **Head of the Meadow** and **Race Point** both welcome cyclists with miles of paved **bike paths** over and around the dunes. The **Head of the Meadow trail** is a leisurely 2 miles (3 km) from the beach parking lot to High Head Road. The hillier **Province Lands trail** includes a 5.5-mile (8.8-km) loop through beech forest and

Dunes in Provincetown

Numerous cycling trails make biking one of the best ways to get around Cape Cod.

low-lying cranberry bogs, plus shorter spurs to Herring Cove, Race Point Beach, and **Bennet Pond.**

The seashore is also home to a surprising number of walking trails, ranging from the kid-friendly 0.3-mile (0.5-km) **Buttonbush Loop** nature trail in front of the Salt Pond Visitor Center to the 8.8-mile (14.2-km) **Great Island Trail** in Wellfleet. The 0.6-mile (1-km) **Doane Trail** loop through pine and oak forest is fully paved, making it accessible to visitors in wheelchairs. The views of Nauset Marsh from **Fort Hill Trail** (1 mile/1.6 km) in Eastham make it especially popular with birders.

The Fort Hill Trail is a birder's paradise.

Parks of New York Harbor

New York Harbor and its surrounding shores are home to a variety of sites administered by the National Park Service, all in an area a fraction of the size of Yellowstone National Park. It would be possible, albeit exhausting, to visit all of these points of interest in a single day, but more enjoyable to spread them out over the course of a weekend or weeklong trip.

The first stop on any New York Harbor itinerary is usually **Castle Clinton National Monument** (*see separate entry in More to See in the Northeast*)

because it's where visitors buy ferry tickets to visit the Statue of Liberty and Ellis Island. Completed in 1811, Southwest Battery (as it was first known) was originally built as a fortress against a British invasion, with 28 cannons capable of firing a 32-pound cannonball a distance of 1.5 miles (2.4 km). The fortress did its job and never had to fire on the enemy.

Renamed in 1917 in honor of New York Governor DeWitt Clinton, the fortress was converted to peacetime use in 1823, with a restaurant and

Fast Facts

Established: NA
Acreage: NA
Visitors (2019): NA
Visitor Centers: Canarsie Pier (Brooklyn), Ryan (Floyd Bennett Field, Brooklyn), Ft. Wadsworth (Staten Island), Jamaica Bay (Queens), Sandy Hook, (NJ)
Nearest Major Airports: John F. Kennedy Intl. (JFK) and LaGuardia (LGA), Queens, NY; Newark Liberty Intl. (EWR), Newark, NJ
Nearest Major Highway: I-278
Fees: Varies by location.
Accessibility: Varies by location.
Contact Information: www.nps.gov/gate, www.nps.gov/cacl, www.nps.gov/gois, www.nps.gov/stli www.nps.gov/elis

The Statue of Liberty stands at the center of New York Harbor.

Castle Clinton once guarded New York against a British invasion. Today it welcomes visitors from the world over.

entertainment venue at its center. Renamed again as **Castle Garden** in 1824, it was at various times an opera house, a theater, an aquarium, and an exhibition hall. Jenny Lind, the "Swedish Nightingale" made her U.S. debut here, thanks to showman P. T. Barnum, who brought the soprano over from Europe. Inventions like the Colt rifle, telegraph, and steam-powered fire engine were also unveiled there.

From 1855–90, Castle Garden started welcoming even more arrivals from Europe in its new role as the nation's official immigrant processing station. More than 8 million people entered the U.S. through its doors. When those functions were moved offshore to nearby Ellis Island, Castle Garden morphed once again into the

New York City Aquarium. After the Aquarium moved to Coney Island in 1941, the Castle was slated for demolition until the National Park Service restored it to its original design. It reopened as Castle Clinton in 1975.

The ferry ride to the **Statue of Liberty** takes only about 15 minutes. An audio tour of Liberty Island is included in the ferry ticket. The 152-foot (46-m) copper statue was a gift from France in 1886 celebrating the alliance of the two nations during the American Revolution. Sculptor Frédéric Auguste Bartholdi designed Lady Liberty's exterior, Gustave Eiffel (he of the Paris tower of the same name) built the metal interior framework, and Richard Morris Hunt, a preeminent American

architect of the era, quite literally put her on a pedestal.

Reservations (up to six months in advance in the peak summer season) are recommended or required for access to the inside of the **pedestal** and to climb the 162 steep and narrow stairs to Lady Liberty's **crown**. Children must be at least 48 inches (22 cm) tall to make the ascent. Visitors taller than 6 feet (183 cm) will need to watch their heads going up and down the stairs. Although the crown delivers knockout views of Manhattan, the best vantage point for photos is on the Fort Wood Level (2P). From there, visitors can take selfies with the statue towering over them.

While the Statue of Liberty might be the most iconic sight in New York Harbor, **Ellis Island** is infinitely more interesting.

Ellis Island

The same ferry that transports visitors from Manhattan (or from New Jersey's Liberty State Park) to Liberty Island also stops at Ellis Island. From 1892–1954, more than 12 million immigrants passed through these halls. The **National Museum of Immigration** does an outstanding job of replicating the immigrant experience of arriving in the New World and telling the stories of the people who went through it.

Gateway National Recreation Area is an urban greenbelt connected by water. Its three units look across New York Harbor at one another, one in Queens' Jamaica Bay (you can take the A train to get there), one in Staten Island, and a third in Sandy Hook, NJ. Together, they offer a staggering array

The Historic Baggage Room, where immigrants checked their luggage while awaiting entry, now serves as the entrance hall to the Ellis Island Museum.

The historic bath house at Jacob Riis Park.

of recreational activities. Run, walk, or hike the multi-use paths at any one of the three areas. On hot days, cool off in the ocean at **Great Kills Beach** (Staten Island), **Jacob Riis Park** (Queens), or four different strands on **Sandy Hook** (New Jersey), all of which are staffed by lifeguards in summer. Canoe or kayak the sheltered waters of Jamaica Bay (a Park Service map of the area outlines five different routes to explore, ranging from 90 minutes to 5 hours long).

Jamaica Bay is also home to a **Wildlife Refuge** that is prime bird-watching territory; over 325 species call Gateway home. There's an **archery range at Floyd Bennett Field** ($75 permits required), but bring your own bow and arrows. In winter, park rangers cut cross-country ski trails through the snow at Sandy Hook's multi-use

path. Fort Wadsworth on Staten Island is a popular sledding site. Riding the **Staten Island Ferry** from lower Manhattan is a terrific way to get a feel for the Big Apple from the water. Best of all, it's completely free.

Sandy Hook is home to the oldest continuously operating lighthouse in the U.S., built in 1764 as New-York Lighthouse. Fort Tilden, next to Jacob Riis Park, was a Nike missile launch site during the Cold War.

Sunset over Sandy Hook beach.

Gettysburg National Military Park

The battle fought here July 1–3, 1863, was the turning point of the Civil War. Union troops repulsed Gen. Robert E. Lee's second and most ambitious invasion of the North in what would become the bloodiest conflict of the war. At the dedication of a national cemetery to inter the more than 3,500 Union soldiers who died in the fighting, Abraham Lincoln delivered the address that would aim to heal the nation's wounds.

The **Museum and Visitor Center** in the middle of the park is the best place to start a visit, if only to pick up the park brochure and map of the outstanding self-guided **Auto Tour** of 16 sites that delve into those three fateful days. The distances between stops are too far to walk, so this is one of the few national parks where a car is essential (although it would be possible to do the tour on horseback or bicycle).

Before departing on the tour (or hiring a **Licensed Battlefield Guide** to enrich the experience), stop in at the **Gettysburg Museum of the American Civil**

Fast Facts

Established: 1895
Acreage: 6,033 (2,441 hectares)
Visitors (2019): 925,117
Nearest Major Airport: Baltimore-Washington Thurgood Marshall Intl. (BWI) Baltimore, MD
Nearest Major Highways: US-15, US-20, I-81
Fees: Battlefield is free to visit, but there are fees for the museum, film, cyclorama painting, and other attractions.
Accessibility: Mostly wheelchair accessible. Information available for visitors with hearing or sight impairments.
Contact Information: 717-334-1124 www.nps.gov/gett

Sunrise over the battlefield at Gettysburg.

A portion of the Cyclorama, Paul Philippoteaux's mural-in-the-round depicting Pickett's Charge.

War and catch a showing of the 20-minute film "**A New Birth of Freedom**," narrated by Morgan Freeman. Both the museum and the film provide outstanding context and background for the battle, and will help orient you to the terrain. The admission ticket to the museum and film also allows you to see the **Cyclorama**, a stunningly elaborate concave mural of Pickett's Charge by French artist Paul Phiippoteaux. Standing 42 feet (13 m) high and extending 377 feet (115 m) in length, the Cyclorama literally envelops viewers into the battle scene.

The tour of the battlefield is riveting. It starts at **McPherson Ridge**, site of the first day's

A statue of Gen. Gouverneur K. Warren overlooks Little Round Top, a key Union stronghold.

battle. The attack by Confederate Maj. Gen. Robert E. Rode forced the Union troops to fall back to **Cemetery Hill**. By the second afternoon, the battle shifted to the south, with Lt. Gen. James Longstreet's Confederates dug in from **Pitzer Woods** all the way across **Warfield Ridge**. Gen. George Meade's Union Army of the Potomac, meanwhile, had taken up positions in **The Peach Orchard**, **The Wheatfield**, **Devil's Den**, and **Little Round Top**. Reinforcements helped the Union troops hold off an attack on their left flank at Little Round Top, but bloody battles in the Wheatfield and Peach Orchard killed or wounded more than 4,000 men from both sides, and forced the Union to retreat again to **Cemetery Ridge.**

July 3 was the most dramatic day of fighting, and the most decisive. Union troops held off Confederate assaults on **Culp's Hill** and **Cemetery Hill**. And by 2 pm, when Maj. Gen. George Pickett led 12,500 Confederates into an all-out charge on the Union center, a corps of 7,000 Federal troops were ready for them. Pickett's army suffered a casualty rate of more than 50%, compared to 1,500 killed and wounded Union troops. The **High Water Mark** denotes the farthest advance of **Pickett's Charge**, and the closest the South came to winning the war. The next day, Robert E. Lee ordered his army to retreat.

The last stop on the tour is **Soldiers' National Cemetery**, located on the hill from which the Union repulsed Pickett's Charge. The final resting place for thousands of Union soldiers killed during the battle is organized by the home states of the men who died. While a few Confederate soldiers are buried at Gettysburg, most were relocated by Southern veterans' societies to cemeteries in Virginia, the Carolinas, and Georgia.

Every weekend from April to October the Park Service stages "**Living History**" demonstrations on the Gettysburg battlefield. Historians in period dress camp out on the battlefield and demonstrate the tools, tactics, and firepower (including shooting real cannons) of the two armies that clashed here. These demonstrations are different than the annual July 4 **Gettysburg**

The site of the Civil War's bloodiest battle is now serene, hallowed ground.

Soldiers National Cemetery, final resting place of more than 3,500 Union troops, and site of Abraham Lincoln's legendary address.

Reenactment, which is held on private land adjacent to the battlefield and is not affiliated with the National Park Service.

Just over Warfield Ridge from the Peach Orchard is the **Eisenhower National Historic Site** (*see separate entry in* More to See in the Northeast). Ike and his wife, Mamie, purchased the home and 189-acre (76-hectare) farm in 1950, two years before his run for president, but his association with Gettysburg dated back to 1915, when as a cadet at West Point, he and his classmates took a field trip to study the legendary military battle. Three years later, during World War I, he was appointed commander of Camp Colt, a U.S. Army Tank Corps Training Center located on the field of

Pickett's Charge. Today, visitors can take guided or self-guided tours of the Eisenhower home, where the 34th president lived until his death in 1967. Almost

all of the Eisenhowers' original 1950s furnishings remain intact, down to the green Formica countertops and linoleum floor tiles.

Volunteers re-enact the Battle of Gettysburg every July 4 on private land near the Battlefield.

MORE TO SEE IN THE NORTHEAST

CONNECTICUT
Weir Farm National Historical Park
Fast Facts

Established: 1990
Acreage: 74 (30 hectares)
Visitors (2019): 38,700
Nearest Major Airport: LaGuardia (LGA), Queens, NY
Nearest Major Highways: US-7, I-684
Fees: $0
Accessibility: The Visitor Center is wheelchair-accessible with temporary ramps. Call ahead so rangers can set up the ramps. The Weir House is wheelchair accessible, but the Weir Studio and Young Studio are not.
Contact Information:
203-834-1896
www.nps.gov/wefa

Contemporary artists intentionally transformed the former summer home of American Impressionist Julian Alden Weir into a site everyone can enjoy . . . and make their own art if they choose. It is the only National Park Service site dedicated to American Impressionist painting.

MAINE
Appalachian National Scenic Trail
Fast Facts

Established: 1937
Length: 2,180 miles (3,508 km)
Visitors (2019): An estimated 3 million people hike some portion of the trail; about 1,000 people hike the entire length each year, or about 25% of those who set out to do so.
Nearest Major Airport: Portland Intl. (PWM), Portland, ME, at the north end; Hartsfield-Jackson Atlanta Intl. (ATL), Atlanta, GA, at the south end.
Nearest Major Highways: I-95 in Maine; GA-52, US-76 in Georgia
Fees: $0
Contact Information:
304-535-6278
www.nps.gov/appa

The "AT" traverses wooded, pastoral, and wild lands of the Appalachian Mountains from Maine to Georgia, passing through a dozen other states in between. Conceived in 1921, it was built by private citizens and completed in 1937. The trail has more than 250 first-come, first-served backcountry shelters for hikers on multi-night trips. The trail is managed in partnership with the U.S. Forest Service, Appalachian Trail Conservancy, numerous state agencies, and thousands of volunteers.

Katahdin Woods and Waters National Monument
Fast Facts

Established: 2016
Acreage: 87,564 (35,436 hectares)
Visitors (2019): NA
Nearest Major Airport: Bangor Intl. (BGR), Bangor, ME
Nearest Major Highways: I-95
Fees: $0. Limited visitor services available.
Accessibility: Mostly inaccessible.
Contact Information:
207-456-6001
www.nps.gov/kaww

Preserves and protects the mountains, woods, and waters east of Baxter State Park, (home of Mount Katahdin, the northern terminus of the Appalachian Trail).

Saint Croix Island International Historic Site
Fast Facts

Established: 1949/1984
Acreage: 6 (3 hectares)
Visitors (2019): 11,613
Nearest Major Airport: Bangor Intl. (BGR), Bangor, ME
Nearest Major Highways: US-1, ME-9
Fees: $0
Accessibility: Mostly inaccessible.
Contact Information:
207-454-3871
www.nps.gov/sacr

The Appalachian Trail starts at Mt. Katahdin, in the Maine woods, and ends 2,180 miles (3,508 km) later at Springer Mountain, Georgia.

Commemorates the short-lived French settlement of Saint Croix Island in the Saint Croix River between Maine and New Brunswick during the winter of 1604–05. Although the French expedition moved on by summer, the French presence in North America had begun.

MASSACHUSETTS
Adams National Historical Park
Fast Facts

Established: 1946/1998
Acreage: 24 (10 hectares)
Visitors (2019): 187,400
Nearest Major Airport: Boston Logan Intl. (BOS), Boston, MA
Nearest Major Highways: I-93
Fees: $15. Free for children under 16.
Accessibility: The first floor of the Old House at Peace Field has limited wheelchair access.
Contact Information:
   617-773-1177
   www.nps.gov/adam

The Adams Family's Old House at Peace Field was home to Presidents John Adams and John Quincy Adams, as well as to U.S. Minister to Great Britain Charles Francis Adams, and literary historians Henry Adams and Brooks Adams. Also on the property are the birthplaces of America's first father-and-son presidents and a library of more than 14,000 historic volumes.

Boston African-American National Historic Site
Fast Facts

Established: 1980
Acreage: 0.59 0.23 hectares)
Visitors (2019): 419,585
Nearest Major Airport: Boston Logan Intl. (BOS), Boston, MA
Nearest Major Highways: I-90, I-93
Fees: $10; $8/student; $8/senior aged 62 and over. $0/child aged 12 and under.
Accessibility: Some of Boston's oldest streets may be too narrow or uneven for wheelchairs or lack

curb cuts. Wheelchairs may be borrowed at the Faneuil Hall Visitor Center.

Contact Information:
617-742-5415
www.nps.gov/boaf

This Beacon Hill site promotes, preserves, and interprets the history of Boston's free Black community in the 1800s, in partnership with the Museum of African American History, the City of Boston, and private property owners. The 15 pre-Civil War structures along the 1.6 mile (2.6-km) Black Heritage Trail were the homes, businesses, schools, and churches of people who fought slavery and injustice. (*See also* Boston National Historical Park.)

Boston Harbor Islands National Recreation Area

Fast Facts

Established: 1996
Acreage: 1,482 (600 hectares)
Visitors (2019): NA
Visitor Centers: Boston Harbor Islands Welcome Center, Georges Island, Spectacle Island, Peddocks Island
Nearest Major Airport: Boston Logan Intl. (BOS), Boston, MA
Nearest Major Highways: I-90, I-93
Fees: $0
Accessibility: The welcome center and ferry center are fully accessible, but the islands are not.
Contact Information:
617-223-8667
www.nps.gov/boha

Some 34 islands and peninsulas in Boston Harbor make up this treasure trove of natural and cultural resources and recreational amenities within a major urban area. The park is managed by a partnership of federal, state, municipal, and non-profit agencies, including the National Park Service.

Frederick Law Olmsted National Historic Site

Fast Facts

Established: 1979
Acreage: 7 (3 hectares)
Visitors (2019): 7,791

Nearest Major Airport: Boston Logan Intl. (BOS), Boston, MA
Nearest Major Highways: MA-9, I-90, I-93
Fees: $0
Accessibility: The multi-level nature of the home and uneven grounds make both difficult to navigate in wheelchairs.
Contact Information:
617-566-1689
www.nps.gov/frla

Preserves the first large-scale landscape architecture office in the U.S., founded by Frederick Law Olmsted Sr. and continued by his sons and other successors. The site includes the Olmsted Archives, which documents over 5,000 projects undertaken by the firm.

John Fitzgerald Kennedy National Historic Site

Fast Facts

Established: 1967
Acreage: 0 (0 hectares)
Visitors (2019): 24,838
Nearest Major Airport: Boston Logan Intl. (BOS), Boston, MA
Nearest Major Highways: MA-9, I-90
Fees: $0
Accessibility: The visitor center is down a flight of stairs inaccessible by wheelchair.
Contact Information:
617-566-7937
www.nps.gov/jofi

Preserves the birthplace and early childhood home of the 35th president. The Kennedy family repurchased the home in 1966 and Rose Kennedy carefully recreated her son's birthplace in the wake of the president's assassination.

Longfellow House-Washington's Headquarters National Historic Site

Fast Facts

Established: 1972
Acreage: 2 (1 hectare)
Visitors (2019): 55,012
Nearest Major Airport: Boston Logan Intl. (BOS), Boston, MA
Nearest Major Highways: I-90, MA-2

Fees: $0

Accessibility: Most of the site is accessible. Visit www.nps.gov/long/planyourvisit/accessibility.htm for descriptions of the inaccessible portions.

Contact Information:
617-876-4491
www.nps.gov/long

George Washington made this home his headquarters during the siege of Boston (1775–76). The poet Henry Wadsworth Longfellow purchased the house in 1837 and lived here until 1850, hosting writers, artists, and statesmen who took part in the flowering of American literature and culture in the 19th century and advocated for the abolition of slavery. The site is home to a vast collection of decorative and fine arts, a library, and a working research archive.

Lowell National Historical Park

Fast Facts

Established: 1978
Acreage: 141 (57 hectares)
Visitors (2019): 481,536
Nearest Major Airport: Boston Logan Intl. (BOS), Boston, MA
Nearest Major Highways: I-495, US-3
Fees: Boott Cotton Mills Museum: $6/adult; $3/student or child aged 6–16; $4/senior. Canal Boat Tours: $12/adult; $10/senior aged 62 and over; $8/student or child aged 6–16
Accessibility: Visit www.nps.gov/lowe/planyourvisit/accessibility.htm for a full description of which sites in the park have limited accessibility.

Contact Information:
978-970-5000
www.nps.gov/lowe

Commemorates the legacy of America's Industrial Revolution through exhibits that tell the story of the transition from farm to factory and chronicle immigrant and labor history and heritage. Guided boat, trolley, and walking tours visit the Boott Cotton Mills Museum with its weave room of 88 operating looms, a "mill girl" boarding house, the Suffolk Mill turbine, and 5.6 miles (9 km) of power canals.

Minute Man National Historical Park

Fast Facts

Established: 1959
Acreage: 1,026 (415 hectares)
Visitors (2019): 1,017,326
Visitor Centers: Minute Man (main), Lexington, Concord, North Bridge
Nearest Major Airport: Boston Logan Intl. (BOS), Boston, MA
Nearest Major Highways: I-495, MA-2
Fees: $0
Accessibility: The visitor centers are wheelchair-accessible; rangers may be able to make accommodations at other sections of the park.

Contact Information:
978-369-6993
www.nps.gov/mima

Commemorates the road traveled by Paul Revere (and his less-remembered compatriots Samuel Prescott and William Dawes) during the midnight ride on April 19–20, 1775. The ensuing battles of Lexington & Concord became known as the "shot heard round the world" that began the American Revolution. The park includes restored sections of the Battle Road, the Minute Man Statue, and the Wayside, home at different times to Louisa May Alcott and Nathaniel Hawthorne.

New Bedford Whaling National Historical Park

Fast Facts

Established: 1996
Acreage: 34 (14 hectares)
Visitors (2019): 143,427
Nearest Major Airport: Boston Logan Intl. (BOS), Boston, MA
Nearest Major Highways: I-195, US-6.
Fees: $0. Admission to the New Bedford Whaling Museum is $19.
Accessibility: Cobblestone streets and historic homes may present challenges to visitors in wheelchairs.

Contact Information:
508-996-4095
www.nps.gov/nebe

The only National Park Service site to commemorate whaling and its contribution to American history includes a National Historic

Landmark District, the schooner *Ernestina*, and the New Bedford Whaling Museum.

Salem Maritime National Historic Site

Fast Facts

Established: 1938
Acreage: 9 (4 hectares)
Visitors (2019): 339,238
Visitor Centers: Salem Armory, Waite & Peirce Museum
Nearest Major Airport: Boston Logan Intl. (BOS), Boston, MA
Nearest Major Highways: I-95, MA-1A
Fees: $0
Accessibility: The Salem Visitor Center, the Scale House exhibit, and all walkways are fully accessible. The replica tall ship *Friendship of Salem* can be accessed via a wheelchair lift.
Contact Information:
978-740-1650
www.nps.gov/sama

The first National Historic Site in the U.S. preserves the maritime history of New England with historic buildings, colonial wharves, and a reconstructed tall ship. The site shares the stories of sailors, privateers, and merchants.

Saugus Iron Works National Historic Site

Fast Facts

Established: 1968
Acreage: 8 (3 hectares)
Visitors (2019): 8,150
Nearest Major Airport: Boston Logan Intl. (BOS), Boston, MA
Nearest Major Highways: I-95, US-1
Fees: $0
Accessibility: The visitor center, museum, and restrooms are fully accessible, but the rest of the site is not.
Contact Information:
781-233-0050
www.nps.gov/sair

As the location of the first fully-integrated ironworks in North America (1646–68), the site interprets the beginning of the American iron and steel industry. It includes a reconstructed blast furnace, forge,

rolling and slitting mill, river basin, and a restored 1600s house.

Springfield Armory National Historic Site

Fast Facts

Established: 1978
Acreage: 55 (22 hectares)
Visitors (2019): 20,979
Nearest Major Airport: Bradley Intl. (BDL), Windsor Locks, CT
Nearest Major Highways: I-90, I-91
Fees: $0
Accessibility: Largely accessible.
Contact Information:
413-734-8551
www.nps.gov/spar

From 1794 to 1968, Springfield Armory was a center for the manufacture of U.S. military small arms and the scene of important technological advances. The Armory Museum preserves one of the world's most extensive firearms collections.

Washington-Rochambeau Revolutionary Route National Historic Trail

Fast Facts

Established: 2009
Length: 680 miles (1,094 km) from Massachusetts to Virginia
Visitors (2019):
Nearest Major Airport: NA
Nearest Major Highways: NA
Fees: $0
Accessibility: Varies by location. Most sites along the trail generally meet accessibility standards for people with disabilities.
Contact Information:
610-783-1006
www.nps.gov/waro

In 1781, Gen. Jean-Baptiste Rochambeau's French Army joined forces with Gen. George Washington's Continental Army to fight the British Army in Yorktown, VA. With the French Navy in support, the allied armies moved hundreds of miles to become the largest troop movement of the American Revolution. Cooperation between the two forces led to victory at Yorktown, securing American independence.

NEW HAMPSHIRE
Saint-Gaudens National Historic Site
Fast Facts

Established: 1977
Acreage: 191 (77 hectares)
Visitors (2019): 31,759
Nearest Major Airport: Boston Logan Intl. (BOS), Boston, MA
Nearest Major Highways: I-91, US-5
Fees: $10/person
Accessibility: The visitor center and parking areas are fully accessible, but many buildings are not. Visit the website for a map showing routes through the park for visitors in wheelchairs. Visually impaired visitors may request curatorial gloves so they can touch some of the statues.
Contact Information:
603-675-2175
www.nps.gov/saga

Includes the home, studios, and gardens of Augustus Saint-Gaudens (1848–1907), one of America's foremost sculptors of the late 1800s and early 1900s. Six historic buildings are open to the public with over 120 sculptures.

NEW JERSEY
Great Egg Harbor Scenic and Recreational River
Fast Facts

Established: 1992
Acreage: 43,311 (17,527 hectares)
Visitors (2019): NA
Nearest Major Airport: Philadelphia Intl. (PHL), Philadelphia, PA
Nearest Major Highways: US-9
Fees: $0
Contact Information:
215-597-5823
www.nps.gov/greg

The Great Egg Harbor River and its tributaries meander through the Pine Barrens of New Jersey. Its remarkable wildlife and abundant recreational opportunities make it a treasured resource.

Morristown National Historical Park
Fast Facts

Established: 1933
Acreage: 1,170 (692 hectares)
Visitors (2019): 271,330
Nearest Major Airport: Newark Liberty Intl. (EWR), Newark, NJ
Nearest Major Highways: I-287
Fees: $0
Accessibility: The visitor center and Washington headquarters museum are fully accessible, as are the paved paths between them and to and from the parking lot.
Contact Information:
973-539-2016
www.nps.gov/morr

America's first National Historical Park preserves, protects and maintains the landscapes, structures, features, archeological resources and collections of the Continental Army winter encampments of 1779–80.

Paterson Great Falls National Historical Park
Fast Facts

Established: 2011
Acreage: 51 (21 hectares)
Visitors (2019): 276,985
Nearest Major Airport: Newark Liberty Intl. (EWR), Newark, NJ
Nearest Major Highways: I-80
Fees: $0
Accessibility: Overlook Park and the Paterson Museum are accessible with some assistance. There are accessible bathrooms at the Paterson Museum and accessible parking spots at Overlook Park.
Contact Information:
973-523-0370
www.nps.gov/pagr

Alexander Hamilton and the Society for Establishing Useful Manufactures founded the city of Paterson in 1792 around the Great Falls of the Passaic River. America's first planned industrial city attracted entrepreneurs, laborers, and immigrants with diverse talents. Paterson's mills produced everything from textiles and Colt firearms to locomotives and aircraft engines.

Thomas Edison National Historic Park preserves the inventor's laboratory and home.

Thomas Edison National Historical Park

Fast Facts

Established: 1955/2009
Acreage: 21 (8.4 hectares)
Visitors (2019): 42,224
Nearest Major Airport: Newark Liberty Intl.
(EWR), Newark, NJ
Nearest Major Highways: I-280
Fees: $15/person. $5/person for the audio tour.
Accessibility: Varies by location. Assistance may be required in some historic buildings.
Contact Information:
973-736-0550
www.nps.gov/edis

Visitors can tour the home and laboratory where Thomas Edison invented the movie camera and nickel-iron-alkaline storage battery and developed the phonograph. The site includes his chemistry lab, machine shop, library, the world's first motion picture studio, and Edison's 29-room Victorian mansion.

NEW YORK
African Burial Ground National Monument

Fast Facts

Established: 2006
Acreage: NA
Visitors (2019): 47,427
Nearest Major Airports: John F. Kennedy Intl.
(JFK), Queens, NY; Newark Liberty Intl. (EWR), Newark, NJ
Nearest Major Highways: I-278, NY-9A
Fees: $0
Accessibility: The visitor center and restrooms are ADA-compliant.
Contact Information:
212-637-2019
www.nps.gov/afbg

The oldest and largest African burial ground in the U.S. was lost to history for centuries until 1991, when construction workers uncovered human skeletal remains 30 feet (9 m) under Broadway. From the 1690s until the 1790s, more than 15,000 free and enslaved Africans and African Americans were buried here. An outdoor memorial in the form of an Ancestral Chamber provides a place to honor this sacred area.

Castle Clinton National Monument c/o Federal Hall National Memorial

Fast Facts

Established: 1950
Acreage: 1 (0.4 hectares)
Visitors (2019): 4,361,034
Nearest Major Airports: John F. Kennedy Intl. (JFK), Queens, NY; Newark Liberty Intl. (EWR), Newark, NJ
Nearest Major Highway: I-278
Fees: $0
Accessibility: Fully accessible.
Contact Information:
 212-344-7220
 www.nps.gov/cacl

Castle Clinton was originally built as a fortress to defend New York Harbor from British forces during the War of 1812. Since then, it has operated as an opera house, an aquarium, and an immigration depot, through which over 8 million people entered the United States from 1855–90. Today, it's where many sightseers purchase tickets for the ferry to the Statue of Liberty and Ellis Island. (*See also* Parks of New York Harbor *on page 234.*)

Eleanor Roosevelt National Historic Site

Fast Facts

Established: 1977
Acreage: 180 (73 hectares)
Visitors (2019): 47,630
Nearest Major Airport: Bradley Intl. (BDL), Windsor Locks, CT
Nearest Major Highways: US-9, I-87.
Fees: $0. Visits to the site are by guided tour only.
Accessibility: Mostly inaccessible.
Contact Information:
 845-229-9442
 www.nps.gov/elro

Eleanor Roosevelt chose Val-Kill for her retreat, her office, her home, and her "laboratory" for social

A statue of George Washington stands outside Federal Hall, where the first president took the oath of office.

change during the prominent and influential period of her life from 1924 until her death in 1962. Here she formulated and put into practice her social and political beliefs. Val-Kill Cottage is the focal point of the historic site. Originally built as a factory building for Val-Kill Industries, it was converted to a residence in 1937.

Federal Hall National Memorial

Fast Facts

Established: 1939/1955
Acreage: NA
Visitors (2019): 264,849
Nearest Major Airports: John F. Kennedy Intl. (JFK), Queens, NY; Newark Liberty Intl. (EWR), Newark, NJ
Nearest Major Highways: I-278, NY-9A
Fees: $0
Accessibility: Fully accessible.
Contact Information:
   212-825-6990
   www.nps.gov/feha

"The Birthplace of American Government" is where George Washington took the oath of office as the first president, and where the first U.S. Congress met in 1789 and adopted the Bill of Rights. The first building on the site hosted the 1735 trial of John Peter Zenger, which helped establish the notion of a free press. The current building was completed in 1842.

Fire Island National Seashore

Fast Facts

Established: 1984
Acreage: 19,580 (7,924 hectares)
Visitors (2019): 391,311
Visitor Center: Fire Island Lighthouse
Nearest Major Airport: John F. Kennedy Intl. (JFK), Queens, NY
Nearest Major Highways: I-495, NY-27
Fees: $0. Ferries to and from the island may charge admission.
Accessibility: Varies by location.
Contact Information:
   516-687-4750
   www.nps.gov/fiis

Cars are prohibited on this skinny barrier island just 50 miles (80 km) from Manhattan, making it a quiet oasis. Ocean beaches, dunes, Fire Island Lighthouse, and the estate of Declaration of Independence signer William Floyd make this park a blend of recreation, preservation, and conservation.

Fort Stanwix National Monument

Fast Facts

Established: 1935
Acreage: 15 (6 hectares)
Visitors (2019): 97,412
Nearest Major Airport: Syracuse Hancock Intl. (SYR), Syracuse, NY
Nearest Major Highways: I-90
Fees: $0
Accessibility: The visitor center is accessible, as are entryways and restrooms.
Contact Information:
   315-338-7730
   www.nps.gov/fost

"The fort that never surrendered" successfully repelled a prolonged British siege in August 1777, and led to American alliances with France and the Netherlands. The current fort is a reconstruction.

Gateway National Recreation Area

Fast Facts

Established: 1972
Acreage: 26,707 (10,767 hectares)
Visitors (2019): 9,405,619
Visitor Centers: Canarsie Pier (Brooklyn), Ryan (Floyd Bennett Field, Brooklyn), Ft. Wadsworth (Staten Island), Jamaica Bay (Queens), Sandy Hook, (NJ)
Nearest Major Airports: John F. Kennedy Intl. (JFK), Queens, NY; Newark Liberty Intl. (EWR), Newark, NJ
Nearest Major Highway: I-278
Fees: $0. Some beaches charge parking fees during summer.
Accessibility: Varies by location.
Contact Information:
   718-354-4606
   www.nps.gov/gate

A large, diverse park spanning two states, Gateway combines recreational activities with natural beauty, wildlife preservation, military history, and more. Visitors can hike, picnic, swim, sunbathe, bike, visit the oldest working lighthouse in the nation or NYC's first municipal airport, see a historic airplane collection, and camp overnight, all in the New York metropolitan area. (*See also* Parks of New York Harbor *on page 234.*)

General Grant National Memorial
Fast Facts
Established: 1959
Acreage: 0.8 (0.3 hectares)
Visitors (2019): 113,852
Nearest Major Airports: John F. Kennedy Intl. (JFK), Queens, NY; Newark Liberty Intl. (EWR), Newark, NJ
Nearest Major Highways: NY-9A, I-87, I-95
Fees: $0
Accessibility: The mausoleum is not wheelchair accessible, but the visitor center is.
Contact Information:
212-666-1640
www.nps.gov/gegr

Who is buried in the largest mausoleum in North America? Ulysses S. Grant, of course, the Union commander who brought the Civil War to an end. His wife, Julia, is also interred here. As president, (1869–77), Grant signed the act establishing the first national park, Yellowstone, on March 1, 1872.

Governors Island National Monument
Fast Facts
Established: 2003
Acreage: 23 (9 hectares)
Visitors (2019): 590,993
Nearest Major Airports: John F. Kennedy Intl. (JFK), Queens, NY; Newark Liberty Intl. (EWR), Newark, NJ
Nearest Major Highway: I-278
Fees: $0
Accessibility: Building 140, the ferry terminal in Manhattan, the Battery Maritime Building, and the ferry boat *Samuel Coursen* are all accessible. Most ranger-led tours follow paved, accessible routes.

Contact Information:
212-825-3045
www.nps.gov/gois

Located half a mile (1 km) off the southern tip of Manhattan, Governors Island is home to two early 1800s fortifications—Fort Jay and Castle Williams—that played strategic roles in defending New York City during the 19th century.

Hamilton Grange National Memorial
Fast Facts
Established: 1988
Acreage: 1 (0.4 hectares)
Visitors (2019): 71,247
Nearest Major Airports: John F. Kennedy Intl. (JFK), Queens, NY; Newark Liberty Intl. (EWR), Newark, NJ
Nearest Major Highways: NY-9A, I-87, I-95
Fees: $0
Accessibility: Largely accessible.
Contact Information:
646-548-2319/2320
www.nps.gov/hagr

The Grange, named after his grandfather's estate in Scotland, was the home of Alexander Hamilton, American statesman and first Secretary of the Treasury.

Harriet Tubman National Historical Park
Fast Facts
Established: 2017
Acreage: 31 (13 hectares)
Visitors (2019): NA
Nearest Major Airport: Syracuse Hancock Intl. (SYR), Syracuse, NY
Nearest Major Highways: I-90, US-20
Fees: $0
Accessibility: Largely accessible.
Contact Information:
646-548-2319/2320
www.nps.gov/hart

Acclaimed abolitionist and suffragist Harriet Tubman acquired this land from U.S. Senator William Henry Seward in 1859 and worked and resided here with her family from 1861 until her death in 1913. In 1903 she donated land to the A.M.E. Zion Church in Auburn, NY, for the establishment of the home "for aged and indigent colored people."

Home of Franklin D. Roosevelt National Historic Site
Fast Facts
Established: 1944
Acreage: 849 (344 hectares)
Visitors (2019): 147,109
Nearest Major Airport: Bradley Intl. (BDL), Windsor Locks, CT
Nearest Major Highways: I-87, US-9.
Fees: $20. Admission is by 1-hour guided tour only. Admission also valid for entrance to the FDR Presidential Library and Museum, which is a self-guided tour.
Accessibility: Fully accessible. Wheelchairs are available free of charge.
Contact Information:
845-229-9115
www.nps.gov/hofr

This was the birthplace and life-long home of America's longest-serving president. He helped design and build the first presidential library on the property. He and his wife Eleanor are buried in the Rose Garden on the property.

Martin Van Buren National Historic Site
Fast Facts
Established: 1974
Acreage: 285 (115 hectares)
Visitors (2019): 20,623
Nearest Major Airport: Bradley Intl. (BDL), Windsor Locks, CT
Nearest Major Highways: I-87, I-90, US-9
Fees: $0
Accessibility: The first floor of the mansion is wheelchair-accessible.
Contact Information:
518-758-9689
www.nps.gov/mava

Lindenwald was the home and farm of eighth U.S. president Martin Van Buren from the time he left office in 1841 until his death in 1862. Van Buren was a primary architect of the American

political party system. He was a contender for the Democratic nomination in 1844 and the presidential candidate in 1848 for the Free Soil Party, the first major anti-slavery party in the United States.

Sagamore Hill National Historic Site
Fast Facts
Established: 1963
Acreage: 83 (34 hectares)
Visitors (2019): 36,738
Nearest Major Airport: John F. Kennedy Intl. (JFK), Queens, NY
Nearest Major Highways: I-495, NY-25A
Fees: $0
Accessibility: Only the first floor of the home is wheelchair accessible. Videos and virtual tours are available at the Old Orchard Museum.
Contact Information:
516-922-4788
www.nps.gov/sahi

This 23-room, shingle-style, Queen Anne mansion was Theodore Roosevelt's Long Island home from 1886 until his death in 1919. From 1901 to 1909, it served as the 26th president's summer White House. Almost all of the furnishings are original. Roosevelt is buried at nearby Youngs Memorial Cemetery.

Saint Paul's Church National Historic Site
Fast Facts
Established: 1980
Acreage: 6 (2.5 hectares)
Visitors (2019): 18,537
Nearest Major Airport: John F. Kennedy Intl. (JFK), Queens, NY
Nearest Major Highways: I-95, US-1
Fees: $0
Accessibility: The visitor center is accessible, but some of the farther reaches of the cemetery are on uneven ground.
Contact Information:
914-667-4116
www.nps.gov/sapa

This 1763 church was home to one of New York's oldest parishes (1665–1980). In 1776 the building served as a hospital following the Battle of Pell's Point.

Saratoga National Historical Park
Fast Facts

Established: 1938
Acreage: 3,410 (1,380 hectares)
Visitors (2019): 145,118
Nearest Major Airport: New York Stewart Intl. (SWF), New Windsor, NY
Nearest Major Highways: I-87, US-4
Fees: $0
Accessibility: Varies by location within the park.
Contact Information:
518-670-2985
www.nps.gov/sara

The American victory over the British on this battlefield in 1777—the first time British troops ever surrendered—marked a major turning point of the American Revolution and one of the decisive battles in world history. The site includes the country estate of Maj. Gen. Philip Schuyler, the 154-foot (47-m) Saratoga monument, and the half-mile (1-km) wheelchair-accessible Victory Woods Trail.

Statue of Liberty National Monument
Fast Facts

Established: Statue of Liberty, 1924; Ellis Island, 1965.
Acreage: 60 (24 hectares)
Visitors (2019): 4,240,461
Visitor Centers: Ellis Island, Liberty Island
Nearest Major Airports: John F. Kennedy Intl. (JFK), Queens, NY; Newark Liberty Intl. (EWR), Newark, NJ
Nearest Major Highway: I-278
Fees: $0. All visitors must purchase ferry tickets ($23.50+) from Statue Cruises, departing from either lower Manhattan or Liberty State Park in New Jersey.
Accessibility: Mostly accessible.
Contact Information:
212-363-3200
www.nps.gov/stli, www.nps.gov/elis

The 152-foot (46-m) copper statue bearing the torch of freedom was a gift of the French people in 1886 to commemorate the alliance of the two nations and the American Revolution. Designed by Frederic Auguste Bartholdi, the statue has come to symbolize freedom and democracy. Nearby Ellis Island, through which nearly 12 million immigrants passed, was reopened to the public in 1990 as the country's main museum devoted entirely to immigration. (*See also* Parks of New York Harbor *on page 234.*)

Stonewall National Monument
Fast Facts

Established: 2016
Acreage: 8 (3 hectares)
Visitors (2019): 2,088,929
Nearest Major Airports: John F. Kennedy Intl. (JFK), Queens, NY; Newark Liberty Intl. (EWR), Newark, NJ
Nearest Major Highways: I-87, NY-9A
Fees: $0
Accessibility: Mostly accessible. Christopher Park is paved with brick and may be uneven.
Contact Information:
212-668-2577
www.nps.gov/ston

Commemorates the uprising that took place the night of June 27–28, 1969, after police raided the Stonewall Inn, a popular gay bar in New York's Greenwich Village that is still privately owned and operated. The spontaneous protests and other acts of resistance that followed the raid marked the

"Gay Liberation," a statue by George Segal, is a focal point of Stonewall National Monument.

beginning of a new era in the gay rights movement in the U.S.

Theodore Roosevelt Birthplace National Historic Site

Fast Facts

Established: 1963

Acreage: NA

Visitors (2019): 25,978

Nearest Major Airport: John F. Kennedy Intl. (JFK), Queens, NY; Newark Liberty Intl. (EWR), Newark, NJ

Nearest Major Highways: I-87, NY-9A

Fees: $0

Accessibility: Wheelchair lifts and elevators make this site fully accessible.

Contact Information:
212-260-1616
www.nps.gov/thrb

The 26th president was born in a brownstone house here in Manhattan's Union Square district on Oct. 27, 1858. Demolished in 1916, the home was reconstructed and rededicated in 1923 and furnished by the president's widow and sisters.

Theodore Roosevelt Inaugural National Historic Site

Fast Facts

Established: 1971

Acreage: 1.2 (0.5 hectares)

Visitors (2019): 26,994

Nearest Major Airport: Buffalo-Niagara Intl. (BUF), Buffalo, NY

Nearest Major Highways: I-190

Fees: $12/adults, $9/students; $9/seniors aged 62 and over, $7/children aged 6–18, $30/family (2 adults and children aged 18 or under). Admission only by guided tour.

Accessibility: Largely wheelchair accessible.

Contact Information:
716-884-0095
www.nps.gov/thri

Following the 1901 assassination of president William McKinley, then-Vice-President Theodore Roosevelt traveled to the Buffalo, NY, home of Ansley Wilcox, where he took the oath of office as the nation's 26th president. The home is now a

museum that celebrates Roosevelt's presidency, a tenure that dramatically altered the course of the nation's domestic and foreign policy.

Vanderbilt Mansion National Historic Site

Fast Facts

Established: 1940

Acreage: 212 (86 hectares)

Visitors (2019): 326,822

Nearest Major Airport: Bradley Intl. (BDL), Windsor Locks, CT

Nearest Major Highways: I-87, US-9

Fees: $10/adult; free for children aged 15 and under. Entry is by one-hour guided tour only.

Accessibility: The elevator is too small to accommodate most wheelchairs.

Contact Information:
845-229-9115
www.nps.gov/vama

This palatial mansion is a fine example of homes built by millionaires during the Gilded Age. Built by Frederick W. Vanderbilt, a grandson of Cornelius Vanderbilt, and designed by the influential firm McKim, Mead, and White, it is an important example of Beaux-Arts architecture and design.

Women's Rights National Historical Park

Fast Facts

Established: 1980

Acreage: 7 (3 hectares)

Visitors (2019): 39,064

Nearest Major Airport: Syracuse Hancock Intl. (SYR), Syracuse, NY

Nearest Major Highways: I-90, US-20

Fees: $0

Accessibility: All sites except the Elizabeth Cady Stanton House are wheelchair accessible.

Contact Information:
315-568-2991
www.nps.gov/wori

Commemorates the first Women's Rights Convention in Seneca Falls in 1848 and celebrates women's efforts to achieve suffrage and equal rights. The park includes the Wesleyan Methodist Chapel where the convention was held; the home of suffragist Elizabeth Cady Stanton; and the M'Clintock House, where the leaders drafted the convention's Declaration of Sentiments.

PENNSYLVANIA
Allegheny Portage Railroad National Historic Site
Fast Facts
Established: 1964
Acreage: 1,284 (520 hectares)
Visitors (2019): 189,189
Nearest Major Airport: Pittsburgh Intl. (PIT), Pittsburgh, PA
Nearest Major Highways: I-99, US-22
Fees: $0
Accessibility: Largely accessible.
Contact Information:
814-886-6100
www.nps.gov/alpo

Traces of the first railroad crossing of the Allegheny Mountains can still be seen here. An inclined-plane railroad, built between 1831 and 1834, permitted transportation of passengers and freight over the mountains, providing a critical link between the Pennsylvania Mainline Canal system and the West.

Delaware Water Gap National Recreation Area
Fast Facts
Established: 1965
Acreage: 67,581 (27,349 hectares)
Visitors (2019): 3,374,866
Visitor Centers: Park Headquarters, Kittatinny Point, Dingmans Falls, Millbrook Village
Nearest Major Airport: Newark Liberty Intl. (EWR), Newark, NJ
Nearest Major Highways: I-80, I-84, US 206, US 209
Fees: $10/vehicle, $2/bicycle or pedestrian at Smithfield Beach, Milford Beach, Bushkill Access, and Dingmans Access in PA, and Turtle Beach and Watergate in NJ.
Contact Information:
570-588-2451
www.nps.gov/dewa

Preserves unspoiled land on both the New Jersey and Pennsylvania sides of the Middle Delaware River for a variety of recreational purposes. The river segment flows through the famous gap in the Appalachian Mountains.

Edgar Allan Poe National Historic Site
Fast Facts
Established: 1980
Acreage 0.5: (0.2 hectares)
Visitors (2019): 15,527
Nearest Major Airport: Philadelphia Intl. (PHL), Philadelphia, PA
Nearest Major Highways: I-95, I-76, I-676
Fees: $0
Accessibility: Only the main house is accessible. Call ahead to arrange a ramp to the entry.
Contact Information:
215-597-7130
www.nps.gov/edal

Interprets the life and work of the American author in a three-building complex at North Seventh Street where Poe lived, 1843–44.

Eisenhower National Historic Site
Fast Facts
Established: 1967
Acreage: 690 (279 hectares)
Visitors (2019): 47,277
Nearest Major Airport: Baltimore/Washington Intl. Thurgood Marshall (BWI), Baltimore, MD
Nearest Major Highways: US-15, US-20, I-81
Fees: $0
Accessibility: The parking area, restrooms, and areas around the home are wheelchair-accessible.
Contact Information:
717-338-9114
www.nps.gov/eise

This was the only home ever owned by President Dwight D. Eisenhower and his wife, Mamie. It served as a refuge when he was president and as a retirement home after he left office.

Flight 93 National Memorial
Fast Facts
Established: 2002
Acreage: 2,320 (939 hectares)
Visitors (2019): 411,226

Nearest Major Airport: Pittsburgh Intl. (PIT), Pittsburgh, PA
Nearest Major Highways: I70-76, US 30, US 219
Fees: $0
Accessibility: Fully accessible.
Contact Information:
 814-893-6322
 www.nps.gov/flni

Preserves the crash site of Flight 93, where 40 passengers and crew perished on September 11, 2001. Their heroic actions thwarted hijackers attempting to crash a plane into the U.S. Capitol.

Fort Necessity Battlefield
Fast Facts
Established: 1931/1961
Acreage: 903 (365 hectares)
Visitors (2019): 312,104
Visitor Centers: National Road Interpretive and Education Center, Mount Washington Tavern
Nearest Major Airport: Pittsburgh Intl. (PIT), Pittsburgh, PA
Nearest Major Highways: US-40, I-68
Fees: $0
Accessibility: Mostly accessible, except for the second floor of the Mt. Washington Tavern.
Contact Information:
 724-329-5512
 www.nps.gov/fone

In a prelude to the American Revolution, colonial troops commanded by 22-year-old Col. George Washington suffered defeat here in the opening battle of the French and Indian War on July 3, 1754.

Friendship Hill National Historic Site
Fast Facts
Established: 1978
Acreage: 675 (273 hectares)
Visitors (2019): 34,159
Nearest Major Airport: Pittsburgh Intl. (PIT), Pittsburgh, PA
Nearest Major Highways: I-79, US-119
Fees: $0
Accessibility: Largely accessible.
Contact Information:
 724-329-2501
 www.nps.gov/frhi

This home on the Monongahela River near Point Marion, PA, belonged to Albert Gallatin, Secretary of the Treasury (1801–13) under Presidents Thomas Jefferson and James Madison. During his tenure, the U.S. purchased the Louisiana Territory and funded the Lewis & Clark expedition.

Hopewell Furnace National Historic Site
Fast Facts
Established: 1938
Acreage: 848 (343 hectares)
Visitors (2019): 49,861
Nearest Major Airport: Philadelphia Intl. (PHL), Philadelphia, PA
Nearest Major Highways: I-76, US-422
Fees: $0
Accessibility: The visitor center and restrooms are accessible, but most of the historic buildings and rocky trails are not.
Contact Information:
 610-582-8773
 www.nps.gov/hofu

Showcases an early American industrial landscape and the role of industrialization in the growth of the early United States. Operating from 1771–1883, Hopewell and other "iron plantations" laid the foundation for the transformation of the United States into an industrial giant. Visitors can tour a variety of buildings, including a blast furnace, a blacksmith's shop, and the ironmaster's mansion.

Independence National Historical Park
Fast Facts
Established: 1939/1956
Acreage: 44 (18 hectares)
Visitors (2019): 4,532,459
Nearest Major Airport: Philadelphia Intl. (PHL), Philadelphia, PA
Nearest Major Highways: I-95, I-76, I-676
Fees: $0
Accessibility: Most of the buildings are accessible. Wheelchairs may be borrowed at the Independence Visitor Center.
Contact Information:
 215-597-8787
 www.nps.gov/inde

The Liberty Bell at Independence National Historical Park

This park has a claim as the birthplace of the United States of America, as the location where both the Declaration of Independence and the U.S. Constitution were signed. The park includes Independence Hall, the Liberty Bell, Congress Hall, the First and Second Banks of the United States, and other structures, sites, and accredited museum collections associated with the founding and growth of the United States.

Visitors (2019): 183,143
Nearest Major Airport: Pittsburgh Intl. (PIT), Pittsburgh, PA
Nearest Major Highways: I-99, I-70-76, US-219
Fees: $0
Accessibility: Mostly accessible. One wheelchair is available for loan at the visitor center.
Contact Information:
814-495-4643
www.nps.gov/jofl

Johnstown Flood National Memorial
Fast Facts
Established: 1964
Acreage: 178 (72 hectares)

The South Fork dam failed on May 31, 1889, unleashing 20 million tons (18 million metric tons) of water that devastated Johnstown, PA. The flood killed 2,209 people, but many around the nation and the world united to aid the "Johnstown sufferers." Clara Barton successfully led the Red Cross in its first major disaster relief effort here.

Middle Delaware National Scenic River
Fast Facts
Established: 1978
Acreage: 1973 (798 hectares)
Visitors (2019): 3,374,866 total
Visitor Centers: Park Headquarters, Kittatinny Point, Dingmans Falls, Millbrook Village
Nearest Major Airport: Newark Liberty Intl. (EWR), Newark, NJ
Nearest Major Highways: I-80, I-84, US-206, US-209
Fees: $10/vehicle, $2/bicycle or pedestrian at Smithfield Beach, Milford Beach, Bushkill Access, Dingmans Access in PA and Turtle Beach and Watergate in NJ.
Contact Information:
570-588-2435
www.nps.gov/dewa

Protected for its outstanding cultural, recreational, scenic, and ecological values, this river flows 40 miles (64 km) through the Delaware Water Gap National Recreation Area. Swimming, boating, and fishing opportunities are available.

Steamtown National Historic Site
Fast Facts
Established: 1986
Acreage: 62 (25 hectares)
Visitors (2019): 105,403
Nearest Major Airport: Newark Liberty Intl. (EWR), Newark, NJ
Nearest Major Highways: I-81, I-84, I-476, US-11
Fees: $0
Accessibility: Mostly accessible except for some train rides and excursions.
Contact Information:
570-340-5200
www.nps.gov/stea

The former Delaware, Lackawanna & Western Railroad yard, including remains of the roundhouse, the switchyard, and other buildings, was transformed into an interpretive museum complex. This complex includes a theater showing the park film, locomotive repair/restoration shops, and

One of many steam locomotives on display at Steamtown National Historic Site.

a collection of working steam locomotives and railroad cars that tell the story of steam railroading in America.

Thaddeus Kosciuszko National Memorial

Fast Facts

Established: 1972
Acreage: 0 (0 hectares)
Visitors (2019): 1,921
Nearest Major Airport: Philadelphia Intl. (PHL), Philadelphia, PA
Nearest Major Highways: I-95, I-76, I-676
Fees: $0
Accessibility: The first floor of the building is accessible, but the restrooms are not.
Contact Information:
215-597-7130
www.nps.gov/thko

Commemorates the life and work of the Polish military leader who served in the Continental Army during the American Revolution. The site is administered by rangers and other staff from Independence National Historical Park, a five-minute walk away.

Upper Delaware Scenic and Recreational River

Fast Facts

Established: 1978
Acreage: 75,000 (30,351 hectares)
Visitors (2019): 215,537
Nearest Major Airport: New York Stewart Intl. (SWF), New Windsor, NY
Nearest Major Highways: I-81, I-84, I-86, NY-17
Fees: $0
Accessibility: Limited.
Contact Information:
570-729-7134
www.nps.gov/upde

Preserves the remarkable cultural, recreational, scenic, and ecological values of this 73-mile (118-km) stretch of river on the Pennsylvania-New York border. The area includes the Roebling Bridge, believed to be the oldest existing wire-cable suspension bridge, and the Zane Grey home.

Reconstructed log cabins at Valley Forge National Historical Park, where the Continental Army spent the winter of 1777–78.

Valley Forge National Historical Park

Fast Facts

Established: 1976
Acreage: 3,468 (1,403 hectares)
Visitors (2019): 2,259,944
Nearest Major Airport: Philadelphia Intl. (PHL), Philadelphia, PA
Nearest Major Highways: I-76, US-422
Fees: $0
Accessibility: Mostly accessible. There is no automatic door to the Washington Memorial Chapel.
Contact Information:
610-783-1000
www.nps.gov/vafo

The site of the 1777–78 Continental Army winter encampment preserves historic landscapes, earthworks, archeological sites, historic structures (including Washington's Headquarters), and a collection of objects illustrating the life of the continental soldier. The park also protects significant natural resources.

RHODE ISLAND
Blackstone River Valley National Historical Park

Fast Facts

Established: 2014
Acreage: 1,489 (603 hectares)
Visitors (2019): NA

Nearest Major Airport: Boston Logan Intl. (BOS), Boston, MA
Nearest Major Highways: I-95, US-1
Fees: $0
Accessibility: Varies by location.
Contact Information:
  401-762-0250
  www.nps.gov/blac

Preserves, protects, and interprets the nationally significant resources that exemplify the industrial heritage of the Blackstone River Valley.

Roger Williams National Memorial
Fast Facts
Established: 1965
Acreage: 5 (2 hectares)
Visitors (2019): 59,419
Nearest Major Airport: Boston Logan Intl. (BOS), Boston, MA
Nearest Major Highways: I-195, US-1
Fees: $0
Accessibility: Mostly accessible.
Contact Information:
  401-521-7266
  www.nps.gov/rowi

Banished from Massachusetts for his religious beliefs, Roger Williams founded Providence in 1636. This memorial commemorates his "outstanding contributions to the development of the principles of religious freedom in this country."

The memorial is a landscaped urban park on the site of the freshwater spring that was the center of the original settlement of Providence.

VERMONT
Marsh-Billings-Rockefeller National Historical Park
Fast Facts
Established: 1992
Acreage: 643 (260 hectares)
Visitors (2019): 45,979
Nearest Major Airport: Burlington Intl. (BTV), Burlington, VT
Nearest Major Highways: I-89, I-91, US-4
Fees: $8/adults aged 16–61, $4/senior aged 62 and over, for guided tours of the mansion. Separate admission fee for Billings Farm & Museum
Accessibility: Fully ADA-compliant.
Contact Information:
  802-457-3368
  www.nps.gov/mabi

Home to pioneer conservationist George Perkins Marsh, the park includes a model farm and forest developed by Frederick Billings and maintained by granddaughter Mary French Rockefeller and her husband, Laurance S. Rockefeller. The park is headquarters for the Conservation Study Institute, designed to enhance leadership in the field of conservation.

THE CAPITAL
REGION

The National Mall and Memorial Parks

"America's Front Yard," is the first stop on most itineraries to the nation's capital. Home of the country's most iconic museums, monuments, and memorials to the people and events that have shaped American history, the National Mall was the site of Dr. Martin Luther King Jr.'s 1963 "I Have a Dream" speech, as well as rallies and protests for countless social issues, including women's suffrage (1913), opposition to the Vietnam War (1969), and the rights of Native Americans (1978). Since 1981, it has also hosted the quadrennial presidential inauguration ceremony.

The Mall is nearly as old as the nation itself. As president, George Washington commissioned the French engineer Pierre L'Enfant in 1791 to develop a landscape plan for the fledgling nation's new capital. L'Enfant originally envisioned a tree-lined "Grand Avenue" at the center of this new city. Today's Washington D.C. still reflects **L'Enfant's urban plan** for a rectangular grid overlapped by wide, majestic,

The original Mall was defined as the green space between the Washington Monument and the U.S. Capitol building.

Construction of the Washington Monument was interrupted in 1853 (note the two different colors) when the Know-Nothing Party couldn't raise enough funds to complete the obelisk.

diagonal boulevards and 15 large plazas where the boulevards intersected the avenues. But his design for the Mall was largely forgotten for the nation's first 100 years. During the Civil War, the land was used to quarter federal troops, slaughter cattle, and produce weapons. After the war, the Baltimore and Potomac Railroad laid tracks and built a rail depot at 6th and B Streets.

It wasn't until after the release of the 1902 McMillan Commission report that L'Enfant's vision was realized. The commission's plan called for a broad grass lawn, similar to what you'd find in a formal European-style garden, flanked by rows of American elm trees and stately public buildings. Since then, the Mall has been a mosaic

of American history, with each generation adding to the story.

The Mall itself is typically defined as the green space between the **Washington Monument** and the **U.S. Capitol Building**. As defined by the Park Service, "**The National Mall**" extends west to include the **Lincoln Memorial** and south to include the **Jefferson Memorial**. "The Reserve" includes all of the above, plus the **Ellipse**, the **White House**, and **Lafayette Square**. This last definition results in a cross-shaped greenbelt, with the Washington Monument at its center, and all other sites within walking distance.

Of those sites, only the White House, the Capitol, the **Smithsonian "Castle,"** and the

lower half of the Washington Monument (construction halted in 1853 when the Know-Nothing Party failed to raise the funds to complete the obelisk) predate the McMillan Commission plan. Since then, however, the Mall has grown ever more crowded, beginning with the **National Museum of Natural History** (1910), the Lincoln Memorial (1922), the **National Gallery** (1941), and the Jefferson Memorial (1943). The popularity of Maya Lin's **Vietnam Veterans Memorial** (1982) inspired a spate of memorials to other American wars, in reverse chronological order: **Korea** (1995), **World War II** (2004) and **World War I** (2014).

Franklin Delano Roosevelt got his own memorial in 1997;

The Smithsonian Museum "Castle" was one of the first buildings on the Mall.

Lei Yixin's statue of **Martin Luther King Jr.** was unveiled in 2011; **Dwight Eisenhower's Memorial** opened in 2020 across the street from the headquarters of the Federal Aviation Administration, which Ike authorized in 1958.

Just as Abraham Lincoln's presidency forever changed the nation, his memorial forever altered the Mall, extending it another mile (1.6 km) west to the Potomac. At the time of Lincoln's death, the area where his memorial now sits was in the middle of the Potomac River. The building sits on landfill that lines up perfectly with the Washington Monument and Capitol to form the Mall's horizontal axis.

Calls for a national memorial to the 16th president began

The Lincoln Memorial, the Washington Monument, and the Capitol line up along the National Mall's horizontal axis.

Dr. Martin Luther King Jr. delivered his "I Have A Dream" speech from the steps of the Lincoln Memorial in 1963.

even as he lingered on his deathbed. But it took another half-century for construction of Henry Bacon's **Parthenon-inspired building** to begin. The 36 Doric columns represent the 36 states in the Union at the time of Lincoln's death, all of which are listed in the frieze above the colonnade, with the year they entered the union. **Daniel French's statue** and **Jules Guerin's murals** were dedicated in 1922; the **Reflecting Pool** was finished a year later.

Like the war it evoked, Maya Lin's **Vietnam Veterans Memorial** was controversial when it first opened. Some veterans complained that it honored only the dead and not the living, and objected to its subterranean location and its color, which one veteran supposedly dubbed "the black gash of shame." The critics were quickly overwhelmed, however, by the thousands of visitors who came and started taking rubbings of the names of fallen comrades and family members. The outpouring was as unexpected as the memorial's architect: at the time her design was chosen out of more than 1,400 submissions, Lin was a 21-year-old Yale student who got a B on the same proposal when she submitted it for grading.

Soon thereafter, veterans of the Korean War lobbied for their own memorial, and in 1995, they got one. The outdoor plaza features a reflective wall engraved

The White House

267

The cherry trees burst into bloom along the Tidal Basin every spring.

stop at the Martin Luther King Jr. and Franklin D. Roosevelt Memorials. Either direction is sure to be replete with other tourists taking selfies, especially in late March and early April, when the **cherry trees** lining the route explode in shocking pink blossoms. The Jefferson Memorial sits at the far end of this loop, lining up with the Washington Monument and the White House to complete the Mall's vertical axis. FDR even ordered the removal of several trees to enhance the view of the Jefferson Memorial from the White House. The 3,000 cherry trees, a gift from the mayor of Tokyo, were added in 1912.

DC Circulator (dccirculator. com) operates a fleet of fully accessible **buses** ($1) that do a figure-eight route around the Mall area, stopping at 14 popular sites as well as Union Station.

not with names, but with images that represent all those who served. Stainless steel statues of soldiers appear to be marching through a triangular field toward an open circle, with a pool ringed by benches, intended as a quiet space for honoring the sacrifices made during the war.

"A grand reunion" of World War II veterans were on hand in 2004 when their memorial opened to the public. Unlike the Vietnam memorial, the **National WWII Memorial** was instantly popular, attracting more than 4 million visitors annually. It has a little something for everyone. The north side represents victory over the European Axis powers, while its south side symbolizes triumph in the Pacific theater. A series of 24 bas-relief panels place the battle heroics abroad side-by-side with the efforts of Americans on the homefront. On the west side, a wall of 4,054 gold stars represents the 405,399 Americans (1 star per 100 people) who lost their lives during the war. Other walls feature statements from Presidents Roosevelt and Truman, as well as some secret

"Kilroy Was Here" engravings of the kind that G.I.s used to draw on buildings throughout Europe.

The WWII Memorial is a good place to start a 2-mile (3-km) loop walk around the **Tidal Basin**. Go clockwise to get to the paddleboat rental stand, or counter-clockwise to

Rudolph Evans's statue of Thomas Jefferson looks toward the White House from the Jefferson Memorial.

Assateague Island National Seashore

Fast Facts

Established: 1965
Acreage: 41,347 (16,733 hectares)
Visitors (2019): 2,344,536
Visitor Centers: Assateague Island, Toms Cove (within the Chincoteague National Wildlife Refuge, VA)
Nearest Major Airport: Norfolk Intl. (ORF), Norfolk, VA
Nearest Major Highways: US-13, US-50, MD-611
Fees: $10/vehicle per day; $25/vehicle weekly pass (valid for 7 days)
Accessibility: All visitor centers are accessible, as are most nature trails, bathhouses, and wayside exhibits. Two accessible campsites may be reserved in advance.
Contact Information: 410-641-1441 www.nps.gov/asis

Like so many of the East Coast's best beaches, Assateague Island National Seashore occupies a **barrier island** off the mainland. Less than a mile south of **Fenwick Island** and the honkytonk atmosphere of **Ocean City**, Assateague is an oasis of quiet. There are no lodgings of any kind, and no restaurants other than a beach hut and a gift shop/snack bar. Just miles and miles—37 miles (60 km), to be precise—of undeveloped sandy beaches, perfect for whiling away a summer afternoon.

Unlike most other beaches, however, this one comes with ponies! About **150 wild horses** roam the island, and while most try to avoid people, a few wander into the parking lots and nose around. Don't touch or feed the ponies; not only is it harmful to their health, it could be harmful to yours. These ponies live in the wild, not a petting zoo, and they can bite and or kick. These wild horses *should* keep you away.

Once a year, usually during the last week of July, the local **Saltwater Cowboys** round up the entire herd so that a

More than 150 wild horses roam the Assateague National Seashore.

269

Every year, the entire herd swims across the Assateague Channel to nearby Chincoteague Island, where new foals are auctioned off.

veterinarian can check their health. The next day, the cowboys swim the herd across the **Assateague Channel** to nearby **Chincoteague Island,** where the horses parade down **Main Street** to the **pony auction** at the **Chincoteague Carnival Grounds.** Selling off the foals prevents the herd from growing too large, and raises money for the Chincoteague Volunteer Fire Company. After the auction, the adult ponies make the **return swim to Assateague,** where they live in the wild for another year. Visitors can watch any part of this week-long spectacle, but the swim, the parade, and the auction are the most popular events. Those in the know head out on the water and watch the swim from a **charter boat** (reserve far in advance).

The other 51 weeks a year, Assateague's primary attraction

is the **beach**. The long, skinny island is divided into two discrete sections, with no road between them (visitors must drive back to the mainland and cross a different bridge to travel between the two sections). The **Maryland** side includes **Assateague State Park. Virginia's** side consists largely of the **Chincoteague National Wildlife Refuge**. Camping is not permitted on the Virginia side, but Maryland is chockablock with campsites, most of which accommodate tents, trailers, and RVs alike, with a few more primitive backcountry sites for tents only. Each site includes a picnic table and fire grill; many campgrounds also feature drinking water, showers, and chemical toilets. An additional 350 campsites are contained within Assateague State Park, where hot-water bathhouse facilities are also available.

A select few nature trails—they're not long enough to be called hikes—lace the island, many on elevated boardwalks over boggy ground. The three trails in the Maryland half (**Life of the Marsh, Life of the Dunes,** and **Life of the Forest**) are all within walking distance of one another at the end of Bayberry Drive and none is more than ¾-mile (1-km) long. Each one introduces visitors to the distinct flora and fauna found on different parts of the island. **Birders** will find snowy egrets and other wading birds in the salt marsh. Eastern towhees, screech owls, and great horned owls proliferate in the forest. The dunes are home to yellow warblers, mourning doves, bobwhite quails, and American goldfinches.

Bicyclists can rent wheels on Chincoteague Island and cross

Snowy egrets are a common sight in Assateague's salt marshes.

over the channel to the **National Wildlife Refuge** via a dedicated paved path. It's also possible to rent bikes from **The Beach Hut**, located in the North Ocean Beach Parking lot just past the entrance to the National Seashore. The longest cycling trails are the 3-mile (5-km) **Wildlife Loop** and the 1-mile (1.6-km) **Black Duck Marsh Trail**. Bikes are also allowed on a 1.25-mile (2 km) stretch of the Refuge's unpaved **service road**. Another 6 miles (10 km) of the service road are open only to walking.

Crabbing is another popular activity on the island, and very little equipment is required. All you need are some chicken legs or necks, string, and a net with a long handle. Bring a ruler to measure crab size (keep nothing smaller than 5 inches (7.5 cm)

at the widest point across the shell for most types) and a cooler with ice. The best spots for catching blue crabs are **Old Ferry Landing** in the Maryland district,

and on the docks by the **National Wildlife Refuge** entrance on the Virginia side.

Surf fishing, on the other hand, involves a bit more gear.

Miles of deserted beaches make Assateague a quiet place to camp . . .

. . . unless you leave your food unsecured.

The Park Service recommends using a 13-foot (4-m) rod and heavy sinkers to keep the line on the bottom under big waves. Summer flounder, kingfish, black drum, and striped bass are the species most frequently caught.

Assateague Outfitters (www.assateagueoutfitters.com; 410-656-9453) is the place to rent canoes or kayaks. It's located on the calm, bay side of the National Seashore, where islands and inlets beckon exploration. For a guided paddle (and expert help in locating ponies in the wild), arrive at 10 a.m. or 1 p.m. for the **Wildlife Discovery Tour** ($50/adult, $30/child; price includes kayak rental but not Park admission).

Pony Express Snack Bar, located across the parking lot from the Assateague State Park Ranger Station, dishes out ice cream, milkshakes, and slushies, in addition to grill favorites like hot dogs, hamburgers, and fish and chips. The only other place to get ice, firewood, beverages, and other provisions, is the Beach Hut.

Crabbing requires little equipment but size minimums must be observed.

Blue Ridge Parkway

Conceived amid a burst of optimism during the depths of the Depression, the Blue Ridge Parkway was the most visited site in the National Park System every year from 1946 to 2012. "America's Favorite Drive" meanders for 469 miles (755 km) between two other landmarks: Shenandoah National Park in Virginia and Great Smoky Mountains National Park in North Carolina and Tennessee. But from the beginning, the parkway was never about getting anywhere quickly. On the contrary, the two-lane road was designed as a leisurely drive and a destination unto itself, with trucks and other commercial vehicles banned from its entire length.

Although the road is narrow, the channel it cuts through the Blue Ridge Mountains is wider than a typical right-of-way. That means the view is constantly framed by the beauty of the surroundings, rather than gas stations, fast-food joints, and other roadside attractions. There are no billboards, stop signs, or traffic lights along the route, and cellphone reception isn't always a sure thing. Even the utilities are buried to preserve sightlines. Entrances and exits appear regularly, but with little indication of where they lead to or from. The speed limit of 45 mph (72 km/h) makes it easy to slow down when you spot wildlife.

Auto touring is, of course, the most popular activity on the parkway. No matter your destination (if you even have one), you're likely to spend some

Fast Facts

Established: 1936
Acreage: 95,974 (38,839 hectares)
Visitors (2019): 14,976,085 (includes visitors in Virginia and North Carolina)
Visitor Centers: Blue Ridge Parkway, Craggy Gardens, Doughton Park, Humpback Rocks, James River, Linn Cove Viaduct, Linville Falls, Peaks of Otter, Rocky Knob, Waterrock Knob
Nearest Major Airport: Richmond Intl. (RIC), VA, at the north end; Charlotte Douglas Intl. (CLT), Charlotte, NC, at the south end.
Nearest Major Highways: I-26, I-40, I-64, I-77, I-81
Fees: $0
Accessibility: Varies by location. Visit www.nps.gov/blri/planyourvisit/accessibility.htm for detailed information about accessibility at 25 locations along the route.
Contact Information: 828-348-3400
www.nps.gov/blri

Drive slowly to avoid harming wildlife on the Blue Ridge Parkway.

Mabry Mill

amount of time getting there, more if you stop at any of the 382 overlooks along the way, where the views must be beheld without a windshield in front of them. Heading south from Shenandoah, the first must-see pullout is **Raven's Roost** (milepost 10.7) for an overview of the entire route. A weathered copper map identifies the **seven mountain peaks** visible from this aerie, which hangs over the side of a high cliff. You might spot mountain climbers rappelling down the cliff face or climbing back up, or hang gliders taking off from the roost.

Mabry Mill (milepost 176) preserves Ed and Lizzy Mabry's century-old Appalachian home, grist mill, sawmill, and blacksmith shop. In summer, cultural demonstrations and Sunday afternoon music and

dancing are an additional reason to take a break here. **Blue Ridge Music Center** (milepost 213) is a dedicated outdoor amphitheater in a pastoral setting, devoted to

maintaining the region's rich heritage of folk music and dance.

The **Linn Cove Viaduct** (milepost 304) is a testament to the parkway's respect for

To minimize damage to the natural setting, Linn Cove Viaduct was built on stanchions.

the natural setting it traverses. The heavy equipment used in traditional road-building techniques would have done serious damage to **Grandfather Mountain**. Instead, the engineers built an elevated highway on stanchions, minimizing excavation. The parkway's "missing link" wasn't completed until 1987, more than half a century after the parkway's first segments were built, but the wait was worth it: the only trees that had to be cut down were those directly below the viaduct.

There's nowhere to stop along the viaduct itself, but if you'd like a closer look at the supporting superstructure, hike for less than a mile along the **Tanawha Trail** from the **Linn Cove Visitor Center** just south of the viaduct.

If you'd like a longer outing, the trail continues over flagstone paths, past boulder formations, and through hardwood forests for 12 miles (19 km) north **to Julian Price Lake**, or south 1.5 miles (2 km) to **Beacon Heights,** two more much-visited overlooks.

Chestoa View Overlook (milepost 320.7) is easy to miss, and requires a short walk (0.7 miles/1 km) to the viewing area: a paved stone patio with a half-moon-shaped rock wall overlooking **Linville Gorge**, with **Table Rock** and Grandfather Mountain in the background.

Mt. Mitchell, the highest peak east of the Mississippi, is 10 miles (16 km) northeast of **Craggy Gardens** (milepost 364). The windswept landscape here is noted for its carpets of

rhododendrons and blueberry heaths. The **Craggy Pinnacle Trail** might be the easiest summit hike in the entire National Park System. The 360-degree views from the peak are just 20 minutes' walk from the parking lot.

Cowee Mountain Overlook (milepost 430) isn't quite the highest point on the drive. That distinction belongs to the **Richland Balsam Overlook** (6,053 feet/1,845 m) located 1.4 miles (2 km) farther south. But the views from Cowee are superior, especially at sunrise and sunset. Here is where you'll get the classic Blue Ridge Mountains view of one range layered behind another behind another.

The parkway's southernmost visitor center, **Waterrock Knob**

The view from Cowee Mountain overlook makes it easy to see how the Blue Ridge Mountains got their name.

(milepost 451.2), is also the highest in elevation (5,820 ft/ 1,774 m). From this lofty perch, visitors can look west over the **Cherokee Indian Reservation**, with the eastern edge of Great Smoky Mountains National Park and several **Appalachian mountain chains** in the distance. Sunrise and sunset are popular visiting hours.

The Maine-to-Georgia **Appalachian Trail** more or less parallels the parkway for its first 100 miles (160 km) in Virginia, and the **Mountains-to-Sea Trail** crosses the parkway around milepost 382, just south of Asheville, NC, on its 1,200-mile (1,929-km) sojourn across North Carolina. Another 369 miles (594 km) of hiking trails leave from various locations along the route.

The parkway dips to its lowest elevation where **Otter Creek** (milepost 60.8) empties into the **James River**. Look for beaver dams on the 0.9-mile (1.4-km) **Otter Lake Loop Trail**, or follow the **Otter Creek Trail,** which crosses the road twice and the creek multiple times over a length of 2.3 miles (3.7 km) each way. The **Green Knob Trail** in **Julian Price Park** (milepost 295.9) is a moderate 2.3-mile (3.7 km) loop along a creek, through rhododendrons, to a view of **Price Lake**. The only hard part is the steep descent at the end, which affords views of **Calloway Peak** on the horizon.

Two different trails leave from the **Linville Falls Visitor Center** (milepost 316.4). The 1.6-mile (2-km) round-trip **Erwins View**

Trail traces the south bank of the Linville River, with overlooks at **Upper Linville Falls**, the chimney-like rock formations at **Chimney View** near the lower falls, **Gorge View**, and a panoramic vista at **Erwins View**. The **Linville Gorge Trail** stays north of the river but is more strenuous. Keep right at the fork for views of the chimneys and the lower falls from **Plunge Basin Overlook**, or bear left to descend to the pool at the bottom of the falls. **Swimming is not permitted anywhere along the Blue Ridge Parkway**, especially here, no matter how inviting the pool might look on a hot day.

The moderate 2.5-mile (4-km) **Crabtree Falls** loop trail (milepost 339.5) leads to a cascade over a 60-foot (18-m)

The Green Knob Trail is an easy hike that ends at Price Lake.

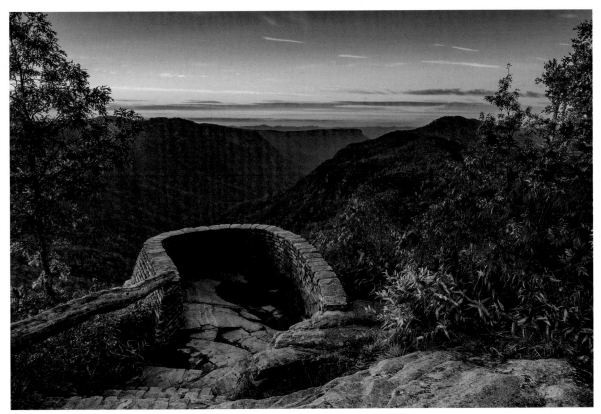

Linville Gorge

cliff face. Ferns and wildflowers thrive on the mist from the waterfall. A series of switchbacks provides a more gradual route back to the parking lot. The 3.2-mile (5.2-km) round-trip **Mt. Pisgah Trail** (milepost 407.6) ascends steeply for 712 feet (217 m) to the summit, with views of the **Shining Rock Wilderness** and the **French Broad River Valley**. An easier option is the **Buck Spring Trail**, a 1.1-mile (1.8-km) section of the Mountains-to-Sea Trail between the **Pisgah Inn** and the **Buck Spring Gap Parking Area**.

The Parkway's leisurely driving speed and well-paved roadway makes it an appealing option for biking. Cyclists should note, however, that there's no dedicated bike lane and limited clearance in the 26 tunnels along the parkway. Distances between developed areas can be long, and the frequent changes in elevation mean constantly changing weather and plenty of hills. The hardest climbs headed southbound are from the **James River Visitor Center** to **Thunder Ridge** (3,300 feet/1,007 m of elevation gain) and between

Balsam Gap and Waterrock Knob (2,450 feet/747 m). Riding north, the first 7 miles (11 km) are a 2,240-foot (683-m) ascent; between **Bull Gap** and **Craggy Gardens**, there's another climb of 2,535 feet (773 m). Visit www.nps.gov/blri/planyourvisit/bicycling-the-parkway.htm for a list of elevation gains up and down the entire Parkway.

Colonial National Historic Park

The two main sites of this park neatly bookend the history of colonial America. **Historic Jamestowne** was established in 1607 as the first permanent English settlement in North America; **Yorktown Battlefield** is where George Washington finally defeated British General Charles Cornwallis's army in 1781, ending the American Revolution. **Colonial Parkway**, a 23-mile (37-km) ribbon of scenic roadway, connects the two historic sites.

It's possible to explore both major sites independently with nothing more than the park brochure and a map. But many visitors find the various guided tour options more informative and enjoyable. The standard **ranger-led tour** of Historic Jamestowne retraces the steps of Captain John Smith and Pocahontas; it lasts about 45 minutes and requires only a little bit of walking. For a deeper dive into the history of the region, join an **Archaeology Tour of James Fort**, an active dig site where you may have the opportunity to ask questions of archaeologists actively working on the excavation. Long thought lost to erosion by the James

Fast Facts

Established: 1930/1936
Acreage: 8,677 (3,511 hectares)
Visitors (2019): 3,327,268
Visitor Centers: Historic Jamestowne, Yorktown Battlefield
Nearest Major Airport: Norfolk Intl. (ORF), Norfolk, VA
Nearest Major Highways: I-64, Colonial Parkway; VA-31 (Jamestowne), US-17 (Yorktown)
Fees: $25/adult (16 and older); free for children 15 and younger.
Accessibility: Most visitor centers, walking paths, restrooms, and other facilities are accessible, with a few exceptions. Visit www.nps.gov/colo/planyourvisit/accessibility.htm for specifics.
Contact Information: 757-898-3400 www.nps.gov/colo

Ranger-led tours of Historic Jamestowne retrace the steps of Captain John Smith . . .

. . . and attempt to separate fact from fiction in the life story of Pocahontas.

River, the Fort has been gradually unearthed since the dig began in 1994, yielding more than 3 million artifacts from the settlement's earliest days. To date, the archaeologists here have uncovered 80% of the original triangular fort.

There are also specialized tours focusing on the contributions of African Americans; the Powhatan, Nanticoke, and Algonquin peoples; and blacksmiths and barrel makers. These tours rotate regularly; check historicjamestowne.org/visit/visit-guide/ for the daily schedule.

A previous excavation in 1948 discovered the ruins of **glass furnaces** built by the early colonists. Today, in a reconstructed interpretive facility, glass blowers in period costumes produce wine bottles,

pitchers, candlesticks, and other common objects using the tools and methods available to 17th-century artisans. One historical anachronism: today's furnaces are heated by natural gas, rather than wood. Many of the objects produced in the **Glasshouse** here are available for sale.

"The Siege at Yorktown," a 16-minute film shown every half-hour at the **Yorktown Battlefield Visitor Center,** provides context you'll need to understand the final conflict of the American Revolution. From there, visitors can take either (or both) of two self-guided driving tours of the battlefield. The free **Yorktown Tour Guide app** includes GPS-enabled audio tours of both routes; free maps of the route are also available from the Visitor Center.

A reconstructed fort at Historic Jamestowne.

Artillery in place at Yorktown, site of the last battle of the American Revolution.

Other highlights of the Yorktown section of the park include the **1730 Nelson House**, a fine example of early Georgian architecture, most of which is original; the restored **Moore House**, where Washington and Cornwallis negotiated the British surrender; and **Yorktown National Cemetery**, where more than 2,000 members of the Union Army (and at least 10 Confederate soldiers) were buried four score and seven years after the American Revolution.

Colonial Parkway was envisioned as a central artery for the park since its inception. Like other national parkways, it is free from development, allowing

The 13 figures at the base of the Yorktown Victory Monument represent the 13 U.S. colonies.

visitors to imagine the landscape as it was in the 17th century. The lack of commerce also makes the parkway an exceptional corridor for spotting 200 species of birds, as well as deer, red foxes, and minks. Not surprisingly, autumn's changing leaf colors bring out people interested in a leisurely drive.

Ten miles northeast of Historic Jamestowne is the city of **Williamsburg**, Virginia's capital from 1699 to 1780 and the third corner of the so-called Historic Triangle of colonial settlements. **Colonial Williamsburg**, the world's largest living-history museum, is privately owned and not affiliated with the national park, but visitors to this region often include it on their itineraries. Those plans might also include stops at **Jamestown Settlement** and **The American Revolution Museum at Yorktown**, two more privately run attractions unaffiliated with the National Park Service.

Colonial Parkway is also a popular **bicycle route** because of its relatively slow-moving traffic. In addition to the 23 miles (37 km) between Jamestowne

and Yorktown, cyclists may pedal **Island Drive**, a 5-mile (8-km) loop around the entire island of Jamestown; a shorter 3-mile (5-km) loop is also possible. Motor homes, buses, and other large vehicles are prohibited from Island Drive. Of the two Yorktown Battlefield driving routes, the 9-mile (14-km) **Encampment Tour** generally has less vehicular traffic than the 7-mile (11-km) **Battlefield Tour.** The Encampment Tour begins at **Surrender Field** and is marked by yellow arrow signs.

Cape Henry Memorial marks the approximate site where the first settlers of Jamestown disembarked in 1607, 13 years before the Mayflower landed on Plymouth Rock. It's technically part of Colonial National Historic Park, but it's located 50 miles (80 km) farther south. There isn't much to do around the memorial other than climb the 165 steps of the spiral staircase to the top of **Cape Henry Lighthouse** ($14). The first federally funded public works project by the U.S. government, the lighthouse is administered not by the Park Service, but by Preservation Virginia.

MORE TO SEE IN THE U.S. CAPITAL REGION

DELAWARE
First State National Historical Park
Fast Facts
Established: 2013/2014
Acreage: 1,115 (467 hectares)
Visitors (2019): NA
Nearest Major Airport: Philadelphia Intl. (PHL), Philadelphia, PA
Nearest Major Highway: I-95
Fees: $0
Contact Information:
  202-824-3560
  www.nps.gov/frst
(Also in Pennsylvania)

Delaware's lone national park consists of six individual sites across the state: the Brandywine Valley, Fort Christina (in Wilmington), Old Swedes Historic Site (in Wilmington), New Castle Court House Museum (in New Castle), The Green (in Dover), and John Dickinson Plantation (in Dover).

DISTRICT OF COLUMBIA
African American Civil War Memorial
Fast Facts
Established: 2004
Acreage: NA
Visitors (2019): NA
Nearest Major Airport: Ronald Reagan Washington National (DCA), Arlington, VA
Nearest Major Highways: I-395, US-1, US-29, US-50
Nearest Metro Station: Memorial/Cardozo
Fees: $0
Accessibility: Fully accessible.
Contact Information:
  202-426-6841
  www.nps.gov/afam

Honors the service and sacrifice of more than 200,000 Black soldiers and sailors who served in the U.S. Army and Navy during the Civil War. Their efforts helped end the war and free over four million slaves. *(A unit of National Mall and Memorial Parks)*

Anacostia Park
Fast Facts
Established: 1914/1933
Acreage: 1,200 (486 hectares)
Visitors (2019): NA
Nearest Major Airport: Ronald Reagan Washington National (DCA), Arlington, VA
Nearest Major Highways: I-295
Nearest Metro Station: Anacostia or Potomac
Fees: $0
Accessibility: The paved Anacostia River Trail that spans the length of the park is wheelchair accessible.
Contact Information:
  202-472-3884
  www.nps.gov/anac

Anacostia Park, site of the 1932 "Bonus March," is a neighborhood park stretching the length of the Anacostia River. The southern portion is a multi-use recreational park with shoreline and river access, ball fields, tennis courts, swimming pool, roller skating pavilion, riverwalk trail, and picnic areas. It provides a breath of fresh air and a space to unwind amid a bustling city. Visitors can exercise along the river trail or relax by the water.

Belmont-Paul Women's Equality National Monument
Fast Facts
Established: 2016
Acreage: 0.34 (0.13 hectares)
Visitors (2019): 9,913
Nearest Major Airport: Ronald Reagan Washington National (DCA), Arlington, VA
Nearest Major Highways: I-395, US-1, US-50

Nearest Metro Station: Union Station, Capitol South
Fees: $0
Accessibility: A series of lifts make the first floor exhibits accessible to visitors in wheelchairs.
Contact Information:
202-543-2240
www.nps.gov/bepa

Home to the National Woman's Party (NWP) for more than 90 years, this house was the epicenter of the struggle for women's rights. In the shadow of the U.S. Capitol and the Supreme Court, Alice Paul and the NWP developed strategies and tactics to advocate for the Equal Rights Amendment and equality for women.

Carter G. Woodson Home National Historic Site

Fast Facts
Established: 2006
Acreage: 0.15 (0.06 hectares)

Visitors (2019): 2,381
Nearest Major Airport: Ronald Reagan Washington National (DCA), Arlington, VA
Nearest Major Highways: I-395, US-29
Nearest Metro Station: Shaw-Howard
Fees: $0
Accessibility: The second and third floor can only be reached by stairs. (There are future plans for an elevator.)
Contact Information:
202-426-5961 (staffed by the Fredrick Douglass National Historic Site)
www.nps.gov/cawo

"The Father of African-American History" founded the Association for the Study of African-American Life in 1915, and established its headquarters on the first floor of the home when he purchased it in 1922. In 1926, Woodson and his organization launched "Negro History Week," which eventually became Black History Month.

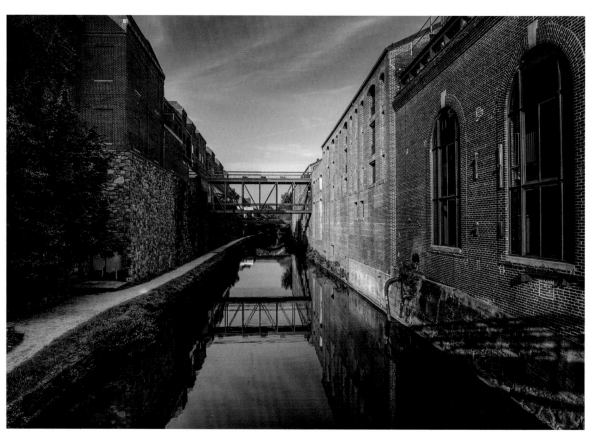

The first mile of the C&O Canal is a popular recreation path in Georgetown.

Chesapeake & Ohio Canal National Historic Park

Fast Facts

Established: 1938/1961/1971
Acreage: 19,612 (7,937 hectares)
Visitors (2019): 1,228,029
Visitor Centers: Brunswick, Cumberland, Georgetown, Great Falls Tavern, Hancock, Williamsport
Nearest Major Airport: Ronald Reagan Washington National (DCA), Arlington, VA
Nearest Major Highways: I-395, US-29
Fees: The Great Falls area is the only portion of the canal that charges an entrance fee: $20/vehicle, $15/motorcycle, $10/pedestrian or cyclist.
Accessibility: The gravel path can be muddy after rainfall. The hiking trails at Great Falls Tavern are not accessible.
Contact Information:
301-739-4200
www.nps.gov/choh
(Also in Maryland and West Virginia)

The C&O Towpath preserves the route of the 185-mile (298-km) canal along the Potomac River between Washington, DC, and Cumberland, MD. The canal was built between 1828 and 1850 and operated for nearly 100 years.

Civil War Defenses of Washington

Fast Facts

Established: 2010
Acreage: NA
Visitors (2019): NA
Nearest Major Airport: Ronald Reagan Washington National (DCA), Arlington, VA
Nearest Major Highways: I-395, US-50
Fees: $0
Accessibility: Varies by location. Many historic facilities are not accessible.
Contact Information:
202-829-2163
www.nps.gov/cwdw
(Also in Maryland and Virginia)

On forested hills surrounding the nation's capital are the remnants of a complex system of Civil War fortifications. These strategic buttresses transformed the young capital into one of the world's most fortified cities. By 1865, 68 forts and 93 batteries armed with over 800 cannons encircled Washington, DC. Today, you can visit 17 of the original sites now managed by the National Park Service (some can be found in Rock Creek Park).

Constitution Gardens

Fast Facts

Established: 1965/1974/1986
Acreage: 40 (16 hectares)
Visitors (2019): NA
Nearest Major Airport: Ronald Reagan Washington National (DCA), Arlington, VA
Nearest Major Highways: I-395, US-1, US-50.
Nearest Metro Station: Smithsonian/National Mall
Fees: $0
Contact Information:
202-426-6841
www.nps.gov/coga

Constructed during the American Revolution Bicentennial in 1976, Constitution Gardens is a living legacy to the founding of the republic as well as an oasis in the midst of a city landscape. A memorial to the 56 Signers of the Declaration of Independence was added in 1984. *(A unit of National Mall and Memorial Parks)*

Dwight D. Eisenhower Memorial

Fast Facts

Established: 2020
Acreage: 3.4 (1.4 hectares)
Visitors (2019): NA
Nearest Major Airport: Ronald Reagan Washington National (DCA), Arlington, VA
Nearest Major Highways: I-395, US-1, US-50
Nearest Metro Station: Archives-Navy Memorial-Penn Quarter, Smithsonian/National Mall
Fees: $0
Accessibility: Fully accessible
Contact Information:
202-426-6841
www.nps.gov/ddem

Commemorates Dwight D. Eisenhower's contributions to America as Supreme Commander of the Allied Expeditionary Force in World War II and as the nation's 34th President. *(A unit of National Mall and Memorial Parks)*

Ford's Theatre National Historic Site

Fast Facts

Established: 1886/1970
Acreage: 0.3 (0.1 hectares)
Visitors (2019): 572,373
Nearest Major Airport: Ronald Reagan
    Washington National (DCA), Arlington, VA
Nearest Major Highways: I-395, US-29
Nearest Metro Station: Metro Center
Fees: $0. Free tickets are required. Advanced
    reservations are $3.
Accessibility: Mostly accessible.
Contact Information:
    202-426-6924
    www.nps.gov/foth

Preserves the location where President Abraham
Lincoln was shot while attending a play on April
14, 1865, and the William Petersen House, across
the street, where the nation's 16th president died
the following morning. The museum beneath the
theater contains objects associated with Lincoln's
life and his assassination. The theater continues to
stage live performances. *(A unit of National Mall and
Memorial Parks)*

Franklin Delano Roosevelt Memorial

Fast Facts

Established: 1959
Acreage: 8.1 (3.2 hectares)
Visitors (2019): 3,303,573
Nearest Major Airport: Ronald Reagan
    Washington National (DCA), Arlington, VA
Nearest Major Highways: I-395, US-1, US-50
Nearest Metro Station: Smithsonian/National Mall
Fees: $0
Accessibility: Fully accessible. Wheelchairs available
    on request.
Contact Information:
    202-426-6841
    www.nps.gov/frde

Four outdoor rooms along the Tidal Basin's cherry tree
walk trace more than 12 years of American history.
Each room corresponds to one of FDR's four terms in

Ford's Theatre, where Abraham Lincoln was assassinated, continues to stage live performances.

Franklin D. Roosevelt's dog Fala is the only canine to be represented in a presidential memorial.

office. Sculptures depict the 32nd president, First Lady Eleanor Roosevelt, and even his dog, Fala, the only canine representation in a presidential memorial. *(A unit of National Mall and Memorial Parks)*

Frederick Douglass National Historic Site
Fast Facts
Established: 1962/1988
Acreage: 8.6 (3.5 hectares)
Visitors (2019): 61,063
Nearest Major Airport: Ronald Reagan Washington National (DCA), Arlington, VA
Nearest Major Highways: I-295
Nearest Metro Station: Anacostia
Fees: $0. All visitors must take the guided tour; reservations are strongly encouraged.
Accessibility: Fully accessible except for the second floor, which can only be reached by stairs. Staff can provide a photo tour of the second floor.
Contact Information:
202-426-5961
www.nps.gov/frdo

Preserves and interprets Cedar Hill, where the "father of the civil rights movement" lived from 1877 until his death in 1895.

George Washington Memorial Parkway
Fast Facts
Established: 1930
Acreage: 7,035 (2,487 hectares)
Visitors (2019): 7,487,265
Nearest Major Airport: Ronald Reagan Washington National (DCA), Arlington, VA
Nearest Major Highways: I-295, I-395, I-495, I-695
Fees: $0, except for Great Falls Park ($20/vehicle, good for 7 days)
Contact Information:
703-289-2500
www.nps.gov/gwmp
(Also in Maryland and Virginia)

Developed as a memorial to the first U.S. president, this parkway preserves the natural scenery along the Potomac River. Over its 30 miles (48 km), it

Steel sculptures march through an open field at the Korean War Memorial.

links historic sites from Mount Vernon, past the Capital, to the Great Falls of the Potomac, where Washington demonstrated his skill as an engineer.

Kenilworth Park & Aquatic Gardens

Fast Facts

Established: 1938
Acreage: 30 (12 hectares)
Visitors (2019): NA
Nearest Major Airport: Ronald Reagan Washington National (DCA), Arlington, VA
Nearest Major Highways: US-50, DC-295
Nearest Metro Station: Deanwood
Fees: $0
Accessibility: The paths around the ponds and the river trail can be muddy and impassable for visitors in wheelchairs, especially after a rainy day.
Contact Information:
202-692-6080
www.nps.gov/keaq

The only NPS park dedicated to cultivating water-loving plants preserves the ponds, water gardens, and original greenhouses built by Walter Shaw in 1880 along the Anacostia River.

Lotuses bloom at Kenilworth Park and Aquatic Gardens.

Korean War Veterans Memorial

Fast Facts

Established: 1986
Acreage: 1.56 (0.6 hectares)
Visitors (2019): 3,841,633
Nearest Major Airport: Ronald Reagan
 Washington National (DCA), Arlington, VA
Nearest Major Highways: I-395, US-1, US-50.
Nearest Metro Station: Smithsonian/National Mall
Accessibility: Fully accessible.
Contact Information:
 202-426-6841
 www.nps.gov/kowa

This grouping of 19 statues of infantry soldiers by sculptor Frank Gaylord stand before a polished granite wall bearing images of uniformed service personnel representing the more than 1,789,000 American soldiers, sailors, airmen, and Marines who served in the Korean conflict from 1950 to 1953. *(A unit of National Mall and Memorial Parks)*

Lincoln Memorial

Fast Facts

Established: 1911
Acreage: 7.29 (2.95 hectares)

Visitors (2019): 7,808,182
Nearest Major Airport: Ronald Reagan
 Washington National (DCA), Arlington, VA
Nearest Major Highways: I-395, US-1, US-50
Nearest Metro Station: Smithsonian/National Mall
Fees: $0
Accessibility: Fully accessible.
Contact Information:
 202-426-6841
 www.nps.gov/linc

Architect Henry Bacon designed this neoclassical tribute to the 16th president of the United States. The 19-foot-high (6-m) marble statue of Lincoln by sculptor Daniel Chester French dominates the memorial, and the Gettysburg Address and Lincoln's Second Inaugural Address are engraved on the north and south interior walls. A promenade of elm trees flanks the Reflecting Pool, completed a year after the memorial. *(A unit of National Mall and Memorial Parks)*

LBJ Memorial Grove on the Potomac

Fast Facts

Established: 1973
Acreage: 17 (7 hectares)

Lincoln Memorial

Visitors (2019): 244,246
Nearest Major Airport: Ronald Reagan
   Washington National (DCA), Arlington, VA
Nearest Major Highways: I-395, US-1, US-50
Nearest Metro Station: Arlington Cemetery
Fees: $0
Contact Information:
   703-289-2500
   www.nps.gov/lydo

A living memorial to the 36th president, the park overlooks the Potomac River vista of the Capital. The design features 500 white pines and inscriptions on Texas granite. *(A unit of National Mall and Memorial Parks)*

Fees: $0
Contact Information:
   202-426-6841
   www.nps.gov/mlkm

Honors Dr. Martin Luther King Jr.'s contributions as a leader of the Black civil rights movement. The figure of Dr. King serves as the forward element of the Stone of Hope, detached from the Mountain of Despair, to reflect victory borne from disappointment. A wall of 16 quotes, presenting Dr. King's ideals of hope, democracy, and love, flanks the Mountain of Despair and encircles the Stone of Hope. *(A unit of National Mall and Memorial Parks)*

Martin Luther King Jr. Memorial
Fast Facts
Established: 1996
Acreage: 2.74 (1.11 hectares)
Visitors (2019): 3,667,562
Nearest Major Airport: Ronald Reagan
   Washington National (DCA), Arlington, VA
Nearest Major Highways: I-395, US-1, US-50
Nearest Metro Station: Smithsonian/National Mall

Mary McLeod Bethune Council House National Historic Site
Fast Facts
Established: 1982/1991
Acreage: 0.07 (0.02 hectares)
Visitors (2019): 3,788
Nearest Major Airport: Ronald Reagan
   Washington National (DCA), Arlington, VA
Nearest Major Highways: I-395, US-1, US-50

The Martin Luther King Jr. Memorial embodies a line from his "I Have a Dream" speech: "With this faith, we will be able to hew out of the mountain of despair a stone of hope."

Nearest Metro Station: Shaw/Howard University, McPherson Square
Fees: $0
Accessibility: Not wheelchair-accessible. A photo tour is available.
Contact Information:
202-673-2402
www.nps.gov/mamc

This was the first headquarters of the National Council of Negro Women, established by Mary McLeod Bethune in 1935. The site commemorates Bethune's leadership in the Black women's rights movement from 1943 to 1949.

Pennsylvania Avenue National Historic Site

Fast Facts
Established: 1965
Acreage: 18 (7 hectares)
Visitors (2019): 125,035
Nearest Major Airport: Ronald Reagan Washington National (DCA), Arlington, VA
Nearest Major Highways: I-395, US-1, US-29, US-50
Nearest Metro Station: Federal Triangle, Archives-Navy Memorial Penn Quarter
Fees: $0
Accessibility: Fully accessible.
Contact Information:
202-426-6841
www.nps.gov/paav

America's Main Street extends from the Capitol to the White House, linking two of the three branches of the U.S. government, and providing a setting for parades and cultural activities. The site comprises parks, plazas, sculpture, and memorials adjacent to the avenue, including John Marshall Park, the U.S. Navy Memorial, and Freedom Plaza. *(A unit of National Mall and Memorial Parks)*

Potomac Heritage National Scenic Trail

Fast Facts
Established: 1983
Length: 710 miles (1,142 km)
Visitors (2019): NA

Nearest Major Airport: Ronald Reagan Washington National (DCA), Arlington, VA; Pittsburgh Intl. (PIT), Pittsburgh, PA
Nearest Major Highways: I-66, I-68, I-70, I-76, I-95, I-395, I-495, US-1
Fees: $0
Contact Information:
202-619-7154
www.nps.gov/pohe
(Also in Maryland, Pennsylvania, and Virginia)

Between the mouth of the Potomac River and the Allegheny Highlands, this evolving trail network provides access to the beauty and heritage of the Potomac and Youghiogheny river corridors. The network includes the Laurel Highlands Hiking Trail and part of the Great Allegheny Passage in Pennsylvania; the Chesapeake & Ohio Canal Towpath in Maryland and Washington, D.C.; the Mount Vernon Trail in Virginia; and numerous bicycling routes, parks, historic sites, and nature areas throughout the region.

President's Park
See the White House. *(A unit of National Mall and Memorial Parks)*

Rock Creek Park
Fast Facts
Established: 1890
Acreage: 1,754 (710 hectares)
Visitors (2019): 2,416,232
Visitor Centers: Nature Center, Old Stone House, Peirce Mill

Rock Creek Park is one of the largest urban parks in the U.S.

Nearest Major Airport: Ronald Reagan
　Washington National (DCA), Arlington, VA
Nearest Major Highways: I-495, US-29
Nearest Metro Station: Cleveland Park
Fees: $0
Accessibility: Varies by location. Visit www.nps.
　gov/rocr/planyourvisit/accessibility.htm for
　details.
Contact Information:
　202-895-6000
　www.nps.gov/rocr

One of the largest natural urban parks in the U.S.,
this wooded preserve also contains a range of
historic and recreational features in the midst of
Washington, D.C.

Star-Spangled Banner National Historic Trail
Fast Facts
Established: 2008
Length: 560 miles (901 km)
Visitors (2019): NA
Visitor Centers: Fort McHenry National
　Monument and Historic Shrine
Nearest Major Airport: Baltimore/Washington
　Intl. Thurgood Marshall (BWI), Baltimore, MD
Nearest Major Highways: I-95, I-895 (Fort
　McHenry)
Fees: $0. Fort McHenry Trail Headquarters has an
　entrance fee of $15/adult (free for children 15
　and younger).
Contact Information:
　410-962-4290
　www.nps.gov/stsp
(Also in Virginia and Maryland)

Through sites and landscapes in Virginia, the
District of Columbia, and Maryland, the Trail tells
the stories of the events, people, and places that led
to the creation of the U.S. national anthem during
the War of 1812, when the Chesapeake Bay region
was choked by shipping blockades and ravaged by
enemy raids.

Theodore Roosevelt Island
Fast Facts
Established: 1932
Acreage: 89 (36 hectares)

Visitors (2019): 151,500
Nearest Major Airport: Ronald Reagan
　Washington National (DCA), Arlington, VA
Nearest Major Highways: I-66, US-29
Nearest Metro Station: Rosslyn
Fees: $0
Contact Information:
　703-289-2500
　www.nps.gov/this
(Also in Virginia)

Landscape architects transformed the former
Mason's Island from neglected, overgrown farmland
into a memorial to America's 26th president. They
conceived a "real forest" designed to mimic the
natural woodlands that once covered the island.
Today, miles of trails through wooded uplands
and swampy bottomlands honor the legacy of its
namesake outdoorsman and conservationist. (*A unit
of National Mall and Memorial Parks*)

Thomas Jefferson Memorial
Fast Facts
Established: 1934
Acreage: 18 (7 hectares)
Visitors (2019): 3,096,895
Nearest Major Airport: Ronald Reagan
　Washington National (DCA), Arlington, VA
Nearest Major Highways: I-395, US-1, US-50
Nearest Metro Station: Smithsonian/National Mall
Fees: $0
Contact Information:
　202-426-6841
　www.nps.gov/thje

Honors the primary author of the Declaration of
Independence, America's first secretary of state, and

Cherry blossoms frame the Jefferson Memorial.

third U.S. president (1801–09). Architect John Russell Pope designed this circular, colonnaded structure in an adaptation of the neoclassical style that Jefferson favored in his own architectural designs. *(A unit of National Mall and Memorial Parks)*

Vietnam Veterans Memorial
Fast Facts
Established: 1980
Acreage: 2.18 (0.88 hectares)
Visitors (2019): 4,580,587
Nearest Major Airport: Ronald Reagan
    Washington National (DCA), Arlington, VA
Nearest Major Highways: I-395, US-1, US-50
Nearest Metro Station: Smithsonian/National Mall
Fees: $0
Accessibility: Fully accessible.
Contact Information:
    202-426-6841
    www.nps.gov/vive

Maya Lin's polished black granite wall is inscribed with the names of over 58,300 men and women who gave their lives in the Vietnam War or remain missing. The site also includes Frederick Hart's bronze statue of three Vietnam War servicemembers, as well as Glenna Goodacre's Vietnam Women's Memorial, dedicated to American women who served in the Vietnam War. *(A unit of National Mall and Memorial Parks)*

Washington Monument
Fast Facts
Established: 1948
Acreage: 106 (43 hectares)
Visitors (2019): 108,410
Nearest Major Airport: Ronald Reagan
    Washington National (DCA), Arlington, VA
Nearest Major Highways: I-395, US-1, US-50
Nearest Metro Station: Smithsonian/National Mall
Fees: $0

Rubbing the etched names of the fallen has become a Vietnam Veterans Memorial tradition.

Accessibility: Fully accessible.
Contact Information:
202-426-6841
www.nps.gov/wamo

The dominating feature of the Capital skyline, this 555-foot (169-m) marble obelisk honors the country's first president. The architect-designer was Robert Mills, but Lt. Col. Thomas Casey of the U.S. Army Corps of Engineers redesigned and completed the monument. *(A unit of National Mall and Memorial Parks)*

White House
Fast Facts
Established: 1792
Acreage: 18 (7 hectares)
Visitors (2019): 454,117
Visitor Centers: White House, Ellipse
Nearest Major Airport: Ronald Reagan Washington National (DCA), Arlington, VA
Nearest Major Highways: I-395, US-1, US-50
Nearest Metro Station: Federal Triangle, McPherson Square, Metro Center
Fees: $0
Accessibility: Fully accessible.

Contact Information:
202-208-1631
www.nps.gov/whho

The White House has been the residence and office of U.S. presidents since 1800. The cornerstone was laid Oct. 13, 1792, on the site selected by George Washington and included in the L'Enfant Plan. *(A unit of National Mall and Memorial Parks)*

Note: *The National Park Service does not schedule White House tours or provide tickets to enter the White House. Public tour requests must be submitted through your member of Congress (or your embassy if you are a citizen of a foreign country). Free self-guided tours are generally available Friday and Saturday, and are scheduled on a first-come, first-served basis. Spaces are limited, so submit requests as far in advance as possible (up to three months, and no less than 21 days). Tours may be subject to last-minute cancelation.*

World War I Memorial
Fast Facts
Established: 2014
Acreage: 1.39 (0.56 hectares)
Visitors (2019): NA

National World War II Memorial

Nearest Major Airport: Ronald Reagan
Washington National (DCA), Arlington, VA
Nearest Major Highways: I-395, US-1, US-50
Nearest Metro Station: Federal Triangle
Fees: $0
Accessibility: Fully accessible.
Contact Information:
202-426-6841
www.nps.gov/nama

Located at Pershing Park, the World War I Memorial honors the 4.7 million Americans who served in the Great War, including the 116,516 who gave their lives. *(A unit of National Mall and Memorial Parks)*

World War II Memorial
Fast Facts
Established: 1993
Acreage: 7.50 (3.04 hectares)
Visitors (2019): 4,831,327
Nearest Major Airport: Ronald Reagan
Washington National (DCA), Arlington, VA

Nearest Major Highways: I-395, US-1, US-50.
Nearest Metro Station: Smithsonian/National Mall
Fees: $0
Accessibility: Fully accessible.
Contact Information:
202-426-6841
www.nps.gov/wwii

Honors the 16 million Americans who served during World War II, along with the millions who supported them on the home front. A wall of 4,054 gold stars symbolizes the 405,399 Americans who died during the war. Architect Friedrich St. Florian designed the memorial, which is adjacent to the Washington Monument. *(A unit of National Mall and Memorial Parks)*

MARYLAND
Antietam National Battlefield
Fast Facts
Established: 1890/1978. Cemetery established: 1866
Acreage: 3,230 (1,307 hectares)

The Observation Tower overlooks Antietam National Battlefield, site of the bloodiest day in American history.

Cemetery acreage: 11.36 (5.60 hectares)
Visitors (2019): 287,343
Nearest Major Airport: Washington Dulles Intl. (IAD), Dulles, VA
Nearest Major Highways: I-70, I-81, MD-65
Fees: $20/vehicle, $10/person. Valid for three days.
Accessibility: Mostly accessible, except for Dunker Church.
Contact Information:
301-432-5124
www.nps.gov/anti

Commemorates the bloodiest day in American history: September 17, 1862, when 23,000 soldiers were killed, wounded, or went missing. The Battle of Antietam repelled the Confederate Army's first invasion into the north, and led President Abraham Lincoln to issue the preliminary Emancipation Proclamation. More than 5,000 of those who died (1,836 of them unidentified), are buried in the adjoining Antietam (Sharpsburg) National Cemetery. No more grave space is available.

Baltimore-Washington Parkway
Fast Facts
Established: 1954
Length: 29 miles (47 km)
Visitors (2019): NA
Nearest Major Airports: Ronald Reagan Washington National (DCA), Arlington, VA, Baltimore/Washington Intl. Thurgood Marshall (BWI), Baltimore, MD
Nearest Major Highways: I-95, US-1
Fees: $0
Contact Information:
301-344-3948
www.nps.gov

Provides a scenic entry to the nation's capital from Baltimore, MD, and other points north of Washington, D.C.

Catoctin Mountain Park
Fast Facts
Established: 1936
Acreage: 5,981 (2,420 hectares)
Visitors (2019): 296,846
Nearest Major Airport: Washington Dulles Intl. (IAD), Dulles, VA

Nearest Major Highways: I-70, US-15
Fees: $0
Contact Information:
301-663-9388
www.nps.gov/cato

Part of the forested ridge that forms the eastern rampart of the Appalachian Mountains in Maryland, this mountain park has 25 miles (40 km) of hiking trails and campgrounds amid sparkling streams and panoramic vistas of the Monocacy Valley. Camp David, the Presidential Retreat, is within park boundaries but closed to the public.

Clara Barton National Historic Site
Fast Facts
Established: 1974
Acreage: 8.59 (3.47 hectares)
Visitors (2019): 4,100
Nearest Major Airport: Ronald Reagan Washington National (DCA), Arlington, VA
Nearest Major Highways: I-270, I-495, MD-614
Fees: $0
Accessibility: The second and third floor are not wheelchair accessible. There are no public restrooms of any kind onsite. Public restrooms are available at adjacent Glen Echo Park.
Contact Information:
301-320-1410
www.nps.gov/clba

Preserves the 38-room home of the founder of the American Red Cross. The house was headquarters of that organization for seven years.

Fort McHenry National Monument and Historic Shrine
Fast Facts
Established: 1925/1939
Acreage: 43 (17 hectares)
Visitors (2019): 419,545
Nearest Major Airport: Baltimore/Washington Intl. Thurgood Marshall (BWI), Baltimore, MD
Nearest Major Highways: I-95, I-895
Fees: $15/adult, free for children 15 and younger.
Accessibility: Largely accessible.
Contact Information:
410-962-4290
www.nps.gov/fomc

Fort McHenry

Preserves the fort whose successful defense in 1814 inspired Francis Scott Key to write "The Star Spangled Banner."

Fort Washington Park
Fast Facts
Established: 1930
Acreage: 341 (138 hectares)
Visitors (2019): 423,868
Nearest Major Airport: Ronald Reagan Washington National (DCA), Arlington, VA
Nearest Major Highways: I-495, US-1
Fees: $0
Accessibility: Parking and restrooms are accessible, as are some paths and trails. Large sections of the River Trail, however, are not. The layout of some historic structures may pose some accessibility challenges.
Contact Information:
301-763-4600
www.nps.gov/fowa

Preserves a fort on the east bank of the Potomac River, built to protect Washington, D.C. Construction began in 1814 to replace a fort destroyed during the War of 1812. One Sunday a month from April to October, the park features Civil War artillery demonstrations. The park also has recreational facilities.

Glen Echo Park
Fast Facts
Established: 1971
Acreage: NA
Visitors (2019): NA
Nearest Major Airport: Ronald Reagan Washington National (DCA), Arlington, VA
Nearest Major Highways: I-270, I-495, MD-614
Fees: $0
Contact Information:
301-320-1400
www.nps.gov/glec

Glen Echo Park began in 1891 as a National Chautauqua Assembly "to promote liberal and practical education." By 1911, it transformed into Washington D.C.'s premier amusement park until it closed in 1968. Since 1971, the National Park Service has owned and operated the site. With the Glen Echo Park Partnership for Arts and Culture, it offers year-round cultural and recreational activities.

Greenbelt Park
Fast Facts
Established: 1950
Acreage: 1,175 (476 hectares)
Visitors (2019): 128,702
Nearest Major Airport: Ronald Reagan Washington National (DCA), Arlington, VA
Nearest Major Highways: I-95, Baltimore-Washington Parkway, MD-193
Fees: $0. Campground fee is $20/night.
Accessibility: The campground has designated accessible campsites. The Perimeter and Azalea Trails are not accessible.
Contact Information:
301-344-3948
www.nps.gov/gree

Just 12 miles (19 km) from Washington, D.C., this woodland park offers urban dwellers access to many forms of outdoor recreation, including camping year-round. The Baltimore-Washington Parkway runs through the park.

Hampton National Historic Site
Fast Facts
Established: 1948
Acreage: 62 (25 hectares)
Visitors (2019): 28,234
Nearest Major Airport: Baltimore/Washington Intl. Thurgood Marshall (BWI), Baltimore, MD
Nearest Major Highways: I-83, I-695, MD-146
Fees: $0
Accessibility: The second floor of the mansion is not accessible.
Contact Information:
410-823-1309
www.nps.gov/hamp

Preserves the remnants of one of America's largest 18th-century Georgian mansions. The park includes the gardens, grounds, and original stone slave quarters.

Harmony Hall
Fast Facts
Established: 1966
Acreage: 63 (23 hectares)
Visitors (2019): NA
Visitor Centers: The nearest visitor center is at Fort Washington Park.
Nearest Major Airport: Ronald Reagan Washington National (DCA), Arlington, VA
Nearest Major Highways: I-495, US-1
Fees: $0
Contact Information:
301-763-4600
www.nps.gov/haha

Preserves an 18th-century estate on open pasture land along the Potomac River. Surrounded by a rich landscape, it offers visitors many chances to connect with colonial history.

Harriet Tubman Underground Railroad National Historical Park
Fast Facts
Established: 2013/2014
Acreage: 480 (194 hectares)
Visitors (2019): NA
Nearest Major Airport: Baltimore/Washington Intl. Thurgood Marshall (BWI), Baltimore, MD
Nearest Major Highways: US-50, MD-335
Fees: $0
Accessibility: Fully accessible.
Contact Information:
410-221-2290
www.nps.gov/hatu

Commemorates the achievements of formerly enslaved abolitionist Harriet Tubman, the Underground Railroad's most famous conductor. The park includes a mosaic of state and federal lands in Dorchester County, MD that are significant to Tubman's early years.

Monocacy National Battlefield
Fast Facts

Established: 1934/1976
Acreage: 1,647 (666 hectares)
Visitors (2019): 144,969
Nearest Major Airport: Washington Dulles Intl. (IAD), Dulles, VA
Nearest Major Highways: I-70, I-270, US-15, US-40
Fees: $0
Accessibility: Fully accessible.
Contact Information:
301-662-3515
www.nps.gov/mono

Commemorates the July 9, 1864, battle in which Union forces, outnumbered three-to-one, held off Confederate Gen. Jubal A. Early's advance on Washington, D.C. Their efforts bought time until reinforcements could arrive, and prevented Confederate forces from taking the nation's capital.

Oxon Cove Park & Oxon Hill Farm
Fast Facts

Established: 1959
Acreage: NA
Visitors (2019): NA
Nearest Major Airport: Ronald Reagan Washington National (DCA), Arlington, VA
Nearest Major Highways: I-295, I-495
Fees: $0
Contact Information:
301-839-1176
301-763-1062
www.nps.gov/oxhi

Preserves an 1812 plantation home that evolved into a therapeutic farm. Hands-on programs and other activities allow visitors to experience farm life and how it has changed over time.

Piscataway Park
Fast Facts

Established: 1961
Acreage: 4,626 (1,872 hectares)
Visitors (2019): 329,729
Nearest Major Airport: Ronald Reagan Washington National (DCA), Arlington, VA
Nearest Major Highways: I-495, MD-210

Fees: $0
Accessibility: The Accokeek Creek boardwalk and the path to the Marshall Hall ruins are accessible, but most other areas of the park are undeveloped and can pose accessibility challenges.
Contact Information:
301-763-4600
www.nps.gov/pisc

Preserves the tranquil view of Mount Vernon from Maryland shore of the Potomac River, and a habitat for bald eagles, beavers, deer, foxes, osprey, and many other species. The park is home to National Colonial Farm, a historic farm museum that demonstrates 18th-century agricultural techniques and methods.

Thomas Stone National Historic Site
Fast Facts

Established: 1978
Acreage: 328 (133 hectares)
Visitors (2019): 8,020
Nearest Major Airport: Washington Dulles Intl. (IAD), Dulles, VA
Nearest Major Highways: I-95, MD-27.
Fees: $0
Accessibility: Varies. Visit www.nps.gov/thst/planyourvisit/accessibility.htm for details about specific locations.
Contact Information:
301-934-6027
www.nps.gov/thst

Preserves the 1771 Georgian mansion of Thomas Stone (1743–87), a signer of the Declaration of Independence and delegate to the Continental Congress. The estate, known as Haberdeventure, includes a tobacco barn, corncrib, family cemetery, and a ¾-mile (1-km) walking trail.

VIRGINIA
Appomattox Court House National Historical Park
Fast Facts

Established: 1935/1954
Acreage: 1,774 (718 hectares)
Visitors (2019): 102,397
Nearest Major Airport: Richmond Intl. (RIC), Richmond, VA

Nearest Major Highways: US-60, US-460
Fees: $0
Accessibility: Largely accessible, except for a 100-yard (91-m) walk uphill from the parking lot. Call the visitor center if you need assistance.
Contact Information:
434-352-8987
www.nps.gov/apco

Preserves the location where Gen. Robert E. Lee surrendered the Confederacy's Army of Northern Virginia to Lt. Gen. Ulysses S. Grant on April 9, 1865, leading to the end of the Civil War.

Arlington House, The Robert E. Lee Memorial

Fast Facts

Established: 1925
Acreage: 28 (11 hectares)
Visitors (2017): 726,059 (closed for renovations from 2018–20)
Nearest Major Airport: Ronald Reagan Washington National (DCA), Arlington, VA

Nearest Major Highways: I-395, US-1, US-50
Fees: $0
Accessibility: The basement and second floor are not accessible.
Contact Information:
703-235-1530
www.nps.gov/arho

Preserves the antebellum home of the Custis and Lee families overlooking the Potomac River and Washington, D.C. Restored outbuildings where enslaved people—including the Syphax, Burke, Parks, and Gray families—lived and worked, are open to the public. The memorial honors Confederate Gen. Robert E. Lee for his role in promoting peace and reunion after the Civil War.

Booker T. Washington National Monument

Fast Facts

Established: 1956
Acreage: 239 (97 hectares)
Visitors (2019): 24,640

Arlington House, former home of Robert E. Lee, overlooks Arlington National Cemetery.

Kitchen cabins at Booker T. Washington National Monument.

Nearest Major Airport: Richmond Intl. (RIC), Richmond, VA
Nearest Major Highways: I-581, US-220
Fees: $0
Accessibility: Largely accessible.
Contact Information
540-721-2094
 www.nps.gov/bowa

Celebrates the legacy of Booker T. Washington, one of the most influential Black leaders of his era. The monument sits on the tobacco plantation where Washington was born into slavery in April 1856.

Captain John Smith Chesapeake National Historic Trail

Fast Facts
Established: 2006
Length: 3,000 miles (4,827 km)
Visitors (2019): NA
Visitor Centers: Trail Headquarters is at Historic Jamestowne; an auxiliary visitor center is located in Gloucester County, VA.
Nearest Major Airport: Norfolk Intl. (ORF), Norfolk, VA
Nearest Major Highways: I-64, Colonial Parkway; VA-31 (Jamestowne)
Fees: $0
Accessibility: Varies by location.
Contact Information
757-898-3400
 www.nps.gov/cajo

When England's John Smith explored the Chesapeake Bay in 1608, he documented hundreds of Native American communities. Today, sites on his map are archeological treasures and sacred sites for tribal citizens. *See also Chesapeake Bay Watershed and Historic Jamestowne and Yorktown Battlefield at Colonial National Historic Park.*

Cedar Creek and Belle Grove National Historical Park

Fast Facts
Established: 2002
Acreage: 3,706 (1,500 hectares)
Visitors (2019): NA
Nearest Major Airport: Washington Dulles Intl. (IAD), Dulles, VA
Nearest Major Highways: I-66, I-81, US-11
Fees: $0
Accessibility: Federal facilities within the park are accessible. Privately owned facilities may not be.
Contact Information:
 869-3051-9176
 www.nps.gov/cebe

Site of the Battle of Cedar Creek, October 19, 1864, this Shenandoah Valley park is also the location of Belle Grove Plantation. The National Park Service manages the park in partnership with several nonprofit and municipal entities. *(The park is within the Shenandoah Valley Battlefields National Historical District.)*

Fort Monroe National Monument

Fast Facts
Established: 2011
Acreage: 328 (133 hectares)
Visitors (2019): NA
Nearest Major Airport: Norfolk Intl. (ORF), Norfolk, VA
Nearest Major Highways: I-64, US-258
Fees: $0
Accessibility: The primary visitor service areas, including the Casemate Museum, are wheelchair accessible. But the fort itself is marked by uneven ground, steep ramps, and other obstacles.
Contact Information:
 757-722-3678
 www.nps.gov/fomr

Interprets the entire span of North American history up through the 21st century, including Native American life there prior to colonization, the arrival of enslaved Africans to the English colony, a safe haven during the Civil War, and as a bastion of defense for Chesapeake Bay.

Fredericksburg and Spotsylvania County Battlefields Memorial National Military Park

Fast Facts

Established: 1927. Cemetery established: 1867
Acreage: 8,340 (3,375 hectares). Cemetery acreage: 12 (5 hectares)
Visitors (2019): 906,800
Visitor Centers: Chancellorsville, Fredericksburg.
Nearest Major Airport: Washington Dulles Intl. (IAD), Dulles, VA
Nearest Major Highways: I-95, US-1, VA-3
Fees: $0. $2 to view each film at the Fredericksburg and Chancellorsville Visitor Centers.
Accessibility: The visitor centers and historic buildings are partially accessible. Basements and second floors are usually inaccessible.
Contact Information:
540-693-3200
www.nps.gov/frsp

Preserves four major battlefields where the Civil War came to its bloody climax: Fredericksburg, Chancellorsville, Wilderness, and Spotsylvania Court House. Four historic buildings associated with those battles are also contained within the park: Chatham, Salem Church, Ellwood, and the house where Stonewall Jackson died.

George Washington Birthplace National Monument

Fast Facts

Established: 1930
Acreage: 662 (268 hectares)
Visitors (2019): 139,666
Nearest Major Airport: Ronald Reagan Washington National (DCA), Arlington, VA
Nearest Major Highways: I-95, US-301, VA-204
Fees: $0
Accessibility: Varies. Visit www.nps.gov/gewa/planyourvisit/accessibility.htm for information about specific locations.
Contact Information:
804-224-1732x227
www.nps.gov/gewa

Preserves the birthplace of the military leader of the American Revolution and the first U.S. president. The park includes the foundation of the house where Washington was born, the archeological remains of outbuildings, a commemorative colonial revival plantation, the family burial ground, picnic grounds, and a public beach.

Great Falls Park

Fast Facts

Established: 1966
Acreage: 800 (324 hectares)
Visitors (2019):
Nearest Major Airport: Ronald Reagan Washington National (DCA), Arlington, VA
Nearest Major Highways: I-495, VA-193
Fees: $20/vehicle, $15/motorcycle, $10/cyclist or pedestrian. Entrance fees are valid for 7 days.
Accessibility: Largely accessible.
Contact Information:
703-757-3101
www.nps.gov/gerfa

At Great Falls, the Potomac River builds up speed and force as it falls over a series of steep, jagged rocks and flows through the narrow Mather Gorge. The Patowmack Canal offers a glimpse into the early history of this country. The park offers many types of outdoor recreation, but swimming, hunting, and camping are all forbidden. (*Part of George Washington Memorial Parkway*)

Green Springs

Fast Facts

Established: NA
Acreage: 14,000+
Visitors (2019):
Visitor Centers: No federal facilities.
Nearest Major Airport: Richmond Intl. (RIC), Richmond, VA
Nearest Major Highways: I-64, US-15, US-33
Fees: $0
Contact Information:
540-693-3200x1020
www.nps.gov/grsp

The privately owned landscapes and structures in this National Historic Landmark District are viewable from public roads. They offer a continuum of rural vernacular architecture with minimal alteration. Many of the farmsteads, often dating to the 19th century and connecting to one another visually, are preserved through easements.

Maggie L. Walker National Historic Site
Fast Facts
Established: 1978
Acreage: 1.29 (0.52 hectares)
Visitors (2019): 9,602
Nearest Major Airport: Richmond Intl. (RIC), Richmond, VA
Nearest Major Highways: I-64, I-95
Fees: $0
Accessibility: The second floor is inaccessible to visitors in wheelchairs.
Contact Information:
804-771-2017
www.nps.gov/mawa

Preserves the Richmond home of Maggie L. Walker, a Black community leader in the early 1900s. Walker was the first African American woman to charter and serve as president of a U.S. bank.

Manassas National Battlefield Park
Fast Facts
Established: 1940
Acreage: 5,073 (2,053 hectares)
Visitors (2019): 510,427
Visitor Centers: Henry Hill, Brawner Farm
Nearest Major Airport: Washington Dulles Intl. (IAD), Dulles, VA
Nearest Major Highways: I-66, US-29, VA-234
Fees: $0
Accessibility: Mostly accessible, with many accommodations for visitors with limited mobility.
Contact Information:
703-754-1861
www.nps.gov/mana

The First and Second Battles of Bull Run were fought here July 21, 1861, and August 28–30, 1862. Confederate Brig. Gen. Thomas J. Jackson acquired his nickname "Stonewall" here.

Petersburg National Battlefield
Fast Facts
Established: 1926/1962. Cemetery established: 1866
Acreage: 2,740 (1,109 hectares). Cemetery acreage: 8.72 (3.53 hectares)
Visitors (2019): 235,691
Visitor Centers: Eastern Front, Five Forks, General Grant's Headquarters
Nearest Major Airport: Richmond Intl. (RIC), Richmond, VA
Nearest Major Highways: I-85, I-95, I-295, VA-36
Fees: $0
Accessibility: All buildings and some trails are fully accessible.
Contact Information:
804-732-3531, ext. 203
www.nps.gov/pete

The Union Army seized Petersburg in 1865 after a 10-month siege. The park includes Grant's Headquarters at City Point in Hopewell, VA. Five Forks Battlefield, in Dinwiddie County, is where the Confederate collapse led to the fall of Petersburg, and a week later, Richmond. Poplar Grove National Cemetery—6,315 interments, 4,110 unidentified—is 10 miles (16 km) south of the park.

Prince William Forest Park
Fast Facts
Established: 1936
Acreage: 16,081 (6,508 hectares)
Visitors (2019): 339,693
Nearest Major Airport: Ronald Reagan Washington National (DCA), Arlington, VA
Nearest Major Highways: I-95, VA-619
Fees: $20/vehicle, $15/motorcycle, $10/cyclist or pedestrian. Entrance fees are valid for 7 days, and do not include nightly camping fees, which range from $13 to $70 (for a 10-person cabin).
Accessibility: Fully accessible.
Contact Information:
703-221-7181
www.nps.gov/prwi

The Piedmont forests of the Quantico Creek watershed shelter hiking trails and five camps built by the Civilian Conservation Corps (CCC) during the 1930s for group and family camping.

Richmond National Battlefield Park

Fast Facts

Established: 1936
Acreage: 8,004 (3,239 hectares)
Visitors (2019): 197,242
Visitor Centers: Cold Harbor, Civil War Visitor Center at Tredegar Iron Works, Chimborazo Medical Museum
Nearest Major Airport: Richmond Intl. (RIC), Richmond, VA
Nearest Major Highways: I-64, I-95, US-301
Fees: $0
Accessibility: Fully accessible.
Contact Information:
    804-226-1981
    www.nps.gov/rich

Commemorates major Civil War battles around Richmond, including Cold Harbor, Beaver Dam Creek, Totopotomoy Creek, Glendale, Fort Harrison, Drewry's Bluff, Malvern Hill, and Gaines' Mill. The park also includes the site of the Chimborazo Confederate Hospital and part of the Tredegar Iron Works, where the main visitor center is located.

Shenandoah National Park

Fast Facts

Established: 1935
Acreage: 199,117 (80,580 hectares)
Visitors (2019): 1,425,507
Visitor Centers: Dickey Ridge, Harry F. Byrd. A mobile visitor center travels throughout the park to answer questions and showcase exhibits.
Nearest Major Airport: Washington Dulles Intl. (IAD), Dulles, VA
Nearest Major Highways: I-64, I-66, I-81, US-33, 211, US-340
Fees: $30/vehicle, $25/motorcycle, $15/cyclist or pedestrian. Children under 16 are admitted for free. Entrance fees are valid for 7 days.
Accessibility: Most buildings and restrooms are accessible.
Contact Information:
    540-999-3500
    www.nps.gov/shen

Preserves a land bursting with cascading waterfalls, spectacular vistas, fields of wildflowers, and quiet wooded hollows along the crest of the Blue Ridge Mountains. Perhaps its most well-known feature is

Little Stony Man Cliffs overlooks both Shenandoah National Park and the Blue Ridge Mountains.

Skyline Drive, a 105-mile (169-km) scenic roadway designed in the 1930s. Forty percent of the park is designated wilderness. The Park boasts abundant wildlife and diverse plant life, 500 miles (804 km) of hiking trails—including 101 (161 km) miles of the Maine-to-Georgia Appalachian Trail—and several historically significant landmarks, including Skyland, Rapidan Camp, and structures built by the Civilian Conservation Corps during the Depression.

Wolf Trap National Park for the Performing Arts

Fast Facts

Established: 1966/2002
Acreage: 130 (53 hectares)
Visitors (2019): 402,580
Nearest Major Airport: Washington Dulles Intl. (IAD), Dulles, VA
Nearest Major Highways: I-495, VA-267
Fees: $0. Ticket prices vary by the performance.
Accessibility: Fully accessible. Call 703-255-1820 for accessible parking spaces closest to the theaters.
Contact Information:
    703-255-1800
    www.nps.gov/wotr

Wolf Trap is the only national park dedicated to presenting the performing arts. From May through September, multiple amphitheaters present musicals, operas, dance performances, and concerts by jazz, country, and popular musicians. The Filene Center, an open-air performing arts pavilion, can accommodate an audience of 7,000, including 3,000 on the sloping lawn in a setting of rolling hills and woods.

U.S. ISLANDS

Hawai'i Volcanoes National Park

This is the only place in the U.S. where visitors can see an **actively erupting volcano** up close and in person. Technically, the park is home to two active volcanoes, **Mauna Loa** and **Kilauea**, but Mauna Loa hasn't erupted since 1984. Kilauea, on the other hand, has been blowing its top almost nonstop since 1983, and with renewed vigor since 2018. Volcanic flows typically last a few months; the fact that Kilauea has been going for nearly 40 years makes it one of the most extraordinary places on earth. UNESCO designated Hawaii Volcanoes a Biosphere Reserve in 1980 and a World Heritage Site in 1987.

The exact location of the lava is constantly changing, so visit the park's website or the NPS app to find the best places to see the bubbling cauldron, steaming vents, or slow-moving red hot rivers down the mountainside. Unlike composite volcanoes like Mt. St. Helens, which suddenly explode and belch out raging torrents of fire, Hawaii's volcanoes are shield volcanoes, which erupt gradually and ooze lava slowly. That gives visitors plenty of time to move, should they happen to get too close.

Even if the lava isn't flowing, the unique landscape carved by previous flows has made for several days' worth of exploration.

Fast Facts

Established: 1916/1961
Acreage: 323,431 (130,888 hectares)
Visitors (2019): 1,368,376
Visitor Centers: Kilauea, Kahuku Visitor Contact Station
Nearest Major Airport: Hilo Intl. (ITO), Hawaii Island (Big Island), HI
Nearest Major Highways: HI-11
Fees: $30/vehicle; $25/motorcycle; $15/pedestrian or cyclist. Entry fees are valid for seven days.
Accessibility: Visitor centers are accessible, but the trails are unpaved and not suitable for wheelchairs. Most of the Sulphur Banks (Ha'akulamanu) Trail is wheelchair accessible if you begin from the Steam Vents parking lot to the west.
Contact Information: 808-985-6000 www.nps.gov/havo

Lava has been flowing at Hawaii Volcanoes National Park nearly nonstop since 1983.

Lava bubbles and steams inside the caldera.

Lodgings within the park include campsites and cabins at the **Namakanipaio campground**, rustic camping facilities at the **Kulanaokuaiki campground**, and historic hotel rooms at the **Volcano House Hotel**. The gateway town of **Volcano Village**, just outside the park, is home to an assortment of hotels, guesthouses, bed and breakfasts, motels, and restaurants.

The best introduction to the park is **Crater Rim Drive**. This road made a complete loop around the **Kilauea Caldera** until 2008, when the **Halema'uma'u crater** within the caldera began to erupt. A 2018 eruption set off more than 60,000 earthquakes, and caused the crater to sink another 1,300 feet (396 meters) deeper. Today, the north end of

Sometimes the lava oozes so slowly, visitors can get close enough to roast a marshmallow.

Crater Rim Drive ends around **Kilauea Overlook**, which has the most dramatic views of both the crater and the larger caldera.

From Kilauea Overlook, visitors will need to turn around and head clockwise around the Crater Rim Drive. At **Steaming Bluff (Wahinekapu)**, hot water that has seeped into the earth returns to the air as vapor, heated by magma underground. A similar action is at play at **Sulphur Banks (Ha'akulamanu)**, a 1.2-mile (2-km) walk from the Visitor Center, except that these steam clouds smell like rotten eggs. When the combination of sulfur dioxide and hydrogen sulfide cool, pure sulfur falls to the ground all around the trail.

If you imagine the Kilauea caldera as a clock face, **Kilauea Iki Overlook** is at around 3 o'clock. From this vantage point, it's hard to believe that in 1959, it was a lake of lava, shooting fountains up to 1,900 feet (580 m) high. To get an even closer look, hike the **Kilauea Iki Trail** down 400 feet (122 m) to the crater floor, which looks like a giant pan of brownies roughly cut with a badly serrated knife. The crater is about a mile long (1.6 km) and about 3,000 feet (914 m) across, translating to a total hike of about 3.3 miles (5.3 km). It's rated as a moderate hike, but it might be the best one in the park. The view from inside the crater is like nothing else in the world. The trail is also a good introduction to the two different kinds of lava formations: pahoehoe, the smooth, ropy formations that look like swirls of chocolate frosting; and a'a, the jagged chunks that can slice you up if you fall on it. Slow-moving flows leave pahoehoe behind, while fast-moving lava creates a'a.

On the way down (or back up) the trail, stop at **Thurston Lava Tube (Nahuku)**, a cave left behind by a river of molten underground lava. Walking through the mile-long (1.6-km) tube is a great way to cool off on a hot day, but keep in mind that crowds are smallest before 9 a.m. and after 4 p.m. The lava tube is lit from 8 a.m. to 8 p.m.

The 2018 eruption made it impossible to drive past Crater Rim Drive's intersection with Chain of Craters Road. But the first mile of Old Crater Rim Drive is still accessible on foot or bicycle, making for an easy hike to **Keanakāko'i (Cave of the Adzes) Crater**. Hawaiian carvers

Kilauea Iki crater

Nahaku (a.k.a. Thurston Lava Tube) is a cave left behind by a river of molten underground lava.

treasured the basaltic rock in this quarry until an 1877 eruption covered it. To extend this walk by another mile (1.6 km), tack on the wheelchair-accessible **Devastation Trail**, so named for the damage caused by the 1959 Kilauea Iki eruption. This easy stroll through a once-flourishing rainforest now looks like a graveyard for trees.

The **Crater Rim Trail** is another easy walk. It more or less parallels Crater Rim Drive, including the portion closed to cars. There are numerous places to join the trail, including Kilauea Overlook, Volcano House, and several pullouts along Crater Rim Drive. It's about 2.2 miles (3.5 km) each way between the Visitor Center and Kilauea Overlook. The **Kūpinaʻi Pali (Waldron Ledge)** portion of the Crater Rim Trail leads to another section

Foliage is surprisingly quick to reclaim landscapes devastated by lava.

The Pu'u Loa Trail ends at the largest field of petroglyphs in the state.

Lava goes wherever it wants.

of the Rim Drive that had to be repurposed after the 2018 eruption (the yellow road lines are still visible). Some locals refer to this as "Earthquake Trail."

The squiggly line seen on the lower half of park maps is **Chain of Craters Road,** which zigzags 19 miles (31 km) down to the sea, passing a half dozen sites of previous eruptions. The drive itself is one of the most scenic in all of Hawaii, not just within the park. Both Chain of Craters and Crater Rim Drive are paved and do not require four-wheel drive.

At the **Pu'u Loa Trailhead**, a 1.5-mile (2.4-km) round-trip takes you to the largest field of **petroglyphs** in the entire state, more than 23,000 images in all. Look for stick figures, canoe sails, and other geometric designs. A short distance from where the road abruptly ends (reclaimed by cooled lava), is **Holei Sea Arch**, formed by lava pouring into the ocean and then eroding.

When the lava is flowing down into the ocean, a great way to watch the spectacle is from the water. Several private tour operators operate **lava boat tours,** but only those with Coast Guard approval can get within 300 meters (984 feet) of the Lava Entry Safety Zone. Check with your outfitter before booking. If the caldera is bubbling, another option, expensive as it may be, is a **helicopter tour**. In addition to delivering a bird's eye view of the volcano, most private companies offering helicopter tours will fly over hidden valleys and waterfalls visible only from the air. For example, Blue Hawaiian (www .bluehawaiian.com) has been operating helicopter tours on four of the Hawaiian islands for over 30 years.

Haleakala National Park

If the Big Island's Volcanoes National Park shows off the power of an actively erupting volcano, Maui's Haleakala National Park offers a glimpse into the landscape those eruptions leave behind generations later. At first glance, Haleakala crater may look dry and barren. But on closer inspection, a wilderness emerges that is unlike any mountain or desert anywhere else in the world. Over 90% of the flora and fauna in Haleakala are endemic to the Hawaiian Islands, and almost half are found only on the island of Maui. No wonder Haleakala has been an International Biosphere Reserve since 1980.

Among these rare (and in many cases, endangered) species is the **nene**, a gray goose familiar to crossword puzzle enthusiasts. The nene, also known as the Hawaiian goose, is Hawaii's state bird, and while the population has been growing since its low point in the mid-20th century, Hawaii still regards it as endangered. There are fewer than 500 nene on Maui, and half of them are in the national park. They are particularly vulnerable to being hit by cars on Haleakala's narrow, winding roads, so drive carefully.

Fast Facts

Established: 1916/1960
Acreage: 33,265 (13,461 hectares)
Visitors (2019): 994,394
Visitor Centers: Headquarters, Haleakala, Kipahulu
Nearest Major Airport: Kahului Intl. (OGG), Maui, HI
Nearest Major Highways: HI-37, HI-377, HI-378
Fees: $30/vehicle; $25/motorcycle; $15 pedestrian or cyclist. Entry fees are valid for three days.
Accessibility: Visitor centers are accessible, but the trails are unpaved and not suitable for wheelchairs.
Contact Information: 808-572-4400 www.nps.gov/hale

The landscape at Haleakala is unlike any other in the world.

The road up the mountain to the park is an adventure in itself.

Silverswords are another Haleakala-only species. The silvery hairs on their spikey succulent leaves collect moisture from the mountain mist, allowing it to thrive in the crater's desert cinder cones. When a silversword reaches maturity, which can be any time from 3 to 90 years, a long stalk covered in hundreds of brilliant purple flowers emerges from its center. When the flowers die, so too does the silversword, scattering thousands of seeds to take root in its place.

Haleakala means "House of the Sun" in the Hawaiian language, a fact that has persuaded many visitors that there's something magical about watching the **sunrise** at the summit. Over the years, sunrise at Haleakala has become a bucket-list excursion on many itineraries.

So many, in fact, that the Park Service requires reservations ($1 per vehicle) for summit visits between 3 a.m. and 7 a.m.

Visitors can reserve spots up to 60 days in advance; additional reservations become available 48 hours before the date.

The nene, Hawaii's state bird.

Silverswords are found in abundance on Haleakala.

Adventure outfitters peddling **bike rides** back down the mountain started proliferating in the 1980s, peaking in the early 2000s, when the Park Service started limiting the number of tour companies. The excursions usually include admission to the park for sunrise; the ride starts just outside the park entrance after the sun comes up.

The, er, downside of riding in a van all the way up to the summit in the chilly predawn and then coasting back to sea level is that you don't get to experience much of the park itself. Moreover, there's nothing particularly sacred about Haleakala at sunrise. Sunset, on

Sunrise at Haleakala summit is a bucket list trip for some, but sunsets are usually less crowded.

the other hand, may be even more breathtaking. At sunrise, the Haleakala crater is in shadow, but by sunset, the western light bathes the colorful crater in a soft glow. Haleakala's sunsets are also more reliable than its sunrises, which can often be obscured by clouds or haze, making the predawn wake-up call a bust. And because Hawaii is so close to the equator, the sun never sets later than 7:15, so visitors who stay for sunset can be back at their lodgings in time for dinner.

A much better itinerary, then, is to sleep in, eat a leisurely lilikoi and guava breakfast, and drive to the park in the late morning. Most of the cyclists will have cleared out by then, leaving you to enjoy the scenery without as much crowding. On the way up, stop at **Leleiwi Overlook** (just beyond mile marker 17, where visitors can get their first glimpse at the crater and the **Ko'olau Gap**. **Kalahaku Overlook** (around mile marker 24) is renowned for its knockout views of the Big Island, and if you're lucky, you might also see a **Hawaiian petrel**, a native seabird that often lays its one egg per year here.

Pu'u'ula'ula is the Hawaiian name for the Summit Observation Deck, the highest point in all of Maui. The summit building provides shelter from the wind (it can be quite cold at 10,023 feet/3,055 meters), while still allowing views through its wraparound windows. The summit is a good place to look for silverswords.

There are essentially just two hiking trails in Haleakala: the **Halemau'u Trail**, which starts at Park Headquarters, and the **Sliding Sands Trail** (a.k.a. Keonehe'ehe'e in Hawaiian). Both are more than

10 miles (16 km) round-trip, with a lot of elevation change, and are rated as difficult. It's also possible to hike down Sliding Sands and up Halemau'u (a total of 11 miles/ 17 km), but you'll need to park one vehicle at each trailhead.

For an easier outing, hike just 1 mile (1.6 km) down the Sliding Sands trail to a natural overlook, before the switchbacks start. From there, you'll get a new perspective on the crater, and you'll only have to climb back about 500 feet (152 m). That's still the equivalent of 50 flights of stairs. The first 1.1 miles (1.8 km) of the Halemau'u trail are also suitable for hikers of moderate abilities. When the ridge drops away on both sides, hikers are rewarded with views into both the crater and the lush valley on the other side.

Easier still is the 0.6-mile (1-km) **Hosmer Grove loop trail** through native shrubland and an "alien forest" planted in 1910 by researcher Ralph Hosmer. Many of the nonnative species survived, including some invasive plants that are now being removed. This trail is as popular with birds as it

is with human visitors. Go slowly and listen carefully.

The **Kipahulu District** of the park stretches all the way down to sea level on Maui's southeastern coast. No roads connect the summit area with Kipahulu. To get there, visitors must drive 12 miles (19 km) past the town of **Hana**, itself a 64-mile (104-km) serpentine, waterfall-studded road trip from the center of Maui. The scenery in the most accessible parts of Kipahulu is tropical rather than alpine desert, more like the rest of Maui than anything in the crater. The 4-mile (6-km) round-trip **Pipiwai Trail** passes **Makahiku Falls** after the first half-mile (1 km), a **bamboo forest** 1 mile (1.6 km) in, and **Waimoku** Falls at the turnaround point.

Three of the **Pools of Oheo**, sometimes known as the "**seven sacred pools**," are accessible from the Pipiwai Trail. The half-mile (1-km) **Kuloa Point Loop Trail** passes two others (the other two are more remote). The pools are one of Maui's most popular attractions, so expect crowds, even in this remote part of the park.

The pools of Oheo Gulch are in the Kipahulu section of the park.

Pearl Harbor National Memorial

Fast Facts

Established: 2008/2019
Acreage: 59 (24 hectares)
Visitors (2019): 1,716,535
Nearest Major Airport:
Daniel K. Inouye Intl. (HNL), Honolulu, HI
Nearest Major Highways:
H-1, H-3
Fees: $0. There is a $1 fee per person fee to reserve a ticket between 1 and 7 days in advance.
Accessibility: Fully accessible. Accommodations are made to assist the visually and hearing impaired.
Contact Information:
808-422-2771
www.nps.gov/perl

Hawaii's most-visited attraction commemorates the tragic events of December 7, 1941. On this "date which will live in infamy," the surprise Japanese attack on the Hawaiian naval base galvanized public opinion and plunged the United States into World War II. A total of 2,341 American service members and 49 civilians lost their lives that day, including 38 sets of brothers.

Nearly half of those killed (1,117) were on the battleship **USS *Arizona***, which burned for two days before sinking to the bottom of the harbor. Completed in 1962, the **USS *Arizona* Memorial** is clearly the centerpiece of any visit to Pearl Harbor. To handle the throngs who want to pay their respects, the Park Service requires **advance reservations** for the ferryboat that shuttles visitors from the visitor center to the building, which straddles the *Arizona*'s sunken hull.

Designed by Alfred Preis, an Austrian immigrant who fled his homeland when Hitler invaded, the 184-foot (56-meter) memorial looks a little bit like a covered bridge. The roof of the building rises at either end, and is lower in the middle, symbolizing America's pride

The USS Arizona *Memorial is Hawaii's most-visited attraction.*

315

The wall of names lists all who perished on the USS Arizona.

before and after World War II, with the Pearl Harbor attack representing the low point of the war in the middle. The interior floor of the Memorial allows visitors to look directly down into the water where the ship remains.

The visit to the *Arizona* begins with an informative 23-minute documentary film about the day's events, followed by the short ferry ride to the Memorial. A hushed solemnity fills the open-air building, anchored by the **wall of names** of the sailors who went down with the ship. Most moving of all, however, may be the 44 names appended to the original list: USS *Arizona* crewmembers who survived the attack, but decades later chose to be interred there, alongside their comrades. Some

Visitors can look down into the water where the USS Arizona *remains.*

of these servicemen went on to live for another 70-plus years, long enough to have children, grandchildren, and even great-grandchildren, but still felt this was where their final resting place should be.

All visitors to the *Arizona* Memorial must **reserve a timed ticket** (every 15 minutes from 8 a.m. to 3:30 p.m. There's a $1 reservation fee. Tickets are released eight weeks in advance, and they sell out fast, so plan far ahead. A few additional tickets are released one day before sailing time, but it would be foolish to count on these being available.

Pearl Harbor is sprawling, often confusing place—it's still an active military base—so plan to arrive at least one hour before your scheduled departure time. There are no refunds and no re-bookings unless space is available if you miss your reservation. While you wait for your boat, check out the **"Road to War"** and **"Attack"** exhibits in the two small galleries between the restrooms and the bell recovered from the *Arizona*.

You'll get your first glimpse of the *Arizona* Memorial at **Remembrance Circle**, a circular monument with plaques listing the names of all the men and women who died on December 7, including civilians. At the center of the monument is a pedestal with a topographical map of Oahu, showing all of the locations that were struck that day. **Contemplation Circle**, like the name suggests, is a waterside plaza meant for tranquility and reflection.

History buffs may want to extend their visit to Pearl Harbor by checking out three other

Plaques at Remembrance Circle list the names of everyone who died on December 7, civilians included.

nearby sites, none of which is managed by the National Park Service. If you plan to visit all three, opt for the Passport to Pearl Harbor combination ticket, which includes admission to all three sites for $80/adults, $40/children aged 4–12.

The **Pacific Fleet Submarine Museum** ($40/adults, $12/children aged 4–12) is adjacent to the National Park Visitor Center. Its primary attraction is the **USS Bowfin**, a fleet attack submarine that fought in the Pacific during World War II. Launched exactly a year after the 1941 attack, the *Bowfin* was nicknamed "the Pearl Harbor Avenger."

The other two attractions require a short shuttle bus ride to Ford Island from the Visitor Center. The **Pearl Harbor Aviation Museum** ($25/adults, $12/children aged 4–12) includes more than 50 aircraft covering 75 years of Pacific aviation history. The **Battleship *Missouri***

Memorial ($30/adults, $14 children 4–12) preserves the last battleship the U.S. ever built. The *Missouri* served in three wars, but is most famous for being the site where Japanese forces surrendered to Gen. Douglas MacArthur in 1945. All tickets include a self-guided tour of the ship, both above and below decks, or a 35-minute guided tour, usually led by a retired veteran.

Virgin Islands National Park

Virgin Islands is the only U.S. national park that is also a tropical paradise. Occupying two-thirds of the island of St. John, the most virgin of the U.S. Virgin Islands, the park is home to unspoiled white sand beaches, vibrant coral reefs, quiet coves, turquoise waters, and green hills. The United Nations designated it a Biosphere Reserve in 1976.

Part of what keeps the park pristine is its remoteness. There are no airports anywhere on the island; visitors must fly into St. Thomas and take a ferry from Red Hook. Accommodations options, in the gateway town of Cruz Bay, range from affordable hotels and guesthouses to luxury private villas.

In September 2017, Hurricanes Irma and Maria destroyed the two lodgings within the park, **Cinnamon Bay Campground** and the upscale **Caneel Bay Resort**. As of June 2021, Caneel Bay had not announced a planned reopening date, but Cinnamon

Fast Facts

Established: 1956
Acreage: 14,948 (6,049 hectares)
Visitors (2019): 133,398
Visitor Centers: Cruz Bay
Nearest Major Airport: Cyril King Airport (STT) on neighboring St. Thomas, VI
Nearest Major Highways: All access is via car barge or passenger ferry from Red Hook, on St. Thomas.
Fees: $0. Day passes for Trunk Bay are $5/adult, $2.50/senior. Overnight anchoring is $26/day, $13/day for seniors.
Accessibility: A few beaches, trails, and paths in the park are wheelchair accessible. Visit www.nps.gov/viis/planyourvisit/accessibility.htm for details.
Contact Information: 340-776-6201 www.nps.gov/viis

There are no airports on St. John; all visitors arrive by ferry boat from nearby St. Thomas.

Cruz Bay

Bay campground announced plans to welcome visitors again in December 2021. The redeveloped campground features 31 bare platforms for tent camping, 55 eco-tents (complete with lamp, fan, electrical outlet, and table and chairs), and 40 new cottages. Bathrooms are communal.

A map of the park looks a bit like an octopus, but with 20 or 30 arms, legs, or fingers sticking out like tentacles into the surrounding waters. Between these peninsulas lie beautiful, calm, azure bays fringed with inviting white sand beaches. The three main National Park beaches—Cinnamon Bay, Trunk Bay, and Hawksnest Bay—lie in neighboring fingers on the island's northwest shore. Restrooms, picnic tables, grills, and accessible beach paths make all three the kind of beach where you can stay all day.

Because it adjoins the campground, **Cinnamon Bay Beach** is one of the most popular on the island. It's also the most commercial beach in the park, with a camp store, watersports rental kiosk, beach volleyball court, and the **Rain Tree Café**, which serves breakfast, lunch, and dinner. **Trunk Bay Beach** is the idyllic one in most of the postcard photos of the park, with **Trunk Cay** standing sentry offshore. Just about every park visitor pays the $5 day use fee, whether it's to snorkel the outstanding **Underwater Trail** or just to snap a selfie before searching for less crowded sands. Snorkel rentals are available at the stand near the snack bar and the beach shop. Trunk Bay gets its name from the Danish settlers who thought the nesting leatherback turtles looked like trunks.

Beyond the three main beaches are dozens of other strands where visitors can get away from crowds and have a deserted stretch to call their own. **Maho Bay**, the next bay over from Cinnamon Bay, is as popular among turtles as it is among people. A private company operates a pavilion here that can be rented for weddings or other gatherings. **Francis Bay**, on the other side of Maho Point, is another good choice for **birding,** snorkeling, or a walk on the 0.7-mile (1.1-km) **Francis Bay Trail boardwalk** around a saltwater pond. **Leinster Bay**, one more bay east of Francis Bay, requires a 1-mile (1.6-km) walk through a tree-lined corridor to get to the beach, but the reward is worth it: the unparalleled snorkeling around **Watermelon Cay**, a short swim away. There's

Trunk Bay Beach is the most popular on the island, and for good reason.

no official underwater trail like Trunk Bay, so you'll have to bone up on your fish recognition skills before visiting.

More than 40% of Virgin Islands National Park is underwater, so it's no wonder people come here to **snorkel.** All of the aforementioned beaches are world-class snorkeling spots with abundant underwater life and coral. The best place for beginners is the **Underwater Trail** on the western side of Trunk Cay, curated with plaques about what to look for along its 225-yard (206-m) length. Parrotfish, yellowtail snapper, and angelfish are all likely sightings in these waters.

Hawksnest Bay is for more advanced snorkelers who can admire the three fragile **Elkhorn coral reefs** without damaging them. In addition to being good turtle territory, Maho and Francis Bays have some of the best visibility of all the waters on the island (unless there's a

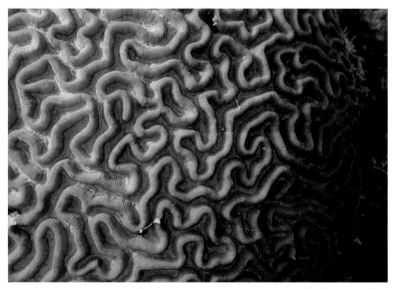

Brain coral is just one of half a dozen coral species found in Salomon Bay.

The Reef Bay Trail passes the ruins of the Annaberg sugar plantation.

north swell). You might even catch a glimpse of an **octopus** here. **Salomon Bay/Honeymoon Beach** require a short walk from the main park road, but the variety of coral species here is unrivaled. These crystal clear waters are home to brain, lettuce leaf, elkhorn, mustard hill, and pillar corals, which are in turn home to colorful fish and other marine life.

Henley Cay, **Whistling Cay**, and a few other islets just offshore are ringed by reefs, but they don't see as many crowds because you need a boat or a kayak to reach them. Keep an eye out for humpback whales, pilot whales, dolphins, green and leatherback sea turtles, and 25 species of sea birds on the journey to and from these reefs.

For such a small island, St. John has a surprising number of hiking trails. Many of the 20-plus trails were originally roads used by the Danish settlers to access the sugar plantations that once dotted the island. The island's population of **feral donkeys** (the unofficial mascot of St. John) are a living reminder of that history.

The easy, but much-traveled **Petroglyph Trail** (3.3 miles/5.3 km) starts at the top of **Mamey Peak** and descends nearly 1,000 feet (304 m) through two forests to a waterfall (rainy season only) and ancient rock carvings left behind by the pre-Colombian Taino people. The moderate **Reef Bay Trail** follows the same route, then continues past the ruins of an old Danish sugar mill on its way down to a shell-strewn beach far from any road. Save some energy for the hike back up the mountain. To extend this hike another 1.6 miles (2 km), start at Maho Bay and climb the **Maria Hope Trail** to **Mamey Peak**.

The **Johnny Horn Trail** starts at Coral Bay, on the east end of the island, climbs up over **Base Hill** and back down to sea level at Watermelon Cay. It's about 3 miles (5 km) round-trip, with 1,000 feet (305 m) of elevation gain and 360-degree views at the top. This trail intersects the Brown Bay Trail, which descends rather steeply to **Brown Bay Beach**, a secluded snorkeling, swimming, and turtle nesting spot inaccessible by car. This portion of the island is a bit more arid and unshaded than other trails within the park, so bring a hat.

There are also plenty of shorter nature walks within the park, including the **Francis Bay Trail**. The **Lind Point Trail** leaves from the Visitor Center in Cruz Bay. From there it's less than a mile (1.6 km) to Salomon Beach, and another half-mile (1 km) to Honeymoon Beach. The **Cinnamon Bay Nature Loop** passes through bay rum trees, planted by the Danish West India Plantation Company to produce St. Johns Bay Rum cologne.

Feral donkeys, St. John's unofficial mascot, roam the island.

MORE TO SEE IN U.S. ISLANDS

AMERICAN SAMOA
National Park of American Samoa

Fast Facts

Established: 1988
Acreage: 8,257 (3,341 hectares)
Visitors (2019): NA
Nearest Major Airport: Pago Pago Intl. (PPG) on Tutuila Island, AS
Nearest Major Highways: NA
Fees: $0
Accessibility: Only the visitor center is accessible.
Contact Information:
684-633-7082
www.nps.gov/npsa

Paleotropical rain forests, coral reefs, and beaches on three volcanic islands in the South Pacific are home to a variety of ocean life, birds, and two species of fruit bats (the only native mammals). Visitors can also experience 3,000-year-old Samoan culture and its traditions. Overnights in villages are encouraged.

GUAM
War in the Pacific National Historical Park

Fast Facts

Established: 1978
Acreage: 2,031 (822 hectares)
Visitors (2019): 432,213
Visitor Center: The T. Stell Newman Visitor Center is open Tuesday, Thursdays, and Saturdays, 9 a.m.–4 p.m.

Tutuila is one of the three islands that comprise National Park of American Samoa.

Nearest Major Airport: Antonio B. Won Pat Intl. (GUM), Guam
Nearest Major Highways: NA
Fees: $0
Accessibility: Varies by unit. Visit www.nps.gov/wapa/planyourvisit/accessibility.htm for details.
Contact Information:
671-477-7278
www.nps.gov/wapa

Seven separate units on the island collectively interpret the 1944 recapture of Guam by American forces during World War II. They range from the summit of Mt. Tenjo (1,033 feet/315 m) to submerged war relics on coral reefs 132 feet (40 m) deep.

HAWAII
Ala Kahakai National Historic Trail
Fast Facts
Established: 2000
Length: 175 miles (282 km)
Visitors (2019): NA
Nearest Major Airport: Ellison Onizuka Kona Intl. (KOA), Kalaoa, Hawaii Island (Big Island), HI
Nearest Major Highways: HI-11
Fees: $0
Contact Information:
808- 326–6012 x 101
www.nps.gov/alka

Preserves, protects, and interprets traditional Native Hawaiian culture and natural resources. The trail encircles the Big Island from Hawaii Volcanoes National Park to Upolu Point at the tip of North Kohala. This "trail by the sea" traverses wahi pana (storied landscapes), ancient Hawaiian sites, and more than 200 ahupua'a (traditional land divisions).

Honouliuli National Historic Site
Fast Facts
Established: 2015/2019
Acreage: 154 (62 hectares)
Visitors (2019): NA
Nearest Major Airport: Daniel K. Inouye Intl. (HNL), Honolulu, HI
Nearest Major Highways: H-1
Fees: $0

Contact Information:
808-725-6149
www.nps.gov/hono

Chronicles the history of internment, martial law, and the experience of prisoners of war in Hawai'i during World War II. Originally established as a National Monument in 2015, it was re-designated a National Historic Site in 2019. As of 2021, it had not yet opened for visitors.

Kalaupapa National Historical Park
Fast Facts
Established: 1980
Acreage: 10,779 (4,362 hectares)
Visitors (2019): 69,401
Visitor Centers: None
Nearest Major Airport: None
Nearest Major Highways: The park is in a remote section of Molokai and cannot be reached by car. Most visitors arrive by mule or by hiking down the 3-mile (5-km) trail from Molokai's main road. Entry to Kalaupapa is by guided tour only. Contact Kekaula Tours (808-567-6088; www.muleride.com) for information about rates, reservations, and visitor permits.
Fees: $0
Accessibility: Largely inaccessible.
Contact Information:
808-567-6802
www.nps.gov/kala

Preserves the site of the Moloka'i Hansen's disease colony, established by King Kamehameha V in 1866. For more than 100 years, Hawaiian residents afflicted with the disease, also known as leprosy, were banished to Kalaupapa, and more than 8,000 people died there. Once a prison, Kalaupapa is now a refuge for the few remaining residents who are now cured, but were forced to live their lives in isolation.

Kaloko-Honokōhau National Historical Park
Fast Facts
Established: 1978
Acreage: 1,163 (471 hectares)
Visitors (2019): 232,921

Nearest Major Airport: Ellison Onizuka Kona Intl. (KOA), Kalaoa, Hawaii Island (Big Island), HI
Nearest Major Highways: HI-11
Fees: $0
Accessibility: Most of the park requires travel over a rough lava trail.
Contact Information:
808-329-6881
www.nps.gov/kaho

This was the site of important Hawaiian settlements before the arrival of European explorers. It includes coastal areas, two large fishponds, and other archeological remnants. The park preserves the native culture of Hawaii.

Puʻuhonua o Hōnaunau National Historical Park
Fast Facts
Established: 1955
Acreage: 420 (170 hectares)
Visitors (2019): 414,410

Nearest Major Airport: Ellison Onizuka Kona Intl. (KOA), Kalaoa, Hawaii Island (Big Island), HI
Nearest Major Highways: HI-11
Fees: $20/vehicle; $15/motorcycle; $10 pedestrian or cyclist. Entry fees are valid for seven days.
Accessibility: The visitor center is fully accessible, but parts of the park are inaccessible to visitors in wheelchairs.
Contact Information:
808-328-2326
www.nps.gov/puho

Preserves a place of refuge for those fleeing punishment (often the death penalty) for violating Hawaii's sacred laws, the *kapu*. The fortress also sheltered vanquished warriors and civilians during times of battle.

Puʻukoholā Heiau National Historic Site
Fast Facts
Established: 1972
Acreage: 86 (35 hectares)

Puʻuhonua o Hōnaunau National Historical Park

Visitors (2019): 133,573
Nearest Major Airport: Ellison Onizuka Kona Intl. (KOA), Kalaoa, Hawaii Island (Big Island), HI
Nearest Major Highways: HI-11
Fees: $0
Contact Information:
808-882-7218
www.nps.gov/puhe

Preserves the ruins of Puʻukoholā Heiau ("Temple on the Hill of the Whale"), built in 1791 by King Kamehameha the Great during his rise to power.

NORTHERN MARIANA ISLANDS
American Memorial Park
Fast Facts
Established: 1978
Acreage: 133 (54 hectares)
Visitors (2019): NA
Nearest Major Airport: Francisco C. Ada/Saipan Intl. (SPN), Saipan, MP
Fees: $0

Contact Information:
(670) 234–7207 x2020
www.nps.gov/amme

Honors the American and Marianas people who gave their lives during the Marianas Campaign of World War II. Memorials stand in tribute to the courage and sacrifice of the servicemen and Chamorro and Carolinian civilians who were killed in battles between the United States and Japan on Saipan, Tinian, and in the Philippine Sea in 1944.

PUERTO RICO
San Juan National Historic Site
Fast Facts
Established: 1949
Acreage: 75 (30 hectares)
Visitors (2019): 1,197,345
Nearest Major Airport: Luis Muñoz Marin Intl. (SJU), Carolina, PR
Nearest Major Highways: None

Fortifications at Castillo San Felipe Del Morro were originally constructed by Spaniards in San Juan in the 1500s.

Fees: $10/person. An annual pass of $35 is valid for up to four adults.

Accessibility: Uneven surfaces, steep ramps, narrow staircases, and tunnels make this site difficult for visitors in wheelchairs. Visit www.nps.gov/saju/planyourvisit/accessibility.htm for details about each of the two castles.

Contact Information:
787-729-6777
www.nps.gov/saju

Countries fought for control of this tiny yet strategic island for centuries. These massive masonry fortifications, the oldest in a U.S. territory, were begun by Spaniards in the 1500s to protect a strategic harbor guarding the sea-lanes to the Americas. Generations of soldiers have lived and worked within the forts ever since. In 1983, UNESCO designated the fortress a World Heritage Site for the ingenuity of its design and engineering.

VIRGIN ISLANDS
Buck Island Reef National Monument
Fast Facts

Established: 1961
Acreage: 19,015 (7,695 hectares)
Visitors (2019): 37,085
Nearest Major Airport: All visitors must arrive by boat from one of the neighboring major islands. Visit the website or NPS app for a list of authorized concessionaires.
Nearest Major Highways: None
Fees: $0
Accessibility: No accessible facilities.
Contact Information:
340-773-1460
www.nps.gov/buis

Preserves some of the finest coral reef gardens in the Caribbean, including coral grottoes, sea fans, and tropical fish. Its interpretive snorkel trail provides a wonderful opportunity to discover the underwater world. The island's beaches and tropical forests are nesting areas for brown pelicans and endangered sea turtles.

Christiansted National Historic Site
Fast Facts

Established: 1952
Acreage: 27 (11 hectares)
Visitors (2019): 103,594
Nearest Major Airport: Henry E. Rohlsen Airport (STX), Christiansted, St. Croix, VI
Nearest Major Highways: None
Fees: $7/adult aged 16 and older. Free for children under 16. Entry fees are valid for three days.
Contact Information:
340-773-1460
www.nps.gov/chri

Commemorates urban colonial development of the Virgin Islands by preserving structures from the

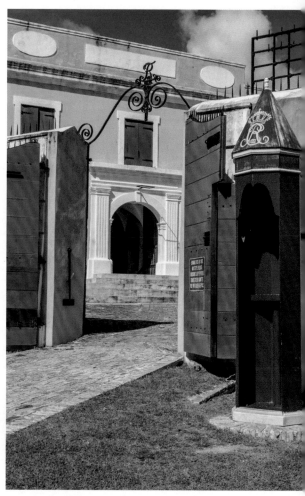

Christiansted National Historic Site preserves Danish colonial structures in St. Croix.

1700s and 1800s in the heart of the capital of the former Danish West Indies on St. Croix Island.

Salt River Bay National Historical Park and Ecological Preserve

Fast Facts

Established: 1992
Acreage: 989 (400 hectares)
Visitors (2019): 5,215
Nearest Major Airport: Henry E. Rohlsen Airport (STX), Christiansted, St. Croix, VI
Nearest Major Highways: None
Fees: $0
Contact Information:
340-773-1460
www.nps.gov/sari

Contains the only known site where members of the 1493 Columbus expedition set foot on what is now U.S. territory. It preserves upland watersheds, mangrove forests, and estuarine and marine environments. The site is marked by Fort Sale, a remaining earthworks fortification from the period of Dutch occupation.

Virgin Islands Coral Reef National Monument

Fast Facts

Established: 2001
Acreage: 12,708 (5,413 hectares)
Visitors (2019): NA
Visitor Centers: Cruz Bay
Nearest Major Airport: Cyril King Airport (STT) on neighboring St. Thomas, VI
Nearest Major Highways: None
Fees: $0
Contact Information:
340-776-6201
www.nps.gov/vicr

This monument is next to submerged lands that are part of Virgin Islands National Park. This tropical marine ecosystem includes mangroves, sea grass beds, coral reefs, octocoral hardbottom, sand communities, and algal plains. The extraordinary blue-green waters and submerged lands are habitat for species like humpback whales, pilot whales, dolphins, green and leatherback sea turtles, reef fish, and 25 species of sea birds.

Starfish, sea urchins, and turtles are just a small sampling of the marine life in Virgin Islands Coral Reef National Monument.

CANADA

Note: All prices in this chapter are in Canadian dollars. Parks Canada charges entry fees daily, unless otherwise noted, but there are no fees for children age 17 and younger.

Banff National Park

If you think Banff is just a Canadian version of Yellowstone, think again. Sure, Banff was Canada's first national park and is still its crown jewel. And yes, it enjoys similarly imposing Rocky Mountain scenery, sulfuric thermal hot springs, and phenomenal wildlife viewing. But unlike Yellowstone, Banff hosts a real town (population 8,000). And Banff's massive glaciers give its lakes a sparkling teal color you won't see anywhere in Yellowstone.

The list of things to do at Banff is practically endless. Name an outdoor activity and you're sure to find an opportunity to pursue it here: hiking, biking, and paddling, of course, but also scrambling up a mountain, fishing, horseback riding, boating, and even **scuba diving** to the bottom of Lake Minnewanka,

where you can see the former village of **Minnewanka Landing**, which was submerged after the construction of a dam in 1941.

And that's just the summer fun. Banff and Lake Louise are a wonderland in winter as well, with three mountains for downhill skiing, dozens of cross-country skiing and snowshoeing trails, frozen waterfalls for ice climbing, frozen lakes for ice skating and hockey, dogsledding, and mineral-rich hot springs for soaking in after a long day of activity in the chilly outdoors.

Start your visit to Banff at the place where it all began: the **Cave and Basin National Historic Site**. Indigenous peoples knew about these thermal springs for millennia. But after employees from the Canadian Pacific Railways publicized them in 1883, private companies rushed

Fast Facts

Established: 1885
Acreage: 1,641,026 (664,100 hectares)
Visitors (2019–20): 4,121,062
Visitor Centers: Banff, Lake Louise
Nearest Major Airport: Calgary Intl. (YYC), Calgary, AB
Nearest Major Highway: Hwy-1 (Trans-Canada Highway)
Fees (CAD): $10/adult; $8.40/senior; $20/family. Camping permits range from $16.05 for a primitive campground in Silverhorn Creek to $39.04 for a site at Tunnel Mountain that includes water and electricity. Fire permits are $8.80 per day. Certain activities and sites charge separate fees.
Accessibility: Varies by location. The Banff Legacy Trail, Bow Riverside Trail, and Fenland Trail are accessible for visitors with impaired mobility, as are many museums, parking lots, and picnic areas. The Cave & Basin National Historic Site has facilities for visitors with impaired hearing, sight, and mobility. Consult the Banff and Lake Louise Visitor Centre (www.banfflakelouise.com/visitor-centres) for the most up-to-date information on accessibility.
Contact Information: 403-762-1550 (Banff) 403-522-3833 (Lake Louise) www.pc.gc.ca/en/pn-np/ab/banff

in to build facilities for bathers to enjoy the waters' supposed curative properties. To prevent overdevelopment, the Canadian government declared the springs Canada's first national park. Several well-curated interpretive trails and boardwalks allow

Elk at Banff National Park

Banff's Cave and Basin National Historic Site is where Parks Canada began.

visitors to explore the birthplace of Canada's national park system.

Swimming or soaking in the Cave and Basin is forbidden, but it's encouraged at the pools of **Banff Upper Hot Springs** (www.hotsprings.ca/banff). There are separate admission fees, but no reservations are needed, and you can rent both swimsuits and towels. The springs are closed Wednesday and Thursday.

Vermilion Lakes Drive is another good introduction to the park. Less than 2 miles (3 km) from the center of town, this scenic, slow-traveled road—with a speed limit of 30 km/h (19 mph)—is a sampler of everything Banff has to offer. You can drive, bike, or walk the entire 2.7-mile (4.3-km) length in a few hours. If you can divert your gaze from the exceptional

views of snow-capped **Mount Rundle**, keep an eye open for birds and other wildlife. Paddlers have half a dozen lakes to choose from along this route.

The drive is a portion of the **Banff Legacy Trail**, a 14-mile (22-km) greenbelt of roads and wheelchair-friendly paved paths extending in both directions

Cyclists love Vermilion Lakes Drive for its views and slow car traffic.

The town of Banff (population 8,000) is surrounded by the National Park.

from the town of Banff. The western end of the Legacy Trail abuts the 30-mile (48-km) **Bow Valley Parkway**. The parkway was the first road to link Banff with Lake Louise and is now an alternative to the busy Trans-Canada highway, allowing visitors to enjoy the views of flower-filled meadows and Castle Mountain. Drivers are advised to travel slowly to protect cyclists, as well as elk, moose, bighorn sheep, and other wildlife crossing the road.

Banff is home to more than 1,000 miles (1,600 km) of maintained **hiking trails**. One of the most popular is **Tunnel Mountain Summit**, partly because the trailhead is walking distance from downtown Banff, and partly because of its sweeping views. The hike is just 1.5 miles (2.4 km) each way but is rated as moderate because it gains 850 feet (260 m) in switchbacks to the summit. The two trails

The short hike to Tunnel Mountain Summit ends in an amazing view of the Bow Valley.

flanking the **Spray River** are longer (3.5 miles/5.6 km each way), but they're relatively flat. A small bridge across the river

Glacial flour gives Lake Louise its unreal teal color.

allows hikers to combine the East and West trails into a loop.

The parking lots at **Lake Minnewanka Day Use Area**, located 6 miles (10 km) northeast of downtown Banff, fill up quickly in summer months. Escape the crowds by walking the mostly flat **Stewart Canyon Trail** (2 miles/3 km round-trip) around the shoreline, or climb the moderate **C-Level Cirque Trail** (5 miles/8km round-trip; 1,492 feet/455 m elevation gain) past an abandoned coalmine to a natural amphitheater carved by a glacier. In winter, Lake Minnewanka is a popular snowshoeing and cross-country skiing destination.

The brilliant Windex-blue hues of **Lake Louise** and **Moraine Lake** (37 miles/60 km and 44 miles/70 km, respectively, northwest of downtown Banff) are so transfixing that you might spend the entire day just staring at them. But that would

be to miss out on some of the best hiking (or skiing) in all of Canada. One of the easiest ways to soak it all in is on the 2-mile (3-km) loop around **Moraine Lake Shoreline**. The **Mount Fay** and **Fay Glacier** reflecting off the lake's surface make a superb backdrop for a selfie.

Two trails leading to adorable teahouses start at the eminent **Fairmont Chateau Lake Louise Hotel**, the premier accommodations in the region, overlooking the lake. The **Lake Agnes Trail** is the shorter of the two: 2.3 miles/3.7 km each way to a small waterfall and the **Lake Agnes Teahouse** (lakeagnesteahouse.com), which is a perfect lunch stop. The exceptional alpine views from **Little Beehive** are another 0.6 miles (1 km) beyond the teahouse. The **Plain of Six Glaciers Trail** traces Lake Louise's northwestern shore for 1.2 miles (2 km) before climbing 1,000 feet

(305 m) into a narrow valley toward **Mount Victoria**. At the 3.7-mile mark, you'll come to another 1924 Swiss-style teahouse. To see all six glaciers, continue another mile past the teahouse to the viewpoint at the end of the trail. If you want to stop at both teahouses on the same hike, take the **Highline Trail** back from the viewpoint for a 10-mile (16-km) loop with nearly 3,000 feet (914 m) of elevation change.

During the peak summer months, the parking lots around Lake Louise and Moraine Lake fill up even before sunrise. Visitors are advised to reserve seats on the **Parks Canada shuttle** from the Banff Park and Ride lot (877-737-3783; reservation.pc.gc.ca). No walk-ons are allowed. The shuttle runs approximately every 20 minutes between 6 a.m. and 6 p.m. A separate connector shuttle (included free with

Moraine Lake

your reservation fee) links Lake Louise with Moraine Lake every 15 minutes from 9 a.m. to 6 p.m. Admission to the connector shuttle is first-come, first served. Neither shuttle is wheelchair-accessible.

Roam, the public transportation system for the town of Banff, runs four bus routes that hit the highlights at the national park, and four more that connect to **Johnston Canyon,** Lake Louise, and Moraine Lake. Roam buses accommodate up to three bikes. To reserve seats and price tickets, visit roamtransit.com/reservations.

For bird's eye views of Banff's glaciers and mountaintops without all the work of hiking, ride a gondola. The **Banff Sightseeing Gondola** whisks visitors to the top of **Sulphur Mountain** (7,486 feet/

2,281 m) in just eight minutes. Each cabin holds four people and is wheelchair-accessible. Best of all, it's free, making it a bargain compared to the **Lake Louise Gondola** or the gondolas and

chairlifts at the three nearby ski resorts, all of which charge $40 or more. In winter, the gondolas and chairlifts at the ski resorts are included in their ticket prices.

You can get a bird's eye view on the free Banff Sightseeing Gondola.

Jasper National Park

Because of their proximity, Banff and Jasper are often thought of (and visited) together. But Jasper plays second fiddle to no one. It's a few hours farther from Calgary than Banff, but that means it gets about half as many visitors. And the drive to Jasper from Banff is a major highlight of any trip to the Canadian Rockies. Keep an eye out for bears on the side of the road—and stay in your car if you see one.

Icefields Parkway between the two parks is one of the most scenic drives in the world, framed by glaciers and waterfalls on both sides. More than half a dozen picnic spots line the parkway, most of them overlooking a lake, river, creek, or other magnificent body of water. **Bow Lake,** located at the parkway's zenith (6,850 feet/2,088 m), is the first such marvel as you head north from Banff. Glacial runoff gives it the same otherworldly blue color

as Lake Louise and Moraine Lake. Four miles (6 km) farther north is the even more aquamarine **Peyto Lake,** whose glassy surface reflects the **Crowfoot Glacier** that looms over it. If you can't get enough of these vistas, you can hike 4 miles (6 km) to **Bow Summit**.

Sunwapta Pass marks the dividing line between the two parks. About 3 miles (5 km) north of the pass, an information center (June–September only) welcomes visitors to Jasper. Visitors of all hiking abilities may embark on the popular **Wilcox Pass Trail**; it's 1 mile (1.6 km) to the iconic **red Adirondack chairs** where people love to take selfies; 2 miles (3.2 km) to **Wilcox Pass,** where you might have to share the trail with mountain goats and bighorn sheep; and 3 miles (4.8 km) through an alpine meadow to **Wilcox Viewpoint** overlooking the **Athabasca Glacier**.

Fast Facts

Established: 1907
Acreage: 2,688,012 (1,087,800 hectares)
Visitors (2019–20): 2,463,419
Visitor Centers: Jasper, Icefield Centre (June-September only)
Nearest Major Airport: Edmonton Intl. (YEG), Edmonton, AB
Nearest Major Highway: Hwy 16 (Trans-Canada Highway); AB-93 (Icefields Parkway)
Fees (CAD): $10/adult; $8.40/senior; $20/family. Camping permits range from $16.05 for a primitive campground in Jonas Creek to $47.84 for a site at Whistlers that includes water, electricity, and a fire pit. Fire permits are $8.80 per day. Certain activities and sites charge separate fees.
Accessibility: Visit the park website for a detailed list of facilities that welcome visitors with impaired mobility.
Contact Information: 780-852-6176 www.pc.gc.ca/en/pn-np/ab/jasper

From June through mid-October, the **Columbia Icefield Adventure** drives visitors right up an impossibly steep road and deposits them on top of the glacier in a six-wheeled studded-tire bus. Prices vary by the day and month, but are usually around $100/person and include admission to the **Skywalk,** a glass bottomed platform cantilevered 918 feet (280 m) over the cliff edge with views of the icefields below. Reservations are recommended but not required.

As you get closer to Jasper, you'll encounter two formidable waterfalls: **Sunwapta Falls**

The Icefields Parkway is one of the most scenic drives in the world.

Bow Lake is most visitors' first stop on the Icefields Parkway drive.

Wilcox Pass is where you'll find Parks Canada's iconic red Adirondack chairs.

Columbia Icefield Adventure drives visitors on top of a glacier in a six-wheeled studded-tire bus.

(30 miles/49 km north of the Icefields Information Centre) and **Athabasca Falls** (at the junction with AB-93A, about 15 miles/ 24 km farther). Athabasca is taller, and arguably the more impressive of the two, but Sunwapta Falls is farther from town, so it gets slightly fewer visitors. **Lower Sunwapta Falls** isn't as impressive as the upper falls, but the 2-mile (3-km) round-trip walk between them is a delightful way to stretch your legs. The **Kerkeslin Goat Lick,** located 4 miles (6 km) south of Athabasca Falls, gets its name from the mountain goats that come here to lick salty mineral deposits.

The turnoff for the **Valley of the Five Lakes** is about 6 miles (10 km) south of Jasper, and is a must for anyone who likes alpine scenery. An easy 3-mile (5-km) hike passes all five lakes (prosaically named first, second, third, fourth, and fifth lake);

Fourth and Fifth Lakes have the best swimming access points.

For an aerial view of the entire region, take a ride on the **Jasper**

A room with a view

SkyTram *(separate fee required).* The 7-minute gondola ride from the base of Whistlers Mountain lifts you 7,425 feet (2,263 m) above the town of Jasper and its six surrounding mountain ranges. From the gondola's upper station, you can hike a little under a mile (1.4 km) to the **Whistlers Mountain summit**, or 4.1 miles (6.6 km) to the bottom station if you don't feel like riding back down.

Once you've arrived at the town of Jasper, take a break from driving and explore on foot or bicycle. Dozens of hiking and biking trails leave from the center of town or a short walk away. Rent bikes or e-bikes (or fat-tired bikes in winter) from **The Bench** (www.thebenchbikeshop.com; 780-852-7768). The 5-mile (8-km) **Discovery Trail** encircles

the town; parts of it are paved, but other parts are too hilly for wheelchairs. The 2.4-mile (3.8-km) **Old Fort Point Trail** is also steep, but well worth it for the views of the town and surrounding valley.

The **Bighorn Alley Trail** leaves from the northeast corner of town and continues for a mostly flat 2.7 miles (4.3 km) to **Lake Edith** and **Lake Annette**, two of Jasper's most popular beaches. The paved 1.5-mile (2.4-km) loop around Lake Annette is wheelchair- and stroller-accessible. Both lakes are relatively small and shallow, ideal for novice paddlers. Pure Outdoors (pureoutdoors.ca; 888-852-4717) rents boats and boards of all sizes and will deliver them to the lake of your choice.

Pyramid Lake and its neighbor **Patricia Lake**, both on the west side of the Trans-Canada Highway, are popular destinations for picnicking, sunbathing, and canoeing. Rent canoes (or rowboats, kayaks, standup paddle boards, electric boats, and mountain bikes) from **Pyramid Lake Resort**. Numerous trails crisscross this section of the park, making it possible to piece together outings of any length and elevation gain. A favorite is the 3.5-mile (5.6-km) **Pyramid Lake Loop**, which doesn't circumnavigate either of the two lakes but delivers superb views of both. Watch out for horse droppings, as this trail is equally popular with **horseback riders**.

Not many driving tours can compare with the Icefields

Patricia Lake is popular for picnicking, sunbathing, camping, and paddling.

Spirit Island sits in the middle of Maligne Lake.

Parkway, but the 30-mile (48-km) road through the **Maligne River Valley** comes close. The fun starts just east of town, where a self-guided interpretive trail walks visitors through narrow but deep **Maligne Canyon**. Situated 17 miles (27 km) south of town, **Medicine Lake** isn't actually a lake, but rather a basin that dams up with snowmelt in summer before ultimately flowing down the Maligne River. For this reason, it is known as the disappearing lake, because the water level changes with the seasons. The misnomer doesn't stop grizzly bears, black bears, bald eagles, and osprey from feeding off Medicine Lake's healthy population of rainbow and brook trout.

Maligne Lake, at the end of the road, is one of the most photographed spots in the world. Visitors are especially drawn to **Spirit Island**, a small copse of evergreens sitting in the midst of a box canyon, surrounded by mountains on three sides. The Stoney-Nakoda people, who consider the mountains physical representations of their ancestors, hold Spirit Island sacred. For most visitors, the only way to see Spirit Island is on a **Maligne Lake Cruise**. From June through mid-October, 90-minute excursions leave from the north end of the lake every 15 minutes starting at 9 a.m.

It's possible to **rent canoes or kayaks** on Maligne Lake, but you won't see the emerald waters surrounding Spirit Island unless you're prepared to paddle four hours each way. For spectacular views of the lake from the trail, take the easy **Mary Schaffer Interpretive Loop**, the equally easy **Moose Lake Loop** (where you are quite likely to see moose), or the steep (2,000 ft/610 m of elevation gain) climb to **Maligne Lake Viewpoint**. All three trails are about 2 miles (3 km) round-trip.

A last word about distances: Jasper is enormous. The park is 20% larger than Yellowstone—almost as big as Los Angeles County, and just as sprawling. Driving from one of the park's five major regions to another can take an hour or more, so you're best off visiting each on a different day. You'll spend less time in your car and more enjoying the wildlife, scenery, and endless opportunities for outdoor recreation.

You are indeed likely to see moose at Moose Lake.

Pacific Rim National Park Reserve

Occupying one of the prettiest shorelines on the southwestern coast of Vancouver Island, Pacific Rim National Park Reserve is a paradise for outdoor recreation. The list of things to do here is as long as a midsummer day. Hikes range from a short easy stroll into the rain forest to a multi-day expedition across seriously rugged terrain. Orcas and humpback whales frequent the ocean waters. Birders travel here in all seasons to spot osprey, great blue heron, and migratory Western Sandpipers, who often bivouac in the park on their way to or from Mexico. And First Nations guest speakers bring to life the history of the Nuu-chah-nulth people who have lived here for centuries.

The park is divided into three discrete sections: **Long Beach**, the **West Coast Trail**, and the **Broken Group Islands**. The Long Beach unit is by far the most popular, and the only one navigable by car. The rain forest and the sea converge here, with often-tempestuous, windswept beaches in between. Before the park was established in 1970, Long Beach was a destination for travelers who sought an escape from civilization.

Hikes in in this area are on the short side. None are longer than the 3.2-mile (5-km) round-trip **Nuu-chah-nulth Trail** between the **Kwisitis Visitor Centre** and **Florencia Bay**. This trail intersects with the 0.5-mile (0.8-km) path to **South Beach**, where gargantuan waves pound a pebbly beach. At the south end of Florencia Bay, the **Willowbrae Trail** (1.7 miles/2.8 km round-trip) begins where Willowbrae Road ends, and

The Long Beach portion of Pacific Rim National Park Reserve is aptly named.

Bears are found everywhere in the park.

continues through old-growth forest to a secluded beach. On the way there (or back), you can take the steep 0.3-mile (0.5-km) detour to a different sandy beach at **Halfmoon Bay**. Whichever way you go, you'll have to climb several long flights of stairs.

Two trails into the rain forest (unimaginatively named **Rainforest A** and **Rainforest B**) flank the park highway about 5 miles (8 km) past the main park entrance. Each trail is a loop of 0.6 miles (1 km) through colossal western red cedars and hemlocks. Birders flock to both trails to scan the canopy for bald eagles, owls, and other avian denizens.

For sightings of osprey, gulls, geese, belted kingfishers, and other shorebirds, there are few better locations than **Long**

Beach itself, especially the 5 miles (8 km) between **Green Point Campground** and Tofino Airport. You don't have to travel far from the parking lot before

you feel like the birds are your only companions.

While the ocean may look enticing, its frigid waters usually deter most visitors from wading in

The surfing is great, but thick wetsuits are a must.

higher than their ankles. Even in summer, the ocean temperature never gets above 57°F (14°C). But that doesn't stop well-insulated **surfers** from hanging ten. Long Beach, **Wickaninnish Beach**, **Cox Bay**, Florencia Bay, and Green Point are all popular surfing spots, and all have areas that are subject to riptides and hazardous currents at various times of year. In general, conditions are rougher (and colder) in winter.

Swimming is an equally chilly proposition on ocean beaches, so for those who venture, a wetsuit is de rigeur. **Combers Beach** has relatively calm waters and an exceptional view of **Sea Lion Rocks**; Wickaninnish Beach is where tide poolers go to see sea anemones, starfish, and other marine life. There's also a designated swim beach at **Kennedy Lake**, 6 miles (10 km) inland from the Pacific Rim Visitor Centre, where the water tends to be a bit warmer.

The park wasn't particularly bike-friendly until recently, but that changed with the addition of the **ʔapsčiik ťašii multi-use pathway**, a paved 16-mile (25-km) route paralleling Highway 4 from the main park entrance all the way north to Tofino. Pronounced *ups-cheek ta-shee*, the name means "going in the right direction on the path" in the Tla-o-qui-aht language. Like the park road, the rec path crosses through or near settlements and villages of First Nations peoples, who are active partners in managing the park and providing programs; visitors are asked to respect their boundaries.

One of the uniquely rewarding activities in Pacific Rim is **storm watching**. From November to March, fierce Alaskan winds cause the Pacific Ocean to rage against the shoreline. The Kwisitis Visitor Center is one of the best places to witness nature's fury, with observation decks located a safe distance from even the most rogue waves. Many oceanfront hotels in Ucluelet and Tofino cater specifically to storm watchers with giant picture windows where you can watch the calamity while curled up by a fire. Some even offer complimentary raincoats and waterproof boots for guests willing to brave the elements.

Driving from Long Beach to the **West Coast Trail** section of the park is a four-hour affair along a circuitous route through Port Alberni. Few visitors make this trip, however, because the appeals of each section are so different. While the hiking trails at Long Beach are short and relatively easy, the West Coast Trail is long: 47 miles (75 km) through some of British Columbia's most challenging terrain. It requires climbing more than 100 ladders, trudging through mud, withstanding driving wind and rain, keeping track of tide tables, and fording fast-flowing rivers or riding self-powered cable cars across.

For serious hikers in peak physical—and mental—condition, the West Coast Trail is a bucket-list trek; most complete it in about a week. The trail is only open from June through September, and reservations are

Storm watching is a favorite winter activity.

To complete the West Coast Trail, you'll have to ride in a cable car across one or more rivers.

required. Hikers seeking a shorter expedition can enter the trail at **Nitinat Narrows** and travel 21 miles (33 km) north to Pachena (near Banfield) or 26 miles (42 km) south to Port Renfrew. There are no other ways in or out of this remote wilderness.

Between these two sections of the park lie the **Broken Group Islands**, an archipelago of more than 100 remote islets and atolls in **Barkley Sound**. In contrast with the rough seas off Long Beach, the sheltered waters here are a haven for boats of all sizes. Multi-day canoeing and kayaking expeditions around the islands have increased in popularity over the last decade, thrilling paddlers but dismaying longtime visitors concerned about too much tourism encroaching on the wilderness and the cultural and archaeological resources.

While the kayaking and canoeing around the islands is gentle enough for beginners, paddling *to* the islands from Bamfield or Ucluelet requires a difficult crossing. For that reason, the **MV *Frances Barkley*** ferries kayakers from Port Alberni to and from the first and last stops on their itineraries. Backcountry permits and reservations are required to camp on the islands, and visitors must stay within designated areas. None of the islands have trash pickup or potable water, but a few have composting toilets.

The sheltered waters in the Broken Islands Group are a haven for canoeing or kayaking expeditions.

Fundy National Park

Fundy National Park takes tidepooling to a new level, thanks to the world's largest tidal range. The difference between high and low tide averages nearly 40 feet (12 m); by comparison, most Atlantic beaches in the U.S. have tidal ranges of no more than 8 feet (2.4 m).

At low tide, park naturalists lead walks along the flats, showing visitors what to look for on the ocean floor. But you can also explore on your own for rock crabs, periwinkles, dog whelk, and other marine life that get exposed every six hours, not to mention the sandpipers and other shorebirds that feed on these creatures. Some younger visitors, meanwhile, may view low tide as the world's largest mud puddle.

As the tide comes in, it funnels into the narrow mouths of several rivers on either side of the bay with such force that it actually reverses the flow of the water. To experience these reversing rapids, however, you'll have to hook up with one of the jetboat or raft operators outside the park, either in St. John and or along the Shubenacadie River across the Bay in Nova Scotia. Be prepared: You will definitely get wet!

For cleaner, drier fun, consider hiking one of Fundy's 31 trails, ranging from the 328-foot (100-m) **Alma Beach** path to the 14-mile (23-km) round-trip **Goose River Trail**. Almost everyone takes the 0.6-mile (1.0-km) wheelchair-accessible loop around **MacLaren Pond**, close to park headquarters. The 328-foot (100-m) **Caribou Plain Boardwalk** is also wheelchair-accessible; the 1.3-mile (2.1-km) **Caribou Plain Loop** trail is not, but it's still an easy walk. Watch for beavers and boreal birds like the White-winged Crossbill, and listen for Black-backed woodpeckers and (in May and June), Spring Peeper frogs.

The 0.6-mile (1-km) round-trip **Shiphaven** trail begins at the quaint **covered bridge** near Point Wolfe and travels boardwalks and stairs, through forests of red spruce. These trees can live 400 years or more and are found only in this part of North America.

For a longer outing, walk, bike, or (in winter) snowshoe the flat 3.5-mile (5.6-km) **East Branch** loop through the **Acadian Forest**, whose mix of evergreen and deciduous trees entice your sense of sight in fall and your sense of smell year-round. The 2.8-mile

Fast Facts

Established: 1948
Acreage: 50,879 (20,590 hectares)
Visitors (2019–20): 296,947
Visitor Centers: Headquarters, Wolfe Lake
Nearest Major Airports: St. John Airport (YSJ), St. John, NB; Greater Moncton Roméo LeBlanc Intl. (YQM), Moncton, NB
Nearest Major Highways: Hwy-2 (Trans-Canada Highway), NB-1, NB-114
Fees (CAD): $7.90/adult; $6.90 senior; $16.00/family (up to seven people); free for children. Certain activities and sites charge separate fees.
Accessibility: The visitor centers, swimming pool, Wolfe Lake, and Salt and Fir Centre are all accessible, as are the Headquarters and Chignecto campgrounds and the boardwalks at Alma Beach, Caribou Plain, and Point Wolfe.
Contact Information: 506-887-6000 www.pc.gc.ca/en/pn-np/nb/fundy

At low tide, you can walk into sea caves at Hopewell Rocks.

Caribou Plain

The Shiphaven Trail begins at the Point Wolfe Covered Bridge.

(4.5-km) **Matthews Head** loop starts at Herring Cove Road and passes through fields once used by Agriculture Canada to develop the best potatoes for French fries. The trail then drops down to Matthews Head, which has postcard-worthy views of the **Bay of Fundy**, before looping back along a moderate section of the otherwise-strenuous **Coastal Trail**.

More experienced hikers who wish to see the park in all its glory should check out the **Fundy Circuit**, a loop connecting seven different trails. The circuit shows off Fundy's finest beaches, lakes, river valleys, waterfalls, and coastal forests. The entire loop is 30 miles (48 km), but you don't have to do it all in one day. Each of the seven segments is a

Dickson Falls

demonstrating your passion for preserving this important natural resource. Snorkels, dry suits, and other necessary equipment are provided to the lucky few who are admitted.

Paddling opportunities in Fundy National Park include ocean, river, and lake adventures. When the tide is coming in, you can sit and wait for the tide to lift your boat. For a ride without the tide, you can rent all manner of boats at Bennett Lake.

Winter activities in the park are concentrated around the **Chignecto Recreation Area**, where **cross-country skiers** will find 11 miles (18 km) of groomed trails. Many of these trails welcome **snowshoers** and **fat bikes** (bicycles with oversized spiked tires on wide rims) as long as they don't muck up the groomed ski trails. Ungroomed hiking trails that remain open in winter include the Caribou Plain trail and East Branch trail. The bowl near park headquarters is a popular sledding spot, in large part because heated restrooms are nearby at the visitor center.

standalone hike of anywhere from 0.6 miles (1 km) to 11-miles (17 km) round-trip. The last leg, the **Upper Salmon River** trail (11 miles/17 km), is steep and requires hikers to ford the river twice. Two other long trails start in the park and connect to points north (the 34-mile/58-km **Dobson Trail**) and south (the 31-mile/49-km **Fundy Footpath**). Both trails are rugged and physically demanding, with lots of elevation gain.

You can download a map and list of trails ranked by difficulty from the park website. It also denotes which trails are open to **mountain biking**. They include two of the trails on the Fundy Circuit: the 4-mile (6.5-km) **Bennet Brook Trail**, where you can cool off in the **swimming hole** below **Bennet Brook Falls**, and the 5-mile (8.5-km) route to **Marven Lake**, where you might spot moose in summertime. You can combine both trails into a single 9-mile (15-km) outing, but you'll have to wade across Point Wolfe River to do it.

Other places to swim include **Bennett Lake** and **Wolfe Lake**, both of which have beaches (but no lifeguards), and a **heated saltwater pool** off Point Wolfe Road. If you want to "**Swim with Salmon**," however, you'll have to do some homework. Parks Canada biologists and First Nations experts lead trips into the Upper Salmon River in search of Atlantic salmon, a species on the verge of extinction in Canada. Admission to this innovative program requires a written application

Bennett Lake is a popular canoeing and kayaking spot.

Prince Edward Island National Park

Located just 15 miles (24 km) north of the provincial capital of Charlottetown, Prince Edward Island National Park is a collection of three separate seashores—**Cavendish, Dalvay**, and the **Greenwich Peninsula**—separated from one another by calm bays perfect for paddling. Motorized watercraft are not permitted within the national park, making for an even more serene environment.

It's possible to drive from one region of the park to another, but once you've settled into a comfortable lounge chair overlooking the Atlantic Ocean, you may not want to get back in the car. If you really want a scenic drive, **Gulf Shore Parkway West** along the Cavendish region delivers unrivaled views of Prince Edward Island's red sandstone cliffs. **Gulf Shore Parkway East** starts at the **Brackley** park entrance and rolls for about 6 miles (10 km) through dunes and salt marshes to **Dalvay**.

The windswept north-facing **beaches** are the big attraction here, drawing most of the park's visitors between June and September. On Canada Day (July 1), Civic Holiday (August 1), and Labour Day (first Monday in September), the parking lots and campgrounds fill up quickly. Early risers capture the most coveted spots on the sand, but the beaches are large enough to accommodate even the biggest holiday crowds. The annual **Cavendish Beach Music Festival** brings some of country music's brightest stars and more than 60,000 fans.

The water only gets above 68°F (20°C) for a brief period in

Fast Facts

Established: 1937
Acreage: 6,672 (2,700 hectares)
Visitors (2019–20): 756,243
Visitor Centers: Cavendish, Green Gables, Stanhope Campground, Greenwich Interpretation Centre
Nearest Major Airports: Charlottetown Airport (YYG), Charlottetown, PE
Nearest Major Highways: Cavendish section: Rte. 6, Rte. 13; Dalvay section: Rte. 2; Greenwich Peninsula: Rte. 313.
Fees (CAD): $7.90/adult; $6.90/senior. Fees are reduced by $4 in June and September. Certain activities and sites charge separate fees.
Accessibility: Largely accessible. Mobility mats and beach wheelchairs at Cavendish, Brackley, and Stanhope Beaches make it easier for visitors in wheelchairs to reach hard-packed sand at water's edge. Cavendish and Stanhope Campgrounds are accessible, and the Greenwich Interpretation Centre is fully accessible.
Contact Information: 902-672-6350 www.pc.gc.ca/en/pn-np/pe/pei-ipe

Broad, windswept beaches are the main attraction at Prince Edward Island National Park.

August, so **swimming** is usually enjoyed most by youngsters and hearty adults. But the park boasts a variety of activities that might get you warm enough for a quick dip: **beach yoga, sandcastle classes, standup paddling, canoeing**, and **kayaking**. Outside Expeditions (800-207-3899; getoutside.com) runs guided kayaking tours ranging from a 90-minute Beginner's Bay outing to a six-hour paddle across the park.

Parks Canada collaborates with local experts to offer classes in sandcastle construction.

A dozen cycling trails lace the park, and most are pancake flat, including two separate bike lanes that parallel the car traffic past the superb views along Gulf Shore Parkway East and West. Rent bikes from Outside Expeditions or from **Outer Limit Sports** (902-569-5690; ww.ols.ca/mystore/bike-rentals-pei). Most of these trails are suitable for walking as well; the Gulf Shore Parkway trails are wheelchair-accessible. For a more remote outing, bike or drive to the end of the paved road at the far western end of the Cavendish region and explore the routes of the **Robinsons Island Trail System**.

The park (and Prince Edward Island in general) has long been a bucket-list destination for fans of the 1908 Lucy Maud Montgomery novel *Anne of Green Gables*. In July and August, Parks Canada operates two tours of the **Green Gables**

Heritage Place, the farmhouse that inspired the novel. A costumed "Anne-imator" leads "**A Cordial Visit**" (a play on Anne's favorite soft drink) Fridays, Saturdays, and Sundays from 6 to 7 p.m. The **"Ropes Down"** tour, led by a Parks Canada guide without the Anne-imation, allows visitors into areas roped off during the regular tour; it's offered twice daily.

Other related attractions around the national park include the home where Montgomery lived and **Montgomery Park**,

Fans of the novel Anne of Green Gables *flock to the farmhouse that inspired its author, Lucy Maud Montgomery.*

Tours lead visitors through the interior of the green-gabled house.

which features a statue of the author. Numerous private companies offer extensive Anne-themed tours of the island, ranging from a few hours to multiple days. Parks Canada has also hidden **geocaches** in four different locations that Montgomery frequented as a child; visit www.pc.gc.ca/en/lhn-nhs/pe/greengables/activ/geocachette-geocaching for coordinates.

The pristine beaches and quiet trails that attract human visitors also appeal to avian ones. Of the hundreds of bird species spotted in the park, the most common include **belted kingfishers**, **ospreys**, **grackles**, **blue jays**, and of course **Canada geese**. The **Tlaqatik** & **Greenwich Dunes** trails are both places where you'll want to keep your binoculars handy. Parks Canada encourages visitors to share their sightings at ebird.org or on the park's Facebook page (www.facebook.com/PEInationalpark).

Red foxes are found throughout the park, but they aren't always red; sometimes they are black or a mix of the two colors. Other mammals that call

the park home include **hares**, **beavers**, **seals**, **whales**, **dolphins**, and **porpoises**. Feeding wildlife is prohibited.

Camping season runs from June through September. The largest campground, **Cavendish**, has more than 200 tent/RV sites overlooking its own beach. **Stanhope Campground** has an additional 100 sites, and is

located less than a mile (1 km) from **Stanhope Beach**. Both campgrounds include showers, flush toilets, a laundromat, and a Parks Canada store.

Never camped before? The park's **Learn to Camp** program, offered on Fridays in July and August, is the perfect introduction. For $93.54, Parks Canada will rent you a 4- or 6-person tent, foam sleeping pads, a camp stove, flashlights, and all the pots, pans, and dishes you'll need for cooking outdoors. Experienced campers will teach you how to set up and break down your tent and how to light a campfire.

The park remains open throughout the winter, but facilities are closed from October through May. Parks Canada plows both sections of Gulf Shore Parkway and several parking lots, so that visitors may cross-country ski or snowshoe, but does not groom trails or remove felled trees.

Prince Edward Island has one of the few east coast beaches where the sun sets over the water.

Saguenay-St. Lawrence Marine Park

The confluence of the St. Lawrence and Saguenay rivers might be the best place in the entire world to see whales. It's also the only place on Earth inhabited by both endangered **Blue Whales** and endangered **Beluga whales**. Three other species of whales, none of them at risk, also frequent these plankton-rich waters: **fin whales** (the second-largest whale species), **humpbacks**, and **minke whales**, whose white-banded flippers can be spotted from shore.

Belugas spend the entire year in the St. Lawrence Estuary, but the four other species visit only from May to October. Even without binoculars, you can often spot these magnificent giants (or at least the spray from their blowholes) from any of the three **interpretation centers**. But to get close enough to see their flukes, you'll want to get out onto the water.

A variety of outfitters offer whale-watching cruises from a handful of locations throughout the park. The following six companies are members of the **Eco-Whale Alliance**, an organization committed to sustainable and responsible whale tourism:

Croisières AML (croisieresaml.com; 800-563-4643), **Croisières Essipit** (vacancesessipit.com; 888-868-6666), **Les Écumeurs Du Saint-Laurent** (lesecumeurs.com; 888-817-9999), **OrganisAction** (croisieresfjordbaleines.com; 418-579-8763), **Parc National Du Fjord-Du-Saguenay** (sepaq.com; 800-665-6527), and **Société Duvetnor** (duvetnor.com; 877-867-1660).

Humpback whales are a common sight in the St. Lawrence Estuary.

Excursion prices vary by time of year, departure location, and the size of vessel, but the rules for how close you can get to the whales are the same whether you're in a motorboat, sailboat, inflatable zodiac raft, or kayak: at least 400 meters (1,312 feet) away from endangered belugas and blue whales, and a minimum of 200 meters (656 feet) from all other species. Most outfitters will provide foul weather gear, but you'll still want to dress warmly, even in the height of summer.

A northern red anemone shines in the opaque waters of the Saguenay fjord.

Departures are most frequent between June and September. You might also spot **harbour seals** (the park's only other year-round resident marine mammal), **grey seals**, **harbour porpoises**, and **harp seals** (usually in winter, but occasionally in summer as well). More than 2,000 animal species have been observed at the park.

If you've brought your own **kayak** or **canoe**, you can travel from one section of the park to another, camping along the way at 13 primitive **paddle-in campsites** along both sides of the fjord. You can also rent kayaks and paddle on your own for a few hours, or on a guided expedition lasting anywhere from 7 hours to three days.

Another great way to take in the sheer 1,000-foot (304 m) cliffs of the Saguenay Fjord is on a **sailboat**. **Voile Mercator** (voilemercator.com; 888-674-9309) offers learn to sail courses lasting from a few hours to a few

weeks. If you prefer to leave the navigation to the professionals, opt for a 3-hour **Sailing & Initiation Tour**. For a fee, you'll depart from **L'Anse-Saint-Jean**, learn some basic sailing techniques, then have the rest of the trip to sit back and enjoy the scenery.

To get close to marine life without a boat, try your hand at **Nordic snorkeling**. In addition to the usual mask, snorkel, and fins, the Québec Federation of Underwater Activities will fit you with a thermal wetsuit, boots, and gloves so you can brave the

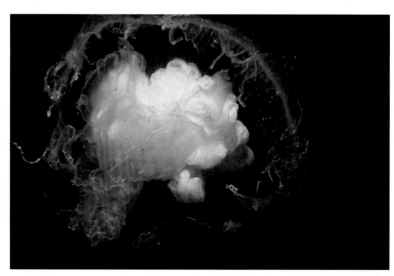

A fried-egg jellyfish

The land on either side of the river is also protected as Saguenay Fjord National Park.

chilly waters of the St. Lawrence. Snorkeling is available Saturdays and Sundays from late May to mid-June and daily from late June to early September.

If cold water snorkeling only whets your appetite for underwater activity, the Federation also offers an introductory **scuba diving** course (no experience required). You'll get a primer on scuba diving basics on land, then take the plunge into the Escoumins region, which is considered one of the finest diving destinations in North America. The available dates for scuba diving are the same as those for snorkeling (above), but the fees for both add up, so check pricing in advance.

Certified scuba divers can explore the St. Lawrence in search of starfish, anemones, and the occasional shipwreck. Or they can take a "**night dive**" in the Saguenay fjord, where the top 30 feet of water is so opaque that no light shines through even in the middle of the day. Just like boats, divers must stay at least of 200 meters (656 feet) from all whales and 400 meters (1,312 feet) away from endangered belugas and blue whales. Contact **Accès Plongée**

Saguenay (accesplongeesaguenay. com; 800-756-6433) for schedule and prices.

While the waters of the Saguenay River are protected as a marine park, the land on either side is preserved as the **Saguenay Fjord National Park.** Despite the name, it is actually a provincial park, administered by Sépaq, (the Société des Établissements de Plein Air du Québec) in coordination with Parks Canada.

In addition to providing access to the fjord, the park offers the land-based activities typically found in national parks. Almost anyone can walk the 0.3-mile (0.5-km) loop to the outstanding viewpoint at **L'Anse de Tabatière**. On the north side of the fjord, the 4-mile (6-km) section of the **Fjord Trail** traces the shores of **Baie Sainte-Marguerite**. For an uphill challenge, try the 4-mile (6-km) ascent to the **Adela Lessard** mountain lookout in the **Tadoussac** region. For a full list of day hikes, ranked by difficulty and location, visit www.sepaq.com.

Thrill-seekers head to the **Baie-Éternité** sector of the provincial park to try their hands (and feet) at the **Via Ferrata des Géants,** a climbing route with ropes, steel cables, rungs, ladders, and other aids drilled into the cliffs to help with the ascent. A highlight is **La Passerelle**, a 279-foot (85-m) steel cable suspension bridge wide enough for just one person, spanning a deep chasm. Participants are clipped into harnesses, but even with all the safety precautions, this activity isn't for those with a fear of heights.

A highlight of the park's Via Ferrata climbing route is La Passerelle, a steel cable suspension bridge wide enough for one person only.

Yoho National Park

Yoho is a Cree word for "awe and wonder," and its dozens (yes, dozens) of 10,000-foot (3048-m) summits are a big reason why. Yoho stands tall at the eastern edge of British Columbia, closer to Alberta's Banff and Jasper National Parks, with which it has much in common, than to Vancouver or Victoria. In fact, Yoho's charming gateway town of **Field, BC**, is just 16 miles (26 km) west of Banff's Lake Louise.

But you might not brave the crowds at Lake Louise once you realize Yoho has some pretty impressive lakes of its own. They're tinted by the same glacial runoff that gives Louise and Moraine Lake their brilliant turquoise color, but they get a fraction of the visitors that Banff and Jasper receive. You could sit and stare all day at the accurately named **Emerald Lake,** or walk the gentle 3-mile (5-km) trail, which delivers incredible mountain and glacier views. Emerald Lake is also a popular paddling spot. You can rent canoes from The Boathouse Trading Company right on the lake.

A visit to the equally spectacular **Lake O'Hara** requires some advance planning, as most private cars are barred

Fast Facts

Established: 1886
Acreage: 324,474 (131,310 hectares)
Visitors (2019–20): 700,902
Visitor Center: The visitor center shares a building with Friends of Yoho and Travel Alberta. It is open only from May 1 through mid October.
Nearest Major Airport: Calgary Intl. (YYC), Calgary, AB
Nearest Major Highway: Hwy-1 (Trans-Canada Highway)
Fees (CAD): $10/adult; $8.40/ senior; $20/family. Certain activities and sites charge separate fees.
Accessibility: Limited. Contact the park for details about specific destinations.
Contact Information: 250-343-6783 www.pc.gc.ca/en/pn-np/ bc/yoho

A teahouse overlooks Emerald Lake.

Reserve a shuttle bus seat to reach the pristine wilderness of the Lake O'Hara region.

from the access road between July 1 and early October. To protect the environment, visitors must ride the shuttle bus to the lake. Reservations are required and usually exceed the buses' capacity, so a random drawing is used to allot seats. Visitors with camping reservations in the Lake O'Hara region are guaranteed a reservation, as are guests with accommodations at the rustic 15-person **Elizabeth Parker Hut** or the much more expensive **Lake O'Hara Lodge**.

The lodge is the starting point for the incredible **Lake O'Hara Alpine Circuit**, a collection of four trails totaling 7 miles (11 km) and forming one of the best one-day outings in this or any national park. Its wide loop around Lake O'Hara travels through the amphitheater of mountains that surround the lake on all sides. The loop passes half a dozen smaller lakes, some of which are warm enough for swimming in summer. The route is rated as moderate, but the 2,900 feet (883 m) of elevation gain (half of it in the first mile)

Yoho is renowned for its waterfalls, including Twin Falls, reached only by a long hike.

might deter hikers who eschew steep ascents and descents.

The mostly flat **Lake O'Hara Shoreline** trail hews closer to the lake, ringing the shore for 2 miles (3 km). You can make this into a longer hike with about 1,000 feet (305 m) of elevation gain by tacking on the 1-mile (1.6-km) side trip to **Lake Oesa.** This trail features a little bit of everything: lake views, stunted forest, mountain meadows, steps carved out of rocky outcroppings, and copper-colored quartzite cliffs.

Yoho is renowned for its abundance of waterfalls, primary among them **Takakkaw Falls,** one of Canada's highest cascades at 1,250 feet (381 m). The falls are perched atop the switchbacks of **Yoho Valley Road,** which is impassable for most RVs or vehicles longer than 23 feet (7 m) year-round (and closed to all vehicles from October to May). A short trail leads from the parking lot to the falls. The much longer **Yoho Valley Trail** also starts at the parking lot and continues 2.5 miles (4 km) each way to **Laughing Falls** or 5 miles (8 km) and 2,500 feet (762 m) each way to **Twin Falls.** Backcountry **campgrounds** at both falls welcome weary backpackers.

The location of **Wapta Falls** at the southwestern corner of the park keeps visitor levels relatively low, even in summer. From the end of Wapta Falls Road, it's a 1.5-mile (2.5-km) walk each way through lush forest to the upper viewpoint and a short scramble down the hillside to the base of the falls.

Mountain biking is permitted on a variety of trails within the

Don't Miss This . . . Suggested Canadian Rocky Itineraries

Day One: Start your trip in Banff, Canada's first and most-visited national park. Visit the **Cave and Basin National Historic Site,** home to the thermal springs that led the Canadian government to safeguard the land against overdevelopment. Have a soak in the **Banff Upper Hot Springs** before exploring **Vermilion Lakes Drive** by bike, car, or on foot. If you like paddling, you can choose from a half-dozen lakes along the route.

Day Two: Get an early start and drive up to the **Lake Minnewanka Day Use Area.** Hike the mostly flat **Stewart Canyon Trail** or the moderate **C-Level Cirque Trail.** Late sleepers can grab breakfast in the charming town of Banff, then stroll to the trailhead for **Tunnel Mountain Summit,** a short trail with tremendous views of the **Bow Valley.**

Day Three: Pack up and head north to strikingly aqua-hued **Lake Louise.** Stop in for a drink or a meal at the stately **Fairmont Chateau Lake Louise Hotel,** which stands sentry over the lake. Then head out on the **Lake Agnes Trail** past a small waterfall to the adorable **Lake Agnes Teahouse.** Leave your car where it's parked and take the bus to nearby **Moraine Lake,** where the brilliant blue water may be even more striking than at Lake Louise. See the lake from every side on a 2-mile (3-km) loop around **Moraine Lake Shoreline.**

Day Four: Head northwest to **Yoho National Park,** adjacent to Banff but off the beaten path. Walk the easy 3-mile (5-km) trail around **Emerald Lake** or rent a canoe or kayak and paddle on the lake as far as you like. Drive up the tight switchbacks of Yoho Valley Road to the very end and picnic at the 1,250-foot (381-m) **Takakkaw Falls.** From there, you can hike another 2.5 miles (4 km) each way to **Laughing Falls** or 5 miles (8 km) and 2,500 feet (762 m in elevation change) each way to **Twin Falls.**

Day Five: Be sure to make reservations in advance to ride the shuttle bus up to the **Lake O'Hara** region, an amphitheater of mountains dotted with gorgeous alpine lakes. Circle the lake on the easy Lake O'Hara Shoreline Trail (2 miles/3 km) or make a bigger (7 miles/11 km) loop through some of the surrounding mountains and other lakes on the Lake O'Hara **Alpine Circuit.**

Day Six: Head back east on Highway 1 to the **Icefields Parkway,** one of the most scenic drives in the world. Stop frequently over its 144-mile (232-km) length between Banff and **Jasper National Park.** Highlights include **Bow Lake, Crowfoot Glacier** (overlooking **Peyto Lake), Sunwapta Pass,** and **Wilcox Pass.** Hop aboard **Columbia Icefield Adventure's** six-wheeled, studded-tire bus and ride on top of a glacier. Walk out onto **Skywalk,** a semi-circular, glass-bottomed platform cantilevered 918 feet (280 m) over a cliff edge with views of the icefields.

Day Seven: Go chasing waterfalls near the southern entrance to Jasper. **Athabasca Falls** is higher, but **Sunwapta Falls** is usually less crowded. Take the easy 3-mile (5-km) walk through **The Valley of the Five Lakes,** or head straight to **Fourth or Fifth Lake** for a swim. Rent bikes in the town of **Jasper** and pedal the 5-mile (8-km) **Discovery Trail,** which encircles the town.

Day Eight: Drive down to the **Maligne River Valley** to see eagles, osprey, and the occasional bear at "disappearing" **Medicine Lake,** then get out on the water at **Maligne Lake.** Rent canoes or kayaks and paddle around the north end of the lake, or hop aboard a 90-minute cruise to the south end, where you'll see **Spirit Island.**

Natural Bridge is really just a hole in the rock that lets the Kicking Horse River cascade through.

park. The two longest routes, the **Ice River Trail** (11 miles/18 km each way) and the **Amiskwi Trail** (12 miles/18 km each way) are on unmaintained terrain and are for advanced cyclists only. Easier rides include the 4-mile (6-km) ride from the Lake O'Hara parking lot to **Ross Lake**, a trail that continues to Lake Louise (another 3 miles/5 km each way). You can also **road bike** 6 miles (10 km) each way to **Lake Louise**

on the Great Divide/Old Hwy 1A, a less-trafficked alternative to the busy Trans-Canada Highway. Yoho Valley Road and Emerald Lake Road are open to bicycles, but you'll be competing with cars on those roads. If you didn't bring your own wheels, you can rent bikes and e-bikes at **Wilson Mountain Sports** next to the Lake Louise Visitor Centre.

The most unique attractions at Yoho are the **Burgess Shale**

fossils, which are some of the oldest and most detailed in the world. Unlike most fossils, they preserve not just the skeletons but also the eyeballs, brains, and other features of multicellular Cambrian organisms that predated the dinosaurs by 250 million years. You can get a sneak peek at some of these artifacts by visiting the **Burgess Shale Virtual Museum** (burgess-shale.rom.on.ca), but to see them

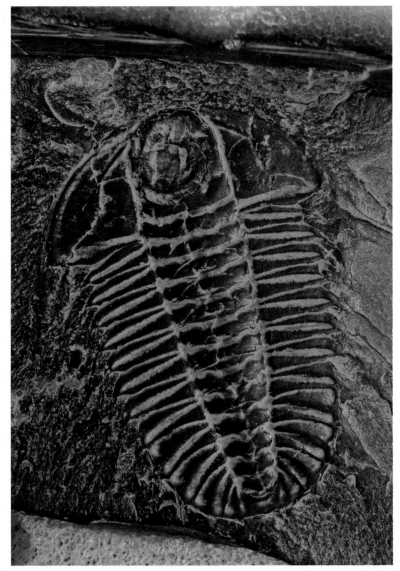

The Burgess Shale fossils, which are some of the oldest and most detailed in the world, can only be visited as part of a guided hike.

Walcott Quarry is an all-day, 13-mile (21-km) affair with 2,710 feet (825 m) of elevation gain. It starts at Takakkaw Falls at 7 a.m. and climbs steeply through spectacular but rugged mountain terrain. Children under age 8 are not permitted on the Mount Stephen or Walcott Quarry hikes.

Wildlife is abundant in Yoho. More than 200 species of birds and 58 species of mammals share their alpine home with visitors. Mountain goats and bighorn sheep are the most commonly spotted animals, but elk, moose, and both black and grizzly bears can appear almost anywhere in the park; backcountry hikers should carry bear spray at all times. There are also small populations of wolves, coyotes, lynx, and mountain lions within the park, though they usually keep their distance from human intruders.

Some of the best birdwatching is in and around the town of Field, where you'll find hummingbirds, warblers, and thrushes. Emerald Lake attracts flycatchers, woodpeckers, swallows, and the same loons that appear on Canada's $1 coin. You may also see osprey or herons on the trail to Wapta Falls where it passes the Leancholi Marsh. Keep your eyes open for beavers too, as well as wolf tracks as you make your way.

in person, you'll have to lace up your hiking boots.

Parks Canada experts lead guided treks to three different fossil sites on different days of the week. The 6-mile (10-km) round-trip outing to Stanley Glacier passes two waterfalls and a turquoise lake along the way. The hike is rated as moderate because of its 2,018 feet (615 m) in elevation gain and a short section of rough trail. In addition

to up-close views of the glacier, you'll see trilobites, brachiopods, and "Stan animal," a recently discovered 505-million-year-old predator.

The 3-mile (6-km) trip to the Mount Stephen trilobite beds is shorter but steeper (2,610 feet/795 m of elevation gain), and hiking poles are mandatory. Railway workers first reported finding "stone bugs" here in the 1880s. The hike to

MORE TO SEE IN CANADA

ALBERTA
Elk Island National Park
Fast Facts

Established: 1913
Acreage: 47,938 (19,400 hectares)
Visitors (2019–20): 391,977
Nearest Major Airport: Edmonton Intl. (YEG), Edmonton, AB
Nearest Major Highway: Hwy 16 (Trans-Canada Highway)
Accessibility: The visitor center, Astotin Theatre, and most restrooms are accessible. Shoreline Trail and several paths in the Astotin Lake area are paved.
Fees (CAD): $7.90/adult; $6.90/senior 65 and older; $16/family
Contact Information:
  780-922-5790
  www.pc.gc.ca/en/pn-np/ab/elkisland

Preserves habitat for elk, bison and more than 250 species of birds. Elk Island's active conservation program replenishes bison herds (once near extinction) around the world. The park is home to some of the best wildlife viewing in North America, especially in July and August, when bison are most active.

Waterton Lakes National Park
Fast Facts

Established: 1895
Acreage: 124,788 (50,500 hectares)
Visitors (2019–20): 457,356
Nearest Major Airport: Calgary Intl. (YYC), Calgary, AB
Nearest Major Highway: AB-5, AB-6
Fees (CAD): $10/adult; $8.40/senior; $20/family

Elk Island National Park preserves the habitat of elk, bison, and more than 250 species of birds.

Red Rock Creek in Waterton Lakes National Park

Contact Information:
403-859-5133
www.pc.gc.ca/en/pn-np/ab/waterton

Protects an exceptional diversity of wildlife and wildflowers in an area where the prairies of Alberta meet the peaks of the Rocky Mountains. Waterton Lakes abuts Montana's Glacier National Park; together, they form Waterton-Glacier International Peace Park. Sometimes nicknamed "The Crown of the Continent," the parks officially acknowledge that ecosystems do not stop at national borders. Bears, moose, wolves, and other wildlife routinely cross between countries at will, but visitors who wish to see both sides of the park must pay separate admission fees and clear immigration and customs at the international border (passports/passport cards required).

BRITISH COLUMBIA
Glacier National Park
Fast Facts

Established: 1886
Acreage: 333,345 (134,900 hectares)
Visitors (2019–20): 801,513 (includes visitors to Mt. Revelstoke National Park)
Nearest Major Airport: Calgary Intl. (YYC), Calgary, AB
Nearest Major Highway: Hwy-1 (Trans-Canada Highway)
Fees (CAD): $10/adult; $8.40/senior; $20/family
Accessibility: From May to October, the park is generally accessible to visitors with mobility impairments. In winter and spring, the only accessible facility is the Rogers Pass Discovery Centre.
Contact Information:
250-837-7500
www.pc.gc.ca/en/pn-np/bc/glacier

Glacier National Park preserves ancient forests, deep valleys, and alpine meadows. It is a place of year-round activity: hiking and biking through cedar forests in spring, summer, and fall; cross-country skiing in winter. Rogers Pass, a linchpin of both the Trans-Canada Highway and the Canadian transcontinental railway, sits at the center of the park. The world's largest mobile avalanche control program uses live artillery to keep the highway and rail line clear. Glacier and Mt. Revelstoke National Parks are so close to each other that people tend to visit both parks on the same trip, so Parks Canada counts their attendance jointly.

Gulf Islands National Park Reserve
Fast Facts

Established: 2003
Acreage: 9,118 (3,690 hectares)
Visitors (2019–20): 24,788
Nearest Major Airport: Vancouver Intl. (YVR), Richmond, BC
Nearest Major Highway: BC-17 to the Swartz Bay ferry to Mayne, Saturna, and Pender Islands. Outlying islands are accessible only by boat or kayak.
Fees (CAD): $17.99 per vehicle per night to camp at the McDonald, Prior Centennial, and Sidney Spit campgrounds.
Accessibility: Largely inaccessible, except for the McDonald campground on Vancouver Island
Contact Information:
250-654-4000
www.pc.gc.ca/en/pn-np/bc/gulf

Scattered throughout the Salish Sea, the Gulf Islands and surrounding waters teem with seals, otters, orcas, and porpoises, while eagles and seabirds soar overhead. The forested islands are a playground for hikers, campers, cyclists, boaters, and kayakers. Visitors may pick apples, pears, cherries, plums, quince, or nuts from any of the park's 17 orchards, which serve as living examples of horticultural practices from the Victorian era.

Gwaii Haanas National Park Reserve, National Marine Conservation Area Reserve, and Haida Heritage Site

Fast Facts

Established: 1988

Acreage: 364,332 (147,440 hectares)

Visitors (2019–20): 2,629

Nearest Major Airport: Vancouver Intl. (YVR), Richmond, BC

Getting There: There are no roads to or in the park reserve; visitors must arrive by boat or plane; permits are required. Visit the park website for a list of licensed tour operators that provide transportation to and from the park.

Fees (CAD): Admission is free. Daily camping fees are $20.03/adult; $16.97/senior. A season pass is $120.29/adult; $100.26/senior.

Accessibility: Mostly inaccessible.

Contact Information:

250-559-8818

www.pc.gc.ca/en/pn-np/bc/gwaiihaanas

Managed in cooperation with the Haida people, Gwaii Haanas offers a window into 12,000 years of human habitation. The 1,800 undeveloped rain forest islands of "Canada's Galapagos" abound with wildlife. Massive moss-draped cedar and Sitka spruce tower above the Haida's ancient carved poles and fallen longhouses.

Kootenay National Park

Fast Facts

Established: 1920

Acreage: 347,529 (140,640 hectares)

Visitors (2019–20): 529,666

Visitor Center: The visitor center is located outside the park in the village of Radium Hot Springs, in the same building as Tourism Radium and Friends of Kootenay.

Nearest Major Airport: Calgary Intl. (YYC), Calgary, AB

Nearest Major Highway: Hwy-1 (Trans-Canada Highway), BC-93 (Banff-Windermere Highway)

Accessibility: Largely inaccessible.

Fees (CAD): $10/adult; $8.40/senior; $20/family. Certain activities and sites charge separate fees.

Kootenay National Park is renowned for its deep canyons.

Contact Information:
250-347-9505
www.pc.gc.ca/en/pn-np/bc/kootenay

With diverse terrain ranging from arid grasslands to glaciers, Kootenay National Park preserves a panoply of Rocky Mountain experiences. Visitors may hike through deep canyons, climb frozen waterfalls, cycle to an abandoned silver mine, or soak in hot springs. The Burgess Shale fossils record an ecosystem from 500 million years ago, long before the dinosaurs. (See Yoho National Park for more details about visiting the fossil beds.)

Mount Revelstoke National Park
Fast Facts
Established: 1914
Acreage: 64,865 (262,500 hectares)
Visitors (2019–20): 801,513 (includes visitors to Glacier National Park)
Nearest Major Airport: Calgary Intl. (YYC), Calgary, AB

Nearest Major Highway: Hwy-1 (Trans-Canada Highway), BC-23
Accessibility:
Fees (CAD): $10/adult; $8.40/senior; $20/family. Additional fees apply for camping and fishing.
Contact Information:
250-837-7500
www.pc.gc.ca/en/pn-np/bc/revelstoke

Mount Revelstoke is renowned for the wildflowers that bloom every summer in meadows just below the summit. The 16-mile (26-km) Meadows in the Sky Parkway winds through cedar and hemlock forests to the summit of Mt. Revelstoke. An interactive sculpture at the top of Big Hill encourages visitors to stand in the boots of legendary ski jumper Nels Nelsen leaning out over his skis. Glacier and Mt. Revelstoke National Parks are so close to each other that people tend to visit both parks on the same trip, so Parks Canada counts their attendance jointly.

Wildflowers carpet the landscape every summer at Mount Revelstoke National Park.

MANITOBA
Riding Mountain National Park

Fast Facts

Established: 1929
Acreage: 733,335 (296,770 hectares)
Visitors (2019–20): 352,218
Visitor Centers: East Gate, South Lake, Lake Audy, Deep Lake, Moon Lake
Nearest Major Airport: Winnipeg James Armstrong Richardson Intl. (YWG), Winnipeg, MB
Nearest Major Highway: MB-10
Fees (CAD): $7.90/adult; $6.90/senior; $16.00/ family
Contact Information:
204-848-7275
www.pc.gc.ca/en/pn-np/mb/riding

Protects a unique landscape where the boreal forest, aspen parkland, and fescue prairie meet. A staggering diversity of wildlife calls this park home, including black bears, moose, elk, lynx, and a colony of wolves that would prefer that you don't spot them. Many places within the park are of sacred cultural and spiritual importance to Cree and Assiniboine First Nations communities, who have lived here for millennia.

Wapusk National Park

Fast Facts

Established: 1996
Acreage: 2,835,534 (1,147,500 hectares)
Visitors (2019–20): 74
Getting There: The closest major airport is Winnipeg James Armstrong Richardson Intl. (YWG), Winnipeg, MB, 870 miles (1,400 km) southwest of the park. The only way to visit is by helicopter from the gateway town of Churchill. In May–September, Hudson Bay Helicopters (www.hudsonbayheli.com; 204-675-2576) carries up to five people per trip; flights range 1–3 hours, depending on the number of passengers. In February and March, Wat'Chee Expeditions (www.watchee.com; 204-675-2114) takes small groups to see polar bear cubs and mothers in their natural habitat.
Accessibility: Hudson Bay Helicopters staff will carry visitors to their seats as needed. Fees (CAD): $0
Contact Information:
204-675-8863
www.pc.gc.ca/en/pn-np/mb/wapusk

Wat'Chee Expeditions takes small groups of visitors into Wapusk National Park to see polar bear cubs and mothers in their natural habitat.

This massive subarctic wilderness lies at the intersection of tundra and boreal forest, and protects one of the world's largest polar bear maternity denning areas. In addition to approximately 1,000 polar bears, wolves, caribou, wolverine, arctic hares, foxes, and more than 200 bird species call this remote park home.

NEW BRUNSWICK
Kouchibouguac National Park

Fast Facts

Established: 1969
Acreage: 59,108 (23,920 hectares)
Visitors (2019–20): 238,957
Nearest Major Airport: Greater Moncton Roméo LeBlanc Intl. (YQM), Dieppe, NB
Nearest Major Highway: NB-11
Fees (CAD): $7.90/adult; $6.90/senior in summer. $3.90/adult; $3.20/senior in April–June and September–November.
Accessibility: Visitors with mobility impairments may borrow all-terrain wheelchairs.
Contact Information:
506-876-2443
www.pc.gc.ca/en/pn-np/nb/kouchibouguac

Located on New Brunswick's Acadian Coast, Kouchibouguac sits at the intersection of mixed-wood forests, colorful salt marshes and estuaries, golden sand dunes, and warm ocean beaches. In winter, the park is a playground for snowshoeing, cross-country skiing, and fat-biking. The park protects and honors the long, rich history of use by the Mi'gmaq First Nations people, whose homes were expropriated when the park was established.

NEWFOUNDLAND AND LABRADOR
Akami-Uapishkᵁ-KakKasuak-Mealy Mountains National Park Reserve
Fast Facts
Established: 2015
Acreage: 2,644,028 (1,070,000 hectares)
Visitors (2019–20): NA
Getting there: Most visitors arrange excursions into the park with private tourism operators. The closest airport is Goose Bay in Happy Valley-Goose Bay, Labrador, which has direct flights from larger airports. There is no road access to the park.
Fees (CAD): $0
Accessibility: No public services or facilities.
Contact Information:
709-896-2394
www.pc.gc.ca/en/pn-np/nl/mealy

The glacially rounded, bare rock summits of Labrador's Mealy Mountains soar 3,871 feet (1,180 m) to overlook Lake Melville. The pristine landscape of mountain tundra, marine coasts, boreal forests, islands and rivers are home to numerous boreal species. The landscapes of this outstanding natural region hold great cultural significance for the Innu, Inuit, and other cultures that have called this place home for thousands of years. The traditional names of the park are Uapishkᵁ, an Innu word meaning "white mountains across," and KakKasuak, a Labrador Inuit word for "mountain."

Gros Morne National Park
Fast Facts
Established: 1973
Acreage: 446,025 (180,500 hectares)
Visitors (2019–20): 238,071
Nearest Airport: Deer Lake Regional Airport (YDF), Deer Lake, NL, is served by direct flights from larger airports in Halifax, Montréal, St. John's, and Toronto.
Nearest Major Highway: Hwy-1 (Trans-Canada Highway), NL-430
Fees (CAD): $10/adult; $8.40/senior; $20/family

Accessibility: Many facilities, campsites, and restrooms are accessible. Portions of the trails at Berry Head Pond, Western Brook Pond, and Shallow Bay Day Use Area are accessible.
Contact Information:
709-458-2417
www.pc.gc.ca/en/pn-np/nl/grosmorne

Soaring fjords and moody mountains tower above a diverse panorama of beaches, bogs, forests, and barren cliffs. Shaped by colliding continents and grinding glaciers, Gros Morne's ancient landscape is a UNESCO World Heritage Site. The barren, orange Tablelands region offers a glimpse into the formation of the Earth's mantle during the creation of the supercontinent Pangea some 400 million years ago.

Terra Nova National Park
Fast Facts
Established: 1957
Acreage: 98,817 (39,990 hectares)
Visitors (2019–20): 44,403
Nearest Major Airport: Gander Intl. (YQX), Gander, NL; St. John's Intl. (YYT), St. John's, NL
Nearest Major Highway: Hwy-1 (Trans-Canada Highway)
Fees (CAD): $5.90/adult; $5.00/senior; $12/family.
Accessibility: The visitor center and some short trails are accessible.
Contact Information:
709-533-2801
www.pc.gc.ca/en/pn-np/nl/terranova

Canada's easternmost national park preserves miles of Atlantic shoreline, boreal forest replete with wildlife, tranquil marshland ponds, and fjords with views of whales and icebergs. As a Dark Sky Preserve since 2018, Terra Nova allows present and future generations to gaze at the stars without light pollution.

Torngat Mountains National Park
Fast Facts
Established: 2005
Acreage: 2,396,922 (970,000 hectares)
Visitors (2019–20): NA
Getting there: Most visitors explore the park by private chartered plane from Happy Valley-Goose

Bay, NL, which has daily scheduled air service from larger airports.

Fees (CAD): $0

Accessibility: Largely inaccessible.

Contact Information:
709-922-1290
www.pc.gc.ca/en/pn-np/nl/torngats

The traditional homeland of the Inuit of Labrador and Nunavik welcomes visitors to experience a dramatic landscape where nature and culture meet. Torngat Mountains preserves jagged peaks, vast glacial fjords and valleys, iceberg-dotted waters, and some of the Earth's oldest rocks.

NORTHWEST TERRITORIES
Aulavik National Park
Fast Facts

Established: 1992

Acreage: 3,014,686 (1,220,000 hectares)

Visitors (2019–20): 15

Visitor Centers: Inuvik, Sachs Harbour

Getting There: There are no roads to the park. Most visitors arrive via chartered flight from Inuvik, 466 miles (750 km) south of the park. The unpaved, gravel Dempster Highway from Dawson City, YT, is the only road to Inuvik. Inuvik Mike Zubko Airport (YEV), Inuvik, NT, is served by larger airports.

Fees (CAD): $0. Backcountry camping permits are $25.04/night. An annual pass is $150.44 and is valid at certain parks.

Contact Information:
867-777-8800
www.pc.gc.ca/en/pn-np/nt/aulavik/visit/tarifs-fees

Preserves unspoiled tundra, pristine rivers, rolling hills, fertile valleys, archaeological sites, and wildlife of Banks Island, in the northernmost reaches of the Northwest Territories. Aulavik, an Inuvialuktun word meaning "place where people travel," is among Canada's most remote national parks. Visitors must be self-sufficient and capable of handling emergencies.

Nahanni National Park Reserve
Fast Facts

Established: 1972

Acreage: 7,413,161 (3,000,000 hectares)

Visitors (2019–20): 770

The Nahanni River is a whitewater paddler's playground.

Getting There: Erik Nielsen Whitehorse Intl. (YXY), Whitehorse, YT, is the closest airport of any size. Most visitors arrive by chartered floatplane from Yellowknife or Fort Simpson. Visit the park website for a comprehensive list of air charter companies and other outfitters and operators.

Fees (CAD): $0. Backcountry camping permits are $25.04/night. An annual pass is $150.44 and is valid at certain other parks.

Contact Information:
867-695-6558
www.pc.gc.ca/en/pn-np/nt/nahanni

The Cirque of the Unclimbables, a collection of remote granite pinnacles in the Mackenzie Mountains, lure top alpinists from around the world. The most famous is the Lotus Flower Tower, a 8,430-foot (2,570-m) sheer rockface first summited in 1960. Nahanni's wild rivers are a whitewater paddler's paradise. The waterfall known as Náįlįcho, or Virginia Falls, is for admiring only; the drop is twice the height of Niagara Falls. Flightseeing trips from British Columbia are a popular way to see the park.

Náats'ihch'oh National Park Reserve
Fast Facts

Established: 2012

Acreage: 1,209,581 (489,500 hectares)

Visitors (2019–20): 119

Getting There: The closest airport is Erik Nielsen Whitehorse Intl. (YXY), Whitehorse, YT. Most visitors arrive by chartered floatplane from Fort Simpson or Yellowknife.

Fees (CAD): $0
Accessibility: Inaccessible.
Contact Information:
867-588-4884
www.pc.gc.ca/en/pn-np/nt/naatsihchoh

Preserves a land near the Yukon border where culture and nature intertwine. Náàts'įhch'oh offers whitewater paddling in the headwaters of the South Nahanni River and hiking through uncharted territory where there are no established trails, but plenty of grizzly bears, Dall sheep, mountain goats, and woodland caribou. There are no services or facilities anywhere in the park. Visitors must reserve and register their trips before arriving.

Thaidene Nene National Park Reserve
Fast Facts
Established: 2019
Acreage: 3,534,842 (1,430,500 hectares)
Visitors (2019–20): NA
Getting There: The nearest major airport is in Yellowknife (YZF), NT, 118 miles (190 km) away, from which there are daily flights to the village of Łutsël K'é. There are no roads to or in the park; most visitors arrive by chartered plane, boat, or snowmobile from Łutsël K'é. Visit the park website for a list of air charter companies, outfitters, lodges, and indigenous tour operators.
Accessibility: Inaccessible.
Fees (CAD): $0
Contact Information:
867-766-8460
www.pc.gc.ca/en/pn-np/nt/thaidene-nene/visit/travel

Preserves the traditional and present-day hunting, fishing, gathering and spiritual areas used by the indigenous peoples of the East Arm of Great Slave Lake, Thaidene Nene means "Land of the Ancestors" in the Dënesųłiné—or Chipewyan—language; the Northwest Territory Métis Nation, Deninu K'ue First Nation, and Yellowknives Dene First Nation peoples also have traditional and cultural ties to the region. Thaidene Nene National Park Reserve is part of a larger group of protected areas around the East Arm and Artillery Lake regions. There are no visitor services or facilities in the park.

Tuktut Nogait National Park
Fast Facts
Established: 1996
Acreage: 4,492,623 (1,818,100 hectares)
Visitors (2019–20): 14
Getting There: The closest airports of any size are in Yellowknife, NT, or Whitehorse, YT, where you can catch a connecting flight to Inuvik, 304 miles (489 km) west of the park. From Inuvik, most visitors reach the park by chartered floatplane. There are no roads to or in the park.
Fees (CAD): $0. Backcountry camping permits are $25.04/night. An annual pass is $150.44 and is also valid at certain other parks.
Accessibility: Inaccessible.
Contact Information:
867-580-3233
www.pc.gc.ca/en/pn-np/nt/tuktutnogait

Located 106 miles (170 km) above the Arctic Circle, Tuktut Nogait preserves wild rivers, steep canyons, rolling hills, and pristine waterfalls that are home to wolves, muskoxen, rare Bluenose west caribou, and other species. All visitors must register with Parks Canada in Inuvik and attend an orientation session.

Wood Buffalo National Park
Fast Facts
Established: 1922
Acreage: 11,064,959 (4,477,830 hectares)
Visitors (2019–20): 3,941
Visitor Centers: Fort Smith (main office), Fort Chipewyan (satellite office)
Getting There: Most visitors fly into Edmonton Intl. (YEG), AB, or Yellowknife Airport (YZF), NT, both of which offer direct flights to Fort Smith and Fort Chipewyan. Visitors can also drive to the park year-round on the Wood Buffalo Parkway (Hwy 5), which connects to the Mackenzie Highway (Hwy 1).
Fees (CAD): $0. Camping fees range from $10.02 per person, per night, in the backcountry to $102.20 for a cabin at Pine Lake (minimum two nights).
Contact Information:
780-697-3662
www.pc.gc.ca/en/pn-np/nt/woodbuffalo

Canada's largest national park (and one of the largest in the world) was created to protect the last remaining bison herds in northern Canada. It

Wood Buffalo, Canada's largest national park, was created to protect the last remaining bison herds in northern Canada.

also preserves a representative example of Canada's Northern Boreal Plains. The Peace-Athabasca Delta, where three rivers converge with Lake Athabasca, is one of the world's most spectacular wetlands, attracting millions of ducks, geese, and other waterfowl on their annual migration. The natural swimming hole known as Pine Lake is actually a series of sinkholes filled with water.

NOVA SCOTIA
Cape Breton Highlands National Park
Fast Facts

Established: 1936
Acreage: 234,256 (94,800 hectares)
Visitors (2019–20): 300,906
Visitor Centers: Chéticamp, Ingonish
Nearest Major Airport: Halifax Stanfield Intl. (YHZ), Goffs, NS
Nearest Major Highway: NS Trunk 8
Fees (CAD): $7.90/adult; $6.90/senior; $16/family.
Accessibility: NA

Contact Information:
902-224-2306
www.pc.gc.ca/en/pn-np/ns/cbreton

One-third of the world-famous Cabot Trail road winds through this park at the far northern tip of Cape Breton Island, closer to Newfoundland than to Halifax. Deep-cut canyons kneel down to sandy beaches with tremendous ocean vistas. Moose and

The Cabot Trail road winds through Cape Breton Highlands National Park.

366

bald eagles may be visible from any of the park's 26 diverse hiking trails, while minke and pilot whales breach in the Atlantic Ocean and Gulf of St. Lawrence.

Kejimkujik National Park and Historic Site
Fast Facts
Established: 1967
Acreage: 99,732 (40,360 hectares)
Visitors (2019–20): 70,756
Visitor Centers: The park visitor center is located in the historic site and is open June 1–October 31. There is no visitor center in the Seaside section.
Nearest Major Airport: Halifax Stanfield Intl. (YHZ), Goffs, NS
Nearest Major Highway: Hwy-15 (Trans-Canada Highway), NS-30. NS-103 leads to the Seaside unit of the park.
Fees (CAD): $5.90/adult; $5.00/senior; $12/family.
Accessibility: Largely accessible. Visit the park website for a detailed list of accessible facilities.
Contact Information:
902-682-2772
www.pc.gc.ca/en/pn-np/ns/kejimkujik

The main section of this two-part park preserves petroglyphs, traditional encampments, and canoe routes that attest to more than 4,000 years of Mi'kmaw culture. Thousands of brilliant stars emerge at night in Nova Scotia's only Dark Sky Preserve, a designation that protects the area from light pollution. The Seaside unit, on the southeast coast, protects white sand beaches, mossy bogs, and the harbor seals who bask in the pristine wilderness.

Sable Island National Park Reserve
Fast Facts
Established: 2011
Acreage: 7,413 (3,000 hectares)
Visitors (2019–20): 394
Visitor Center: Main Station is the only facility in the park that is staffed year-round.
Nearest Major Airport: Halifax Stanfield Intl. (YHZ), Goffs, NS
Getting There: The island is accessible only by small plane from Halifax or by boat. Both options often involve delays and/or cancellations.

Fees (CAD): $24.22
Accessibility: Inaccessible. There are few visitor facilities in this backcountry.
Contact Information:
902-426-1500
www.pc.gc.ca/en/pn-np/ns/sable

Wild horses outnumber people on this remote smile-shaped island 200 miles (320 km) off the coast of Nova Scotia. Some of eastern Canada's largest sand dunes dominate the landscape. The world's largest breeding colony of grey seals inhabit the many miles of deserted beaches. The island is often called "the graveyard of the Atlantic" due to the more than 350 ships that have wrecked here due to fog, rough seas, or submerged sandbars.

NUNAVUT TERRITORY
Auyuittuq National Park
Fast Facts
Established: 1972
Acreage: 4,716,995 (1,908,900 hectares)
Visitors (2019–20): 356
Getting There: Iqaluit Airport (YFB), Iqaluit, NU, is the closest regional airport. Most visitors arrive by boat or snowmobile. Call 867-473-2500 for a list of licensed boat operators who provide access to the park.
Fees (CAD): Admission is free. There are fees for day and overnight guided excursions into the backcountry.
Accessibility: Largely inaccessible.
Contact Information:
867-473-2500 or 867-927-8834
www.pc.gc.ca/en/pn-np/nu/auyuittuq

The first Canadian National Park located above the Arctic Circle, Auyuittuq (an Inuktitut word meaning "Land that Never Melts") preserves a zig-zag of craggy granite peaks and glittering glaciers overlooking tundra valleys and steep-walled fjords whose winding waterways teem with narwhal and ringed seals. Icy thundering streams and wildflower-dotted meadows mark this remote landscape. Akshayuk Pass, a natural corridor through towering rocks, beckons experienced mountaineers and backcountry skiers. Snow geese and Arctic foxes are among the many species that bask in the midnight sun.

Qausuittuq National Park

Fast Facts

Established: 2015
Acreage: 2,720,136 (1,100,800 hectares)
Visitors (2019–20): NA
Getting There: The only way to access the park is by private plane from Resolute Bay (YRB), Resolute, NU. Resolute Bay has regular air service from Ottawa (with multiple stops).
Fees (CAD): $0. There are fees for guided excursions into the backcountry ranging from $12.26 to $25.04 per person.
Accessibility: Largely inaccessible
Contact Information:
> 867-975-4673
> www.pc.gc.ca/en/pn-np/nu/qausuittuq

Protects rolling tundra on a cluster of islands in a frozen sea. Qausuittuq, an Inuktitut word meaning "place where the sun doesn't rise," is a haven for endangered Peary caribou. This traditional hunting and fishing area has sustained Inuit populations of Resolute Bay since the time of their relocation in the 1950s. All visitors must register prior to entering the park and sign out when leaving.

Quttinirpaaq National Park

Fast Facts

Established: 1986
Acreage: 9,334,406 (3,777,500 hectares)
Visitors (2019–20): 18
Getting There: The only way to access the park is by private plane from Resolute Bay (YRB), Resolute, NU. Resolute Bay has regular air service from Ottawa (with multiple stops).
Fees (CAD): $0. There are fees for guided excursions into the backcountry ranging from $12.26 to $25.04 per person.
Accessibility: Largely inaccessible.
Contact Information:
> 867-975-4673
> www.pc.gc.ca/en/pn-np/nu/quttinirpaaq

In the "Land at the Top of the World," massive glaciers fuel wild rivers, while jagged black peaks puncture shimmering ice caps. Muskoxen and caribou roam the tundra, heedless of human activity. Lake Hazen, one of the largest and deepest lakes above the Arctic Circle, is a thermal oasis with remarkably lush vegetation. Ellesmere Island, on which the park is located, is often used as a base camp for North Pole expeditions.

Sirmilik National Park

Fast Facts

Established: 1999
Acreage: 5,485,739 (2,220,000 hectares)
Visitors (2019–20): 298
Getting There: Call the Nattinak Visitor Centre (867-899-8226) for licensed operators who can arrange transportation to and from the park from Pond Inlet. For transportation from Arctic Bay, call 867-439-8483.
Fees (CAD): $0. There are fees for guided excursions into the backcountry ranging from $12.26 to $25.04 per person.
Accessibility: Largely inaccessible
Contact Information:
> 867-899-8092
> www.pc.gc.ca/en/pn-np/nu/sirmilik/visit

Sirmilik, an Inuktitut word meaning "place of glaciers," is home to the ultimate Arctic adventure under the midnight sun. Polar bears, ringed seals, and walruses populate this expansive landscape of glaciers, valleys and red-rock hoodoo spires, where nesting seabirds crowd sheer cliffs. Intrepid visitors may ski across glaciers or paddle among seals and floating ice, listening for narwhals and beluga whales.

Ukkusiksalik National Park

Fast Facts

Established: 2003
Acreage: 5,159,560 (2,088,000 hectares)
Visitors (2019–20): NA
Getting There: Most visitors access the park via a 7-hour boat ride from Repulse Bay or via charter plane from Baker Lake or Rankin Inlet.
Fees (CAD): $0. There are fees for guided excursions into the backcountry ranging from $12.26 to $25.04 per person.
Accessibility: Largely inaccessible.
Contact Information:
> 867-462-4500
> www.pc.gc.ca/en/pn-np/nu/ukkusiksalik

Ukkusiksalik's rolling ochre hills and lush tundra thrive with polar bears, grizzlies, Arctic wolves, and caribou, while its waters are rich with seals, beluga whales, and other marine life. The park is home to more than 400 documented archaeological sites, including tent rings, food caches, fox traps, and other reminders of human cultures present in this remote wilderness for millennia. There are no facilities, services, or campgrounds in the park.

ONTARIO
Bruce Peninsula National Park
Fast Facts

Established: 1987
Acreage: 30,938 (12,520 hectares)
Visitors (2019–20): 490,388
Visitor Centers: The Visitor Centre is located in the town of Tobermory. A campgrounds office is located on the southeast shore of Cyprus Lake. Both are only open from May to October.
Nearest Major Airport: Toronto Pearson Intl. (YYZ), Toronto, ON
Nearest Major Highway: ON-6
Fees (CAD): $7.90/adult; $6.90/senior; $16/family.
Accessibility: Many restrooms and campsites are accessible.
Contact Information:
  519-596-2233
  www.pc.gc.ca/en/pn-np/on/bruce

A variety of wild landscapes occupy the very tip of the Bruce Peninsula, which juts into Lake Huron. Hikers travel through large tracts of forest, black bears roam, and rare reptiles find refuge in diverse wetlands rich with orchids and ferns. The waters of Singing Sands Beach are warm enough for swimming. Advance reservations are required to park at the popular Grotto.

Georgian Bay Islands National Park
Fast Facts

Established: 1930
Acreage: 3,459 (1,400 hectares)
Visitors (2019–20): 35,780
Visitor Centers: Cedar Spring Campground
Nearest Major Airport: Toronto Pearson Intl. (YYZ), Toronto, ON
Getting There: The park is accessible only by boat. The closest departure point from the mainland is in Honey Harbour, where Honey Harbour Road (Musoka Road 5) ends. If you don't have

your own boat, you can take the Parks Canada DayTripper vessel round-trip from Honey Harbour to Beausoleil Island. Reservations are required; visit the park website to reserve passage and see prices.
Fees (CAD): $5.90/adult; $5.00/senior; $12/family.
Accessibility: Largely inaccessible
Contact Information:
  705-526-8907
  www.pc.gc.ca/en/pn-np/on/georg

Protects the world's largest freshwater archipelago: a nature preserve in the clear waters of Lake Huron accessible only by boat. Windswept white pines and the granite shores of the Canadian Shield give way to dense deciduous woodland. Hiking and cycling trails meander between the ecosystems. Beausoleil Island, the largest in the chain, preserves evidence of the Anishinaabeg presence during the mid-19th century. The landscape was the setting for numerous paintings by Canada's Group of Seven artists between 1920 and 1933.

Point Pelee National Park
Fast Facts

Established: 1918
Acreage: 3,756 (1,520 hectares)
Visitors (2019–20): 396,168
Nearest Major Airport: Detroit Metropolitan Wayne County Airport (DTW), Detroit, MI, U.S. (international border crossing required). The closest Canadian airport is Toronto Pearson Intl. (YYZ), Toronto, ON.
Nearest Major Highway: ON-3, Essex-33
Fees (CAD): $7.90/adult; $6.90/senior; $16/family.
Accessibility: The visitor center, the DeLaurier building exhibits and parking lot, group camping facilities, and most restrooms are accessible. Visitors may reserve use of an all-terrain wheelchair at the visitor center and at the Marsh Boardwalk in June through September.
Contact Information:
  519-322-2365
  www.pc.gc.ca/en/pn-np/on/pelee

Canada's second-smallest national park is also its most ecologically diverse. Point Pelee's forest hosts diverse habitats that provide a sanctuary for plants and animals rarely found elsewhere in the country. The park is renowned as the best place in inland

Monarch butterflies return to Point Pelee National Park every fall.

North America to witness the northward migration of songbirds. Monarch butterflies return here every fall. A free shuttle is available for visitors who cannot walk to The Tip, the southernmost point in mainland Canada.

Pukaskwa National Park

Fast Facts

Established: 1971
Acreage: 464,014 (187,780 hectares)
Visitors (2019–20): 9,107
Visitor Centers: The visitor center, located on the shore of Hattie Cove, is open June 1 through September 30.
Nearest Major Airport: Thunder Bay Intl. (YQT), Thunder Bay, ON
Nearest Major Highway: ON-17 (Trans-Canada Hwy.), ON-627
Fees (CAD): $5.90/adult; $5.00/senior; $12/family.
Accessibility: The Beach Boardwalk trail and some of the walking paths near the Visitor Center and Anishinaabe Camp are accessible, as are two campsites in Hattie Cove Campground.

Contact Information:
807-229-0801 ext. 248
www.pc.gc.ca/en/pn-np/on/pukaskwa

Preserves Ontario's only wilderness national park, a landscape of pink-and-slate granite shores, miles of Lake Superior coastline, and stretches of spruce, fir, pine, and hardwoods. Wetlands, lakes, and forests meet in this biodiverse park, which is home to iconic species like bald eagles, moose, Canada lynx, and the endangered peregrine falcon.

Rouge National Urban Park

Fast Facts

Established: 2015
Acreage: 19,546 (7,910 hectares)
Visitors (2019–20): NA
Visitor Center: Construction is scheduled to begin in 2023 and be complete by 2025.
Nearest Major Airport: Toronto Pearson Intl. (YYZ), Toronto, ON
Nearest Major Highway: ON-401, ON-407
Fees (CAD): $0.

Accessibility: Varies. Visit the park website for
  a detailed list of facilities that are accessible to
  visitors with impaired mobility.
Contact Information:
  416-264-2020
  www.pc.gc.ca/en/pn-np/on/rouge

The largest urban park in North America lies an
hour's drive from downtown Toronto. It protects
a rich array of natural, cultural and agricultural
resources, including amazing biodiversity, Toronto's
only campground, one of the region's largest
marshes, some of the last remaining working farms
in the Greater Toronto Area, unspoiled beaches
on Lake Ontario, and some of Canada's oldest
known indigenous sites, some dating human history
back more than 10,000 years. The park is home
to hundreds of species of wild mammals, birds,
reptiles, and fish, and dozens of additional species in
captivity at the Toronto Zoo.

Thousand Islands National Park

Fast Facts

Established: 1904
Acreage: 5,807 (2,350 hectares)
Visitors (2019–20): 72,625
Visitor Centers: The visitor center is on the
  mainland, in Mallorytown.
Nearest Major Airport: Ottawa/Macdonald-Cartier
  Intl. (YOW), Ottawa, ON
Nearest Major Highway: ON-401, Thousand
  Islands Parkway. Visitors who don't have their
  own boats may rent one in Mallorytown, take
  a water taxi, or join a cruise from other points.
  Visit the park website for a list of operators.
Fees (CAD): $0. Admission to the park is free,
  but there are fees for boat launching, mooring,
  parking, camping, and heritage presentation
  programs.
Accessibility: Mostly inaccessible, although some
  cruises can accommodate visitors with impaired
  mobility.
Contact Information:
  613-923-5261
  www.pc.gc.ca/en/pn-np/on/1000

Preserves 19 granite islands in the St. Lawrence
River between Kingston and Brockville. The
location is a transition zone between the Canadian
Shield and the Adirondack Mountains. The islands
are home to rare species of birds and vulnerable
turtles and other reptiles. Recreation opportunities
include hiking, boating, paddling, cycling,
kitesurfing, birding, scuba diving, and wildlife
viewing.

QUÉBEC
Forillon National Park

Fast Facts

Established: 1970
Acreage: 53,622 (21,700 hectares)
Visitors (2019–20): 169,825
Nearest Major Airport: Québec City Jean Lesage
  Intl. (YQB), Québec City, QC
Nearest Major Highway: QC-132, QC-198
Fees (CAD): $7.90/adult; $6.90/senior; $16/family.
  Additional fees for camping vary by season and
  location.
Contact Information:
  418-368-5505
  www.pc.gc.ca/en/pn-np/qc/forillon

Preserves a naturally vibrant environment on the
northeast tip of the Gaspé Peninsula, where the
Bay of Gaspé meets the Gulf of St. Lawrence. The
park encompasses four major ecosystems—aquatic,
coastal, marine, and forest—and is renowned for its
exceptional views of seaside cliffs and the wildlife
that frequent the area.

La Mauricie National Park

Fast Facts

Established: 1970
Acreage: 132,473 (53,610 hectares)
Visitors (2019–20): 219,824
Visitor Centers: Saint-Jean-des-Pies, Saint-Mathieu,
  Rivière à la Pêche Service Centre
Nearest Major Airport: Québec City Jean Lesage
  Intl. (YQB), Québec City, QC; Montréal-
  Trudeau Intl. (YUL), Dorval, QC
Nearest Major Highway: QC-155
Fees (CAD): $7.90/adult; $6.90/senior; $16/family.
  Additional fees for camping vary by season and
  location.
Accessibility: The visitor centers have accessible
  restrooms, as do the Mekinac, Lac Edouard,
  Esker, and Shewenegan picnic areas. Some
  campsites have been modified for visitors with
  disabilities. The Lac Etienne Trail and portions of

the Les Cascades Trail can accommodate visitors with impaired mobility.

Contact Information:

819-538-3232

www.pc.gc.ca/en/pn-np/qc/mauricie

Preserves hardwood and conifer forests, dotted with more than 150 lakes. Spread over 12 of these lakes are 136 backcountry campsites accessible only by canoe. The 39-mile (63-km) parkway through the park is wide enough to accommodate groups of cyclists. (Note: Park admission may at times be limited to visitors who already have reservations for boat rentals or accommodations.)

Mingan Archipelago National Park Reserve

Fast Facts

Established: 1984

Acreage: 37,239 (15,070 hectares)

Visitors (2019–20): 41,381

Visitor Centers: Havre-Saint-Pierre, Longue-Ponte-de-Mingan; Aguanish Reception Center, Baie-Johan-Beetz Reception Center. All are open only from early June to mid-September.

Nearest Major Airport: Québec City Jean Lesage Intl. (YQB), Québec City, QC

Nearest Major Highway: QC-138

Fees (CAD): $5.90/adult; $5.00/senior; $12/family.

Accessibility: Facilities on the mainland are accessible, as are portions of Petite île au Marteau.

Contact Information:

418-538-3285

www.pc.gc.ca/en/pn-np/qc/mingan

Protects 20 large islands and sedimentary islets in addition to more than 1,000 Precambrian islands stretching along the Minganie coast, more than 540 miles (870 km) northeast of Québec. Wildlife includes whales, seals, Atlantic puffins, and some unique flora and fauna found nowhere else in Canada. Many campers and hikers island hop by kayak or on a cruise.

Monoliths at Mingan Archipelago National Park Reserve

SASKATCHEWAN
Grasslands National Park
Fast Facts

Established: 1981
Acreage: 180,387 (73,000 hectares)
Visitors (2019–20): 17,477
Nearest Major Airport: Regina Intl. (YQR), Regina, SK
Nearest Major Highway: West Block: SK-4, SK-18; East Block: SK-18. Access roads to both blocks are gravel.
Fees (CAD): $5.90/adult; $5.00/senior; $12/family. Camping fees range from $10.02 for backcountry sites to $102.50 for an oTENTik, a cross between a tent and a cabin.
Contact Information:
West block: 877-345-2257; East block: 306-476-2018
www.pc.gc.ca/en/pn-np/sk/grasslands

Expanses of dinosaur fossils harken back to a time before human habitation. Tipi rings are testament to First Nations communities, and ruins of prairie homesteads recall new arrivals intent on inhabiting the prairie. Guided rides in traditional wagons to cowboy campfires bring Grasslands' more recent history to life. The park is divided into two parts: the west block, which centers on the Frenchmen River Valley, and the east block, home to the Killdeer Badlands and the Wood Mountain Uplands. The Dark Sky Preserve here, which shelters the region from light pollution, is one of the largest and darkest in Canada.

Prince Albert National Park
Fast Facts

Established: 1927
Acreage: 957,435 (387,460 hectares)
Visitors (2019–20): 283,873
Nearest Major Airport: Saskatoon John G. Diefenbaker Intl. (YXE), Saskatoon, SK
Nearest Major Highway: SK-2, Hwy-263, Hwy-264
Accessibility: Varies. Visit the park website for a comprehensive list of accessible facilities.
Fees (CAD): $7.90/adult; $6.90/senior; $16/family. Additional fees for camping vary by season and location
Contact Information:
306-663-4522
www.pc.gc.ca/en/pn-np/sk/princealbert

Prince Albert National Park's variety of habitats attracts more than 200 recorded species of birds.

Preserves an accessible wilderness in central Saskatchewan, with extensive opportunities for outdoor recreation. Visitors hike boreal forests, canoe pristine lakes, see free-range plains bison, and hear wolves howling. Waskesiu Lake is the center of most activity, with 10 vehicle-accessible beaches and eight mostly flat hiking trails of varying lengths. Located at the intersection of aspen parkland and boreal forest, the park provides a variety of habitats, attracting more than 200 recorded species of birds.

YUKON TERRITORY
Ivvavik National Park
Fast Facts

Established: 1984
Acreage: 2,409,277 (975,000 hectares)
Visitors (2019–20): 98
Getting There: There are no roads to the park. Most visitors arrive via chartered flight from the town of Inuvik, NT, 124 miles (200 km) east of the park. The unpaved, gravel Dempster Highway from Dawson City, YT, is the only road to Inuvik.
Accessibility: Mostly inaccessible.
Fees (CAD): Backcountry excursion/camping fees are $25.04/night; $150.44/year.
Contact Information:
867-777-8800
www.pc.gc.ca/en/pn-np/yt/ivvavik

Created as the result of an Aboriginal land claim, Ivvavik protects the calving grounds of the

Porcupine Caribou herd for the Inuvialut First Nations people. In the Inuvialuktu language, Ivvavik means "a place for giving birth." The park is adjacent to Alaska's Arctic National Wildlife Refuge. Rafters make the trek here to paddle the renowned Firth River, which cuts through mountain valleys on its way to the Arctic Ocean.

Kluane National Park and Reserve
Fast Facts
Established: 1972
Acreage: 5,451,392 (2,206,100 hectares):
Visitors (2019–20): 29,055
Visitor Centers: Kluane, Thechàl Dhâl'
Nearest Major Airport: Erik Nielsen Whitehorse Intl. (YXY), Whitehorse, YT
Nearest Major Highway: YT-1 (Alaska Highway)
Accessibility: Both visitor centers are accessible, as is the Kathleen Lake Day Use Area. The Kokanee Trail is an accessible boardwalk.
Fees (CAD): $0. oTENTiks, a cross between a tent and a cabin, cost $122.64/night, plus a reservation fee.
Contact Information:
867-634-7207
www.pc.gc.ca/en/pn-np/yt/kluane

Kluane is the site of Canada's largest icefield and 17 of the country's 20 highest peaks, including Mount Logan, the tallest of all at 19,551 feet (5,959 m). Dall sheep, mountain goats, and North America's most genetically diverse grizzly bear population call the park home. Hiking and rafting past calving glaciers are popular activities.

Vuntut National Park
Fast Facts
Established: 1993
Acreage: 1,073,673 (434,500 hectares)
Visitors (2019–20): NA
Getting There: Most visitors arrive by charter flight from Old Crow (YOC), YT.
Accessibility: Largely inaccessible.
Fees (CAD): $24.50/day; $147.20/year
Contact Information:
867-667-3910
www.pc.gc.ca/en/pn-np/yt/vuntut

Preserves a remote and untouched Arctic wilderness, where the Vuntut Gwitchin First Nation people have lived for millennia, following the migration of caribou. Every May, the Caribou Days celebration in Old Crow commemorates the connection between the Vuntut and the Porcupine Caribou herd. Some years, the park receives no visitors.

Mount Logan, Canada's highest peak, straddles the Continental Divide in Kluane National Park and Reserve.

Index

#

1.5 Mile Resthouse, 68
1st Burroughs Mountain, 38
1730 Nelson House, 280

A

Abbotts Bridge, 191
Abbotts Lagoon, 15
Abraham Lincoln Birthplace National Historical Park, 156
Abrams Falls, 178
Absaroka range, 115
Acadia National Park, 220–223
Acadian Forest, 344
Adams National Historical Park, 243
African American Civil War Memorial, 281
African Burial Ground National Monument, 248–249
Agate Fossil Beds National Monument, 163
Ahwahnee Dining Room, 5
Ahwahnee Hotel, 4, 5
Akami-Uapishkᵘ-KakKasuak-Mealy Mountains National Park Reserve, 363
Alabama, 196–198
Alagnak Wild River, 49
Ala Kahakai National Historic Trail, 323
Alaska, 44–48, 49–56
Alberta, 330–334, 358
Alberta Falls, 122
Alcatraz Island, 6
Aleutian Islands World War II National Historic Area, 49
Alibates Flint Quarries National Monument, 99
All-American Road, 120
Allegheny Portage Railroad National Historic Site, 255
Alma Beach, 344
Alpine Visitor Center, 121
Alum Cave Trail, 180
American Memorial Park, 325
American Samoa, 322
Amiskwi Trail, 356
Amistad National Recreation Area, 99
Anacostia Park, 281
Andersonville National Historic Site, 203
Andrew Johnson National Historic Site, 213
Angels Landing, 72
Aniakchak National Monument and Preserve, 49–50
Annie Creek Trail, 43
Annie Spring Entrance Station, 43
Antelope Canyon, 80
Antelope Point, 80

Anthony Creek, 180
Antietam National Battlefield, 293–294
Apgar Village, 126
Apostle Islands National Lakeshore, 170
Appalachian National Scenic Trail, 242, 276
Appalachian Trail, 176
Appomattox Court House National Historical Park, 297–298
Arches National Park, 103–104
Arizona, 66–70, 84–92
Arkansas, 181–184, 198–200
Arkansas Post National Memorial, 198–199
Arlington House, The Robert E. Lee Memorial, 298
Arlington Lawn, 184
Armco Ferro House, 140
Assateague Island National Seashore, 269–272
Assateague Outfitters, 271
Athabasca Falls, 337
Athabasca Glacier, 335
Aulavik National Park, 364
Aurora Ridge, 29
Auyuittuq National Park, 367
Avalanche Peak, 114
Avenue of Flags, 152
Aztec Ruins National Monument, 93

B

Badlands National Park, 169
Baie Sainte-Marguerite, 352
Bajada Nature Trail, 12
Baker Beach, 7
Balsam Gap, 277
Baltimore-Washington Parkway, 294
Bandelier National Monument, 93
Banff Legacy Trail, 331–332
Banff National Park, 330–334
Banff Upper Hot Springs, 331
Bar Harbor, 220
Bar Island, 222
Barker Dam Nature Trail, 12
Barkley Sound, 343
Bathhouse Row, 181
Bath Road Heronry, 147
Battleship *Missouri* Memorial, 317
Beach 4, 32
Beach Hut, 271
Beacon Heights, 275
Bear Lake, 122
Bear Lake Corridor, 122
Bear Lake Road Corridor, 124
Bears Ears National Monument, 83

Bear Valley Trail, 15
Bear Valley Visitor Center, 13
Beaver Creek, 118
Beaver Marsh, 147
Beaver Pond, 126
Beech Flats, 177
Bell Route, 192
Belmont-Paul Women's Equality National Monument, 281–282
Benge Route, 192
Bennett Lake, 346
Bennett Pond, 233
Bent's Old Fort National Historic Site, 129
Bering Land Bridge National Preserve, 50
Bicentennial Campground, 8
Big Bend National Park, 99
Big Bend of Zion Canyon, 73
Big Cypress National Preserve, 200
Big Hole National Battlefield, 133
Bighorn Alley Trail, 338
Bighorn Canyon National Recreation Area, 133
Big Slick Ridge, 177
Big South Fork National River and Recreation Area, 213
Big Spring, 74
Big Thicket National Preserve, 100
Birmingham Civil Rights National Monument, 196
Biscayne National Park, 200–201
Black Canyon of the Gunnison National Park, 129–130
Black Duck Marsh Trail, 271
Black Heritage Trail, 229
Black Hills National Forest, 150
Black Lake, 122
Black Rock, 12
Blackstone River Valley National Historical Park, 259–260
Blacktail Ponds, 114
Blue Angels, 188
Blue Ridge Music Center, 274
Blue Ridge Parkway, 176, 209, 273–277
Bluestone National Scenic River, 215
Bogachiel Peak, 30
Boggerman Loop, 179
Bolinas Ridge Trail, 7
Booker T. Washington National Monument, 298–299
Boston African American National Historic Site, 229, 243–244

Boston Common, 225
Boston Harbor, 227
Boston Harbor Islands National Recreation Area, 244
Boston Latin School, 226–227
Boston Mill Visitor Center, 149
Boston National Historical Park, 224–229
Bow Lake, 335, 336
Bow Valley Parkway, 332
Brackenridge Nature Trail, 188
Bradley Lake, 118
Brandywine Falls, 149
Brices Cross Roads National Battlefield Site, 207
Bridalveil Creek, 5
Bridalveil Falls, 2, 5
Bridal Veil Falls, 149
Bridge Bay Marina, 115
Bridge Mountain, 72
Bright Angel Point Trail, 70
Bright Angel Trail, 68
Bristle Cone Pine Trees, 79
British Columbia, 340–343, 353–357, 359–361
Broken Group Islands, 340, 343
Brown Bay Beach, 321
Brown v. Board of Education National Historic Site, 155
Bryce Canyon National Park, 76–79
Bryce Point, 77
Bubble Pond Bridge, 220
Buck Island Reef National Monument, 326
Buck Spring Gap Parking Area, 277
Buck Spring Trail, 277
Buckstaff, 181–182
Buffalo National River, 199
Buford Dam, 189, 191
Bullfrog, 80
Bullfrog Bay, 80
Bull Gap, 277
Bunker Hill Monument, 229
Burgess Shale, 356–357
Burr Trail Road, 83
Buttonbush Loop, 233
Bynum Mounds, 195

C

Cabrillo National Monument, 16
Cades Cove, 179
Cades Cove Loop Road, 179–180
Cadillac Mountain, 220–221
Cadillac North Ridge Trail, 221
Cadillac South Ridge Trail, 221
Calf Creek Recreation Area, 79
California, 1–24

California Tunnel Tree, 5
Calloway Peak, 276
Calumet Bike Trail, 141
Camera Obscura, 8
Camp Nelson National Monument, 156
Canada, 128, 330–374
Canaveral National Seashore, 201
Caneel Bay Resort, 318
Cane River Creole National Historical Park, 206
Canyon de Chelly National Monument, 84
Canyonlands National Park, 83, 104–105
Canyon Lodge Eatery, 115
Canyon Rim Trail, 67
Canyon Trail Rides, 73
Canyon Village, 113–114
Canyon Vista, 69
Cape Breton Highlands National Park, 366–367
Cape Cod National Seashore, 230–233
Cape Hatteras National Seashore, 209
Cape Henry Lighthouse, 280
Cape Henry Memorial, 280
Cape Krusenstern National Monument, 50
Cape Lookout National Seashore, 209
Cape Royal, 70
Capital Region, 264–302
Capitol Reef National Park, 79, 83, 105
Cap Rock, 12
Captain John Smith Chesapeake National Historic Trail, 299
Capulin Volcano National Monument, 94
Caribou Plain, 344
Carl Sandburg Home National Historic Site, 209–210
Carlsbad Caverns National Park, 94
Carter G. Woodson Home National Historic Site, 282
Casa Grande Ruins National Monument, 84
Cascade Canyon, 118, 119
Cascade Lake Trail, 114
Castillo de San Marcos National Monument, 201
Castle Clinton National Monument, 234, 249
Castle Garden, 235
Cataloochee Campground, 179
Cataloochee Creek, 179
Cathedral Rocks, 2
Cat Island, 188
Catoctin Mountain Park, 294
Cave and Basin National Historic Site, 330

Cedar Breaks National Monument, 105–106
Cedar Creek and Belle Grove National Historical Park, 299
Cedar Ridge, 68
Cemetery Hill, 240
Cemetery Ridge, 240
César E. Chávez National Monument, 16
Chaco Culture National Historical Park, 95
Chain of Craters Road, 310
Chamberlain's Ranch, 74
Chamizal National Memorial, 100
Channel Islands National Park, 16–17
Charles Pinckney National Historic Site, 211
Charlestown Navy Yard, 228–229
Charles Young Buffalo Soldiers National Monument, 166
Chattahoochee River National Recreation Area, 189–191
Checkerboard Mesa, 75
Cherokee Indian Reservation, 276
Chesapeake & Ohio Canal National Historic Park, 283
Chessmen, 79
Chicha Foka Multi-Use Trail, 195
Chickamauga and Chattanooga National Military Park, 203–204
Chickasaw National Recreation Area, 168
Chief Mountain International Highway, 128
Chignecto Recreation Area, 346
Chimney Rock, 14
Chimney View, 276
Chincoteague Island, 270
Chincoteague National Wildlife Refuge, 270
Chiricahua National Monument, 84–85
Chittenden Road, 114
Cholla Cactus Garden, 12
Christian Pond, 119
Christiansted National Historic Site, 326–327
Christine Falls, 34, 35
Cinnamon Bay Beach, 319
Cinnamon Bay Campground, 318
Cinnamon Bay Nature Loop, 321
City of Rocks National Reserve, 56–57
Civil War Defenses of Washington, 283
Clara Barton National Historic Site, 294
Cleetwood Cove, 41
Clements Mountain, 128
C-Level Cirque Trail, 333
Cliff House, 8
Clingmans Dome, 177

Cloudcap Overlook, 41
Clover Lake, 37
Coast Guard Beach, 230
Coast Trail, 15
Cochran Shoals, 191
Coconino Overlook, 70
Colonial National Historic Park, 278–280
Colonial Williamsburg, 280
Colorado, 120–124, 129–133
Colorado Desert, 11
Colorado National Monument, 130
Colorado River, 68, 70
Colter Bay Village, 118
Columbia Icefield Adventure, 335
Combers Beach, 342
Congaree National Park, 211
Connecticut, 242
Constitution Gardens, 283
Contemplation Circle, 317
Continental Divide, 120, 128
Copp's Hill Burying Ground, 227
Coronado National Memorial, 85
Court of the Patriarchs, 71
Cowee Mountain Overlook, 275
Cowles Bog Trail, 139
Cowpens National Battlefield, 211
Crabtree Falls, 276–277
Craggy Gardens, 275, 277
Craggy Pinnacle Trail, 275
Crater Lake, 111
Crater Lake Lodge, 40
Crater Lake National Park, 39–43
Crater Lake Trolley, 41
Crater Rim Drive, 307
Crater Rim Trail, 309
Craters of the Moon National Monument and Preserve, 57
Crissy Field, 8
Crowfoot Glacier, 335
Culp's Hill, 240
Cumberland Gap National Historical Park, 157
Cumberland Island National Seashore, 204
Curecanti National Recreation Area, 130
Curry Village, 5
Cuyahoga Valley National Park, 146–149
Cuyahoga Valley Scenic Railroad, 148–149
Cypress Log Cabin, 140

D
Davis Bayou, 187–188
Dayton Aviation Heritage National Historical Park, 166–167
Death Valley National Park, 17
Deer Lake, 30
Delaware, 281
Delaware Water Gap National Recreation Area, 255

Denali Bus Depot, 44
Denali National Park and Preserve, 44–48
Desert View, 67
Desert View Campground, 66
Desert View Drive, 67
De Soto National Memorial, 201
Devastation Trail, 309
Devil's Den, 240
Devils Postpile National Monument, 18
Devil's Punchbowl, 29
Devils Tower National Monument, 134–135
Dewey Point, 5
Diablo Lake, 63
Diana Dunes Dare, 139
Dinosaur National Monument, 130–131
Discovery Point, 40
Discovery Point Trail, 42
Display Spring, 184
Doane Trail, 233
Dobson Trail, 346
Drakes Bay, 14
Drakes Beach, 15
Dream Lake, 122
Dry Tortugas National Park, 201–202
Dunbar Beach, 141
Dunes Kankakee, 141
Dunewood Campground, 141
Dwight Eisenhower Memorial, 266, 283

E
Eagle Lake, 220
East Palisades Trail, 191
Ebey's Landing National Historical Reserve, 60
Echo Lake Beach, 222
Edgar Allan Poe National Historic Site, 255
Effigy Mounds National Monument, 154
Eielson Visitor Center, 45
Eisenhower National Historic Site, 241, 255
El Camino Real de los Tejas National Historic Trail, 100
El Camino Real de Tierra Adentro National Historic Trail, 95
El Capitan, 2, 5
Eleanor Roosevelt National Historic Site, 249–250
Elephant Seal Overlook, 14
Elkhorn coral reefs, 320
Elk Island National Park, 358
Ellipse, 265
Ellis Island, 235–236
El Malpais National Monument, 95
El Morro National Monument, 95
El Tovar, 66
Emerald Lake, 122, 353
Emerald Mound, 195
Emerald Pools, 72
Emmons Glacier, 38
Emmons Vista Overlooks, 38

Erwins View Trail, 276
Estes Park, 124
Eugene O'Neill National Historic Site, 18–19
Everglades National Park, 202

F
Fairmont Chateau Lake Louise Hotel, 333
Fairyland Loop, 78
Fall Hollow, 194
Faneuil Hall, 227
Fay Glacier, 333
Federal Hall National Memorial, 249, 250
Fenwick Island, 269
Firehole Lake Drive, 112, 115
Fire Island National Seashore, 250
First Ladies National Historic Site, 167
First State National Historical Park, 281
Fish Creek, 127
Flight 93 National Memorial, 255–256
Florencia Bay, 340
Florida, 185–188, 200–203
Florida National Scenic Trail, 188
Florida Tropical House, 140
Florissant Fossil Beds National Monument, 131
Floyd Bennett Field, 237
Ford's Theatre National Historic Site, 284
Fordyce Bathhouse, 183
Forillon National Park, 371
Forney Ridge, 178
Fort Bowie National Historic Site, 85
Fort Caroline National Memorial, 202
Fort Davis National Historic Site, 100–101
Fort Donelson National Battlefield, 213
Fort Frederica National Monument, 204
Fort Funston, 7
Fort Hill Trail, 233
Fort Laramie National Historic Site, 135
Fort Larned National Historic Site, 155
Fort Matanzas National Monument, 202–203
Fort McHenry National Monument and Historic Shrine, 294–295
Fort Monroe National Monument, 299–300
Fort Necessity Battlefield, 256
Fort Pickens Tram Service, 187
Fort Point National Historic Site, 6, 19
Fort Pulaski National Monument, 204
Fort Raleigh National Historic Site, 210
Fort Scott National Historic Site, 155

Fort Smith National Historic Site, 199
Fort Stanwix National Monument, 250
Fort Sumter and Fort Moultrie National Historical Park, 212
Fort Union National Monument, 96
Fort Union Trading Post National Historic Site, 133–134
Fort Vancouver National Historic Site, 60–61
Fort Washington Park, 295
Fossil Butte National Monument, 135
Fountain Paint Pot, 112, 115
Fourth and Fifth Lakes, 337
Francis Bay, 319
Francis Bay Trail, 321
Franklin Delano Roosevelt Memorial, 265–266, 284–285
Frederick Douglass National Historic Site, 285
Frederick Law Olmsted National Historic Site, 244
Fredericksburg and Spotsylvania County Battlefields Memorial National Military Park, 300
Freedom Hills Overlook, 194
Freedom Riders National Monument, 196
Freedom Trail, 224, 225
French Broad River Valley, 277
Frenchman Bay, 222
Friendship Hill National Historic Site, 256
Frozen Lake, 38
Fundy National Park, 344–346

G
Garfield Peak, 43
Garnet Hill Trail, 115
Garrison Creek, 194
Gates of the Arctic National Park and Preserve, 50
Gateway Arch National Park, 142–145
Gateway National Recreation Area, 236–237, 250–251
Gauley River National Recreation Area, 215
General Grant National Memorial, 251
George Rogers Clark National Historical Park, 154
George Washington Birthplace National Monument, 300
George Washington Carver National Monument, 162
George Washington Memorial Parkway, 285–286
Georgia, 189–191, 203–206

Gettysburg National Military Park, 238–241

Gettysburg Reenactment, 240–241

Gila Cliff Dwellings National Monument, 96

Glacier Bay National Park and Preserve, 51

Glacier Creek Stables, 124

Glacier Falls, 122

Glacier Gorge Trail, 122

Glacier National Park, 125–128

Glacier National Park (Canada), 359

Glacier Park Lodge, 127

Glacier Point Road, 4, 5

Glen Canyon National Recreation Area, 80–83

Glen Echo Park, 295–296

Goat Haunt, 128

Godfrey Glen, 42

Going-to-the-Sun Road, 125

Golden Gate Bridge, 6

Golden Gate National Recreation Area, 6–8

Golden Spike National Historical Park, 106

Goose River Trail, 344

Governors Island National Monument, 251

Granary Burying Ground, 226

Grand Canyon Junction, 67

Grand Canyon Lodge, 69

Grand Canyon National Park, 66–70

Grand Canyon of the Yellowstone, 115

Grand Canyon-Parashant National Monument, 85–86

Grand Canyon Railway, 69

Grand Canyon West, 70

Grandfather Mountain, 275

Grand Lake, 124

Grand Loop Road, 110

Grand Portage National Monument, 160

Grand Prismatic Spring, 112

Grand Promenade, 184

Grand Staircase Escalante National Monument, 79, 83

Grand Teton National Park, 116–119

Grandview Point, 68

Grand View Point, 119

Grand View Terrace, 152

Granite Park Chalet, 126

Grant-Kohrs Ranch National Historic Site, 134

Grant Village, 112

Grasslands National Park, 373

Grayback Drive, 41

Great Egg Harbor Scenic and Recreational River, 247

Great Falls Park, 300

Great Fountain Geyser, 112, 115

Great Island Trail, 233

Great Kills Beach, 237

Great Marsh Trail, 139

Great Northern Route, 127

Great Sand Dunes National Park and Preserve, 131

Great Smoky Mountains National Park, 176–180

Great White Throne, 71

Greenbelt Park, 296

Green Gables Heritage Place, 348

Green Knob Trail, 276

Green Point Campground, 341

Green Springs, 300–301

Grizzly Giant Loop, 5

Gros Morne National Park, 363

Grotto, 72

Grotto Falls, 178

Grove of the Patriarchs, 36

Guadalupe Mountains National Park, 101

Guam, 322–323

Guilford Courthouse National Military Park, 210

Gulf Islands National Park Reserve, 359

Gulf Islands National Seashore, 185–188

Gulpha Gorge Campground, 184

Gwaii Haanas National Park Reserve, 360

H

Hagerman Fossil Beds National Park, 57–58

Haida Heritage Site, 360

Haleakala National Park, 311–314

Hale Bathhouse, 183

Halemaʻumaʻu crater, 307

Halemauʻu Trail, 314

Half Dome, 2, 3, 5

Halfmoon Bay, 341

Hall of Mosses, 30, 31

Hall of Records, 150

Halls Crossing, 80

Hamilton Grange National Memorial, 251

Hampton National Historic Site, 296

Hanging Gardens, 83

Happy Hollow Spring, 184

Harmony Hall, 296

Harpers Ferry National Historical Park, 215–216

Harriet Tubman National Historical Park, 251–252, 296

Harry S. Truman National Historic Site, 162

Hawaiʻi, 311–314, 315–317, 323–325

Hawaiʻi Volcanoes National Park, 306–310

Hawk Campground, 8

Hawksnest Bay, 320

Hayden Valley, 113–114

Haypress Campground, 8

Head of the Meadow, 232

Heart Oʻ the Hills Campground, 28

Henley Cay, 321

Henry M. Jackson Visitor Center, 35

Herbert Hoover National Historic Site, 154

Hermits Rest, 67

Herring Cove, 231–232

Hetch Hetchy Reservoir, 5

Hidden Falls, 118

Hidden Lake, 37, 128

Hidden Lake Overlook, 125, 128

Hidden Valley, 12

Highland Run, 194

Highline Trail, 128, 333

Hill Wheatley Plaza, 184

Historic Pierce Point Ranch, 14

Hi-View trail, 12

Hobie Cat Beach, 80

Hohokam Pima National Monument, 86

Hoh Rain Forest Visitor Center, 30

Hoh River, 31

Hole-in-the-Wall, 32

Holei Sea Arch, 310

Home of Franklin D. Roosevelt National Historic Site, 252

Homestead National Historic Monument, 163–164

Honeymoon Beach, 321

Honouliuli National Historic Site, 323

Hopewell Culture National Historical Park, 167

Hopewell Furnace National Historic Site, 256

Horn Island, 186, 188

Horseshoe Bend, 82

Horseshoe Bend Military Park, 196–197

Horseshoe Lake Trial, 48

Horse Trail, 15

Hosmer Grove, 314

Hotel Hale, 183

Hot Springs National Park, 181–184

Hot Water Cascade, 184

House of Tomorrow, 140

Hovenweep National Monument, 131–132

Hubbell Trading Post National Historic Site, 86

Hurricane Pass, 118

Hurricane Ridge, 28

I

Ice Age Floods National Geologic Trail, 61–62

Ice Age National Scenic Trail, 170–171

Ice Creamery, 115

Icefields Parkway, 335, 336

Ice River Trail, 356

Idaho, 56–58

Igloo Creek, 48

Illinois, 153–154

Independence National Historical Park, 256–257

Indiana, 138–141, 154

Indiana Dunes National Park, 138–141

Indian Garden, 68

Inn at Brandywine Falls, 149

Inspiration Point, 77, 118, 180

Iowa, 154

Island Drive, 280

Isle Au Haut, 220

Isle Royale National Park, 158

Ivvavik National Park, 373–374

J

Jackson Falls, 194

Jackson Glacier, 125

Jackson Lake, 117, 118

Jackson Lake Dam, 118

Jacob Lake, 69

Jacob Riis Park, 237

James A. Garfield National Historic Site, 167

James River, 276

James River Visitor Center, 277

Jamestown Settlement, 280

Jasper National Park, 335–339, 355

Jean Lafitte National Historical Park and Preserve, 206

J. Earle Bowden Way, 188

Jeff Busby Campground, 193–194

Jefferson Memorial, 265, 268

Jenny Lake, 118

Jenny Lake Boating, 118

Jenny Lake Campground, 118

Jenny Lake Lodge and Cabins, 118

Jewel Cave National Monument, 169

Jimmy Carter National Historic Site, 204–205

John Day Fossil Beds National Monument, 58, 59

John D. Rockefeller, Jr. Memorial Parkway, 135

John Fitzgerald Kennedy National Historic Site, 244

John Muir National Historic Site, 19

John Muir Trail, 3

Johnny Horn Trail, 321

Johnson Beach, 186

Johnston Canyon, 334

Johnstown Flood National Memorial, 257–258

Jordan Pond Loop, 220

Jordan Pond Loop Trail, 221–222

Joshua Tree National Park, 9–12

Julian Price Lake, 275

Julian Price Park, 276

Juney Whank Falls, 178

K

Kalahaku Overlook, 314

Kalaupapa National Historical Park, 323

Kaloko-Honokōhau National Historical Park, 323–324

Kansas, 155–156

Kantishna, 45

Katahdin Woods and Waters National Monument, 242

Katmai National Park and Preserve, 51–52

Kawuneeche Valley, 122

Kayenta Trail, 72

Keanakākoʻi (Cave of the Adzes) Crater, 308–309

Kehoe Beach, 15

Kejimkujik National Park and Historic Site, 367

Kelham Beach, 15

Kenai Fjords National Park, 52–53

Kenilworth Park & Aquatic Gardens, 286

Kennedy Lake, 342

Kennesaw Mountain National Battlefield Park, 205

Kentucky, 156–157

Kerkeslin Goat Lick, 337

Keweenaw National Historical Park, 158

Keys View, 12

Kilauea, 306

Kilauea Caldera, 307

Kilauea Iki Overlook, 308

Kilauea Iki Trail, 308

Kilauea Overlook, 308

Kings Canyon National Park, 19

King's Chapel, 226

Kings Mountain National Military Park, 212

Kipahulu District, 314

Kirby Grove Campground, 8

Klapatche Ridge, 38

Klondike Gold Rush National Historical Park, 53

Kluane National Park and Reserve, 374

Knife River Indian Villages National Historic Site, 165

Kobuk Valley National Park, 53

Kodachrome Basin State Park, 79

Koʻolau Gap, 314

Kootenay National Park, 360–361

Korean War Memorial, 265, 267–268, 287

Kouchibouguac National Park, 362–363

Kulanaokuaiki campground, 307

Kule Loklo, 13

Kuloa Point Loop Trail, 314

Kūpinaʻi Pali (Waldron Ledge), 309–310

L

Labyrinth Canyon, 80

Lafayette Square, 265

Laguna Trail, 15

Lake Agnes Teahouse, 333

Lake Agnes trail, 333

Lake Annette, 338

Lake Butte Overlook, 115

Lake Chelan National Recreation Area, 63

Lake Clark National Park and Preserve, 53–54

Lake Crescent, 29

Lake Crescent Lodge, 29

Lake Edith, 338
Lake Haiyaha, 122
Lake Louise, 36, 333, 356
Lake Louise Gondola, 334
Lake McDonald, 126
Lake Mead National
    Recreation Area, 87
Lake Meredith National
    Recreation Area, 101–102
Lake Michigan Water Trail,
    141
Lake Minnewanka Day Use
    Area, 333, 355
Lake Oesa, 355
Lake of Glass, 122
Lake O'Hara, 353–354
Lake Powell, 80
Lake Powell National Golf
    Course, 83
Lake Quinault, 32
Lake Quinault Lodge, 33
Lake Roosevelt National
    Recreation Area, 62
Lakes Trail Loop, 36
Lake View Beach, 141
Lake Wood, 222
Lamar Bathhouse, 182
Lamar Valley, 112
La Mauricie National Park,
    371–372
Lands End, 8
Langdon Beach, 186
L'Anse de Tabatière, 352
L'Anse-Saint-Jean, 351
La Passerelle, 352
Lassen Volcanic National
    Park, 19–20
Laughing Falls, 355
Lava Beds National
    Monument, 20
LBJ Memorial Grove on the
    Potomac, 287–288
Lee's Ferry, 82
Leinster Bay, 319
Leleiwi Overlook, 314
Lewis and Clark National
    Historic Park, 59
Lewis and Clark National
    Historic Trail, 164
Life of the Dunes, 270
Life of the Forest, 270
Life of the Marsh, 270
Limantour Beach, 14
Lincoln Boyhood National
    Memorial, 154
Lincoln Home National
    Historic Site, 153
Lincoln Memorial, 265,
    266–267, 287
Lind Point Trail, 321
Linn Cove Viaduct,
    274–275
Linville Gorge, 275
Lipan Point, 68
Little Beehive, 333
Little Bighorn Battlefield
    National Monument, 134
Little Mountain Overlook,
    193
Little River Canyon
    National Preserve, 197
Little Rock Central High
    School National Historic
    Site, 199
Little Round Top, 240

Little San Bernardino
    Mountains, 11–12
Live Oaks Bicycle Route,
    187
Lodge at Bryce Canyon, 79
Logan Pass, 127
Lone Rock Beach, 80
Longfellow House-
    Washington's
    Headquarters National
    Historic Site, 244–245
Longmire Museum, 34
Longs Peak, 123, 124
Look Rock Tower Trail, 180
Loop Trail, 126–127
Lost Canyon, 115
Lost Creek Campground, 43
Lost Eden, 80
Lost Lake, 115
Lost Palms Oasis Trail, 12
Louisiana, 206–207
Lover's Lane Trail, 30
Lowell National Historical
    Park, 245
Lower Emerald Pool, 72
Lower Sunwapta Falls, 337
Lower Yosemite Falls, 2, 5
Luftee Gap, 177
Lyndon B. Johnson National
    Historical Park, 102
Lynn Camp Prong Cascades,
    178

M
M66 Bar & Grill, 115
Mabry Mill, 274
MacLaren Pond, 344
Madison River, 114
Maggie L. Walker National
    Historic Site, 301
Maho Bay, 319
Makahiku Falls, 314
Maligne Canyon, 339
Maligne Lake, 339, 355
Maligne River Valley, 339
Mamey Peak, 321
Mammoth Cave National
    Park, 157–158
Mammoth Hot Springs,
    112, 115
Manassas National
    Battlefield Park, 301
Manhattan Project National
    Historical Park, 62, 96,
    213–214
Manitoba, 362
Many Glacier, 127
Many Glacier Hotel, 127
Manzanar National Historic
    Site, 20–21
Marconi Beach, 231
Maria Hope Trail, 321
Marias Pass, 128
Marietta Paper Mill, 191
Marin Headlands, 7
Mariposa Grove of Giant
    Trees, 3, 4, 5
Marsh-Billings-Rockefeller
    National Historical Park,
    260
Martin Luther King Jr.
    Memorial, 266, 288
Martin Luther King Jr.
    National Historic Site,
    205

Martin Van Buren National
    Historic Site, 252
Marven Lake, 346
Maryland, 269–272,
    293–297
Mary McLeod Bethune
    Council House National
    Historic Site, 288–289
Marymere Falls, 29
Massachusetts, 224–229,
    230–233, 243–247
Massachusetts State House,
    225–226
Mastodon Peak, 12
Mather Campground, 66
Mauna Loa, 306
Maurice Bathhouse, 183
Mazama Village, 42
McGurk Meadow, 4–5
McPherson Ridge, 239–240
Medgar & Myrlie Evers
    Home National
    Monument, 207–208
Medicine Lake, 339, 355
Menors Ferry Historic
    District, 118
Merced River, 5
Mesa Verde National Park,
    132
Metal Ford, 194
Michigan, 158–160
Middle Delaware National
    Scenic River, 258
Middle Pool, 72
Midway Geyser Basin, 112
Midwest, 138–171
Milky Way, 12
Million Dollar Road, 79
Mills Lake, 122
Mill Springs Battlefield
    National Monument, 158
Mingan Archipelago
    National Park Preserve,
    372
Mingo Falls, 178
Minidoka National Historic
    Site, 58
Mink Lake, 30
Minnesota, 160–162
Minnewanka Landing, 330
Minuteman Missile National
    Historic Site, 169–170
Minute Man National
    Historical Park, 245
Mirror Lake, 3
Mississippi, 185–188,
    207–209
Mississippi National River
    and Recreation Area, 160
Missouri, 142–145,
    162–163
Missouri National
    Recreational River, 164
Mist Trail, 3, 5
Miwok village, 13–15
Mojave Desert, 11
Mojave National Preserve,
    21
Moments in Time trail, 29
Monocacy National
    Battlefield, 297
Montana, 125–128,
    133–134
Montara Mountain, 6
Montezuma Castle National
    Monument, 87–88

Monument Valley, 83
Moore House, 280
Moores Creek National
    Battlefield, 210
Moose-Wilson road, 119
Moraine Lake, 333
Moraine Park Stables, 124
Moran Point, 68
Mormon Pioneer National
    Trail, 153
Mormon Row, 119
Mormon Row Historic
    District, 117
Morristown National
    Historical Park, 247
Moulton Barn, 119
Mountains-to-Sea Trail, 276
Mount Fay, 333
Mount Mazama, 39
Mount Rainier National
    Park, 34–38
Mount Revelstoke National
    Park, 361
Mount Rundle, 331
Mount Rushmore National
    Memorial, 150–152
Mount Scott, 43
Mount Victoria, 333
Mt. Adams, 36
Mt. Desert Island, 220
Mt. Healy Overlook Trail,
    48
Mt. Hood, 36
Mt. Mitchell, 275
Mt. Pisgah Trail, 277
Mt. Reynolds, 128
Mt. St. Helens, 36
Mt. Washburn, 114
Mt. Weaver, 177
Muir Beach, 8
Muir Woods National
    Monument, 6, 7, 21
Myrtle Falls, 35

N
Nááts'ihch'oh National Park
    Reserve, 364–365
Naches Peak, 37
Nahanni National Park
    Reserve, 364
Namakanipaio campground,
    307
Narada Falls, 34
Narrows, 73
Natchez National Historical
    Park, 208
Natchez Trace National
    Scenic Trail, 208
Natchez Trace Parkway,
    192–195
National Gallery, 265
National Mall, 264–272
National Museum of
    Immigration, 236
National Museum of
    Natural History, 265
National Park Inn, 34
National Park of American
    Samoa, 322
Natural Bridges National
    Monument, 83, 106–107
Nauset Light, 231
Nauset Lighthouse, 231
Navajo National
    Monument, 88
Naval Live Oaks Area, 188

Navarre Beach Marine Park,
    188
Nebraska, 163–165
Nevada, 92–93
Nevada Fall, 3
New Bedford Whaling
    National Historical Park,
    245–246
New Brunswick, 344–346,
    362–363
Newfound Gap, 177
Newfoundland and
    Labrador, 363
New Hampshire, 247
New Jersey, 247–248
New Mexico, 93–99
New Orleans Jazz National
    Historical Park, 207
New River Gorge National
    Park and Preserve, 216
New York, 248–255
Nez Perce National
    Historical Park, 58
Nicodemus National
    Historic Site, 155–156
Nike Missile Site, 7
Ninety Six National Historic
    Site, 212
Niobrara National Scenic
    River, 164
Nisqually Gate, 34
Nisqually Glacier, 35
Nitinat Narrows, 343
Noatak National Preserve,
    54
Noland Divide, 177–178
Norris Geyser Basin, 112,
    115
North Carolina, 176–180,
    209–211
North Cascades National
    Park, 62–63
North Country National
    Scenic Trail, 165
North Dakota, 165–166
Northeast, 220–260
Northeast Creek, 223
North End, 227
Northern Mariana Islands,
    325
North Kaibab Trail, 70
North Rim, 69
North Rim Campground, 69
North Rim Scenic Drive, 70
Northwest Territories,
    364–366
Nova Scotia, 366–367
Nunavut Territory, 367–369
Nuu-chah-nulth Trail, 340

O
Obed Wild and Scenic
    River, 214
Oberlin Bend, 127
Observation Point, 112, 115
Ocean Beach, 8
Ocean Path, 222
Ocean Springs, 188
Ocmulgee Mounds National
    Monument, 205–206
Oconaluftee River Trail, 180
Ohio, 146–149, 166–168
Ohio & Erie Canal, 148
Ohio Water Trail, 148
Oklahoma, 168–169
Oklahoma City National
    Memorial, 168–169

Old Corner Book Store, 227
Old Faithful, 111–112, 115
Old Fall River Road, 121
Old Ferry Landing, 271
Old Fort Point Trail, 338
Old North Church, 227
Old South Meeting House, 227
Old Spanish National Historic Trail, 88–89
Old State House, 227
Old Trace Drive, 194
Old West Lookout, 115
Olmsted Point, 5
Olympic Discovery Trail, 29
Olympic National Park, 28–33
Ooh Aah Point, 68
Opal Beach, 186
Oregon, 39–43, 58–60
Oregon Caves National Monument and Preserve, 60
Oregon National Historic Trail, 60
Organ Pipe Cactus National Monument, 89
Orion, 12
Otter Creek, 276
Otter Point, 222
Ouachita Mountains, 181
Overmountain Victory National Historic Trail, 210
Oxbow Bend, 117, 119
Oxon Cove Park & Oxon Hill Farm, 297
Ozark Bathhouse, 183
Ozark National Scenic Riverways, 162

P
Paces Mill, 191
Pacific Crest Trail, 43
Pacific Fleet Submarine Museum, 317
Pacific Northwest, 27–63
Pacific Rim National Park Reserve, 340–343
Padre Island National Seashore, 102
Page Rimview Loop, 83
Painted Desert, 70
Painted Hills, 59
Palisades Lake Trail, 37
Palo Alto Battlefield National Historical Park, 102
Panorama Point, 35–36
Park Boulevard, 11
Parks of New York Harbor, 234–237
Park Street Church, 226
Pa'rus Trail, 71
Paterson Great Falls National Historical Park, 247
Patricia Lake, 338
Paul Revere House, 227
Peach Orchard, 240
Peal Harbor Aviation Museum, 317
Peal Harbor National Memorial, 315–317
Pea Ridge National Military Park, 199–200

Pecos National Historical Park, 96
Pennsylvania, 238–241, 255–259
Pennsylvania Avenue National Historic Site, 289
Perdido Key, 188
Perry's Victory and International Peace Memorial, 167–168
Petersburg National Battlefield, 301
Petit Bois Island, 186
Petrified Forest National Park, 89–90
Petroglyph Beach, 82
Petroglyph National Monument, 97
Petroglyph Trail, 321
Peyto Lake, 335
Phantom Ranch, 67
Phantom Ship Island, 40, 41
Pharr Mounds, 195
Pickett's Charge, 240
Pictured Rocks National Lakeshore, 159
Piegan Pass, 126
Pinery Narrows, 147
Pinnacles National Park, 21–22
Pinnacles Overlook, 41
Pipe Spring National Monument, 90
Pipestone National Monument, 160–161
Pipiwai Trail, 314
Piscataway Park, 297
Pisgah Inn, 277
Pitzer Woods, 240
Place of a Thousand Drips, 178
Plaikni Falls, 42
Plain of Six Glaciers Trail, 333
Pleasant Valley, 115
Plunge Basin Overlook, 276
Point Bonita Lighthouse, 7
Point Imperial, 70
Point Reyes Beach, 15
Point Reyes Hostel, 15
Point Reyes Lifeboat Station, 14
Point Reyes Lighthouse, 14
Point Reyes National Seashore, 13–15
Pools of Oheo, 314
Port Angeles, 28
Port Chicago Naval Magazine National Memorial, 22
Potkopinu, 194
Potomac Heritage National Scenic Trail, 289
Poverty Point National Monument, 207
Powers Island, 191
Prairie Duneland Trail, 141
Presidential Trail, 150
President William Jefferson Clinton Birthplace Home National Historic Site, 200
Presidio of San Francisco, 6
Prince Albert National Park, 373

Prince Edward Island National Park, 347–349
Prince William Forest Park, 301
Province Lands trail, 232–233
Puerto Rico, 325–326
Pu'ukoholā Heiau National Historic Site, 324–325
Pukaskwa National Park, 370
Pullman National Monument, 153
Pumice Castle Overlook, 40–41
Pu'uhonua o Hōnaunau National Historical Park, 324
Pu'u Loa Trailhead, 310
Pu'u'ula'ula, 314
Pyramid Lake, 338

Q
Qapaw, 182
Qausuittuq National Park, 368
Québec, 350–352, 371–372
Queen's Garden, 77–78
Quincy Market, 227
Quttinirpaaq National Park, 368

R
Race Point, 232
Rainbow Bridge National Monument, 83, 107
Rainbow Falls, 178
Rain Tree Café, 319
Ramsey Cascades, 178
Rancho Corral de Tierra, 6
Raven's Roost, 274
Reconstruction Era National Historical Park, 212–213
Redwood National Park, 22, 23
Reef Bay Trail, 321
Reflecting Pool, 267
Reflection Canyon, 83
Reflection Lakes, 34
Remembrance Circle, 317
Rhode Island, 259–260
Rialto Beach, 31
Richland Balsam Overlook, 275
Richmond National Battlefield Park, 302
Riding Mountain National Park, 362
Riley Creek Campground, 48
Rim Drive, 39
Rim Trail, 42, 43, 78
Rim Village, 42
Rio Grande Wild and Scenic River, 102–103
River Raisin National Battlefield Park, 159–160
Riverside Walk, 71
Riverview Road, 148
Roaring Fork Motor Nature Trail, 178
Robinsons Island Trail System, 348
Rock Creek Park, 289–290
Rock Spring Nature Trail, 194

Rocky Mountain National Park, 120–124
Rocky Mountains, 109–135
Rocky Pledge, 124
Rocky Springs, 195
Roger Williams National Memorial, 260
Roosevelt Lodge Dining Room, 115
Rosie the Riveter National Historical Park, 23
Ross Barnett Reservoir, 194
Ross Lake, 356
Ross Lake National Recreation Area, 63
Roswell Mill, 191
Rouge National Urban Park, 370–371
Ruby Beach, 32
Russell Cave National Monument, 197
Ryan Mountain, 12

S
Sable Island National Park Reserve, 367
Sagamore Hill National Historic Site, 252
Saguaro National Park, 90
Saguenay Fjord National Park, 352
Saguenay-St. Lawrence Marine Park, 350–352
Saint Croix Island International Historic Site, 242–243
Saint Croix National Scenic Riverway, 171
Saint-Gaudens National Historic Site, 247
Saint Paul's Church National Historic Site, 252–253
Salamander Glacier, 125
Salem Maritime National Historic Site, 246
Salinas Pueblo Missions National Monument, 97–98
Salmon Crusades, 29
Salomon Bay, 321
Salt River Bay National Historical Park and Ecological Preserve, 327
Samuel Taylor Park, 7
San Agustin, 13
San Antonio Missions National Historical Park, 103
Sanctuary River, 48
Sand Beach, 222
Sand Creek Massacre National Historic Site, 132–133
Sandy Hook, 237
San Juan Island National Historical Park, 63
San Juan National Historic Site, 325–326
Santa Monica Mountains National Recreation Area, 23–24
Santa Rosa Island, 186
Saratoga National Historical Park, 253
Saskatchewan, 373

Saugus Iron Works National Historic Site, 246
Savage Alpine Trail, 48
Savage River, 44
Savage River Campground, 48
Savage River Loop Trail, 48
Scenic Loop Drive, 116
Schoodic Peninsula, 220
Schoolroom Glacier, 118
Scotts Bluff National Monument, 165
Sculptor's Studio, 152
Sculptured Beach, 15
Sea Lion Overlook, 14
Sea Lion Rocks, 342
Selma to Montgomery National Historic Trail, 197
Sequoia National Park, 24
Seven Lakes Basin, 30
Seven-Mile Hole Trail, 114, 115
Shadow Lake, 38
Sheep Lakes, 124
Shenandoah National Park, 302
Shiloh National Military Park, 214–215
Shining Rock Wilderness, 277
Ship Island, 186
Shoshone Point, 68
Siesta Lake, 5
Signal Mountain, 118
Signal Mountain Lodge, 118
Silent City, 77
Silver Falls Trail, 36
Silver Forest Trail, 38
Sirmilik National Park, 368
Sitka National Historical Park, 55
Skeleton Point, 68
Skull Rock, 10
Skyline Trail, 35
Sky Pond, 122
Sky Trail, 15
Sled Dog Kennels, 47
Sleeping Bear Dunes National Lakeshore, 160
Sliding Sands Trail, 314
Smithsonian Castle, 266
Snake River, 118, 119
Snake River Overlook, 117
Soldiers' National Cemetery, 240
Sol Duc Falls, 30
Sol Duc Hot Springs and Resort, 29
Sol Duc River Valley, 29
Somes Sound, 220
Sope Creek, 191
South, 176–216
South Carolina, 211–213
South Dakota, 150–152, 169–170
South Kaibab Trail, 68
Southwest, 65–107
Sperry Chalet, 126
Sperry Glacier, 125
Sperry Trail, 126
Spirit Island, 339
Split Rock, 31
Spray River, 332–333

Springfield Armory National Historic Site, 246
Spruce Nature Trail, 31
Spruce Railroad, 29
Stanford House, 149
Stanhope Beach, 348
Stanton Beach, 80
Stanton Creek, 80
Star-Spangled Banner National Historic Trail, 290
Staten Island Ferry, 237
Station Road Bridge Trailhead, 147
Statue of Liberty, 235, 253
Steaming Bluff, 308
Steamtown National Historic Site, 258–259
Ste. Genevieve National Historical Park, 162–163
Stevens Canyon Entrance, 36
Stewart Canyon Trail, 333, 355
Stinson Beach, 8
St. Mary's Falls, 126
Stones River National Battlefield, 215
Stonewall National Monument, 253–254
Sulphur Banks, 308
Sulphur Mountain, 334
Sunrise Nature Trail, 37
Sunrise Point, 37
Sunrise Visitor Center, 37
Sunset Crater Volcano National Monument, 90–91
Sunset Point, 77
Sunset Trail, 184
Sunwapta Falls, 335–336, 355
Sunwapta Pass, 335
Supai Tunnel, 70
Superior Bathhouse, 183–184
Superior Bathhouse Brewery, 184
Sutro Baths, 7
Swan View Overlook, 194
Swiftcurrent Lake, 127

T
Table Rock, 275
Tadoussac, 352
Taft Creek, 31
Taggart Lake Trail, 118
Takakkaw Falls, 355
Tallgrass Prairie National Preserve, 156
Tanawha Trail, 275
Tattoosh Ridge, 36
Teewinot, 118
Teklanika River, 46
Teklanika River Campground, 48
Telescope Tree, 5
Temple of Sinawava, 71
Tenaya Canyon, 2
Tenaya Lake, 5
Tennessee, 176–180, 192–195, 213–215
Tennessee Valley Divide, 194
Tennessee Valley Trail, 7
Terra Nova National Park, 363
Texas, 99–103

Thaddeus Kosciuszko Memorial, 259
Thaidene Nene National Park Reserve, 365
Theodore Roosevelt Birthplace National Historic Site, 254
Theodore Roosevelt Inaugural National Historic Site, 254
Theodore Roosevelt Island, 290
Theodore Roosevelt National Park, 165–166
Thomas Edison National Historical Park, 248
Thomas Jefferson Memorial, 290–291
Thomas Stone National Historic Site, 297
Thor's Hammer, 77
Thousand Islands National Park, 371
Three Sisters, 231
Thunderbird Lodge, 66
Thunder Hole, 222
Thunder Ridge, 277
Thurston Lava Tube, 308
Tidal Basin, 268
Timbered Island, 119
Timberline Falls, 122
Timpanogos Cave National Monument, 107
Timucuan Ecological and Historic Preserve, 203
Tinkers Creek Gorge, 149
Tioga Road, 5
Tipsoo Lake, 37
Tlaqatik & Greenwich Dunes, 349
Toklat River, 44–45
Tomales Bluff, 14
Tomales Point, 14
Tomales Point Trail, 14
Tonto National Monument, 91
Torngat Mountains National Park, 363–364
Tower Bridge, 78
Towers of the Virgin, 72
Towpath Trail, 148
Trail of Tears National Historic Trail, 200
Trail of the Shadows, 34
Trail Ridge Road, 120
Transept Trail, 70
Trashcan Rock, 10
Trillium Gap Trail, 178
Triple Arch, 127
Triple Divide Peak, 128
Trout Lake Trail, 114, 115
Trunk Bay Beach, 319
Trunk Cay, 319
Tuktut Nogait National Park, 365
Tule Springs Fossil Beds National Monument, 93
Tumacacori National Historical Park, 91
Tundra Wilderness Tour, 46
Tunnel Mountain Summit, 332
Tunnel View, 2
Tuolumne Meadows, 5
Tupelo National Battlefield, 208

Tusayan, 67
Tusayan Museum Ruin, 67
Tuskegee Airmen National Historic Site, 197–198
Tuskegee Institute National Historic Site, 198
Tuzigoot National Monument, 91
Twentymile Creek Cascade, 178
Two Bridges, 78

U
Ukkusiksalik National Park, 368–369
Ulysses S. Grant National Historic Site, 163
Unkar Delta, 70
Upper Delaware Scenic and Recreational River, 259
Upper Linville Falls, 276
Upper Salmon River, 346
Upper Yosemite Falls, 3
U.S. Capitol Building, 265, 266
U.S. Islands, 306–327
USS Arizona, 315
USS Cassin Young, 228
USS Constitution, 228
Utah, 71–75, 76–79, 80–83, 103–107

V
Valles Caldera National Preserve, 98
Valley Floor, 5
Valley Forge National Historical Park, 259
Valley of the Five Lakes, 337
Vanderbilt Mansion National Historic Site, 254
Vermilion Cliffs, 82
Vermilion Lakes Drive, 331, 355
Vermont, 260
Vernal Fall, 3, 5
Via Ferrata des Géants, 352
Vickery Creek Trail, 191
Vicksburg National Military Park, 208–209
Vidae Falls, 41
Vietnam Veterans Memorial, 265, 267, 291
Virginia, 273–277, 297–302
Virginia Falls, 126
Virgin Islands, 326–327
Virgin Islands Coral Reef National Monument, 327
Virgin Islands National Park, 318–321
Voyageurs National Park, 161–162
Vuntut National Park, 374

W
Waco Mammoth National Monument, 103
Wahweap, 80
Waimoku Falls, 314
Wall of Windows, 79
Wall Street, 78
Walnut Canyon National Monument, 91–92
Walter's Wiggles, 73
Wapama Falls Trail, 5
Wapta Falls, 355
Wapusk National Park, 362

Warfield Ridge, 240
War in the Pacific National Historical Park, 322–323
War of 1812 Memorial, 194
Warren Peak, 12
Washington, 28–38, 60–63
Washington Monument, 265, 266, 291–292
Washington-Rochambeau Revolutionary Route National Historic Trail, 246–247
Washita Battlefield National Historic Site, 169
Watchman Overlook, 40, 42
Watchman Peak, 43
Watchman Point, 72
Watchman Trail, 71–72
Watchtower, 67
Watermelon Cay, 319
Waterrock Knob, 275–276
Waterton-Glacier International Peace Park, 128
Waterton Lake, 128
Waterton Lakes National Park, 128, 358–359
Waterton Lake Trail, 128
Wawona Point, 5
Wawona Road, 2, 5
Wawona Stables, 5
Weir Farm National Historical Park, 242
West Side Loop, 12
West Thumb, 112
West Virginia, 215–216
Wheatfield, 240
Whiskeytown National Recreation Area, 24
Whistlers Mountain, 338
Whistling Cay, 321
White Cliffs of Dover, 10
White Gulch, 14
White House, 265, 292
White River Entrance, 37
White Sands National Park, 98–99
White Wolf Campground, 5
Whitman Mission National Historic Site, 63
Whittington Spring, 184
Wickaninnish Beach, 342
Wieboldt-Rostone House, 141
Wilcox Pass Trail, 335, 355
Wilcox Viewpoint, 335
William Howard Taft National Historic Site, 168
Williamsburg, 280
Willowbrae Trail, 340
Wilson's Creek National Battlefield, 163
Wind Cave National Park, 170
Windy Gap, 14
Wisconsin, 170–171
Wizard Island, 40
Wolfe Lake, 346
Wolf Trap National Park for the Performing Arts, 302
Women's Rights National Historical Park, 254–255
Wonder Lake, 45, 48
Wonderland Trail, 34

Wood Buffalo National Park, 365–366
World War II Home Front National Historical Park, 23
World War II Memorial, 265, 268, 293
World War I Memorial, 265, 292–293
Wotan's Throne, 70
Wrangell-St. Elias National Park and Preserve, 55–56
Wright Brothers National Memorial, 211
Wupatki National Monument, 92
Wyoming, 110–115, 116–119

Y
Yellowstone Falls, 110, 115
Yellowstone Lake, 112
Yellowstone National Park, 110–115
Yockanookany, 194
Yoho National Park, 353–357
Yorktown Battlefield, 278, 279
Yorktown National Cemetery, 280
Yosemite National Park, 2–5
Yosemite Valley, 2
Yovimpa Point, 76
Yucca House National Monument, 133
Yukon-Charley Rivers National Preserve, 56
Yukon Territory, 373–374

Z
Zig Zag, 181
Zion Canyon, 71
Zion Canyon Overlook Trail, 75
Zion-Mt. Carmel Tunnel, 75
Zion National Park, 71–75
Zion National Park Lodge, 72, 73
Z Ranch Trail, 15